T0247708

PROVIDING FOR THE PEOPLE

The Civilization of the American Indian Series

PROVIDING FOR THE PEOPLE

Economic Change among the Salish
and Kootenai Indians, 1875–1910

Robert J. Bigart

UNIVERSITY OF OKLAHOMA PRESS : NORMAN

Library of Congress Cataloging-in-Publication Data

Names: Bigart, Robert, author.
Title: Providing for the People : economic change among the Salish and
    Kootenai Indians, 1875–1910 / Robert J. Bigart.
Other titles: Civilization of the American Indian series ; v. 280.
Description: Norman : University of Oklahoma Press, [2020] | Series:
    The civilization of the American Indian series ; volume 280 | Includes
    bibliographical references. | Summary: "Examines the economic
    transition of the Salish and Kootenai Indian tribes of the Flathead
    Indian Reservation from a hunter-gatherer to a ranching-farming
    economy between 1875 to 1910 and their ability to remain self-
    supporting"—Provided by publisher.
Identifiers: LCCN 2020001835 | ISBN 978-0-8061-6630-8 (hardcover)
ISBN 978-0-8061-8361-9 (paperback) Subjects: LCSH: Salish Indians—
Montana—Flathead Indian Reservation—
    Economic conditions—19th century. | Kootenai Indians—Montana—
    Flathead Indian Reservation—Economic conditions—19th century.
Classification: LCC E99.S2 B545 2020 | DDC 978.6004/979435—dc23 LC
record available at https://lccn.loc.gov/2020001835

Providing for the People: Economic Change among the Salish and Kootenai Indians, 1875–1910 is Volume 280 in The Civilization of the American Indian Series.

The paper in this book meets the guidelines for permanence and durability of the Committee on Production Guidelines for Book Longevity of the Council on Library Resources, Inc. ∞

Contents

Acknowledgments   vii

Introduction   1
1. The End of the Buffalo Economy, 1875–1881   12
2. Crafting a New Economy, 1882–1888   40
3. Hunting, Horses, and Cattle, 1889–1904   69
4. Farming, Government Aid, and Wage Work, 1889–1904   91
5. Commercial Exchanges and Business Enterprises,
   1889–1904   123
6. Turmoil and Progress, 1905–1910   138
   Afterword: The Post-1910 Economic Implications
   of Allotment on the Flathead Indian Reservation   162

Appendix A: Flathead Reservation Chiefs, 1875–1910   167
Appendix B: Flathead Reservation Indian Agents, 1875–1910   186
Notes   205
Bibliography   257
Index   267

Acknowledgments

This book is one of the fruits of over fifty years of research into the history of the Salish and Kootenai Indian people of the Flathead Indian Reservation. The project began as an independent study as an undergraduate student in 1968 and has continued, full-time and part-time, ever since.

Over these years, in chronological order, my research work has been supported and supervised by Tony Kusniewski, John Ewers, K. Ross Toole, Clarence Woodcock, Jerry Slater, and Joe McDonald. I cannot express enough my thanks for their ideas and encouragement over this long period.

During these years, I have had the assistance of more than a hundred archivists and librarians from all over the United States and even beyond. I cannot name them all. I have benefited from the generous help from several generations of archivists at the National Archives in Washington, D.C. The newspaper collection at the Montana Historical Society proved especially valuable in my research. The MHS staff has changed over the years but has always been kind and courteous with remarkable patience. I have found considerable material in the manuscript and general collections at the Mansfield Library, University of Montana, Missoula. Other collections from Yale University, the National Library of Canada, Dartmouth College, Los Angeles, and many different locations have given me access to countless additional material. I cannot thank you enough, but I hope this book and the other materials that have grown out of my research will be some small consolation for putting up with all my requests and questions.

My biggest debt over the years has been to the people and tribal community on the Flathead Indian Reservation. They all have been remarkably kind and understanding of my quixotic interests. This monograph is based on the written historical material, so it is only a starting point for further research. The Salish–Pend d'Oreille and Kootenai Culture Committees of the Confederated Salish and Kootenai Tribes are working on oral histories of the tribes, which will greatly expand our understanding of the history of the tribes from the tribal perspective. Hopefully, tribal member researchers will use both the oral and written sources to delve into their tribal heritage. This book has full footnotes citing the sources I used, which should make it possible for community members and other researchers to follow up on my research.

Social and intellectual debts accumulated over more than fifty years of research are hard to summarize. I hope and pray that this book will provide some ideas and evidence that will prove valuable to future historical researchers and others. The history of the Flathead Indian Reservation includes a remarkable number of brave and capable leaders who have made the survival of the tribes possible through two centuries of danger and challenge.

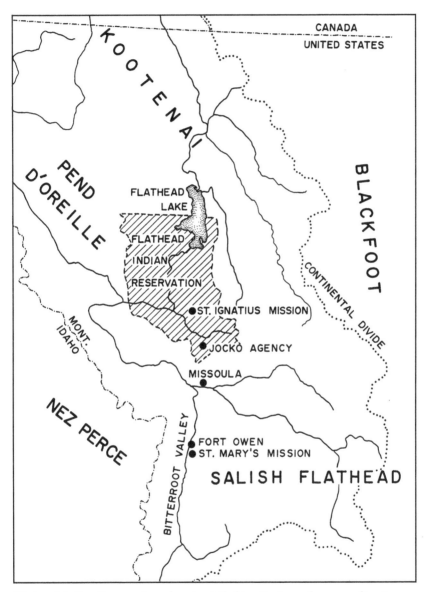

Flathead Indian Reservation, showing tribal territories and surrounding towns. Map by Marcia Bakry, Smithsonian Institution, Washington, D.C.

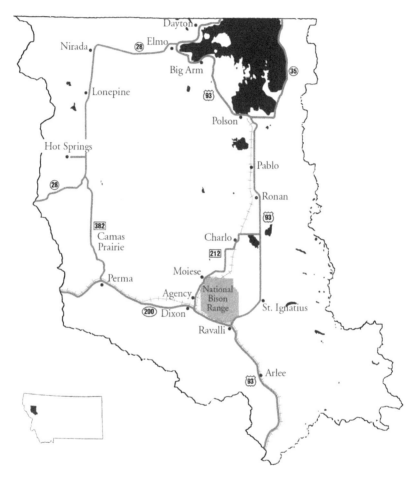

Flathead Indian Reservation, showing towns and roadways. Map by Wyatt Design, Helena, Mont.

Introduction

For centuries the Salish and Kootenai Indian tribes of the northern Rocky Mountains lived off the bounty of the land. They affiliated in tribal communities and hunted and gathered meat and plant foods on an annual cycle. Their villages were in the Rocky Mountains and the adjacent northwest Great Plains. Important changes swept the tribes in the eighteenth century. Horses arrived from the south, and the Blackfeet and other Plains tribes used their access to guns to expand into former Salish and Kootenai territory on the plains. The 1780 smallpox epidemic killed many tribal members and forced the Salish and Kootenai villages back into the Rocky Mountain valleys. When the white traders and trappers arrived in the early nineteenth century, they allied with the Salish and Kootenai for mutual protection. In the middle of the century the tribes welcomed Christian missionaries at St. Mary's and St. Ignatius Missions for spiritual power. In 1855 they formalized their relationship with the United States government through the Hellgate Treaty. By 1875 the tribes had endured wrenching adjustments, but even more was to come during the next thirty-five years.

Between 1875 and 1910 major changes in the tribal economy were accompanied by the growing power of the Flathead Indian agent on the reservation. The new order of things was not preferred by most tribal members, but they never stopped fighting to have their voices heard and to maintain their economic independence and self-support. The tribes and tribal members could not be defined as just victims of an unjust system.

1

They were independent historical actors who were often victimized, but who never stopped fighting to protect their interests. The traditional chiefs and the agents cooperated in some areas of mutual interest and competed in other fields.

An Economic Revolution

The economy of the Flathead Reservation tribes was revolutionized between 1875 and 1910. In 1875 the tribes supported themselves through hunting—especially buffalo—and gathering plants in their season. The tribes had some cattle and gardens in 1875, but those were still a minor part of the tribal economy. Thirty-five years later, in 1910, cattle herds and farming were the foundation of the economy, supplemented with some big game hunting and gathering of wild plants. The Flathead Reservation tribes were able to remain self-supporting through this time of dramatic change. The tribes did not receive general rations and did not allow the government to get control of their food supply. Government assistance was limited to the old and infirm or recent arrivals on the reserve. Assistance was short-term for the Kalispel and Spokane Indians, who moved to the Flathead in the 1880s, and for the Bitterroot Salish in the 1890s. Most government aid was bartered to tribal members in exchange for labor, firewood, hay, and other products used in running the agency.

The Salish and Kootenai tribes of the Flathead Reservation showed a remarkable ability to change and adapt through hard times. The traditional economy before 1875 had supported the tribes well, but when faced with the resource crisis of the late nineteenth century, the Salish and Kootenai adapted and survived. Few tribal members probably preferred the new economic order, but they did what they needed to do to feed and provide for themselves and their families.

The bedrock of the 1875 Salish and Kootenai economy had been hunting and gathering. The flood of white settlers and miners moving to Montana played havoc with resources. In the late nineteenth century the plains buffalo herds were exterminated, and other big game populations crashed from overhunting. The Flathead Reservation tribes added seasonal labor on their farms to the annual hunting schedule and expanded their farms and livestock herds to compensate for the declining game populations. By the early twentieth century, hunting was further complicated by Montana state hunting regulations, which tried to reserve big game for sports hunters over subsistence hunters. Access to wild plants and fruits was complicated by the land claims of white settlers, but the surviving evidence is sketchy.

A growing aspect of the economy between 1875 and 1910 was the open-range herds of horses and cattle on the reservation. Agent W. H. Smead, especially, worked to develop the market for horse sales off the reservation. Cattle competed with horses for grass, but horse buyers from the Midwest and other regions steadily reduced the Flathead herds. Some reservation horses even went to southern Africa for the Boer War and to Japan for the Russo-Japanese War in the early twentieth century.

Cattle herds kept expanding between 1875 and 1910 and became the primary export from the reservation. The largest herds were owned by a few mixed-blood families, but apparently most Indian families either had a few cattle or worked seasonally for their richer tribesmen, or both. In addition to regular exports of cattle to Chicago and other markets, the Pablo-Allard buffalo herd was rounded up in the early twentieth century and sold to the Canadian government. The Allard family made several attempts to start a Wild West show business to exhibit tribal buffalo and reservation cowboys. Unfortunately, the shows never proved viable in the long run.

Another growing facet of the tribal economy between 1875 and 1910 was agriculture. Farming on the reservation covered both family garden plots and grain and hay fields. Most of the garden produce was consumed by families, but in a few cases, surplus produce was sold. Wheat was often grown to be ground into flour, but much of the grain, and most of the hay crop, was fed to livestock. Two irrigation ditches were constructed by the government in the Jocko Valley. Other farmers dug private ditches to water their crops. Some hay and grain were sold to off-reservation customers in good years. As mentioned previously, most tribal members integrated the agricultural work into the seasonal hunting and gathering schedule.

Many tribal members—especially mixed-bloods—worked for money or supplies. A few worked for the Jocko Agency and St. Ignatius Mission, but many others found seasonal or casual short-term work. Agriculture and ranching needed extra labor during harvest, roundups, and driving herds. Casual labor ranged from catching runaway horses to giving somebody a wagon ride from the railroad station to the Jocko Agency. Such incidental work would have been valuable to many tribal members, but there is no way to determine how extensive it was.

Tribal members also operated businesses and traded with white-owned businesses on and off the reservation. Tribal businesses included Duncan

McDonald's hotel at Ravalli, Charlie Allard's stagecoach line to Flathead Lake, and Baptiste Eneas's ferry at the foot of Flathead Lake. Little documentation has survived to describe Indian trade with on-reservation traders, but Missoula, Plains, and Kalispell newspapers carried frequent references to tribal members shopping in their communities.

Part of the tribal economic activity off the reservation included whiskey. Off-reservation businesses made money selling alcohol to Indians, either directly or indirectly. Some tribal members developed businesses bootlegging alcohol on the reservation.

Government aid, such as wagons and agricultural implements, was useful but, in most cases, was bartered for firewood, logs, grain, hay, or other commodities needed by the agency. Except for a few short-term cases covering failed hunts or crops or helping relocated tribal members get established, government aid was not free.

A final part of the reservation economy that can be documented was theft, both by tribal members and other tribes. Horses were stolen by some tribal members, especially from hostile tribes.

The economic turmoil on the reservation between 1875 and 1910 raises several questions that can be partially answered by the historical evidence. The first problem would be the distribution of economic assets in the 1910 economy. There was no question a few rich families—such as the Allards, Pablos, and McDonalds—owned the largest herds, farms, and businesses. As discussed in the following section, however, most tribal members had at least a few horses and cattle and small gardens. Many probably also benefited from seasonal and casual work for their richer neighbors. The economic distribution was not equal, but most families were self-supporting and survived.

The other question of the new tribal economy was how economically well-off the tribes were. There is evidence suggesting that by 1905, the tribes were as well-off as most rural Montana white communities. In this case, the tribal community was not poor in 1905. As could be expected, however, the forced sale of tribal assets—land—at below-market prices through allotment reduced their future income and pauperized many tribal members.

Comparisons to Other Tribes

But how was the Flathead Reservation experience between 1875 and 1910 similar to that of other tribal communities? And how was it different?

The backdrop of intertribal comparisons of the power of agents compared to that of traditional chiefs was general rations. The ability of chiefs to resist agent demands was considerably compromised where the agent controlled the food supply for tribal members. On the Flathead Reservation, government assistance only complimented the income from hunting and gathering, cattle, horses, and farming, which allowed the chiefs to resist government policies in the 1880s and 1890s.

The available reservation histories allow some limited comparisons to the Flathead Reservation in economic change and development between 1875 and 1910. All American Indian tribes were faced with the loss of the buffalo and other big game and predatory white people occupying farming and gathering locations. Indian tribes in the nineteenth century were forced to find other economic resources to survive.

All of the reservation case studies showed Indian people with surprising initiative and drive to develop alternative economic resources to replace their traditional sources of support. Those tribes that were forced onto general rations suffered almost complete devastation. They had a much bigger hole to climb out of in order to survive and support their families in the new economic order. The Flathead Reservation was fortunate to have embryonic farming and livestock industries to fall back on.

Many of the case studies included general assertions about tribal economic change without describing the incidents and events that back up their observations. It is also possible that the limited number of studies presented here are not a representative sample of the American Indian experience during the late nineteenth century. Hopefully, future researchers will test the assertions against a broader range of sources and data.

The Piegan Blackfeet were an example of a reservation that faced economic desperation after the loss of the buffalo herds in the early 1880s. The tribes were forced to rely on government rations, which were sometimes inadequate to feed the tribe. The winter of 1883–84 in particular became known as the starvation winter. Farming on the Blackfeet Reservation was curtailed by the limited agricultural bottomland, the short growing season, and the shortage of equipment and supplies. Efforts to construct an irrigation system in the 1890s were largely a failure. The one promising development was the foundation of a livestock industry on the reservation. The agent issued cattle in the 1890s, and the Blackfeet tribe began a long, slow effort to build a new tribal economy.[1]

The Crow Indians relied on rations, but they showed remarkable initiative and energy in developing agriculture on their reservation between 1890 and 1920. The tribe could call on memories of farming along the Missouri River at the start of the nineteenth century. Cooperative farms on the reservation at the end of the nineteenth century proved productive. The district farms, combined with family farms, produced wheat that supplied both the Crow and Northern Cheyenne Agencies. The Crows agreed to use proceeds of land sales to develop an irrigation system. The Crows and Cheyennes proved willing laborers in constructing ditches. Unfortunately, pressure from the government expanded the irrigation system to the point that Crow farmers could not afford the water charges. Political and economic pressures moved more tribal farmers into leasing or selling land to white and commercial farmers.

Cattle production on the Crow Reservation offered great promise at the end of the nineteenth century. Unfortunately, the grazing pressure from white-owned trespassing cattle, and later from white ranchers who leased reservation land, competed with Crow-owned cattle on the range. Crow Indians succeeded in finding new sources of economic production after losing the buffalo, but they failed in the political battle to keep their white neighbors from appropriating the benefits from Crow resources.[2]

One of the most remarkable pieces of evidence of the energy and drive of Crow and Northern Cheyenne Indians to prosper in the new economic order was provided in the details of Indian labor constructing irrigation ditches and doing freighting work in the late nineteenth century. Historian Frank Rzeczkowski examined agency records and found that the Northern Cheyennes in the 1890s and early twentieth century were eager for wage work, freight hauling, and other agency work. Agriculture on the Northern Cheyenne reservation was marginal at best, which made wage labor especially attractive.

In addition to freighting, both the Crows and Cheyennes looked to profit from the construction jobs provided by the new Crow irrigation project. Surviving construction reports showed that the jobs attracted many Crow, Cheyenne, and even Cree workers. Indian workers were willing to work for money to support their families when the opportunity presented itself. In one case in 1895 the Northern Cheyenne agent secured a contract for the Cheyennes to supply 400 cords of wood for the army post at the agency. The agent had to rush to stop the woodcutting parties because they were harvesting too much wood. By the time the agent stopped the woodcutters, 517 cords of wood were delivered.[3]

The neighboring Coeur d'Alene Indians developed agriculture with the help of the Jesuit missionaries and had farms to take up the slack from the declining hunting resources. The farms developed by tribal members in the second half of the nineteenth century were successful in supporting the tribe and avoiding general rations. The Coeur d'Alenes tried to develop a timber industry but failed to receive government assistance to buy a sawmill. They finally had to rely on contracting with white lumbermen, and the jobs and most of the profits went outside the tribe. There was one case of a tribal member operating a successful stage line in the area, but evidence of other Indian enterprises remains to be researched.[4]

The Northern Arapaho Indians in Wyoming also worked hard to find new ways to support themselves after the end of the buffalo. Council chiefs and headmen operated large communal farms where their followers shared in the labor and harvest. Many Arapahos worked "cutting and selling wood, hauling coal, laboring on government irrigation ditches, and raising hay, grains, and vegetables for sale." Tribal members took wage work for the army, agency, and missions to earn money. Their labor did not provide all the support the Arapahos needed. The agent was still able to use rations to control the Indians and coerce cultural change.[5]

The Southern Cheyennes and Southern Arapahos in Oklahoma were dependent on rations, but they took advantage of those economic opportunities open to them. In the late nineteenth century they started gardens in the river bottoms, built up cattle herds, and took all the freighting jobs they could find. Some farmers lived in central camps and went out daily to work their fields. Traditional cooperative practices were continued through common fields and sharing of food and other products. Tribal members worked to incorporate the new opportunities into their traditional values and community organization. They suffered from a lack of legal protection, which made Indians open prey for white thieves and attackers preying on tribal assets and members.[6]

The Comanches were also ration Indians, but they found support from new economic opportunities in the late nineteenth century. They developed cooperative farming, freighting jobs, and cattle herds as new sources of income to partially replace the buffalo. They also generated some income from grazing rentals paid by white cattlemen. The Comanches worked to cope with the new white-dominated economic order without adopting white American values.[7]

The Ojibwa Indians on the White Earth Reservation in Minnesota did not receive regular rations. In the late nineteenth century they expanded their gardens, sometimes selling their surplus to white men. They continued subsistence gathering of wild plants and found a ready market for wild rice and snakeroot. Hunting continued but was supplemented by wage labor, timber work, and craft sales. Government annuities helped support the Ojibwas, and the agent worked to use the annuities to control tribal members.[8]

The Indians of Puget Sound, Washington, also survived without regular rations. The arrival of white settlers increased the competition for fishing, but the Indians were able to find employment opportunities working for their white neighbors. Some Indians survived by developing farms but most combined as much fishing as possible with wage employment.[9]

The Klamath Indians in Oregon received treaty annuities in the late nineteenth century, but only the old and needy received subsistence rations. Tribal members tried to develop farms, but the high elevation of the reservation resulted in many failures due to frost and lack of rainfall. Some families were able to raise cattle and hay. Others sold logs to white men and the agency and worked for the agency and traders—especially freighting government supplies. Many families continued to rely on traditional fishing and gathering in season. The Klamaths developed new economic opportunities as available, and they continued traditional activities as much as possible.[10]

The Menominee Indians in Wisconsin lost access to much of their traditional land used for hunting and gathering. During the late nineteenth century most Menominees supported themselves with logging work in the reservation forest. The tribesmen had to contend with a series of federal laws and government politics that worked to disrupt the tribal logging industry, but the Menominees were able to support themselves from the employment and log sales from their forest.[11]

These comparative case studies of reservation economics in the late nineteenth century are neither exhaustive nor random. They do suggest, however, that tribes other than just the Salish and Kootenai examined in this monograph were actively seeking new sources of support to cope with the devastating economic changes of the loss of traditional hunting and gathering resources. Like the Flathead Reservation tribes, other tribes continued as much of their traditional economic life as possible, but they worked to develop new sources of support to limit or avoid dependence on government rations. The Indian people on Flathead and other reservations were resourceful and independent.

Table 1.1. Flathead Indian Reservation Statistics, 1875–1904

Year	Population	Acres cultivated	Acres broken	Wheat	Oats/Barley
1875	1,566	1,500	74	4,000	1,000
1876	1,629	1,800	402	4,500	3,150
1877	1,542	1,920	100	5,000	4,200
1878	1,585	2,000	NA	8,000	4,510
1879	1,607	3,460	660	20,200	4,150
1880	1,338	3,300	300	25,000	7,000
1881	1,292	1,500	250	20,000	15,970
1882	1,391	1,800	300	23,500	19,710
1883	1,693	2,200	400	26,200	21,000
1884	1,734	2,500	3,000	24,000	6,850
1885	1,816	6,490	8,000	28,000	28,250
1886	2,280	6,860	500	34,000	40,500
1887	2,016	7,063	550	35,550	41,715
1888	2,018	8,000	1,140	40,500	47,000
1889	1,914	8,900	900	45,200	45,500
1890	1,784	9,000	500	8,790	12,750
1891	1,788	10,000	600	23,030	20,460
1892	1,801	13,255	3,255	42,675	45,050
1893	1,914	10,600	680	20,200	19,800
1894	2,065	10,700	700	20,700	21,000
1895	2,101	10,800	600	50,000	75,000
1896	1,993	10,000	400	15,000	10,000
1897	1,998	10,000	300	13,500	12,000
1898	1,998	10,000	300	13,500	12,000
1899	1,998	11,000	1,000	38,650	33,268
1900	1,621	12,000	1,000	41,061	34,380
1901	1,638	14,000	1,500	45,000	37,000
1902	1,581	17,000	3,000	65,000	43,000
1903	1,670	25,000	8,000	75,000	45,000
1904	1,835	28,000	3,000	82,000	50,000

Population 1880–85 does not include Bitterroot Valley Flatheads.

Numbers of "Indian families engaged in civilized occupations" were not consistent from year to year. Some years "civilized" pursuits were listed separately, and some years Indian and mixed-blood families were listed separately.

Vegetables	Hay	Horses	Cattle	Swine	Indian families engaged in "civilized" occupations	Acres fenced
2,100	150	2,500	1,800	450	75	NA
3,475	112	1,800	800	350	75	NA
3,425	100	2,100	1,100	520	156	NA
3,425	10	2,286	3,323	175	120	NA
4,709	NA	9,335	5,785	500	145	NA
7,025	100	10,000	6,900	690	150	NA
11,340	300	2,443	2,619	125	96	NA
12,370	540	2,710	3,585	200	143	2,700
14,402	NA	3,100	5,450	220	165	3,200
12,080	1,110	3,400	6,500	400	133	3,700
17,150	2,335	3,900	8,000	950	240	13,490
23,011	4000	4,800	11,400	1,050	345	13,800
7,856	4,400	5,250	10,400	1,350	505	14,350
23,717	6,000	5,607	13,200	1,250	377	15,000
27,680	6,040	5,782	13,250	1,460	380	15,500
7,181	2,000	5,227	13,190	1,275	500	16,000
13,475	4,040	4,782	14,400	1,400	600	17,000
35,020	4,720	4,833	15,880	1,500	700	20,255
13,915	4,200	6,766	15,010	1,100	620	18,000
7,290	6,600	7,000	15,000	1,000	NA	19,000
19,000	6,000	16,000	15,000	1,200	NA	19,000
11,000	7000	18,000	17,000	1,300	NA	19,000
10,500	7000	15,012	11,000	1,200	NA	20,000
10,500	7000	15,012	11,000	NA	NA	20,000
12,050	8,500	15,000	10,000	1,500	NA	25,000
15,000	10,000	16,000	12,000	1,500	NA	30,000
15,000	12,000	16,000	20,000	1,500	NA	37,000
23,300	18,000	17,000	27,000	1,800	NA	40,500
20,900	25,000	23,000	27,000	2,000	NA	50,000
23,070	27,000	21,000	28,000	2,300	NA	NA

CHAPTER 1

The End of the Buffalo Economy, 1875–1881

The period between 1875 and 1881 was a time of seismic change in the economic life of the Salish, Pend d'Oreille, and Kootenai Indian people living on the Flathead Indian Reservation. In 1875 traditional hunting and gathering were still the most important economic activities for the Flathead Reservation tribes. The plains buffalo hunt was the base of their economy. The buffalo provided the tribes with generous provisions of meat, skins, and other products, which sustained the tribes. Other big game, such as deer, elk, and mountain goats, together with wild berries and roots, combined with the buffalo to support the tribes. Horse and cattle herds and grain and vegetable crops on the reservation were valuable, but secondary in 1875. In the late 1870s the tribes were developing an economic life that inserted livestock and agricultural work into the seasonal round of buffalo hunts and gathering plants.

But the buffalo herds and other wildlife populations were beginning to crash, and 1881 saw the last known buffalo hunt by the Flathead Reservation tribes. With some government assistance—but no general government rations—the reservation tribes were able to maintain their economic independence and in 1881 were still self-supporting. They expanded their cattle and horse herds and planted new fields of grain and vegetable gardens. Some tribal members found part-time employment with white men and better-off Indian ranchers. Most traded with white merchants in off-reservation towns. A few took to the whiskey trade or benefited from the hospitality of white settlers. Through a variety of strategies, the Flathead Reservation tribes were able to cope with the loss of the buffalo without giving the government control of their food supply.

The economic importance of the buffalo to the Flathead Reservation tribes was attested to in an 1874 letter from St. Ignatius Mission. The letter was unsigned, but may have been written by Omar G. V. Gregg, a Confederate Civil War veteran who worked for the St. Ignatius Mission as a printer in the middle 1870s.[1] The November 1874 buffalo hunt consisted of 183 lodges of the Pend d'Oreille, Coeur d'Alene, Kootenai, Spokane, and Colville tribes, aggregating to six hundred men for protection against the larger Plains tribes. According to this letter, five of the hunters succeeded in killing 104 fat buffalo cows and bulls. The writer calculated that these five hunters harvested 52,000 pounds of meat on the hunt. The five returned with buffalo tongues and products from the hides, sinews, and other parts of the animals. The anonymous writer estimated the entire hunting party, including all the allied tribes, got 3,240,000 pounds of meat on the hunt. In Chicago that amount of meat would have cost half a million dollars.[2] In the middle 1870s a successful plains buffalo hunt provided abundantly for the Flathead Reservation tribes.

But even in 1875, the buffalo hunt could be a capricious provider. Some hunters returned with much less success. On May 1, 1875, Flathead agent Peter Whaley reported that at least one group of buffalo hunters "returned poorly clad and in other respects poorly supplied."[3]

The Flathead Reservation farmers integrated their buffalo hunts into the seasonal schedule working their farms. Peter Whaley noted on June 1, 1875, that many tribal members who had farms had left on a buffalo hunt after their crops were planted.[4] The farmers returned from the summer hunt later to harvest their crops and have their grain ground into flour before traveling to the plains in the fall for the winter buffalo hunt.[5]

During the summer of 1875 the governor of Montana complained about the buffalo hunters passing through the white settlements without U.S. Army escorts. The chiefs, however, pointed out the provision in the 1855 Hellgate Treaty that guaranteed the right of the tribes to travel off the reservation to hunt on unoccupied lands.[6]

The buffalo hunt could be intertwined with physical violence and horse theft. During the autumn of 1875 one group of Pend d'Oreille buffalo hunters on the plains engendered considerable hostility from the Blackfeet Indians. During July 1875 twenty-two lodges of Pend d'Oreilles visited the

Blackfeet Agency. They had a letter or permit from the commanding officer of Fort Shaw allowing them to hunt buffalo on the Blackfeet Reservation. The Piegan head chief, White Calf, reluctantly acquiesced to allow the Pend d'Oreilles to hunt buffalo north of the Marias River.[7]

That fall, as the Pend d'Oreilles were preparing to return to the Flathead Reservation, they stole ten horses belonging to two of the Blackfeet chiefs. The Blackfeet caught up with the Pend d'Oreilles at Cadottes Pass and forced the Pend d'Oreille to return the stolen horses.[8] At about the same time, Agent Charles S. Medary identified some other Pend d'Oreille warriors who had stolen Blackfeet horses. According to Medary, he had the guilty parties punished and returned the horses to their original owners.[9]

In October 1875, just before the last of the Pend d'Oreille buffalo hunters returned home west of the mountains, two young Pend d'Oreille warriors came across two Blackfeet women some distance from the Blackfeet Agency. They lassoed the women and started to drag them off when some nearby white men intervened and obtained their release. One of the women was the wife of Blackfeet chief Little Plume. Little Plume was "greatly incensed." The entire Pend d'Oreille hunting party departed from the Blackfeet Reservation as quickly as possible. The Blackfeet Agency personnel pleaded with Little Plume to not attack the fleeing Pend d'Oreilles.[10]

In February 1876 two Pend d'Oreille Indians stole twenty head of horses from the Gros Ventres. About half of the stolen horses were retrieved by the Montana civil authorities and U.S. Army soldiers and returned to the Gros Ventres.[11]

Later that month a Flathead Reservation mixed-blood—apparently Basham Finley—took time out from the buffalo hunt to steal two Piegan horses on the Marias River. Finley was tracked back to the Flathead by Capt. Andrew Dusold, a U.S. Indian detective. Dusold arrested Finley near St. Ignatius Mission with the assistance of a reservation chief. He was held in the Helena jail.[12]

Pend d'Oreille chief Big Canoe visited Deer Lodge on February 27, 1876, while returning from the buffalo country with a U.S. Army escort. While at Deer Lodge, the Pend d'Oreille traded buffalo robes and buffalo tongues with the whites.[13] Another Pend d'Oreille buffalo hunting party—without an army escort—followed the Big Canoe band back to the Flathead in early April 1876. This band was accused in the newspapers of killing white-owned cattle on the Dearborn River.[14]

The buffalo hunt was a critical part of the economy of the Flathead Reservation tribes in the middle 1870s, but it soon became entangled in the panic and hysteria that gripped the Montana white population and federal government after the Sioux victory in the Battle of the Little Big Horn. On August 22, 1876, the commissioner of Indian affairs issued an order that all Indian traders in Montana were prohibited from selling guns or ammunition to Indians or whites.[15]

No information was found about how the commissioner of Indian affairs' order impacted the buffalo hunting trips of the Flathead Reservation tribes. The predicament of the Flathead Reservation tribes was described in a note in the *Weekly Missoulian* on September 13, 1876. According to this article, Missoula was full of friendly Indians — probably including many Pend d'Oreilles or Flathead Reservation Salish. They had large herds of horses and mules and were "well armed with needle Sharp and Spencer guns and well supplied with ammunition." The writer pointed out that these Indians had shown "many proofs of their friendship in their dealings with the whites," but some Missoula whites were still suspicious they might ally with the Sioux.[16] This was despite the traditional hostility between the Sioux and the Rocky Mountain tribes.

During the winter of 1876–77 a large camp of reservation Salish, Pend d'Oreilles, Coeur d'Alenes, Spokanes, Gros Ventres, and Blackfeet were in north-central Montana hunting buffalo. Chief Arlee of the reservation Salish led a religious service on Christmas 1876. Father Philip Rappagliosi, S.J., spent part of the winter in the camp baptizing children and teaching.[17] By the end of February 1877 the Pend d'Oreille buffalo hunters were on their way back home to the Flathead Reservation.[18]

The 1876 prohibition of guns and ammunition sales by Indian traders in Montana may not have had a devastating impact on Pend d'Oreille, Salish, and Kootenai buffalo hunters from the reservation, but events in 1877 struck much closer to home. The Nez Perce hostiles in 1877 were traditional allies of the Flathead Reservation tribes, and they fled through western Montana during the war. Avoiding hostilities with Montana whites while securing guns and ammunition for hunting and protection became critical for the tribes in 1877.

In response to the passage of the Nez Perce hostiles through Montana during the summer of 1877, the federal government issued orders prohibiting the sale of guns and ammunition to any Indian in Montana — friendly or hostile. Apparently this order, unlike the order in 1876, was enforced, causing immediate problems for the Flathead Reservation tribes. The new Flathead Indian agent Peter Ronan was upset because those Indians who still depended on the hunt for food could be forced to either starve or fight for food. On August 21, 1877, Ronan petitioned his political patron, Montana delegate Martin Maginnis, to secure an exemption for the Flathead Reservation tribes from the ammunition sales ban. Ronan pointed out that for thirty years the reservation tribes had been able to purchase all the ammunition they needed, and there had never been any reason to question their loyalty or friendship toward their white neighbors. And now, after they had stood forth to protect the white settlers during the Nez Perce War, they were being deprived of their ability to support themselves by hunting.[19] A few days later, on September 2, 1877, Ronan met with U.S. Army general W. T. Sherman, who was then in Missoula, to press the case for modifying the order.[20]

In order to encourage the Flathead Reservation tribes to remain on the reservation during the height of the panic among white Montanans in the summer of 1877, Ronan purchased and distributed subsistence supplies on his personal credit.[21] Later in 1877, the reservation chiefs decided to take what guns and ammunition they had and proceed to the buffalo grounds by a northern trail that avoided the white settlements. The reservation party returned home safely after the hunt without incident. The Bitterroot Salish under Chief Charlo were hit especially hard by the ban on ammunition sales because their crops had been destroyed by a hailstorm, and they had been unable to tend them while the Nez Perces were transiting the Bitterroot Valley.[22]

On May 1, 1878, Ronan forwarded a letter from the reservation chiefs to the commissioner of Indian affairs. The letter had the marks of Arlee, the Salish chief; Michelle, the Pend d'Oreille chief; and Eneas, the Kootenai chief. The chiefs pointed out that they had made good progress in developing their farms, but they still needed to hunt buffalo to help support themselves. The crops were planted, and the young men wanted to hunt for meat while the old people stayed at home to tend the growing plants. By this time the government had approved the sale of powder, lead, and caps to the Flathead Reservation tribes, but this was little help because they did not have any muzzle-loading guns, and none were available for purchase. They needed metallic ammunition that worked in the new guns they owned. The chiefs tried to explain how the tribes integrated farming and hunting into their annual economic cycle:

We are doing our best to bring our children up to work, but when the crops are planted and nothing to do, we feel that it would be a great wrong to force our children to stay at home when they so much love to hunt the buffalo and return at the time work commences, cheerful and happy and well supplied with meat and furs.[23]

As 1878 progressed, there was a war between the government and the Bannock Indians in neighboring Idaho and rumors and murders of whites by small bands of hostile Nez Perce Indians transiting Montana on their way back to their Idaho homeland. In his annual report on August 12, 1878, Ronan credited the reservation chiefs with helping minimize the chance that the explosive situation would erupt into further violence. Ronan and the chiefs were afraid that some of the white settlers might mistake Flathead Reservation hunters for hostiles and that an attack would plunge the reservation tribes into war.[24]

A week later, Ronan complained to the commissioner of Indian affairs that no provision had been made to subsist the Bitterroot Salish or the Flathead Reservation tribes if they abandoned the buffalo hunt. The Bitterroot Salish particularly relied on the buffalo hunt over the last winter because they had lost their 1877 crop while rallying to protect the Bitterroot Valley whites. They had remained on the buffalo grounds in the Judith Basin until the summer of 1878. The only friction when they returned to the Bitterroot was when their dogs killed some sheep. Soon they would need to return to the plains, and Ronan suggested they be provided with a small escort of army soldiers while going through the settlements.[25]

Few of the Flathead Reservation tribes went on the buffalo hunt during the 1877–78 period, and most of those traveled by a northern route to avoid the white settlements. A small band of Salish and Pend d'Oreilles went to the plains in 1878 by way of the Big Blackfoot and Fort Shaw, but they were led by a very trustworthy chief—probably Big Canoe. Ronan had received no complaints against this party. Many reservation tribal members were engaged in raising grain and cattle, but there were still a number who relied on hunting to help support their families. Since the government had not provided him with the funds to purchase rations, how could Ronan try to keep them from the buffalo hunt? Besides, the 1855 Hellgate Treaty guaranteed the tribes the right to hunt, fish, and gather plants off the reservation.[26] On October 1, 1878, a band of hunters under Chief Big Canoe left Missoula for the buffalo grounds with an army escort.[27]

Another Pend d'Oreille buffalo hunting party during the summer of 1878, under Chief Andre, returned to the reservation without having killed any buffalo. When they arrived on the plains, the Blackfeet and Assiniboine threatened to attack the party if they killed any of "their" buffalo. Andre decided to return to the Flathead Reservation in order to avoid an all-out war with the Plains tribes. Ronan thought the failure of the hunt would encourage more tribal members to concentrate on their cattle herds and farms. In the meantime Ronan asked the commissioner of Indian affairs for authority to purchase 6,000 pounds of beef and 6,000 pounds of flour to help fill in the gap from the failed hunt.[28]

The government's 1877 order prohibiting the sale of guns and ammunition to the Flathead Reservation tribes had kept the regulated Indian traders and white merchants from supplying the buffalo hunters. This forced the reservation tribes to rely on small-time traders on the plains. No evidence has been found describing these sales during the winter of 1877–78, but Andrew Garcia left a detailed record of such dealings in the Musselshell during the winter of 1878–79. The Pend d'Oreilles who camped with Garcia that winter might have been Lower Pend d'Oreilles living west of the Flathead Reservation. According to Garcia, the Pend d'Oreilles asked for guns and ammunition on credit, but he refused. Garcia then traded with both the Blackfeet and the Pend d'Oreilles, exchanging guns and ammunition for buffalo robes.[29] The small itinerant traders on the plains might have charged more for guns and ammunition, but they probably paid less attention to legal technicalities.

By 1879 the declining plains buffalo herds were making the buffalo hunts less productive, while the expanding cattle herds and farms on the reservation were playing a more important role in supporting the Flathead Reservation tribes. On March 3, 1879, Ronan reported that the twenty lodges of Pend d'Oreilles under Chief Big Canoe, who had left the reservation in September 1878, were, according to his knowledge, the only ones that had gone on the 1878–79 winter hunt. On January 29, 1879, Pend d'Oreille chief Michelle wrote to Big Canoe's group, then on the plains, assuring them that the buffalo hunters' cattle on the reservation were in good shape. Michelle also exhorted the buffalo hunters to be careful to not steal any horses from white men while on the hunt.[30] According to Ronan, the buffalo "hunting parties are growing less every year as the Indians are brought to see the great benefits that accrue to those who remain at home and take care of their farms and stock, and but a short time will elapse until the habit will entirely cease."[31]

In late March, Chief Arlee of the reservation Salish, learned that the Bitterroot Salish under Chief Charlo were returning from their winter hunt with poor and worn out horses. Arlee sent a band of fresh horses to their relief, driven by four reservation Salish. Ronan provided a letter of introduction for the herders to explain their relief mission to white authorities.[32]

The three reservation chiefs—Salish chief Arlee, Pend d'Oreille chief Michelle, and Kootenai chief Eneas—in May 1879 requested permission and an escort for some of the young men to go on a summer buffalo hunt. The chiefs argued that the buffalo hunt was a reward and incentive for the young men to do their plowing, harrowing, fencing, and sowing. They had completed the spring labor, and some now wanted to go on the buffalo hunt, while others stayed on the reservation to watch the cattle and growing crops. The commissioner of Indian affairs approved the request, and the army supplied an escort to the buffalo range.[33]

Chief Arlee and five lodges of reservation Salish passed through Helena in June 1879 on their way to the plains.[34] About a month later they stopped at Helena on their return trip to the Flathead Reservation.[35]

A Salish buffalo hunting party passed through Helena in October 1879 on their way east. The group seems to have included both reservation and Bitterroot Salish and some Pend d'Oreilles.[36] Some of their horses were stolen a few days later, and white men were suspected.[37] The hunters returned to the reservation in spring 1880, possibly in two parties.[38] Pend d'Oreille chief Big Canoe died in Missoula on the return trip, and his body was taken to the reservation for burial.[39]

The 1880–81 buffalo hunt ended in tragedy. On their way home in spring 1881, a combined group of Bitterroot and reservation Salish and Pend d'Oreilles met a whiskey trader near Martinsdale. Antoine Arlee was killed by a Pend d'Oreille in the resulting drunken fight. The survivors returned to the reservation in early April 1881. In May 1881 Chief Arlee put on a large memorial dinner at the agency for his dead son.[40]

A few weeks later in June 1881, Chief Arlee led a small band on what was probably the last buffalo hunt for the Flathead Reservation tribes. After a short buffalo hunt, he retrieved his son's body from a grave in the Mussel-shell Valley to rebury Antoine on the reservation. The hunters returned through Deer Lodge in August 1881.[41] The Bitterroot Salish had their last buffalo hunt over the winter of 1882–83.[42] The plains buffalo were killed off by the middle 1880s. Once the foundation of the Flathead Reservation tribes' economies, the resource was no more. They were forced to find other ways to support themselves.

The buffalo hunt was not the only traditional economic activity to support the Flathead Reservation tribes between 1875 and 1881. Fishing, gathering roots and berries, and hunting deer, elk, mountain goats, and other big game were also important economic activities. The buffalo hunt was fairly well documented in the historical sources, but only limited information has survived about these other activities.

Four references to Flathead Reservation Indians hunting big game, other than buffalo, have been found. The Pend d'Oreilles who became embroiled in a July 1879 altercation with a party of white men in the Lincoln area started out hunting deer. After alcohol was introduced, an Indian named Moses was killed in a fight. The white murderer, Evans, was arrested, but charges were dropped when the Indian witnesses failed to appear at Evans's trial.[43] On October 25, 1879, a Helena newspaper noted that seven lodges of Pend d'Oreilles were hunting game in the mountains near town.[44] Another documented incident was a Salish hunter who killed a mountain goat on the reservation in January 1880.[45] During the summer of 1881, while a Northern Pacific Railroad survey crew was working about eight or ten miles above Plains on the Clark's Fork, a reservation Indian named Bighead was in the area hunting deer with dogs. Bighead chased a deer into the river where it was then killed by the white surveyors. The story was related by Clarence Prescott, a member of the survey party.[46]

Fishing was another economic activity that paralleled hunting. In July 1881 a party of about eighty Pend d'Oreilles was camped at the mouth of Prickly Pear Canyon between Helena and Fort Benton. The Pend d'Oreilles caught a number of large trout.[47] In his 1881 annual report Agent Peter Ronan mentioned that Horse Plains was a popular fishing place for tribal members.[48] The Jocko River on the reservation was a prime trout fishery. On November 1, 1879, a correspondent in a Helena newspaper commented on the large trout caught by Indian fish traps on the Jocko.[49] In 1881 a Salish fisherman caught a fifteen-pound trout on the Jocko.[50] Despite the poor documentation, fishing would have been important as the Flathead Indians worked to support themselves between 1875 and 1881.

The final traditional food source was gathering root crops, such as bitterroot, berries, and other plant foods. These activities were not noticed in the historical sources, but they must have continued to be valuable. Some problems must have developed as white men established farms in western

Montana that occupied food-gathering sites, but we do not know how much this interfered with the annual economic cycle for the tribes before 1881.

New Economic Resources, 1875–1881

New, nontraditional economic resources such as cattle, horses, and gardens were of growing importance between 1875 and 1881. These assets would have become especially valuable as the buffalo, big game, and wild food harvests declined.

Before motor transport, horses were the most effective means for moving people and baggage around Montana. The annual reports of the commissioner of Indian affairs include yearly estimates of horses, cattle, and agricultural production on the Flathead Reservation. The numbers were little more than informed estimates, but they do suggest there were more horses than people on the reservation. Most of the 1875–81 estimates range between 2,000 and 2,500 horses for 1,300 to 1,500 people.[51] During this period the horses and cattle were on open range and had to fend for themselves during the winter. Agent Peter Ronan wrote in his 1878 annual report that stock owners did not put up hay for winter feeding, because they believed there was "no necessity to provide hay or shelter for stock, as the winters are too mild to require it."[52] The winter of 1880–81 was severe, and tribal stock owners' losses were great, which established the need for winter feeding.[53] In July 1881 a correspondent for a Chicago newspaper encountered Indian men and women putting up hay in the Jocko Valley.[54]

Most of the historical sources indicate the Flathead Reservation tribes were relatively well-off in horses. In July 1877 Capt. C. C. Rawn of Fort Missoula wrote that "a great number" of the Pend d'Oreilles and Salish on the reservation were "rich in horses."[55] Agent Ronan estimated in his 1877 report that the Kootenais on the reservation owned three hundred horses.[56] A month later, when the Pend d'Oreilles were trying to get ammunition for a buffalo hunt despite the government ban on sales to Indians, some Pend d'Oreilles in Fort Benton attempted to trade horses for ammunition.[57]

Ronan completed a census of stock owners on the reservation on March 19, 1878. He found tribal members owned 2,286 horses.[58] In March 1878 the reservation Salish had enough surplus horses to send a band of fresh horses to relieve the Bitterroot Salish buffalo hunters returning from the plains.[59] The Pend d'Oreille buffalo hunters traveling through Helena in October 1879 sold "a good many" horses to local whites.[60] About the same time, an eight-year-old horse that had been sold by an Indian to a white man in Frenchtown strayed back to the reservation.[61] The available evidence suggested that between 1875 and 1881, the Flathead Reservation tribes had adequate numbers of horses to provide transport and even a surplus to sell to white men in Montana.

Since much of the reservation was good grazing land, tribally owned cattle herds were the best prospect for replacing the sustenance lost with the extinction of the plains buffalo herds. The numbers of reservation cattle listed in the annual reports were quite erratic between 1875 and 1881, but tended to run between 2,000 and 3,000 head.[62]

In the late 1870s many of the cattle on the reservation were owned by white men, most of whom had married into the tribes. In 1875 and 1876 the Missoula County economy was depressed after the decline of the gold mining camps, and the county was desperate for more tax revenue. The county commissioners attempted to tax the horses and cattle of the Bitterroot Valley Salish, which led to considerable bitterness on the part of Chief Charlo.[63] As part of their effort to increase Missoula County tax revenue, the commissioners tried to tax the cattle owned by mixed-bloods and white men married into the tribes. According to Charles Medary, the white cattlemen who lived on the reservation had been on the reservation from five to eight years and had considerable improvements on their property.[64]

According to one source, William Irvine led a drive of 1,200 head of cattle from the Flathead Reservation to Cheyenne, Wyoming, in May 1876. Irvine led similar drives in 1877, 1879, and 1880. Unfortunately, the source does not say whom Irvine was working for when he made the cattle drives.[65]

The most detailed record of cattle ownership on the reservation in the late 1870s was the March 19, 1878, inventory by Agent Ronan. Ronan counted 3,323 Indian-owned cattle on the reservation. He found 755 owned by white men (not counting those held by the agency and St. Ignatius Mission). The census listed 105 tribal cattle owners. Most of the larger herds were owned by mixed-bloods or white men, but Ronan listed 67 cattle owners who were full-blood Indians. The only full-blood owners with 100 or more head were Chief Arlee and his family, who had 100 head. Five mixed-bloods had sizable herds: Duncan McDonald and his four brothers (500 head), Antoine Revais (100 head), Michel Pablo (320 head), Raphael Bisson (110 head), and Jim Grass (125 head). Two white men had herds on the reservation with the permission of the chiefs: James Dugan (355 head) and Daniel Sullivan (275 head). Both of these white men had their herds in the Little Bitterroot River area. The second-largest herd on the reservation—410 head—was owned by James Burns, a white man who lived in the Mission Valley with his Pend d'Oreille wife.[66]

In August 1878 one visitor to the reservation wrote that reservation cattlemen had been purchasing high-quality cattle from farmers in the Bitterroot Valley to improve their herds.[67] That same month, Agent Ronan wrote to the commissioner of Indian affairs about procedures for replacing a lost check in payment for 6,000 pounds of beef. Ronan bought the beef from Duncan McDonald for $240.[68]

As mentioned previously, Pend d'Oreille chief Michelle wrote to the Pend d'Oreille buffalo hunters on the plains in January 1879 with news about events on the reservation. The letter assured the buffalo hunters their cattle on the reservation had come through the winter in good shape.[69]

Sabine, the widow of a white man who lived on the reservation, sold over two hundred head of cattle in May 1879. She deposited the proceeds in a Missoula bank for the benefit of her children.[70]

The Flathead Agency did help some tribal members get a start in the cattle business. In September 1880 Ronan distributed one hundred head of cattle to tribal members. He planned to turn the cattle over to the three head chiefs on the reservation who, in turn, would select the individuals to receive the cattle.[71] During the summer of 1881, blackleg, a cattle disease, broke out in the reservation herds.[72]

Cattle drives and roundups provided employment for a number of tribal members. Several tribal elders in 1940 recalled an 1879 cattle drive of over 1,000 head from Lewiston, Idaho, to the Upper Flathead Valley. The cattle were owned by T. J. Demers, the Frenchtown merchant who married a Pend d'Oreille woman, but most of the trail crew were Indian.[73] Charles Allard was in charge of the crew that drove cattle to the Dakotas in the spring of 1880. The cattle were not sold until 1881 due to a business depression in the Dakotas.[74]

Between 1875 and 1881, the cattle industry on the Flathead Indian Reservation proved an important, and probably growing, asset to the reservation tribes. Cattle helped fill the hole in the tribal economy left by the extermination of the plains buffalo herds.

Another economic resource the tribes expanded to help compensate for the declining hunting and gathering resources was the production of tribal member farms. Most of the farms produced wheat and oats, which were both used by the farmers for food and fed to livestock, and vegetables.

Many of the farms were small, especially during the first part of the 1875–81 period. As mentioned previously, tribal members fit their farming schedule into the seasonal cycle of hunting and gathering. Several sources discuss buffalo hunters putting in their crops and then leaving for the summer buffalo hunt while the crops were growing.

The Flathead Reservation statistics bounced around between 1875 and 1881, but they suggest 1,500 to 2,000 acres were cultivated during this period. Wheat production grew from 4,000 to 20,000 bushels. Oats and barley started at 1,000 bushels, but rose to 15,000 bushels. The vegetable harvest grew from 2,000 bushels to 11,000 bushels. The figures indicate that agricultural production on the reservation grew especially fast at the end of the period as the returns from the buffalo hunts crashed.[75]

In January 1875 Agent Peter Whaley reported that 1,102 acres were then cultivated by Indians in small patches of ten to fifty acres each.[76] On May 1, 1875, Whaley said the agency gristmill had been busy for two weeks grinding six hundred bushels of Indian grown wheat into flour. The wheat had been raised on small patches of two to ten acres each.[77] In his next monthly report, on June 1, 1875, Whaley wrote that the Pend d'Oreille and Kootenai farmers had sowed their crops and left for the summer buffalo hunt on the plains.[78] Unfortunately, the 1875 crop largely failed due to weather. The seasonal hunts took up the slack.[79]

Later that year, on September 13, 1875, the new agent, Charles Medary, mentioned that Pend d'Oreille chief Michelle and a few fellow tribesmen operated a small farm, four miles from the Jocko Agency.[80] The Indian farmers only had small crops of wheat in 1875, but the agency gristmill ground the harvest into flour before the tribal members headed to the plains for their buffalo hunt.[81]

Farming in 1875 was labor-intensive, especially during the sowing and fall harvest. The need for seasonal labor must have provided work for many tribal members who did not themselves farm. In October 1875 Eli Glover passed the farm located along the Clark's Fork River below Frenchtown and owned by a white man married to an Indian woman. The farmer drove the plow to harvest the potatoes. A crew of eighteen Indian men and women were gathering up the potatoes.[82]

One early farmer was Baptiste Eneas (Iroquois/Kootenai), who also operated the ferry at the foot of Flathead Lake. In spring 1877 Baptiste was raising oats and vegetables, some of which he sold to travelers heading north.[83] Agent Ronan sent a sample of Baptiste's wheat crop to the commissioner of

Indian affairs in December 1878. He had harvested sixty bushels per acre without irrigation.[84]

Some sources claimed that Agents Whaley and Medary exaggerated the progress the Flathead Reservation tribes were making in farming. An unnamed correspondent writing in the *Rocky Mountain Husbandman*, a newspaper in Diamond City, Montana, claimed only forty acres were under cultivation before the 1877 growing season.[85] In his 1877 annual report, however, Agent Ronan found six families who had "excellent crops of wheat, oats, potatoes, onions, turnips, &c," just among the Kootenais.[86]

Chiefs Arlee, Michelle, and Eneas made their marks on a May 1, 1878, letter asking the commissioner of Indian affairs for authorization to take the young men to the plains buffalo herds. The letter was probably written by Agent Ronan but had been translated for the chiefs by Michel Revais, the agency interpreter. The letter claimed, "A great many of us have houses to live in—have good farms fenced in—had good crops now planted." Since the crops were in, they wanted the young men to go on the buffalo hunt "while the old people stay at home and look after the crops until they ripen when all return from the hunt and help to gather them." Farming was folded into the seasonal round of hunting and gathering.[87]

In June 1878 Frank Decker, the white agency miller, told the Missoula newspaper that he had ground about eight thousand bushels of wheat from the 1877 crop into flour. He also said Indians had made forty thousand rails to erect fences on the reservation.[88] A correspondent for a Helena newspaper later that summer wrote that Indian farms filled a significant portion of the Jocko Valley.[89]

In his 1877 report Agent Ronan claimed that, despite grasshoppers, the crops of the Indian farmers would "be an abundance." In 1877 more Indians had planted successful vegetable gardens. Ronan was especially proud to report that Chief Eneas of the Kootenais had used his government salary as a chief to personally purchase a combined mowing and reaping machine for use on Kootenai farms.[90]

Agent Ronan made a long, detailed report to the commissioner of Indian affairs on December 30, 1878, about the confused contest for the ownership of a farm in the Horse Plains area. An Indian woman named Elize had claimed the farm and made an agreement with a white settler named John for John to build a fence on the land while Elize furnished the seed wheat. The crop was to be split between the two. Unfortunately, John later sold his interest in the farm to another white man named James Laughlin without explaining his arrangement with Elize. The resulting conflict between Laughlin and Elize and her son Louie Cultis-toe was further complicated by language and cultural differences. Ronan recommended that, since the farm was off the reservation, Laughlin should pursue his claims in Montana Territory courts. No record has been found indicating how this case was settled, but informal oral agreements might also have complicated land tenure and farming arrangements on the reservation.[91]

In February 1879 Ronan purchased one thousand pounds of oats from Espaniole Finley, a mixed-blood tribal member.[92] A newspaper correspondent visiting the agency in the spring of 1879 wrote that small Indian farms dotted the Jocko Valley. Most of the farms were from thirty to eighty acres.[93] That same spring, the three head chiefs of the reservation requested government permission for a summer buffalo hunt after the spring farm work was completed.[94] Ronan also wrote, about that time, that farmers and stockmen needed to travel to off-reservation towns to sell their surplus crops and livestock.[95]

Ronan wrote to the commissioner of Indian affairs on August 15, 1879, to argue for the need for a new threshing machine on the reservation. The old machine had been worn out with use.[96] In response to a circular regulation from the commissioner of Indian affairs, Ronan explained on November 5, 1879, that reservation farmers and stockmen exchanged their surplus crops and animals for groceries and articles for family consumption. Most did not sell their goods for cash.[97]

The only account of farming on the reservation in 1880 was in Ronan's annual report. Ronan claimed that "a number of new farms had been fenced in during the past season."[98] On January 1, 1881, Ronan wrote that the new threshing machine the agency received had worked well, but there was now enough demand to justify a second machine.[99]

Ronan was worried in June 1881 that a partial drought would damage the 1881 crop.[100] By August 1, 1881, Ronan expected a "fair average crop of grain and vegetables" despite a cold spring and a very dry summer.[101] In his annual report Ronan pointed out that while only ninety-six Indians had farms in 1881, "a great number of their relatives and friends" assist those farmers with seasonal help.[102]

By 1881 farming on the reservation was not as extensive as stock raising, but both enterprises were being expanded to help fill in the gap left in the reservation economy by the loss of the buffalo herds and other big game.

The loss of the hunting resources was a crisis for the tribes, but they had other resources to fall back on to maintain their economic independence.

Labor and Business, 1875–1881

Some Indians worked for the agency or took part-time work for white settlers in Missoula and surrounding towns. Labor for white people was not a major part of the new reservation economy, but it did help.

The Flathead Reservation tribes demonstrated their business acumen when in 1877 they were asked by Capt. C. C. Rawn of Fort Missoula to serve as scouts to warn the army and white settlers of the approach of any hostile Nez Perce. The chiefs assured Rawn and Ronan of their friendship toward the whites, but they insisted on getting pay and uniforms if they were to work as scouts. Since the agency and the army were not able to authorize pay, the reservation tribes only agreed to pass on what information they obtained without actively scouting the passes.[103]

Beginning in 1877 and continuing to 1898, the Ronan family employed a series of Indian women as laundresses. Mary Ronan's memoirs do not give the years of employment, but they included a Kootenai woman named Milly; To-a-pee, a Spokane Indian; Agatha Grandjo; Old Sophie; Katherine Barnaby; and finally, Felicitas Barnaby. The Ronans also hired Anastasia Morrigeau and Agnes Polson as nursemaids for their young children.[104]

In February 1878 an article in the *Weekly Missoulian* summarized the role of Indian workers and customers in the Missoula economy. The article noted that Indian workers "have made themselves useful in washing and scrubbing, sawing wood, carrying water in the winter, and pulling weeds from gardens in summer; in fact, they have supplied a kind of help that was needed by the [white] people."[105]

In November 1878 Duncan McDonald, a tribal member trader, hired Kootenai chief Eneas and another Indian to guide his pack train loaded with flour through the Upper Flathead Valley.[106] During the winter of 1878–79 Andrew Garcia, an itinerant white trader in the Musselshell Valley, paid Pend d'Oreille buffalo hunters to do several short-term jobs. Garcia bought the outfit and goods of another white trader to add to his stock. He needed help hauling the newly acquired wagon to his camp. Garcia paid a Pend d'Oreille, Pa-kal-k (Young Eagle), a needle gun and two boxes of cartridges for hauling the wagon to Garcia's camp. Afterward, Garcia hired two Pend d'Oreille, Charl and Petoe, and one mixed-blood, Samwell, to guide two white men to the Bozeman Trail. He paid each of the first two an Indian blanket and two boxes of Henry cartridges. Samwell, the mixed-blood Pend d'Oreille, earned two blankets and two boxes of fifty-caliber cartridges for making the trip.[107]

According to Clarence Prescott, in February 1879 several parties of white prospectors were traversing the Flathead Reservation looking for a rumored gold strike just west of the reservation boundary. Accompanied by Alex Morrigeau, a mixed-blood tribal member, the party got caught up in a winter blizzard and ended up at the banks of the Flathead River opposite the mouth of the Jocko River. They looked for a ford but could not find one. They finally offered a passing Indian $5 if he could find a crossing. The Indian did not find a safe place to cross and so did not get paid. The prospectors eventually made it back safely to Missoula by themselves.[108]

In 1879 and 1880 the Flathead Agency ran an apprenticeship program for young tribal members. The apprentices received subsistence and possibly a stipend. Since the boys wanted to join the seasonal buffalo hunts, it proved impossible to keep or discipline the apprentices. Ronan requested in December 1880 that the program be ended on the Flathead Reservation.[109]

Paid labor and services for whites were not a big part of the reservation economy between 1875 and 1881, but it was important for some families and individuals. Another facet of the Flathead Reservation economy from 1875 to 1881 involved tribal member trade with white merchants, including those in off-reservation towns. A few tribal members—mostly mixed-bloods—who worked as traders and ferrymen serving tribal members and white travelers through the reservation will be discussed. A special case— the whiskey trade—will also be considered. Since most of the Indian business with reservation traders and off-reservation merchants involved cash or trade, very little documentation has survived in the written record.

The commercial trade of Alex Morrigeau, a mixed-blood reservation rancher, was important enough in 1876 that a squabble broke out when he moved his business. Morrigeau had shopped at T. J. Demers's store in Frenchtown but started patronizing Missoula merchants because he felt Demers had cheated him. Since Demers was a politician as well as a merchant, he had Missoula County assess Morrigeau's wagon and horses for taxes despite Morrigeau being a tribal member living on the reservation.[110]

The Missoula newspaper on February 8, 1878, observed that Indian trade with local merchants "from the proceeds of their labors and sale of furs and skins, has been considerable."[111] That fall, Alex Matt entered into another economic exchange when he ran a two-year-old horse in a half-mile race at the Missoula County Fair. His horse placed second and won ten dollars.[112] Andrew Garcia traded guns and ammunition to the Pend d'Oreilles in the Musselshell for buffalo robes during the winter of 1878 and 1879.[113]

In another exchange that made it into the historical record, on April 15, 1879, Grand Joe paid the $1.50 balance due on a flute he purchased from the W. H. H. Dickinson store in Missoula. On July 10, 1879, Duncan McDonald ordered a one-year subscription to *Harper's Weekly* at the same store.[114] That fall, Joseph Loyola, a Colville Indian living on the reservation, paid for a subscription to the *Weekly Missoulian*.[115] A horse owned by Charles Allard took third in a race at the 1879 Missoula County Fair. Unfortunately, only first and second won monetary prizes.[116]

The reservation Salish who stopped at Helena in June 1881, on their way to buffalo, sold surplus horses to Helena whites.[117] Agent Ronan wrote in his 1881 annual report that it would be "a great hardship and injustice" to tribal members to force them to stop dealing with off-reservation merchants.[118] In September 1881 Grand Joe raced a horse in Missoula during the county fair. Grand Joe's horse lost, so he did not win any prizes or bets.[119] Ronan reported on November 1, 1881, that tribal members who had surplus grain, vegetables, or hay were able to sell them for good prices given the economic boom from the influx of railroad construction workers.[120]

A number of tribal members, again mostly mixed-bloods, had charge accounts at the Missoula Mercantile Company during this period. Only the 1881 ledger of the company itemized the purchases. A summary of a few accounts will give an idea of the custom involved. These accounts were paid in cash, furs, grain, and even breaking horses.

In 1881 Senecal bought whiskey, food, clothes, tobacco, and other items and paid for them partly with oats. Peter Irvine bought whiskey, clothes, and tobacco and paid cash. Charles Allard purchased food, household items, and fabric and settled his account with cash. Dandy Jim bought blankets and food paid with cash. Archie McDonald bought clothes and fabric and paid cash and broke two horses. Anthony Plant bought food, fabric, and household items and settled his account with cash. Michel Pablo bought food, clothes, blankets, fabric, ammunition, traps, and household items and paid his account in cash, furs, and freighting. Louis Valley bought blankets, fabric, and shoes and settled the account with cash. Peter Matt bought food, a wagon, and ranch supplies and paid with cash, oats, and freighting. Alex

Matt bought a trunk and paid by repairing picks and cash. Joseph Morrigeau bought whiskey and clothes and paid the bill off in cash. Alex Morrigeau bought whiskey, fabric, clothes, household items, and food and paid in cash, a horse, furs, butter, oats, and credit for goods furnished to the crew, who was building an access wagon road through the reservation for the Northern Pacific Railroad construction.[121] Many of the account holders were successful reservation ranchers who employed other tribal members both full-time and seasonally.

Most tribal members before 1881 relied primarily on hunting, gathering, ranching, and farming for support. But they were also occasional participants in the white capitalistic economy that surrounded the reservation.

A few tribal members actually operated businesses in the 1875–81 period. Duncan McDonald was the most prominent. On May 17, 1876, McDonald returned to Missoula after spending the winter trading in furs and buffalo robes.[122] That fall, McDonald traveled to Missoula to purchase goods for his new trading post near the Flathead Agency.[123] Earlier in 1876 Duncan had purchased the business and trade goods of William Goodyer, a white man who had operated a store at the agency for less than a year.[124] In August 1878 Agent Ronan requested a replacement check for one that was lost paying for 6,000 pounds of beef the agency purchased from McDonald.[125] A few months later, in November 1878, McDonald took a pack train loaded with flour to sell in the Canadian mining and cattle camps.[126] At the end of 1879, Agent Ronan did not mention McDonald in a report on traders on the reservation, so McDonald had closed his store by then.[127] In the fall of 1880 and 1881 McDonald ran pack trains of apples from Washington State to Missoula. In 1880 Missoula merchant Christopher Higgins hired McDonald to make the trip. In 1881 McDonald packed 6,000 pounds of apples for the Missoula market.[128]

The other tribal member who was most active as a businessman between 1875 and 1881 was Baptiste Eneas, Iroquois/Kootenai. Baptiste operated the ferry across the Flathead River at the foot of the lake where Polson is now located. He rented sailboats to white tourists who vacationed on Flathead Lake in the summer of 1876. In 1878 Agent Ronan purchased 1,248 pounds of white clay from Baptiste to use in whitewashing agency buildings.[129]

Antoine Revais, a mixed-blood, operated a ferry and small store on the Lower Flathead River in 1879.[130] In 1881 he advertised his "improved and enlarged" ferry across the Flathead River on the road through the reservation.

He promised reduced rates for Northern Pacific Railroad employees and pack trains headed for the Kootenai River country.[131]

Other tribal members engaged in commerce and operated trading establishments on the reservation. Joseph Loyola maintained a small establishment at St. Ignatius Mission.[132] Telesphore Guillium Demers, the mixed-blood son of Telesphore Jacques Demers, the Frenchtown merchant, applied for trading privileges on the reservation in August 1881.[133]

A special category of economic exchange with whites between 1875 and 1881 was the whiskey trade. Since the whiskey trade was illegal and clandestine, only limited evidence has survived describing it. Whiskey drained resources from more productive economic enterprises and engendered violence that was a challenge for tribal leaders.

Agent Medary reported on a September 1875 incident involving alcohol at the head of Flathead Lake. According to his information, a party of white men on their way to the Whoop Up Country in Canada were drinking in the Upper Flathead Valley. The drunken whites quarreled with several mixed-bloods, who were probably drinking with the whites. One of the mixed-bloods was knifed to death by a white man named Allen. Kootenai chief Eneas confronted the white men and demanded that Allen surrender to the white government authorities for trial. When Allen refused, Eneas and the Kootenais followed the white men and shot and killed Allen from ambush. The other whites were not harmed, and no property was stolen by the Kootenais.[134]

In the February 8, 1878, article in the *Weekly Missoulian* about the economic role Indians played in Missoula, the writer despaired of keeping white outlaws from selling whiskey to Indians camped near Missoula. During the preceding week, a group of drunken Indian women had started a fire against a wood stable to keep warm. The town night watchman discovered the flames before they could spread, but the writer felt it was impossible to stop the sale of liquor to Indians because if "they want liquor, they find means to get it."[135]

A party of Pend d'Oreilles stopped at Blackfoot, a small camp near Helena, in June 1878 and requested the whites share food in the traditional sign of hospitality. They later obtained whiskey—presumably by purchase or trade—and several knife fights broke out. The newspaper report did not indicate any injuries or deaths resulted from the scuffle.[136]

Many Montana whites in the 1870s and 1880s seem to have interpreted the laws against selling liquor to Indians as only applying to full-blood

Indians, not mixed-bloods. In 1878 Lorette Pablo, a mixed-blood, was indicted by the grand jury for providing whiskey to Indians near Lincoln Gulch. The newspaper account was vague, but presumably the whiskey was purchased, shared, or sold to the full-blood Indians who accompanied him.[137] (This attitude was also seen in the 1881 charge accounts at the Missoula Mercantile Company abstracted previously, where many mixed-blood customers charged whiskey to their accounts.)

A writer in the *Weekly Missoulian* on April 25, 1879, blamed the whiskey traffic more on the Indian appetite for alcohol than the white desire for illegal profits. The article lamented:

> The demoralization of both reds and whites from Indians about town is manifest. It is in the nature of things impossible to keep Indians sober when opportunities to be otherwise are so abundant. So long as there is no restraint upon an Indian, and he is at liberty to meet some lawless white man in a secluded place for illicit traffic in liquors, so long will Indians continue to be debauched by drunkenness.[138]

Agent Ronan argued that most of the drinking and carousal by Indians in Missoula was the doing of outlaw Indians visiting Missoula from the lower Columbia River country—not the better behaved Indian people from the Flathead Reservation.[139]

A July 1879 Lincoln Gulch drunken fight between several white men and a party of Flathead Reservation Indians—including a Pend d'Oreille named Moses and August Finley, a mixed-blood—resulted in the deaths of an Indian and a white man. The surviving white man, Richard Evans, was arrested for murder, but not convicted.[140] The accounts were contradictory, but presumably the Indians obtained the whiskey by purchase or trade.

A March 18, 1880, article in the Missoula newspaper summarized the problem of alcohol sales to Indians: "as a general thing, the Indians and whites in Missoula county get along very smoothly. If we could keep evil-disposed whites from selling them liquor we would never have any cause for complaint."[141] In the spring of 1881 a camp of Salish buffalo hunters from the reservation and the Bitterroot Valley were camped near Martinsdale, in central Montana. A white trader sold them whiskey and Chief Arlee's son, Antoine Arlee, was murdered by a Pend d'Oreille in a resulting drunken melee.[142]

Agent Ronan wrote in his August 1881 monthly report that two white men had been arrested in Missoula for selling whiskey to Indians. He claimed that he had broken up the whiskey trade on the reservation. Liquor was still available in off-reservation towns, but Ronan felt the local authorities were making progress in breaking up the off-reservation whiskey trade.[143] In August 1881 the volunteer Indian police force on the reservation under the direction of the traditional chiefs arrested John Bobier, a merchant from Kootenai. Bobier was accused of selling whiskey to tribal members, but he argued the Indians forced him to sell the whiskey to them. Bobier was incarcerated in Missoula and charges were filed against him.[144]

The whiskey trade between Indian customers and white suppliers was a significant part of the economy of the Flathead Reservation tribes between 1875 and 1881. Unfortunately, this particular component of the new economy brought violence, injury, and death to tribal members.

Federal Economic Aid, 1875–1881

Government aid was another economic asset for the tribes from 1875 to 1881. The amount of aid was quite limited during this period except for the Bitterroot Salish under Chief Arlee. Between 1875 and 1879, the tribes received the final payments under the 1855 Hellgate Treaty. Since the treaty was ratified in 1859, the twenty-year payments ran only through 1879. During the late 1870s the payments were $3,000 annually for general support— for about 1,500 tribal members—and $500 annual salaries for each of the three principal chiefs.[145] Salish chief Arlee's band received $5,000 per year under the agreement with Congressman James Garfield, which was supposed to be enough to assist all of the Bitterroot Salish. Most of the Salish, however, had remained in the Bitterroot Valley, leaving much larger shares for those few who moved to the Jocko with Arlee.[146] The government bureaucracy had trouble fulfilling some promises. In March 1875 Chief Arlee complained he never received six hundred bushels of wheat promised in the 1872 Garfield Agreement.[147]

There were no general rations. Government aid was useful, however, in helping tribal members expand their farming and ranching assets to make up for the loss of the buffalo. For example, in 1875 the agency distributed vegetable seeds to Indian farmers.[148]

To emphasize the limited amount of government assistance received, the December 1876 testimony of Chiefs Arlee and Michelle to the federal grand jury in Deer Lodge complained about unfulfilled promises from 1855 and 1872. They especially objected because no government school or hospital had been established on the reservation. They also pointed out that the government employees under the 1855 Hellgate Treaty, who were supposed to provide services for tribal members, were actually doing clerical and other work to keep the Flathead Agency functioning.[149]

The economic crisis confronting the Flathead Reservation tribes in 1877 and 1878, when their access to guns and ammunition was restricted by the government, emphasized that the tribes were basically self-supporting during the late 1870s. Only the reservation Salish under Chief Arlee had government aid that was a significant part of their income. In 1877 Ronan reported in his annual report that Chief Arlee's band was in "comfortable circumstances."[150] The rest of the reservation tribes received only incidental government aid and relied mainly on their own efforts. The guns and ammunition restrictions threatened an important component of their economic livelihood—hunting. Ronan argued that to suddenly cut the tribes off from the hunting resources would force them to fight to survive. Cattle and farms might be growing in importance in the tribal economy, but many families still relied at least partially on hunting. If the tribes could not hunt, they needed general rations to survive.[151]

During the Nez Perce War crisis, Ronan used his personal funds to purchase emergency supplies for those Indians camped near the agency.[152] Ronan received authority to purchase some general supplies in October 1877, but it is not clear which funds paid for the supplies.[153] In December 1877 Ronan distributed the goods and gave priority to the old and decrepit. Young men had to perform work on their farms or for the general community in return for their supplies.[154]

In July 1878 Ronan reported that tribal members viewed the goods distributed as recompense for the government order prohibiting the purchase of guns and ammunition. Therefore, they felt they should not be required to do labor in order to receive the goods. They wanted the Hellgate Treaty money used to purchase plows and other agricultural equipment.[155]

Ronan made a special plea for agricultural implements, wagons, and harness for the Kootenai Indians who were starting farms. Ronan proudly pointed out that Kootenai chief Eneas had used the money the government paid him personally for his work as chief to purchase a mowing and reaping machine, a set of carpenter tools, and a set of blacksmith tools for the use of his tribe.[156]

In August 1878 Ronan wrote that the $3,000 a year from the Hellgate Treaty was not enough to cover the needs of the aged, infirm, and indigent. There were no appropriations to cover general rations.[157] As mentioned previously, an emergency arose later that year when Chief Andre and the Pend d'Oreille buffalo hunting party returned to the reservation empty-handed. When the Pend d'Oreilles had arrived on the plain, the Blackfeet and Assiniboines threatened them with all-out war if they killed any buffalo. Ronan asked for authority to purchase 6,000 pounds of beef and 6,000 pounds of flour to subsist the hunters through the winter.[158]

According to a newspaper reporter visiting during spring 1879, the agency blacksmith had repaired ninety-three plows for tribal members.[159] A year later, the agency contributed candles, pipes, and tobacco to the wake for Pend d'Oreille chief Big Canoe, who died as he was returning from the buffalo hunt.[160] Ronan reported in his 1880 annual report that, during the fiscal year, the agency had ground 9,000 bushels of Indian wheat into flour and sawed 100,000 feet of lumber.[161]

The government purchased two hundred head of stock cattle for distribution in 1880. Half were given by the chiefs to young men starting their herds in the fall of 1880.[162] Ronan wrote that the other half of the animals were distributed in June 1881.[163] In his May 1, 1881, monthly report, Ronan mentioned that the agency flour mill "was overrun with work" and that the blacksmith was busy sharpening plows and repairing wagons and agricultural implements.[164]

The account of the July 1881 visit of a Chicago journalist to the reservation mentioned both the Flathead Agency and St. Ignatius Mission as sources of agricultural aid to tribal members. The agency grist and sawmills must have mostly served tribal members living in the Jocko Valley. Few descriptions have been found, but the grist and sawmills at St. Ignatius Mission served tribal members living in the Flathead Valley. The central location of the mission on the reservation made the mills at St. Ignatius more useful to the tribal economy than those at the Jocko Agency.[165]

On September 16, 1881, Ronan wrote to the commissioner of Indian affairs asking that the salaries of the three principal chiefs on the reservation be continued. The $500 a year payment had been provided for by the Hellgate Treaty through 1879. The commissioner of Indian affairs funded the salaries for 1880, but they were not budgeted for 1881.[166] Ronan did mention another government-provided economic asset on November 1,

1881. The agency provided threshing services for tribal member farmers, mainly in the Jocko Valley.[167]

Between 1875 and 1881 government rations were only provided to the old and infirm except in a few special emergencies. The government did provide agricultural equipment and seed cattle stock to help farmers get started. The blacksmith shop and grist and saw mills provided valuable assistance to some farmers in the Jocko Valley. Government assistance was a useful but very limited economic asset for the tribes in the late 1870s.

Other Economic Resources, 1875–1881

The last part of the Flathead Reservation economy between 1875 and 1881 that can be documented would be sharing/theft. The exchange of property through sharing/theft was bound up in cultural norms. For the Flathead Reservation tribes in the 1870s, stealing Blackfeet horses was a courageous honor, not a crime. The other culturally determined part of "theft" was Indian-white difference in the social concept of hospitality. In tribal culture, hosts were obligated to share with guests. Giving food, tools, or everyday objects to a visitor was normative, not a special act of benevolence. The white visitor to an Indian home was treated generously, and Indians calling on white people expected the same munificence. The boundary between theft and sharing could lead to friction and hard feelings.[168]

One incident mentioned previously that illustrated Pend d'Oreille interest in Blackfeet horses took place in October 1875. The Pend d'Oreilles stole ten horses that were hobbled close to the Blackfeet camp and then fled west. Five of the horses belonged to Blackfeet head chief Little Plume, and the other five were the property of Tall Hat, a band chief. The Blackfeet pursued the Pend d'Oreilles and caught up with them at Cadottes Pass. The Blackfeet demanded the return of the horses, and they were reluctantly surrendered by the Pend d'Oreilles.[169] Also, as mentioned in the discussion of the buffalo hunt, Pend d'Oreille warriors stole twenty horses from a Gros Ventres camp on the plains in January 1876. The Pend d'Oreilles were then camped on the Teton River opposite Fort Shaw.[170] In traditional Pend d'Oreille culture, horse theft was an accepted economic activity that increased a warrior's prestige and wealth in horses.

In the summer of 1876 there were at least two incidents of Indians on the reservation being accused of making use of white-owned rafts or skiffs maintained by mail carriers on the Flathead and Clark Fork River. The sources do not explain how the Indians might have viewed this form of sharing.[171] Later that year Agent Charles S. Medary reported several cases of reservation Indians stealing white-owned horses. According to Medary, the chiefs assisted him in recovering the animals and punishing the thieves. Medary did not provide details about any of the cases, so there is no way to evaluate his claims.[172]

A couple of incidents of sharing/theft in the Paradise-Plains area during the Nez Perce War period in late summer 1877 illustrate the cultural confusion surrounding the sharing of personal property. In one case Neptune Lynch discovered some Lower Pend d'Oreille children helping themselves to vegetables in his garden. The children probably looked at taking the garden vegetables much like helping themselves to wild foods. To Lynch, however, the plants he had sowed and cared for were his personal property, and the children were thieves. The disagreement escalated into an armed standoff. Fortunately, no one pulled a trigger, and the confrontation dissipated.[173]

In another cross-cultural incident about the same time in nearby Paradise, Denver Laughlin talked to the passing Indians. It turned out, the Indians wanted food from the whites as a sign of hospitality. Laughlin responded to the request and even presented some chickens to the Indian travelers, who went peacefully on their way.[174] Another incident in the Sun River area on the plains happened around early October 1877. A party of Pend d'Oreilles visited the camp of a large sheep owner and helped themselves to provisions and a gun.[175]

Mary Ronan, the wife of Agent Peter Ronan, described a visit to her house by an elderly Indian gentleman that showed the type of cross-cultural social exchanges involved. The man entered and sat near the fireplace. After several requests of, "What does your heart want?" he replied, "My throat is thirsty for sugar and my heart is hungry for fifty cents." The request was filled, giving the whites an opportunity to demonstrate their hospitality and proper social conduct.[176]

An incident of the "theft" of a ferry boat by a Pend d'Oreille Indian named Maxime in spring 1878, showed just how entangled such exchanges could become. George Conford accused Maxime of stealing his ferry boat from the Superior area and taking it down the Clark's Fork River and up the Flathead River. Maxime used the boat to ferry travelers across the Flathead River. Maxime had contacted T. J. Demers, the local white merchant, to see if the boat had been abandoned by its owner. After checking, Demers told Maxime that several boats had been lost on the river, and Maxime could take them if he could locate them. Based on these general assurances, Maxime took Conford's boat by mistake.[177]

An unnamed Indian was arrested in April 1878 for stealing money out of the cash register in a Missoula hardware store. He was able to discard the bills while he was being searched. The Missoula sheriff was about to release him when other Indians accused him of having murdered a prominent mixed-blood near Big Blackfoot in the summer of 1877.[178]

Another unnamed Pend d'Oreille and a Spokane Indian entered the home of Gaspard Deschamps just below Missoula in June 1878. They took food and some other items. They were pursued by the Missoula sheriff and a posse but escaped.[179]

On January 29, 1879, Pend d'Oreille chief Michelle wrote to remind Chief Big Canoe and the Pend d'Oreille buffalo hunters on the plains to not let anyone steal horses from Indians or whites. Michelle insisted any stolen horses be returned to their owners and the thieves punished.[180]

A Pend d'Oreille Indian named Moses was killed by white men in a drunken row that probably started over a blanket. The blanket had been stolen from the white men by another Indian who claimed the white men had swindled him.[181]

Finally, in August 1881, John Edward Bobier, a white man, accused reservation Indians of stealing whiskey from his pack goods. At the time, Bobier was being charged in court with selling whiskey to Indians.[182]

Despite the cultural differences that entangled the exchanges, sharing/theft played a small but significant role in the reservation economy. No documentation has survived, but presumably hospitality and sharing among tribal members were much more important than gifts or stolen commodities received from other tribes or white settlers.

Conclusion

The years between 1875 and 1881 were a period of dramatic change for the economy of the Flathead Reservation tribes. The plains buffalo herds were exterminated, and big game populations in western Montana crashed as a result of overhunting. At the same time, access to some traditional gathering sites for roots and berries was lost because they were occupied by white farmers.

Fortunately, the tribes had herds of horses and cattle and the produce of reservation farms to fall back on. With the growing importance of stock, the open range on the reservation proved a valuable and growing resource. More tribal members were also fencing in fields of grain and vegetable gardens. The livestock and agricultural resources combined with limited part-time work, trade with merchants, and some government aid to keep the Flathead Reservation tribes basically self-supporting and economically independent. Unlike other Montana Indians, the Flathead Reservation tribes never lived on general government rations. The economic adjustments that accompanied the loss of the buffalo herds must have been painful, but the Salish, Pend d'Oreilles, and Kootenais rose to the challenge. They survived the changes and were able to avoid giving the government control over their food supply.

CHAPTER 2

Crafting a New Economy, 1882–1888

The Flathead Reservation economy between 1882 and 1888 continued its pivot from the traditional hunting-gathering activities to stock raising and farming. Hunting, gathering, and fishing were getting less productive as the expanding white population added to the pressure on the available resources. The buffalo herds were gone, other wild game populations were crashing, and many gathering sites for native plants were occupied by white settlers. For most tribal members, traditional economic activities continued in their seasons, but they were no longer able to support the tribes. To fill in the gap, tribal members expanded their cattle and horse herds on reservation ranges and increased their farming of grain and vegetable crops.

Tribal members received some economic assistance from the Flathead Agency and the St. Ignatius Mission, but the tribes were basically self-supporting through these changes. The tempo of change increased after 1882 to culminate in the first recorded shipment of reservation cattle to off-reservation markets in trainload lots in 1888. The expansion of cattle exports from the reservation signified the tribes' increased integration into the larger American economy, as well as tribal efforts to be self-supporting and to limit government control of the reservation economy.

One of the most significant economic developments on the Flathead Indian Reservation between 1882 and 1888 was the right-of-way sale and construction of the Northern Pacific Railroad across the southern end of the reservation. The sale money and the construction work by tribal members had an important impact on reservation economic growth. The railroad also had a number of indirect impacts on the reservation economy. It facilitated the transport of goods from the outside onto the reservation. Presumably this lowered the price of goods for the traders and some of the mixed-blood cattlemen. Even more important, the railroad eased the process and cost of shipping the cattle, grain, and other bulk products produced on the reservation to off-reservation markets. As will be discussed, the production of these commodities expanded greatly during the 1880s. In the view of many tribal members, an undesirable impact was the increased traffic of white people traveling through the reserve and sometimes seeking employment. Only a few of the indirect economic impacts of the railroad can be documented through the historical sources.

Flathead Indian agent Peter Ronan learned in January 1882 that the Northern Pacific Railroad had definitely selected a route that passed through the reservation. Many tribal members opposed letting the railroad cross the reservation, and tensions were already strained over the work of the railroad surveyors laying out a route through the reserve. Ronan pleaded for instructions from Washington and for negotiations with the tribes for the purchase of the right-of-way and timber needed for the railroad.[1] About two weeks later, on January 16, 1882, Ronan wrote a second letter to reinforce the need for negotiations.[2] After two months of simmering tension, Ronan wrote Martin Maginnis, Montana Territory delegate to Congress, and his political mentor, to plead for help in pushing the bureaucracy to speed up arrangements to negotiate with the tribes for purchase of the right-of-way.[3]

Meanwhile in January 1882, some tribal members objected to survey work on the reservation to locate the railroad right-of-way. Some of the work involved cutting trees and brush in established Indian fields. One confrontation in January 1882, which involved threats with a knife, was exasperated by language difficulties.[4] In another incident along the Flathead River in March 1882, a survey crew paid Dominick five dollars for damage done in his field.[5] The surveyors and Agent Ronan negotiated with the tribal chiefs to allow the survey work to proceed.[6] Ronan repeated his plea for negotiations, and the railroad hired tribal member Duncan McDonald to mediate friction.[7]

As construction crews drew nearer to the reservation, the Montana white population became more concerned that the lack of a right-of-way agreement on the reservation could delay the work. On July 9, 1882, the *Helena Independent* editorialized that the Hellgate Treaty provision allowing for public roads through the reservation meant no further tribal consent was needed.[8] The *Independent* repeated this argument on July 12, 1882, and the *Helena Daily Herald* chimed in with agreement the next day.[9] It was quite likely that some news of this argument made it back to tribal members, increasing their apprehension over the government's willingness to respect tribal rights.

Meanwhile, the lack of agreement with the tribes was starting to interfere with railroad construction work.[10] The Missoula newspaper suggested that grading work on the reservation begin before an agreement was reached with the tribes.[11]

After an appeal by the railroad to initiate work on the reservation before an agreement was reached, Ronan called a general council of tribal members in July 1882. The decision of the council was to refuse permission for the work to proceed ahead of negotiations.[12] The commissioner of Indian affairs had instructed Ronan to not allow any work to begin without tribal consent. On July 19, 1882, the commissioner of Indian affairs telegraphed Ronan, "Allow nothing to be done by Rail Road Company on reservation without full consent of Indians. This is absolute."[13]

The federal government finally sent Joseph McCammon, United States assistant attorney general, to negotiate with the tribes for the right-of-way. Between August 31 and September 2, 1882, McCammon met with Flathead Reservation tribal members to hammer out an agreement. Tribal leaders complained about possible negative impacts from the railroad and wanted it to proceed west from Missoula to avoid the reservation. In an effort to keep the railroad off the reservation, the chiefs asked for a million dollars for the right-of-way. Kootenai chief Eneas stated that the reservation was "a small country; it is valuable to us; we support ourselves by it; there is no end to these lands supporting us; they will do it for generations." Salish chief Arlee argued, "You seem to like your money, and we like our country; it is like our parents."[14] McCammon offered $15,000 or $10 an acre and finally proposed $16,000. McCammon's condescension was palpable in the transcript as he pressured and threatened the chiefs to force an agreement.

The chiefs reluctantly agreed to sell the right-of-way but insisted on getting the payment in cash rather than annuities. They complained that the tribes had not gotten many of the goods and services promised in the 1855 Hellgate Treaty. The chiefs also made McCammon agree to use his influence to get the northern boundary of the reservation extended to the Canadian border. McCammon presented the proposed boundary move to the commissioner of Indian affairs in a November 21, 1882, letter.[15] A year later, when Senator G. G. Vest visited the reservation, the chiefs and headmen had changed their minds and withdrawn the request, fearing that any adjustments in the boundary might be manipulated against the interests of the tribes.[16]

The written terms of the right-of-way sale agreement, signed by 219 tribal members on September 2, did not agree with the verbal agreement reached during the negotiations. According to the transcript, the railroad was getting use of the land, not full title. Pend d'Oreille chief Michelle stated, "It is like the railroad borrowing the strip of land." McCammon agreed, "It is just buying the use of the strip of land." The written agreement, however, provided that the tribes "do hereby surrender and relinquish to the United States all the right, title, and interest" they had in the right-of-way land.[17] Emotions ran high at the negotiations, and according to Duncan McDonald, one young tribal member had to be prevented from assaulting one of the government negotiators.[18]

The Helena newspapers were impressed with the negotiating skills the tribes demonstrated. The *Helena Daily Herald* opined on September 7, 1882, "Why, the shrewdest of our real estate dealers can't hold a candle to these savages as land traders, and it is fortunate for the inhabitants of our rising cities that the Flathead Reservation is as far away as it is."[19]

Much to the relief of Montana whites, construction work commenced immediately after the agreement was negotiated—even before the land was paid for.[20] Ronan pointed out that despite considerable tribal opposition to running the railroad through the reservation, construction work proceeded without violence.[21] Some confrontations over damage to property owned by individual tribal members were mediated by Agent Ronan.[22] Presumably Duncan McDonald helped avoid misunderstandings and conflict while he worked for the railroad, but no accounts have survived.

Some tribal members found employment during the railroad construction delivering piles to bridge sites and possibly some other work. Details are scarce, but Ronan wrote on December 1, 1882,

that Indians who desire employment are now receiving good wages from the Northern Pacific Rail-road Company in various Capacities.— Several Indians have taken Contracts from the Division Engineer for the delivery of Piles at points where it is necessary to build bridges on the Reservation, and the Wagons and Harness, furnished by the

Indian Department have been a great Source of revenue to them, as they can get plenty of employment for their teams at more than a fair remuneration.[23]

In his 1883 annual report Ronan mentioned that tribal members had furnished "piles, ties, and cord-wood" for the railroad construction and the "high prices lately paid by beef contractors connected with the railroad afforded the Indians an excellent market for surplus steers."[24]

The other direct impact of the railroad right-of-way sale on the reservation economy was the money the railroad paid the tribes for the right-of-way and the compensation to tribal members who were displaced by the right-of-way. Unfortunately bureaucratic delays in Congress held up the money for many months.

In May 1883 Ronan wrote to McCammon asking him to lobby the secretary of the interior to speed up the payments. Secretary H. M. Teller decided to approve the payouts to individual farmers displaced by the right-of-way even though Congress had not yet approved the agreement with the tribes.[25] In early July 1883, some ten months after the agreement was reached, the individual farmers received their remuneration.[26]

Secretary Teller objected to paying the right-of-way purchase funds to tribal members in cash.[27] As mentioned previously, the tribes had insisted during the negotiations that they get the payment in cash to reduce the chance that the funds or goods would be stolen. The right-of-way money and the payment for reservation timber used in the construction was finally paid to tribal members in a per capita cash payment of $14.21 per person in January 1885—almost two and half years after the agreement was reached on September 2, 1882.[28]

Another economic impact of the railroad on the reservation was the payment for livestock injured and killed by trains. In the first few years of operation, the railroad dragged its feet in settling claims, which resulted in hard feelings among tribal members.[29] On August 30, 1884, Ronan sent the commissioner of Indian affairs a long list of dead and injured cattle and horses for which the railroad had yet to pay the owners.[30] Newspaper reports claimed the growing animosity resulted in vandalism of railroad property on the reservation.[31] Ronan blamed the destruction on Indians visiting Flathead from other reservations.[32] The railroad finally settled the claims in November 1884, and according to newspaper accounts, the tribal members who had suffered losses were satisfied with the compensation.[33]

Traditional Tribal Economic Activities

Traditional economic activities, such as hunting, fishing, and gathering plant foods, continued after the last buffalo hunt in 1881. These sources of food and material were no longer the base of the tribal economy, but they were still valuable. The buffalo herds were gone and other big game populations depressed, but many tribal members were skilled hunters and still able to harvest animals to supplement their diet. Fishing was a source of food for many tribal families. Hunting continued as a seasonal activity fitted into the annual agricultural cycle. The expanding white population increased the competition for game, fish, and wild plants, but tribal members found it worthwhile to continue traditional economic work.

Several historical sources suggest most of the reservation Indian population took part in the annual fall hunt. On November 1, 1882, Ronan reported that "a large majority of the Indians have gone into the mountains to hunt and will probably be out until Christmas." In 1882 tribal members had an extra motivation to go on the fall hunt because they wanted to avoid the surrounding white communities, which were battling a smallpox outbreak.[34] In spring 1883 the Deer Lodge newspaper complained Flathead Reservation Indians were killing elk in that area during the closed hunting season.[35]

Again, on October 14, 1885, Ronan wrote that "a large number of Indians of this Reservation" left on their fall hunt after their crops had been harvested. The hunters wanted dried meat for winter use, but they were also motivated by the Montana Territory bounty laws. The territory paid hunters eight dollars for each bear killed outside the reservation.[36] That month some white Montanans complained about Indians hunting in the Big Blackfoot area, and Ronan sent out messengers to "order" the hunters to return to the reservation.[37] They returned but complained that if white men could hunt and fish on the reservation, they should be able to hunt off the reservation, especially since the right was guaranteed in the 1855 Hellgate Treaty.[38] On October 27, 1885, Ronan sent a long letter to the *New North-West* in Deer Lodge, defending the right of tribal members to freely leave the reservation and hunt and fish off the reservation.[39]

The number of tribal hunters picked up again in the fall of 1886 as a consequence of a drought that reduced the harvest that year.[40] On May 28, 1887, Ronan sent another letter to the *New North-West* outlining the off-reservation hunting rights of Flathead Reservation Indians. The Deer Lodge newspaper editor added his interpretation to Ronan's letter. According to the editor, the provision that the reservation Indians had the right to hunt off the reservation "in common with citizens of the Territory" meant tribal members had to obey the restrictions of Montana fish and game laws.[41] Despite the disagreement regarding the application of Montana laws to tribal hunters, seasonal hunting continued to be a common economic activity for tribal members. On November 8, 1888, Father Jerome D'Aste noted in his diary that, except for one family and an elderly woman, there were "no Indians around, all gone hunting."[42]

During the 1880s there were several records that document fishing as an economic activity for tribal members. On September 28, 1883, Alex Staveley Hill purchased four freshly caught trout from a daughter of Baptiste Eneas, the Iroquois mixed-blood ferry operator at the foot of Flathead Lake. The next day Eneas's wife and Mrs. Angus McDonald rode past Hill's camp and took their horses into the Flathead River. The two women sat on their horses and used grasshoppers as bait for the fish.[43] Later that year, on October 5, 1883, Ronan wrote that an Indian had caught thirteen trout the day before, presumably in the Jocko River.[44] In the summer of 1884 the priests at St. Ignatius told journalist Eugene V. Smalley that after the crops were planted, many Indian families went to the mountains or to the lake to dig camas, fish, and recreate.[45] A number of unnamed Indians were arrested and fined in October 1885 for putting a fish trap in the Swan River in violation of Montana game laws.[46] L. Casper Berray remembered his wife buying fish from Indian fishermen in the late 1880s in the Noxon area.[47]

No direct evidence was found of tribal members from the Flathead Reservation gathering traditional plant foods between 1882 and 1888. Presumably some seasonal gathering continued, but possibly less than earlier in the nineteenth century. Hunting, fishing, and probably gathering were less important than they were traditionally, but they were still a valuable resource for the tribes.

The New Economy

While traditional economic activities were slowly declining in importance in the reservation economy, new opportunities linked to the white economy were expanding. Stock raising and farming were of growing importance on the reservation. Between 1882 and 1888, the number of horses on the reservation doubled according to the estimates furnished by Agent Peter

Ronan in his annual reports. In 1882 Ronan set the horse herds at 2,700, and in 1888 they were given as 5,600.[48]

In the 1880s horsepower was a critical economic asset for both transport and labor. In June 1882 a group of Pend d'Oreilles visited Helena with a band of horses to sell to the white residents.[49] About the same time, E. V. Smalley, a visiting journalist, reported that those Flathead Reservation tribal members who still supported themselves with hunting and gathering used horse sales to earn enough cash to purchase blankets, tobacco, and powder.[50]

Given the economic value of horses in the 1880s, they were occasionally exchanged in horse theft. Flathead Reservation tribal members were both victims and perpetrators of these transactions. In October 1882 Alex Morrigeau, who lived near Jocko Canyon, recovered a horse worth $180. It had been stolen from him in the summer of 1881.[51] In April 1883 Suassa, a Salish, and Pe-elli, a Pend d'Oreille, were accused of stealing seventeen horses on the Blackfeet Reservation and driving them to the Flathead Reservation. One of the two men was arrested in Missoula, but he was released by the white authorities because no formal charges were filed. Agent Ronan convinced Chief Arlee to take custody of the seventeen stolen Blackfeet horses. Arlee, however, objected to returning the horses to the Blackfeet until the Blackfeet returned Flathead Reservation horses they had recently stolen.[52]

At the Fourth of July celebration at Missoula in 1883, an unnamed Indian from St. Ignatius entered his horse in two horse races. Unfortunately, his horse lost both races.[53] A *New York Times* correspondent reported in early September 1883, that he saw large herds of cattle and horses on the reservation along the Northern Pacific Railroad line.[54] Senator G. G. Vest and Montana Territory delegate Martin Maginnis visited the reservation in September 1883. Chief Michelle told the two visiting officials that many tribal members were selling horses in order to buy more cattle.[55] The next spring, May 1884, Charles Allard, a mixed-blood tribal member, drove a band of about one hundred horses from the reservation for sale in the Sun River country.[56]

Agent Ronan submitted a list of cattle and horses owned by tribal members and killed or maimed by Northern Pacific Railroad trains in 1883 and 1884. The list is not easy to follow but included some thirty horses and fifty-one cattle. Many of the horses were identified as work horses and several were valued at $100 each.[57]

On February 12, 1885, Ronan submitted a set of proposed "Rules governing the Court of Indian Offences." The rules included jail sentences of 30 to 90 days for stealing horses and driving them on the reservation. Anyone who caught a horse that did not belong to them and rode the horse away from its range was to serve 10 to 30 days in the reservation jail.[58]

Two reports were found of white men on the reservation buying horses for use east of the Continental Divide. On May 8, 1885, Sam Mitchell and Frank Higgins were purchasing horses for sale on the cattle ranges of Chouteau County.[59] Later that summer on July 24, 1885, Percy Kennett and Reese Anderson purchased reservation horses to herd their cattle near Fort Maginnis. They secured several railroad carloads of horses.[60]

According to Peter Ronan's 1885 annual report, "a great majority" of tribal members owned herds of cattle and horses and "take as good care of them and have as much pride in the ownership as the average white farmer or stockman. They use their own brands and marks, have their regular 'round ups' and the property of individuals is respected and protected."[61]

Sometimes the trade in horses went beyond simple exchanges. On August 14, 1885, tribal rancher Roman Nose advertised that two stray horses had returned to his ranch. He had sold the horses to a white man, but he did not know the buyer's name. Roman Nose wanted the white buyer to pick up the horses and pay for the advertisement and keep of the horses.[62] The next year, Ronan advertised another stray horse was being held by an Indian rancher.[63] In a more convoluted case in November 1886, a party of Flathead Reservation Indians forcibly took a horse from the field of a white Deer Lodge area rancher. They insisted the horse had been stolen from them, but the white rancher claimed he had purchased the horse from another white man.[64]

Years later as an old man, Charlie Young remembered Salish Indians camped in the Ovando area in the middle 1880s. He recalled as many as fifty tepees at once with hundreds of head of horses.[65] Father Lawrence Palladino wrote that the horse culture was popular among the Indian students at the St. Ignatius Mission boys' school in the 1880s. Vocational classes in harness- and saddle-making were especially popular among the students. John B. Guidi, S.J., the apostolic delegate to the Philippines and younger brother of Joseph Guidi, S.J., stationed at St. Ignatius, visited the Flathead Reservation in the fall of 1886. He was so impressed with the quality of the student leatherwork that he obtained a saddle for his use and one for a friend in the royal court in Portugal.[66]

An unnamed Indian stole a horse from Max Couture on the reservation and two horses from Couture's father in May 1887. The thief sold Max

Couture's horse to a white ranchman in Bearmouth. Couture pursued the culprit, and the thief received one hundred lashes punishment.[67]

In the summer of 1888 Malcolm McLeod, a young mixed-blood on the reservation, got a job from an old Indian near Arlee to break horses. Malcolm got to keep every fourth horse he broke.[68]

Horses were an integral part of the new economy on the reservation. They were productive assets used in labor, sold, and exchanged by theft.

Cattle were another growing economic asset on the reservation between 1882 and 1888. According to the estimates supplied by Agent Ronan in his annual reports, cattle herds on the reservation grew from about 3,600 head in 1882 to about 13,200 head in 1888. This was an over threefold increase over the period.[69] As the reservation cattle herds grew, tribal stockmen moved to a more intensive model of ranching. Instead of year-round open range, many tribal members combined summer open range with harvesting hay for winter feeding. Ronan's estimates for hay harvested on the reservation increased from 540 tons in 1882 to 6,000 tons in 1888. That was more than a tenfold increase.[70] The end of this period, in 1888, marked the first record of reservation cattle being shipped to off-reservation markets by the trainload. Organized cattle exports from the reservation represented a new level of integration of the Flathead Reservation into the larger white American economy.

In June 1882 journalist E. V. Smalley noted that probably nine-tenths of the Flathead Reservation Indians were self-sustaining and saw thousands of sleek cattle and fine horses on the reservation open range.[71] Ernest Ingersoll traversed the reservation from west to east in the summer of 1882. He mentioned seeing "wide crops" of hay as soon as he entered the reservation. One member of his party helped himself to pans of sour milk found at an unattended Indian ranch. Finally, when they reached the Jocko Valley, they encountered a mixed-blood woman whose white husband was away at Flathead Lake attending to his cattle.[72] In 1882 a Colonel Warrington visited Chief Arlee in the Jocko Valley and estimated Arlee was well-to-do and worth $15,000 or $20,000. Arlee had accumulated much of his wealth trading cattle and other economic enterprises.[73]

Agent Ronan proudly recorded in his August 13, 1883, annual report that "quite a number" of Indians were then engaged in putting up hay.[74] About the same time in summer 1883, Paul Dana visited the reservation and remarked that "the hay fields [in the Jocko Valley] look like any in the country of white men." While Dana's party was camped near Flathead Lake an Indian brought them a large pail of strawberries and about a gallon of "delicious cream." Their benefactor raised short-horned cattle of "first-rate quality." Dana thought the reservation cattle were as fine as those found on any range in Montana.[75]

The chiefs charged white men for grazing cattle on the reservation, especially in the Little Bitterroot Valley. According to one account, the white stockmen paid about $1,500 per year.[76]

During the September 1883 visit of Senator G. G. Vest and Montana delegate Martin Maginnis to the reservation, Chief Michelle observed that tribal members were selling ponies and investing the proceeds in cattle.[77]

As mentioned previously, during 1883 and 1884, the Northern Pacific Railroad was slow in paying tribal members for cattle and horses killed by the railroad trains.[78] In Ronan's listing of outstanding claims, he listed fifty-one cattle and thirty horses. Many of the cattle killed were milk cows valued at up to $60 each. The value of stock cattle killed was up to $40 per animal.[79]

A Northern Pacific Railroad photographer, F. Jay Haynes, toured the reservation in 1884. He took several pictures of a prosperous Indian farm and cattle herd.[80]

W. F. Wheeler visited the reservation in May 1885 and noted that tribal farmers milked cows to make butter. According to Wheeler, "During the whole distance from the Agency to the Lake, herds of cattle and horses were in sight." A recent general council of tribal members had decided to force all white-owned cattle off the reservation so there would be more grazing left for tribal-member-owned herds.[81]

In December 1886 A. L. Demers, a white trader, opened butcher shops at St. Ignatius and Arlee. Two mixed-bloods, Max Couture and Isadore Laderoute, worked as butchers.[82]

Several sales of Flathead Reservation cattle were noted in 1888. In February 1888 T. J. Demers, the white Frenchtown merchant who had married into the tribes, advertised five hundred head of Durham cattle for sale. They were being raised by some of Demers's Indian relatives at Hot Springs.[83] Late that summer, two white cattle buyers from Ohio, A. Campbell and George C. Campbell, passed through Missoula on their way to buy cattle. They said they planned to purchase two trainloads of cattle on the reservation.[84] This was the first reference found for large purchases of trainloads of reservation cattle for the off-reservation market. An Interior Department inspection report on October 20, 1888, found about three thousand acres on the reservation devoted for raising hay for winter feed. According to the inspector, the majority of the cattle on the reservation were owned by mixed-bloods and white men married to Indian women.[85]

Two of the reservation stockmen—Michel Pablo and Charles Allard— raised buffalo as well as cattle and horses. They purchased twelve or fourteen head of buffalo from Indian Samuel in April 1885 for $2,000.[86] Allard sold a large buffalo to a Missoula meat market during the Christmas season of 1888. According to newspaper accounts, the resulting 1,300 or 1,400 pounds of buffalo meat sold quickly.[87]

Between 1882 and 1888 stock raising on the Flathead Reservation was a rapidly growing concern. Cattle herds were increasing, and more tribal ranchers were harvesting hay to use for winter feeding. Ownership brands were used. Open range during the summer was combined with winter feeding. A small herd of buffalo on the reservation was growing as an echo of the traditional hunts of wild plains buffalo.

Farming on the reservation between 1882 and 1888 expanded greatly as more and more families took up agriculture to replace the declining hunting resources. Many families started farms, while others expanded existing fields. A common practice was to integrate the agricultural calendar of planting and harvesting into a schedule of seasonal hunting. Agent Peter Ronan's annual reports showed a population increase of 45 percent between 1882 and 1888, from just below 1,400 Indians in 1882 to just over 2,000 in 1888. The 1882 figure did not include the Salish living in the Bitterroot Valley, who were counted in the 1888 number. The rest of the population increase resulted from the natural growth of births over deaths and Indian people moving to the reservation from eastern Washington and northern Idaho. The population increase was dwarfed by the 350 percent growth in the number of acres cultivated on the reservation, from 1,800 acres in 1882 to about 8,000 acres in 1888.

Flathead Reservation farming in the 1880s included both grain crops and vegetable gardens. The wheat crop, which was probably mostly used for flour, grew from an estimated 23,500 bushels in 1882 to 40,500 bushels in 1888. Oats and barley, which were fed to stock, grew even more from about 19,700 bushels in 1882 to 47,000 bushels in 1888. The production of tribal member vegetable gardens almost doubled from about 12,400 bushels to just over 23,700 bushels in 1888. A few of the historical sources criticize Ronan's estimates as inflated, but the general trend was still an increase in agricultural efforts by tribal members.[88]

On February 1, 1882, Ronan reported that "quite a number" of tribal members were engaged in splitting and hauling rails to build fences to enclose fields.[89] Many of the farms must have been small scale operations. In July 1882 a journalist noted that a number of tribal members were fencing fields and "cultivating little patches of grain and potatoes."[90]

Ronan advised T. C. Power at Fort Benton on July 27, 1882, that it might be cheaper for Power to purchase grain to fulfill his government contract from a reservation trader than to ship grain in from off the reservation. The trader would purchase the grain from tribal member farmers.[91] In 1883 a bad harvest of oats on the reservation meant there was no local grain for Power to purchase. In 1884 Power filled his contract for oats for the agency from local farmers.[92]

Ernest Ingersoll, who traversed the reservation during the summer of 1882, visited the farm of an unnamed Indian where he found

> two log cabins, a big conical lodge (made of poles, green cowhides and matting) and a root-cellar. All around it were fields of oats, barley and wheat, with a patch of potatoes and kitchen vegetables left to grow pretty much as they pleased. He had no barn, stacking his grain and using his cabins for storehouses as well as winter quarters, his teepee serving as a summer house. The kitchen was an outdoor fire.[93]

In September 1882 Joseph McCammon, a United States assistant attorney general, compiled a list of twenty-nine individual tribal members whose improvements would be taken for the Northern Pacific Railroad right-of-way along the Jocko and Flathead Rivers in the southern part of the reservation. All but four of the displaced improvements involved cultivated land or gardens. For example, Alexander Morrigeau lost almost 14 acres of cultivated land, and a house and a barn valued at $1,000. Maxime Couture gave up 45 acres of cultivated land and a house, all valued at $600. Pend d'Oreille chief Michelle lost almost 15.5 acres of cultivated land worth $325. Basile Finley gave over 35 acres of cultivated land and four houses, all worth $700. The railroad right-of-way followed the valley bottoms where many tribal members had established farms.[94]

Etienne Xavier DeRouge, S.J., wrote a description of agriculture on the Flathead Reservation in 1882. He emphasized the widespread participation in small scale farming: "Nearly all of them have their little fields round their houses, with a few cows and fowl."[95]

S. S. Benedict, an Indian inspector, filed a report on July 10, 1883, stating that the majority of Indians living in the Jocko Valley were mixed-bloods who were "really in a very prosperous condition." A few full-bloods had small farms in 1883 and considerable stock—especially horses—but "most of the land under cultivation upon the reservation is worked" by mixed-bloods.[96]

In August 1883 an alcohol-fueled robbery in Evaro rolled out U.S. Army troops from Fort Missoula. Apparently, some of the robbers were young relatives of Chief Arlee. The sources are not clear about who else was involved, but Arlee's relatives escaped into the mountains. They avoided arrest by promising to reform and help Chief Arlee with his harvest work.[97]

Duncan McDonald, a mixed-blood trader, complained to an Indian inspector in December 1884 that Ronan would not grind for free the wheat McDonald purchased from Indian farmers. Ronan argued that if he ground McDonald's wheat with agency employees, McDonald would be able to monopolize the benefits of the gristmill. McDonald could extend credit to the farmers, collect their wheat at harvest, have it ground into flour, and then sell the flour back to the farmers for a profit.[98]

A correspondent in the Missoula newspaper on August 22, 1884, commented on Chief Arlee's "fine farm and an abundant crop." Alexander Matt, a mixed-blood, had recently established a farm and blacksmith shop near Arlee. The writer described an Indian crew harvesting an Indian grain crop in the Jocko Valley.[99]

Indian inspector Robert S. Gardner visited the Flathead Agency in January 1885. At that time, an irrigation ditch was being constructed to irrigate 5,000 acres of land in the Jocko Valley. Practically all the excavation work was being done by Indian labor. Gardner listed the names and crops of the principal Indian farmers on the reservation. The list included 23 Indian farmers in the Jocko Valley including Chiefs Arlee, Big Sam, and Louison. Gardner also noted 24 major Indian farmers in the Mission Valley, 23 along the Flathead River and mouth of the Jocko River, and 9 in Camas Prairie. Of special interest was the 200-acre Kootenai farm at Dayton Creek. The farming was done in common by Kootenai tribal members, and the estimated crop was 1,000 bushels of wheat, 500 bushels potatoes, and 500 bushels of turnips. The entire reservation-wide list totaled 9,050 acres fenced and an 1884 production of 26,290 bushels of grain and vegetables. Many small farms of 10 or 20 acres were not included. Since Gardner visited the reservation in January, he must have gotten his information from Ronan and the agency staff.[100]

W. F. Wheeler wrote that, during a May 1885 trip through the reservation, he found "well fenced and cultivated fields" along all the waterways and the foothills of the Mission Mountains. He also remarked that in addition to raising and marketing cattle, horses, and pigs, the farmers also harvested grain and sold the surplus in Missoula.[101]

Ronan had a list of reservation farmers in his August 1885 annual report, which included some of the smaller farms. This list had 39 farmers in the Jocko Valley, some as small as 10 acres. In a partially successful effort to induce the Bitterroot Valley Salish to remove to the Jocko Agency, Ronan had promised to help the newly relocated families establish farms. The government built them houses, fenced and plowed 10 acres per family, and provided basic seed, implements, and cows. This second list had 51 Indian farmers in the Mission Valley; the smallest was 50 acres. Another 24 farms were along the Pend d'Oreille River and the mouth of the Jocko River, and 10 were in Camas Prairie.[102]

The custom of integrating agriculture with traditional big game hunting continued. In October 1885 Ronan noted that a "large number" of tribal members were off the reservation hunting after the crops had been harvested.[103]

Ronan proudly pointed to tribal progress in agriculture on March 29, 1886. He claimed 139 families were "engaged to a considerable extent in agricultural pursuits." Sixteen families had ordered young fruit trees from a New York State nursery. Ronan asked for more funding to construct irrigation ditches to expand Indian farming.[104]

During the summer of 1886 Ronan was able to open a new six-mile-long irrigation ditch in the Jocko Valley to make room for newly arrived Bitterroot Salish farmers. The first two miles required blasting and construction of wooden flumes, which probably employed white carpenters. The lower four miles were excavated by Indian workers. During the spring of 1886 high water threatened to destroy the new flume, but Ronan had the diversion breached until the water receded. Ronan requested funds for another threshing machine to use in the fall of 1886.[105] On June 3, 1886, Ronan asked for money to employ a ditch rider to protect the irrigation ditch and distribute the water to individual farms.[106] In his 1886 annual report Ronan wrote, "A greatly increased number of farms have been fenced in during the past winter and spring," and he had run out of plows to issue to new farmers. The Kootenais at the north end of the reservation continued to operate a large farm in common, which Ronan wanted broken up into individual family farms.[107]

Indian inspector George B. Pearsons filed a report on the Flathead Agency on November 11, 1886. Pearsons found that some tribal members "have large farms and quite an amount of stock and are doing finely while others are terribly poor and cling to their old customs and traditions with tenacity." According to Pearsons, there were 108 Indian houses located near the St. Ignatius Mission, whose occupants worked farms in the country-side. Duncan McDonald, the mixed-blood trader, and Father Leopold Van Gorp, S.J., of the mission, complained that the 1886 harvest was consider-ably less than Agent Ronan had claimed in his annual report.[108]

In his December 1, 1886, monthly report, Ronan wrote that the crops had been reduced by a late drought, which seriously lowered the yield.[109] There was enough grain harvested in 1886 that A. L. Demers, the St. Igna-tius trader, offered to sell reservation wheat and oats to the T. C. Power & Co., to fulfill Power's government contract.[110]

Ronan included a list of thirty tribal farmers who had purchased fruit trees from a Minnesota nursery in the spring of 1887. The purchasers included Pend d'Oreille chief Michelle.[111]

An October 20, 1888, inspection report by E. D. Bannister included a list of the larger farm operators on the reservation. Bannister found that thirteen full-blood Indians, eight mixed-bloods, and six white men married to Indians had the largest farms.[112]

Between 1882 and 1888 more Indian families established farms on the reservation. Most of the farmers raised grain for flour, stock feed, and sale off the reservation. Many tribal members also had vegetable gardens to grow food for domestic use. Farming was becoming an increasingly valuable economic activity on the reservation.

Government Assistance

As mentioned, the Flathead Reservation tribes never became dependent on government rations, but the Flathead Agency did provide some useful aid. There was significant temporary economic help given to groups—especially the Bitterroot Salish—to help them locate and start farming operations. For most tribal members, government aid was very limited, and it was usually given in payment for work done for the Flathead Agency. The economic impact of government aid was restricted both by the parsimonious appro-priations and the location of the agency at the extreme southern end of the reservation.

One outcome of the early 1884 Washington, D.C., visit by Agent Ronan and five Bitterroot Salish leaders was that the federal government authorized government aid for the Bitterroot Salish. The aid was to help the Salish establish farms and went to those who removed to the Jocko Reservation and to those who remained in the Bitterroot Valley. To each Salish family that removed, Ronan promised provisions until the first harvest, two cows, a wagon and harness, a plow and other agricultural implements, and seed for the first year. Those families who agreed to remove to the reservation also got their choice of 160 acres of unoccupied land, assistance in the erection of a house, and help in fencing and breaking up a field of ten acres.[113] Unfortunately after waiting for appropriations and procurement, most of the equipment was not delivered until early 1885.[114] Ronan hired tribal members for the unskilled work providing assistance for the Bitterroot Salish, such as splitting rails for fencing and breaking up land for farming.[115] The aid given to the Bitterroot Salish who removed to the reservation was significant but temporary. Ronan received funds to assist the first seventeen families who removed, but he never did receive funds to assist fifteen more families who removed in 1887.[116] Ronan was limited to what he could give those later families from the scant general appropriation for the agency.

In 1887 part of the Lower Kalispel tribe was relocated to the reservation from Washington State. Government negotiators agreed to give them assistance in starting farms on the reservation, but Congress never approved the agreement. Ronan was reduced to providing the assistance he could squeeze from the regular agency appropriations.[117]

The general Flathead Agency funds between 1882 and 1888 were useful, but far too limited to support the tribes. According to journalist E. V. Smalley in July 1882, the government supplied plows and wagons, a sawmill, gristmill, blacksmith shop, and threshing machine. Only the old and sick received blankets and subsistence. Smalley thought nine-tenths of the tribal members were self-sustaining.[118] As Ronan explained to merchant T. C. Power on September 25, 1882, most of the wagons and larger agricultural implements were not just given to tribal members, but they were exchanged for labor in putting up hay, getting firewood, and supporting other agency operations.[119]

The main point that Ronan repeated several times was that government money to assist the Flathead Reservation tribes was extremely limited. He pointed out that the 1883–84 appropriations for the Flathead Agency provided only $13,000, which also had to cover the pay of agency employees.

That worked out to only $8 per Indian for the year, totally inadequate to "support" the tribes.[120] In his 1886 annual report Ronan calculated the subsistence supplies each Indian would receive, if they were divided among all tribal members. Each Indian would receive only 6 1/4 pounds of bacon, 4/5 of a pound of beans, 1 3/4 pounds of coffee, 12 1/2 pounds of flour, 13/20 of a pound of rice, 7/20 of a pound of oatmeal, 4 3/4 pounds of sugar, 7/20 of a pound of tea, and 7/10 of a pound of salt, *per year*, which was obviously not enough supplies to subsist the tribe.[121] On March 29, 1886, Ronan reported that the limited number of plows he had received were already gone, given to new farmers in exchange for labor for the agency.[122]

According to Ronan, the agency workforce was so limited that it could barely keep up with the requests for services. On November 1, 1882, he wrote that the gristmill was full of Indian wheat waiting to be ground into flour, and the sawmill yard was piled high with logs tribal members had hauled in to be sawed into lumber. The carpenter's shop was filled with broken wheels and other articles needing repair, and many Indians had ordered sashes and doors for construction. The blacksmith shop was crowded with items needing work, but due to the shortage of employees, the blacksmith had to make his own charcoal before he could work on the orders.[123] On July 10, 1883, Indian inspector S. S. Benedict recommended that the volume of goods supplied to the agency be reduced so those funds could be used to expand the agency workforce. Tribal members then would not have to furnish labor and wood fuel to have their lumber sawed and grain ground.[124] Ronan agreed in most cases to using agency employees to provide more services, except for Duncan McDonald, a tribal member who operated a trading post near the agency. Ronan felt that agency employees already provided ample services for McDonald. If McDonald did not have to supply help to operate the gristmill, he could monopolize the value of the government gristmill services.[125]

One very positive aid that the government provided the farmers in the Jocko Valley was the construction of an irrigation ditch finished in time for the 1886 growing season. The six-mile ditch, built largely with paid Indian labor, moved water from the Jocko River to new farms established in the Jocko Valley for the removed Bitterroot Salish.[126]

An important handicap limiting the economic benefit of agency services on the Flathead Reservation economy between 1882 and 1888 was the poor location of the agency. The agency was near the extreme southern boundary of the reservation. Given the poor state of the roads in the 1880s, it was very difficult for farmers living in other parts of the reservation to get supplies or services from the agency in the Jocko Valley. The many farmers and other tribal members living in the Flathead Valley would often not want to haul grain or logs to the agency and then make a separate trip to retrieve the flour or lumber. Tribal members living in the Jocko Valley must have benefited most from the goods and services provided by the agency.[127] St. Ignatius Mission in the Flathead Valley was located near the center of the tribal population and provided many of the same services to tribal members. The mission had a sawmill, gristmill, carpentry shop, blacksmith, and threshing machine. We know that the shops and craftsmen at the mission provided services to tribal members in the Flathead Valley, but no detailed accounts or descriptions of these services have survived.[128]

The Flathead Agency did provide some economic goods and services to tribal members between 1882 and 1888. The importance of government aid for the development of the reservation economy was limited by parsimonious appropriations and the inconvenient location of the agency.

Other Economic Assets

Another economic resource for some tribal members between 1882 and 1888 was employment. A few tribal members took regular jobs at the agency or mission, but many tribal members did casual work for the agency, mission, traders, or white men traveling through or recreating on the reservation.

In the first part of this period, in 1882, some tribal members were receiving "good wages from the Northern Pacific Rail-road Company in various Capacities." The railroad contracted with some tribal members to cut reservation logs and haul them to locations where they were needed as piles for bridges.[129] In his 1883 annual report Ronan mentioned that tribal members had been employed by the railroad to furnish piles, ties, and cordwood for the construction.[130] Unfortunately he did not describe in detail the work tribal members did for the railroad or identify which Indians held the jobs.

Between February 1882 and September 1883, Duncan McDonald worked for the Northern Pacific Railroad as guide and mediator while the line was being constructed through the reservation. No detailed account of McDonald's railroad work has survived, but he traveled through the reservation with some of the survey crews and railroad officials. In one case, McDonald mediated between an Indian farmer named Dominic and a railroad survey crew that wanted to cut brush in Dominic's field.[131]

The best documented part of McDonald's work was arranging a tour of the reservation for some prominent guests at the last spike ceremony completing the Northern Pacific Railroad in 1883. The railroad employed McDonald to construct a wagon road to McDonald Peak in the Mission Mountains. When the special train stopped at Ravalli, Duncan's brother Angus guided the more energetic guests on a ride and climb up the mountain. Duncan took the less adventurous guests on a tour of St. Ignatius Mission and Lake McDonald.[132]

The Flathead Agency also employed some tribal members, especially after the agency police force was established in 1885. In 1887, for example, Michel Revais was paid $300 a year as interpreter. The miller in 1887 was a white man married to a tribal member.[133] That year Antelli was paid $10 a month as captain of the agency police, and fourteen other tribal members were paid $8 a month as police privates. The Indian judges were not paid until shortly after the 1882–88 period.[134] In some years, other tribal members worked as agency employees. In 1881, for example, Alexander Matt got $900 a year as the blacksmith, Peter Finley earned $600 as the gunsmith, and Gonsague Matt was paid $600 as the herder. These were in addition to the $300 Michel Revais was paid as interpreter that year.[135]

Most of the employment provided by the agency was casual, and few records have survived to detail its extent. As mentioned previously, tribal members were contracted to do the excavation work for the new irrigation ditch in the Jocko Valley. According to one newspaper report on May 8, 1885, about one hundred Indians were then working on digging the irrigation ditch.[136] The seasonal ditch rider was probably a tribal member. Also as noted previously, tribal members put up hay for the agency stock, gathered firewood, and provided other services for the Flathead Agency in exchange for wagons, harness, plows, and agricultural equipment.

Before 1882 the principal chiefs on the reservation were paid for their work to help keep order on the reservation. The salaries had been a provision of the 1855 Hellgate Treaty ratified in 1859. However, that treaty provision expired in 1879, and salaries were only continued for a few years afterward.[137]

In 1883 Ronan hired two temporary Indian employees to help him locate the markers from the survey of the northern boundary of the reservation. One was to serve as herder and interpreter and the other, who had seen the boundary surveyed eleven years before, was to work as Ronan's guide and packer.[138]

During the winter of 1883–84 Agent Ronan acted as intermediary for T. C. Power, who had the contract to supply oats for the agency. Ronan hired Indians to haul the oats from the Arlee railroad station to the Jocko Agency. Having the work done by Indians was less efficient, because they did not have the best equipment, but it ensured that the Indian farmers would benefit from the employment:

> You say that you "Could get the Same Amt. recd. hauled and deliv-ered here (at Helena) the Same distance for half the money." Now, I dont for a moment doubt the fact—Even had you said less than half I should have believed it. By decent freight teams it would have all been done in one or two days and at a few loads. But had you required to get it Stored where there are no warehouses, and hauled by *pairs* of Indian Ponies which could not haul more than 12 or 1400 at a time and by men who took a month to do it, I fancy you would be prepared to admit that circumstances alter cases. . . . I omitted to notice the last remark of your letter to the effect that "if the Indians did the hauling all right"—I hardly understand its drift, but I may state thereanent that Indians did it and did it all.[139]

Photographer F. Jay Haynes made an 1884 tour through the Flathead Reservation. One of the pictures he took was of the Flathead Agency sawmill with an Indian crew. It was likely that the Indian laborers were working in exchange for lumber, but they also could have been the casual hires of the tribal member getting the lumber.[140]

Ronan requested authority in March 1886 to employ tribal members in breaking land for farms for those Bitterroot Salish recently removed to the Jocko Valley. Ronan mentioned he "was overtaxed with applications for work" from tribal members. The commissioner of Indian affairs approved $210 to pay Indians to break seventy acres of land.[141]

At the end of 1886, Ronan proposed using Indian labor in exchange for wagons, harness, plows, and other equipment to get logs to saw for a new jail building. He hired tribal members to harvest the logs, but the commis-sioner of Indian affairs did not approve his request for funds to pay other construction expenses.[142]

The St. Ignatius Mission was a significant, but poorly documented, source of employment for tribal members during the 1880s. The mission account books are very hard to follow, but they do record the employment of tribal members and white men married to Indians. For example, the account books for the late 1880s had wages paid to Joseph Pain, John Battise Finley, Frank Ducharme, Isaac Tellier, Alex McLeod, and Herman Felsman. There were also very vague and frustrating references to "cash for wages" with no indication of who the casual laborers were.[143] Most of the farm work at the mission was performed by students and brothers, but presumably the range riders hired to care for the mission cattle herds were mainly tribal members.

Much of the employment of tribal members between 1882 and 1888 probably consisted of seasonal and occasional short-term work. According to journalist E. V. Smalley, who visited the reservation in 1882, "The Indians are kind and hospitable to travelers, — ready to lend and row a boat for a small fee, or to hire themselves and their ponies for long trips in the mountains."[144]

In the summer of 1883 a party of Northern Pacific Railroad officials was waiting in the Jocko Valley for instructions. To pass the time, the white men paid for prizes for contests in Indian "native sports of horse-racing and running." The young people of Chief Arlee's band competed for the prize money.[145]

A tourist party of white hunters from Connecticut hired tribal members to help with a pack trip to the headwaters of the Jocko and Blackfoot Rivers in August 1884. Three tribal members worked as cook, packer, and guide for the party.[146]

Another example of casual employment that can be documented in the historical record was in the expenses of John T. Wallace, a special agent for the U.S. Department of Justice. On February 21, 1886, he paid one dollar for a ride in an "Indian hack" from the Arlee railroad station to the Flathead or Jocko Agency.[147]

On December 4, 1883, Indian inspector C. H. Howard reported that one former Indian student at St. Ignatius Mission was working on the new school building as a painter.[148] A month later an eloping couple of tribal members were cutting firewood in Missoula when located by a pursuing party of Indian policemen. They were working for Andrew Logan, a white man living in Missoula.[149]

In Malcolm McLeod's account of his life, he described working for A. L. Demers, the Indian trader in St. Ignatius in 1887. McLeod hauled hay and split and hauled firewood for Demers. In 1888 he broke horses for an "Old Indian" at Arlee in exchange for a fourth of the horses he broke. Later that year he took another job as a cowboy for a white man in the Bitterroot Valley.[150]

A few tribal members operated businesses serving white and tribal member customers. As in the 1875–81 period, two prominent tribal members—Antoine Revais and Baptiste Eneas—operated ferries across the Lower Flathead River during the 1880s. Baptiste Eneas's ferry was at the foot of Flathead Lake near the present-day town of Polson. In September 1883 Alex Staveley Hill traveled through the reservation and mentioned in his travelogue that he paid Eneas six dollars to ferry eight horses and four men across the foot of Flathead Lake. When Hill headed south two days later, he hired a wagon from Eneas for a dollar a day. The men driving the hired wagon were to deliver forty pounds of freight to Eneas on the return trip from Ravalli railroad station.[151] Two months later on October 12, 1883, an anonymous writer in the *Weekly Missoulian* was patronizing Eneas's ferry when a party of young Indians staged a drunken melee at the ferry landing. Nobody seemed to have been hurt in the ruckus, and that night Eneas's daughter brought out an accordion, and the music led to a vigorous but peaceful gala.[152] In the summer of 1884 journalist Eugene V. Smalley reported that Eneas charged two dollars for each team and wagon transported on his ferry. According to Smalley, Eneas was "making a fortune" from the increasing traffic to the Upper Flathead Valley.[153] Mathew Eccles, an early white settler in the Upper Flathead Valley, reported that by 1886 the fare for Eneas's ferry had increased to $2.50.[154]

Antoine Revais was the mixed-blood tribal member who operated a ferry further south across the Lower Flathead River for travelers heading east and west through the reservation. In July of 1882 E. V. Smalley spent a night at Revais's house before taking his ferry across the Flathead River. According to Smalley, Revais "prepared us a supper of bacon and flapjacks, and cleared a space on the dirty floor of his cabin for us to spread our blankets." The next morning, Smalley took Revais's ferry across the river and continued westward.[155] About the same time in 1882, Ernest Ingersoll used Revais's ferry to travel east across the Flathead River. Ingersoll asked Revais for food and coffee, but Revais sent the traveler on to his ranch. Ingersoll described the Revais ranch as "a score or so of loghouses and stables huddled together and surrounded by redskin teepees, corrals, and small stagings sustaining harness, etc., out of reach of dogs and coyotes." Ingersoll found no one home at the Revais ranch and so continued eastward.[156]

On August 1, 1882, Peter Ronan wrote the commissioner of Indian affairs that Revais wanted to sell his ferry because he was getting too old to keep up with the traffic generated by the construction of the Northern Pacific Railroad through the reservation. Ronan explained that in the fall of 1881 he had provided Revais with lumber to build a larger ferry and Revais had borrowed money to pay for the other equipment needed to upgrade the ferry. With his age and the increased traffic, Revais needed to sell his business, or the Northern Pacific Railroad might install a competing service. The commissioner of Indian affairs only agreed to Revais's selling the ferry to another Indian.[157] Revais retired from the business, but it is not known if he was able to sell the ferry and get back his investment.

As in the years before 1882, Duncan McDonald continued to be the most active tribal member businessman and entrepreneur between 1882 and 1888. In the first few years of the period, McDonald spent most of his time working for the Northern Pacific Railroad as a guide and mediator to negotiate disagreements with tribal members during the construction of the railroad through the reservation. Sometime while he was working for the railroad, McDonald opened his first businesses serving travelers at the new railroad station at Ravalli. The earliest reference to his Ravalli businesses was on October 1, 1883, when Alex Staveley Hill mentioned McDonald's store and restaurant.[158]

In 1883 McDonald complained to C. H. Howard, an Indian inspector, that Ronan refused to grind wheat he had purchased from Indian farmers. Ronan argued that it would be unfair to use the agency gristmill to grind wheat that McDonald would then sell back to the Indian farmers as flour and get all the profit for himself.[159]

McDonald hired a white man named C. A. Stillinger as his clerk at the Ravalli store in 1885. Stillinger was recently discharged from the U.S. Army and went to work for McDonald for $35 a month. He worked for McDonald until 1892, when he bought out most of McDonald's Ravalli businesses and another tribal member business, Charles Allard's Ravalli-Kalispell stage line.[160] Stillinger's management skills probably played a critical role in the financial success of McDonald's enterprises at Ravalli.

McDonald traveled to Missoula in December 1885 and left his Ravalli store in charge of a clerk—probably Stillinger. The evening after he left Ravalli, a drunken Indian threatened the clerk, who refused to give the Indian something he wanted. The disappointed patron pulled out a knife and menaced the clerk. Two sober Indian customers escorted the inebriated gentleman out of the store. McDonald proceeded to the Missoula Mercantile Company, where he purchased a Winchester gun, a revolver, and a hundred rounds of ammunition. He took the arms back to Ravalli in case of future trouble.[161]

In the later part of the 1882–83 period, McDonald's business establishments at Ravalli grew and prospered. In June 1887 McDonald began work on a new, larger hotel building.[162] Among McDonald's enterprises were a hotel, restaurant, stage line to Flathead Lake, and a steamboat on the lake.[163] McDonald and Charles Allard announced on March 7, 1888, that they had jointly formed a new company, the Selish Express Company, to transport passengers and freight between Ravalli and the foot of Flathead Lake.

Agent Peter Ronan filed a report with the commissioner of Indian affairs on October 23, 1886, which enumerated the reservation traders and their annual business. Two of the traders were Indian, but all did business with tribal members. A. B. Hammond, a white man from Missoula, had a license for a store at Arlee railroad station in the Jocko Valley. Ronan reported that the store did $14,335 in annual business. McDonald had a trading post near the Ravalli railroad station, which did $13,000 in business annually. Alex Demers, a white man, was the trader at the St. Ignatius Mission in the Flathead Valley. His business was given as $8,000 a year. At the foot of Flathead Lake, H. A. Lambert had a trading post. Lambert had only done $3,500 in business the year before, but was hoping the business would grow. Finally Telesphore Guillium Demers, who was part Pend d'Oreille, operated a store near the Kootenai village in the northern part of the reservation. His trade was $7,000 per year. While all the Indian traders were patronized by tribal members, there is no way to tell how much of the annual trade was with white men traveling through the reservation.[164]

From 1883 to 1888, A. L. Demers, the Indian trader, took wheat and oats from Indian farmers in payment on their charge accounts. Demers then sold the grain to dealers such as T. C. Power, who had the federal contract to furnish grain for the Flathead Agency.[165]

Some other tribal members operated businesses on the reservation, but details are not available. An April 1884 newspaper notice stated that Louis Couture, a mixed-blood tribal member, had established a bridge and "public stopping place" at Mud Creek north of St. Ignatius. The short article did not describe what services Couture offered to travelers and Indians in that area.[166]

The most important economic exchange between the tribes and the surrounding white community in the first couple of years of this period, however, was the sale of the Northern Pacific Railroad right-of-way and its construction. The economic impact of the railroad on the reservation was detailed at the start of this chapter. Each tribal member received a per capita payment of $14.21 in January 1885 as their share of the $21,458 the railroad paid for the right-of-way and timber through the reservation.[167] Tribal members who were displaced by the right-of-way were paid a total of $7,624 in July 1883.[168]

Two purchases by tribal members in 1882 were unusually expensive. In early July, Charles Allard paid a Mr. Levasseur $200 for Missoula Belle, a sorrel filly racehorse.[169] In December 1882 Duncan McDonald purchased a wagonload of oats, four horses, wagon, and harness from Zeb Harris. Harris met McDonald while driving through the reservation to the railroad. McDonald paid $900 for the lot.[170]

Other examples of trade or exchange between tribal members and the surrounding white economy have survived in the sources. One example was an unnamed Salish man in 1882 who paid a white undertaker in the Musselshell Valley a horse to provide a coffin and white man's burial for a Pend d'Oreille who died while on a buffalo hunt.[171]

In June 1882 E. V. Smalley, the journalist, witnessed the shopping customs of a group of unnamed Indians patronizing a saddler's shop in Missoula. Smalley did not specify which tribe the Indian customers were from, but offered the exchange as a typical example of the "Indian way of dealing" with merchants. The Indian customers browsed and sat down in front of the shop, and after a quarter of an hour the saddler came out and asked what they wanted. According to Smalley, if the merchant "had noticed them at first, they would have gone away without buying."[172]

The experiences of Tyson D. Duncan, who settled in the Kalispell area in 1883, illustrated some typical Indian-white economic exchanges in the period. Duncan's wife traded with the Kootenais and other Indians in the area for buckskin, venison, and fish.[173] In August 1884 an unnamed Indian at Arlee brought in an eleven-pound trout, which he sold to a white man.[174] One of the most celebrated economic transactions of the 1880s was between two tribal members in April 1885, when Michel Pablo paid Indian Samuel $2,000 for his herd of twelve or fourteen head of buffalo.[175] According to one account, in October 1885, an Indian from St. Ignatius mistook a Missoula lawyer's office for a bookstore and asked to buy a dictionary.[176] The December 1885 conflict between two intoxicated Indians and the white postmaster and trader at Arlee apparently resulted from a disagreement over a gun that had been hocked as security for an earlier ten dollar purchase.[177] Charles Allard was in Missoula doing his Christmas shopping in December

1885.[178] A correspondent for a Portland, Oregon, Catholic newspaper in May 1886 wrote that Indian farmers raised wheat, corn, potatoes, and other crops and found a "ready market . . . for all produce at Missoula and Horse Plains," which gave the farmers "a chance to have some money."[179] That same month, Maggie McDonald from the reservation visited Missoula on a shopping expedition.[180] Charles Allard slaughtered and sold a buffalo to a Missoula meat market in December 1888 for Christmas sales.[181] On December 29, 1888, Peter na'ia' borrowed $5 from Father Jerome D'Aste, S.J., at St. Ignatius.[182]

Whiskey purchases were a special economic traffic between Indians and whites in the 1882 and 1888 period. In most instances the surviving evidence only documented the disorder or violence that resulted, not the economic exchange.

In a few cases tribal members did not purchase the alcohol. For example, in March 1885 a party of Flathead Reservation Indians was placing obstructions on the Northern Pacific Railroad below the reservation. A conflict arose between the partying Indians and the railroad section crew, which was finally resolved by Agent Ronan and the reservation Indian police. Apparently, the celebration started when the Indians discovered and tapped a barrel of whiskey that had been lost by freighters three years before.[183] In most cases, however, tribal members had to buy the whiskey.

The June 1882 murder of Frank Marengo by Koonsa Finley occurred while Finley was drunk on whiskey purchased from an unnamed seller at Camas Prairie. Chief Arlee argued, "This man has committed a murder under the influence of whisky. Why do you not go to Camas Prairie, and get the man who sold him the whisky. Strike at the heart of the disease; not at the victims." Ronan replied that there was not enough evidence to convict the dealer in court. Finley was released by the federal court because he had already been punished by the chiefs for the murder, but the whiskey dealer was never charged.[184]

In September 1882 there were complaints about Indians causing trouble in the Plains area while drunk.[185] Later that month, Ronan got two tribal members to try to make purchases and then bring the whiskey to the authorities. One saloon keeper was arrested and charged with selling liquor to Indians.[186] It is not known how this case worked out in the courts.

A series of events in January 1883 illustrated the economic aspect of the liquor traffic. In that month a stepson of Chief Arlee got drunk and tried to attack his stepfather. In disgust, Arlee worked with Ronan to charge two whiskey sellers in Missoula, a white man named Kibble and a white woman named Belle Ross. They sent "two trusty Indians" to purchase whiskey at the Kibble-Ross saloon. They made the purchase, and charges were filed against the pair. Ronan, Modeste Finley, and Sam Flathead appeared as witnesses against them. Kibble and Ross found a "railroad 'rounder'" who swore that no Indians purchased whiskey from the saloonkeepers. The judge dismissed the charges, much to Ronan's disgust.[187] One of Arlee's stepsons—possibly the same one who had attacked Arlee—was found beaten to death near Finley Creek in May 1887 as a result of a drinking party.[188]

In early August 1883 a saloon keeper doing business just south of the reservation boundary at Evaro sold whiskey to a group of Indians. According to Agent Ronan, most of the Indians were from the Lower Columbia River country, but they induced five local Indians to join the party. While drunk, they committed a strong-arm robbery and took $210 from a local white man. The Evaro railroad agent telegraphed for help, and soldiers commanded by Col. Thomas Ruger were sent from Fort Missoula. The soldiers drove the off-reservation Indians out of the area, but the stolen money was not recovered.[189]

When tribal members were employed to dig portions of the Jocko Valley irrigation ditch in May 1885, two mixed-bloods set up a bootlegging business. Tallo Aslin and Larry Finley purchased whiskey at an off-reservation saloon and then resold it to the recently paid workers on the reservation.[190]

In most cases, however, the historical sources only describe the incidents of violence growing out of the alcohol purchases. For example in January 1884, C. H. Howard, an Indian inspector, reported that three recent cases of murder on the reservation were caused by whiskey. One woman was killed with an ax by her brother-in-law, another Indian stabbed and killed his brother at St. Ignatius, and one woman stabbed another in the northern part of the reservation.[191]

In another example, a newspaper article described an October 1885 incident that occurred after a group of Indians "obtained six bottles of whisky from some soldiers." Presumably the Indian customers paid the soldiers for the alcohol.[192] In yet another of many examples, in October 1886 an unnamed group of Indians attacked a white man on Finley Creek with knives.[193]

The last type of economic activity between 1882 and 1888 found in the historical sources was theft. In 1883 there was still some traditional inter-tribal horse theft activity, but no reports appeared in later years. In April

1883 there were charges of Flathead Reservation tribal members stealing horses from the Crow and Blackfeet tribes.[194]

In October 1883 a group of Indians, including Koonsa Finley from Flathead, attacked and robbed Chinese miners in the Nine Mile area near Frenchtown.[195] Finley and the other Indians were arrested and tried in the Missoula court, but they were released when the Chinese victims would not identify the robbers in court.[196]

Some of the theft victims were other tribal members. In May 1887 an unidentified Indian stole a horse from tribal member Max Couture and two horses from his father. Couture pursued the thief to Bearmouth and retrieved the horses.[197] A few days later, there was a report in the newspaper that the thief had received one hundred lashes on the reservation as punishment.[198]

Tribal member Bendois was arrested in October 1887 for stealing two horses from a Finley at the Jocko Agency. Bendois was tried for horse theft in the Missoula court. This was his second trial for horse theft.[199]

Conclusion

The years between 1882 and 1888 saw the continued development of a new economy on the Flathead Reservation. Traditional economic activities declined in importance, but they were not abandoned. Cattle ranching, farming, and wage labor increased in value as the people of the Flathead Reservation community worked to maintain their economic independence and adjust to the invasion of white settlers into western Montana.

CHAPTER 3

Hunting, Horses, and Cattle, 1889–1904

The late nineteenth century and the opening of the twentieth century saw continued growth in the new Flathead Reservation economy of cattle, horses, grain farming, paid labor, and small business exchange. Hunting and gathering continued, but they could no longer support the majority of the tribal population. Cattle and horse raising on the reservation open range grew to be the most important export industry on the reservation. Much of the tribal population seemed to have been engaged in stock raising, especially during roundups, haying, and harvesting seasons.

Hunting and Gathering, 1889–1904

Traditional economic activities, such as hunting, fishing, and gathering, continued between 1889 and 1904 for the Flathead Reservation tribes. Hunting had become a largely seasonal activity on the reservation, but most Indian families probably took part. For example, Father Jerome D'Aste mentioned on September 21, 1890, that a "good many Indians are starting off for hunt" and a few days later on September 25, 1890, "Most of the Indians are going away."[1] Again on October 4, 1902, D'Aste wrote, "Many Indians are gone hunting."[2]

Most Indian families on the reservation had integrated seasonal hunting trips into the annual agricultural cycle. Agent Peter Ronan wrote the commissioner of Indian affairs on November 20, 1889:

Some of the Indians of this reservation, after harvest season, are in the habit of leaving the reservation to hunt; their object is to obtain a winter supply of meat, which they dry and cure and pack home to the reservation for family use. The hides are dressed by the Indian women and sold at the Traders stores for cash and trade. I know of no instance where Indians of this reserve slaughter game for any other purpose than to supply food and to dress the hides for sale to supply their necessities.[3]

While hunting continued to be a valuable supplementary resource for the tribal economy between 1889 and 1904, two new challenges developed during the period limiting the value of hunting for the tribes. First, big game populations in the northern Rocky Mountains crashed during the late nineteenth century under the increased hunting pressure that came with the exploding white population in the area. The second new development was conflict with Montana state authorities over hunting regulations. The state hunting laws were passed to protect big game populations from extermination, but they were structured in favor of seasonal recreational hunting by the white population.

The 1855 Hellgate Treaty had included a provision by which the government recognized the continued right of tribal members to "the privilege of hunting, gathering roots and berries, and pasturing their horses and cattle upon open and unclaimed land." The same section also secured the right of Indians to fish, and by implication hunt, "at all usual and accustomed places, in common with citizens of the Territory."[4]

During the late nineteenth century and early twentieth centuries, the Flathead Agency and the Indian Office in Washington, D.C., interpreted "in common with citizens" to mean that tribal members were required to follow Montana state regulations while hunting off the reservation. The policy limiting tribal off-reservation hunting rights was illuminated by a confrontation between game warden J. S. Booth and Flathead Reservation hunters in the Thompson River country in March 1896. Booth attempted to arrest fifteen Indians who were charged with hunting out of season. But the Indians refused to submit, and one held Booth off at gunpoint. Booth had arrest warrants sworn out for the Indians and attempted to get Agent Joseph Carter's cooperation in apprehending the offenders. Carter refused to permit their arrest until he got instructions from the commissioner of Indian affairs.[5]

Agent Carter wrote the commissioner of Indian affairs on April 16, 1896, that it was his opinion that tribal members "were amenable to the state laws while off their reservation," but that the accused Indian hunters had been misled that a letter of introduction they obtained from the Plains merchant J. A. McGowan gave them permission to hunt out of season.[6] On May 1, 1896, the commissioner of Indian affairs replied, "In my judgement it is certainly the wisest course, for the Indians to construe their treaty to mean that they are allowed to hunt in common with the citizens and are therefore amenable to the game laws of the State of Montana. This will avoid much trouble and confusion in the future." The commissioner did argue that in this case, due to the misunderstanding generated by McGowan's letter, the charges against the Indian hunters should be dropped by the state.[7]

In 1903 the federal government made a claim that would have seriously curtailed the tribes' off-reservation treaty hunting rights. On August 25, 1903, J. B. Weber, the forest supervisor in Hamilton, wrote Agent W. H. Smead that land in the national forests was no longer "open and unclaimed" and therefore the tribes had no treaty hunting rights in the national forests that covered most of the northern Rocky Mountains.[8] The General Land Office, which then supervised the forest reserves, insisted that Flathead tribal members needed a permit from the Indian agent to enter a forest reserve, were only permitted to take two horses per person, and were subject to all state hunting laws. The restriction on horses was intended to limit the amount of meat and hides Indian hunters could transport back to the reservation. The General Land Office supported a commissioner of Indian affairs decision that "the Indians under their treaty referred to by you now have no right whatever to hunt or to pasture their stock upon the public domain or any of the forest reservations in violation of the State laws and such rules and regulations as may be made by this Department or the Forest Supervisor acting under its direction."[9]

The early state hunting regulations emphasized closed seasons and bag limits. Closed seasons were tailored for sports hunters over subsistence hunters who needed food throughout the year. Bag limits served the needs of white men who used hunting as a supplement to their food supply. They did not work well for those Indian families who relied on hunting for their primary food supply.[10]

The state efforts to restrict Indian hunting led to continuing conflict in the 1890s. A few examples were: in March 1890 the *Weekly Missoulian* published several complaints about Kootenai Indians hunting in the Upper

Flathead Valley. One of the complaints claimed the Indian hunters used dogs to chase deer.[11] Three Kootenai Indians were arrested in March 1893 for killing elk outside of the state hunting season. The Kootenais claimed treaty hunting rights in defense.[12] A report in December 1894 recorded that reservation hunters were using dogs and exceeding the bag limits hunting deer west of Missoula.[13] Reports of Indian hunters in the South Fork Flathead River in February 1896, however, were ignored in order to avoid the expense of sending a warden to make an arrest.[14] A year later, in April 1897, state authorities arrested two Flathead Indians near Drummond for killing game out of season. The correspondent complained that the arrests, trial, and incarceration could cost the taxpayers $1,000.[15]

The continuing conflict with Montana state game wardens occurred against a backdrop of crashing big game populations in the Northern Rockies. The hunting pressure from the rapidly expanding white population combined with Indian subsistence hunting to greatly reduce available game. Two authors have documented the scarcity of big game in western Montana before the white mining boom of the 1860s. Both of them combed the journals of the early white travelers for references to how abundant game was before 1900.[16] Elers Koch, a longtime U.S. Forest Service employee in western Montana, concluded from his historical research and personal experience that the big game populations in western Montana reached their lowest level in the 1890s and early twentieth century. Koch wrote that he "was brought up in the Gallatin Valley in Montana, and usually spent most of the summer in the hills through the nineties, yet at that time game was so scarce that the sight of a single deer, elk, or sheep was most unusual. I often traveled for weeks, with a pack outfit, through the high country without seeing any big game."[17] In 1900 Joseph Barlow Lippincott reported on a summer 1897 U.S. Geological Survey reconnaissance of the Bitter Root Forest Reserve, which included the Bitterroot Mountains and the adjacent area of east-central Idaho. Lippincott traveled 876 miles through the reserve and saw only one elk and two deer.[18] In October 1900 an unnamed Stevensville correspondent wrote: "The elk is fast becoming extinct in this region, or being driven from Montana into Wyoming and Idaho."[19]

The most egregious example of white Montanans' efforts to impede Indian hunting rights was a 1903 law making it illegal for Indians to leave their reservation while armed. In September 1903 deputy game warden Arthur Higgins confiscated Alex Bigknife's guns when Bigknife was in Missoula shopping for his fall hunt. The newspaper reported Bigknife "was much surprised and put out."[20] Bigknife returned to the reservation and he and the traditional chiefs immediately hired a Missoula lawyer, Harry H. Parsons, to sue the warden. On September 3, 1903, the Montana state game warden wrote to Smead apologizing for the confiscation and instructed the Missoula warden to return Bigknife's gun.[21] Bigknife refused to accept the return of his gun and he and the chiefs raised $1,000 to pay the lawyer to pursue the lawsuit against Warden Higgins.[22] The state dragged the Big-knife case out in the courts on technicalities, but did stop enforcing the law against Indian hunters.

Between 1889 and 1904, tribal members also faced increased obstruction from Montana state officials while fishing, but fish continued to supplement the tribal larder. In the summer of 1890 journalist Palmer Henderson visited the farm of Antoine Moise and his family in the Jocko Valley. Moise returned with a string of trout for the family table.[23] In later years Harry Nesbitt remembered Indian parties camping on the Clark Fork River and Bull River below Thompson Falls about 1890. They came in the autumn to fish, hunt, and pick berries.[24]

Some white fishermen on Flathead Lake, probably during 1894, heard that nearby Kootenai fishermen had caught trout weighing forty pounds.[25] In the Missoula Justice Court on October 23, 1895, Alex, an Indian, was convicted of selling fish and fined $1 and costs. A year and a half later, on April 5, 1897, Frank Lamoose was convicted of selling trout fish and sentenced to thirty days in jail.[26] Also in 1897, T. C. McKeogh, a Jesuit scholastic at St. Ignatius described Indians fishing in Mission Creek at night with lights. The fish attracted to the lights were speared by the Indian fishermen.[27] Morton J. Elrod, a University of Montana professor, wrote about an Indian fishing party on Lake McDonald on the reservation in the late 1890s. After a particularly harsh summer rainstorm, Elrod's party helped the Indians out with dry wood, matches, and food.[28] Finally, Agent W. H. Smead denied a fishing permit for a white man on May 7, 1903, because the reservation streams were being fished out, and a "good many" of the old Indians depended quite largely on the supply of fish for their food.[29]

Even less documentation has survived describing gathering of wild roots and berries between 1889 and 1904. Harry Nesbitt, a white settler on Bull River below Thompson Falls, remembered Indian families coming to the area to pick berries in about 1890 when Nesbitt was a child.[30] On June 2, 1901, Father Jerome D'Aste noted in his diary that many of the Jocko Agency Indians were in Missoula digging bitterroot.[31] Finally Dan Longpre, a white man living in the Nine Mile area, remembered Indians coming to the valley in the fall to harvest huckleberries about 1902.[32]

Between 1889 and 1904, hunting, fishing, and gathering continued to be a valuable part of the Flathead Reservation economy. These traditional activities were no longer the base of the tribal economy, but they still made a valuable cultural and economic contribution to the tribal community. Low game populations and Montana state efforts to favor sports hunters through hunting regulations, however, complicated life for tribal members hunting to support their families.

Horses, Range, and Horse Meat

Horses had been a critical economic asset for the Salish and Kootenai tribes for the entire nineteenth century. Between 1889 and 1904, horses transported people and goods and provided the power to plow and farm. Much of the reservation was open range, and according to many sources, the range was overstocked with horses and cattle. During the later part of the period, tribal-member-owned horses competed with cattle for grass. The 1890s also saw large herds of horses driven to the Flathead Reservation from other Pacific Northwest reservations that were among the first to be allotted.

The Flathead agent's annual estimates of reservation horse herds between 1889 and 1904 were only estimates, but they indicate the number of horses grew dramatically over these years. The 1904 estimate of 21,000 head was almost four times the 1889 estimate of 5,782 horses on the reservation.[33]

Since horses played such an important economic role in Flathead Reservation life in the late nineteenth century, there were persistent problems settling accounts when they were stolen or lost. Cases involving misappropriated horses appeared regularly in the historical documents between 1889 and 1904. Even more cases must have occurred, because most of the problems over horse ownership would probably have been settled between the parties or by the local chief or judge without being mentioned in the surviving written records.

A few examples of these continuing problems over horse ownership give a taste of the importance of horses for individual tribal members. In early 1890 a Jewish peddler named Sieff bought a pinto horse, which was stolen from him by an unknown thief while Sieff was in Missoula. In the spring of 1890 Sieff heard that his horse was on the reservation in the possession of a mixed-blood. The mixed-blood traded the pinto to Mr. M. C. Morris for another horse. Morris returned the stolen pinto horse to Sieff and wanted to get back the horse he had traded to the mixed-blood for the pinto. Shortly after, Sieff was traveling through the reservation and encountered the mixed-blood. The unnamed mixed-blood agreed to return Morris's horse. In the meantime Morris consulted a local justice of the peace, who proceeded to file a case against Sieff for "stealing" Morris's horse. After a convoluted legal proceeding, the jury found Sieff not guilty, and the justice of the peace agreed to return the pinto horse to Sieff.[34]

In January 1892 a case against Antoine Finley in Missoula District Court for horse stealing was dismissed. Since the alleged theft had occurred on the reservation, the judge decided the court did not have jurisdiction. No further information on this incident has been found.[35]

Duncan McDonald, on the reservation, had a horse, saddle, and blankets stolen in September 1893. The thief was reported to be headed north past the foot of Flathead Lake.[36] During Agent Joseph Carter's term from 1893 to 1898, very few accounts have survived of daily events on the reservation. The Flathead Agency building burned down in 1897, and none of the Flathead Agency records before 1898 have survived.[37]

In contrast, the Flathead Agency correspondence for 1898 through 1904 is available and provides documentation of many controversies over horse ownership. For example, on February 9, 1898, Mr. C. W. Howe of Missoula complained that the Indian bitterroot diggers camped south of Missoula in May 1897 had taken his yearling colt with their horses when they returned to the reservation.[38] On May 8, 1898, Agent Smead wrote to Lackery, an Indian in Missoula, that Battice, the son of Pierre Joseph, had gambled off a horse belonging to Pierre Joseph's wife. Now Pierre Joseph wanted the horse back.[39] A few days later, on May 20, 1898, Smead wrote to Judge Joseph Standing Bear in St. Ignatius that Paul Andre had a horse claimed by Grand Joe. Paul Andre had won the horse gambling with an unnamed Cree who did not own the horse.[40] Anne Sapierre complained to Smead on July 5, 1898, that Sac Arlee had sold a horse belonging to her to John Peter in Missoula.[41] Similar complaints of lost, stolen, or missing horses run throughout Agent Smead's correspondence.

Some of the contests over horses became very complex and convoluted. One example from November 1898 illustrated just how complicated they could become. At some point, Charles Allard sold a bay mare branded with Allard's brand to Malcolm McLeod. It afterward passed through the possession of Richard McLeod, Dan McLeod, Alex Matt, Henry Matt, and then Antoine Moise. Antoine Moise lost the bay mare and another horse in May 1898. Somehow Allard picked up the horse (with Allard's brand) and traded it to George Guardipee for a mare. Now Moise wanted the bay mare back, and Guardipee wanted his mare returned to him.[42]

On August 23, 1899, Smead wrote about a case where someone stole a horse from an unnamed Indian and then traded the horse with a white man named Horatio Cook in the Upper Flathead Valley. Cook later traded the horse with his brother-in-law, Ebb Fordham. Fordham traveled on the stolen horse through the reservation, where the original Indian owner recognized the horse and claimed it. Fordham surrendered the horse to the Indian.[43]

One of Antoine Ninepipe's sons rode a horse belonging to his father to Missoula in 1900 and put the horse up in the Missoula Feed Corral, a stable. When the younger Ninepipe was ready to leave, he did not have enough money to pay the stable bill. He sold the horse to the stable owner and received the proceeds less the stable charges in cash. But Antoine had never given his son permission to sell the horse. The stable owner in turn sold the horse to another white man. The new owner let the horse get away, and the horse returned to the reservation on its own.[44]

These persistent conflicts over lost and stolen horses occurred against a backdrop of broader economic developments on the reservation between 1889 and 1904. During much of the period there are reports that the reservation range was overstocked, and many of the horses on the range belonged to Indians who had rights on the Nez Perce and Umatilla Reservations—not on Flathead.

No range surveys were made, but the available contemporary observations suggest that the cattle and horse herds on the reservation had reached the carrying capacity of the land. In 1893 Olin D. Wheeler, a journalist visiting the reservation, reported that the reservation was "pastured to its full capacity."[45] In a similar vein, in a May 1896 interview, Agent Joseph Carter claimed the range on the reservation was "fully occupied by the herds of the Indians."[46] Carter lamented in his 1897 annual report that "the range is fast deteriorating, and will soon be ruined by the countless ponies . . . that cover this reserve."[47]

F. M. Cory appeared on the reservation in 1895, and among other things, Cory organized a roundup of horses on the range belonging to white men and Indians from the Nez Perce and Umatilla Reservations. One newspaper account maintained that 2,000 horses on the reserve did not belong there.[48]

Two of the Nez Perce horse owners hired a Missoula lawyer to protect their interests.[49] Cory's efforts to remove nonmember horses from the reservation grasslands stumbled when it was discovered that he was an imposter and not a government agent.[50]

Agents Carter and Smead maintained that a large proportion of the horses on the reservation were owned by Nez Perce Indians from the Umatilla Reservation. On August 20, 1897, Carter wrote that one-third of the 15,000 horses on the Flathead Reservation range were owned by Indians allotted on the Umatilla Reservation.[51] Smead claimed on February 21, 1899, that a Umatilla Indian named Johnson had a large number of horses on Flathead, but did not give a number.[52] In 1900—according to a report by Indian inspector Cyrus Beede—Allicott, Johnson, and Kiola, Nez Perce Indians living on Flathead, had about 3,000 horses grazing on the Flathead range.[53]

Soon after Agent Smead took office in 1898, he initiated an active campaign to reduce the horse herds on the reservation open range and improve the quality of the horses that remained. Smead's plan called for forcing non-Salish and Kootenai horse owners to either sell or move their horses from the range. He particularly targeted Indians from the Umatilla Reservation who had recently relocated to Flathead. He also pressured Indians from other tribes who lived on the reservation to reduce their horse stocks. Some of those Indians from other tribes were later adopted into the Confederated Salish and Kootenai Tribes.

Smead worked to develop a market so tribal stockmen could sell their horses to off-reservation buyers. He lobbied for reduced freight rates for shipping from Flathead to eastern markets. One market he cultivated was reservation pig farms where the pigs were fattened with slaughtered horse meat.

Many of the horse buyers Smead attracted to the reservation came from across the country, but one important purchaser was C. C. Willis of Plains. Thanks to a February 1900 interview in the *Anaconda Standard*, we have an outline of the economics of Willis's business as a horse buyer. In six months Willis had purchased five hundred horses from reservation Indian owners for an average cost of $1.75 each. He slaughtered the horses and sold the hides for about $2 each. Then he fed the horse meat to hogs. The horse meat was supplemented with grain for the last couple of weeks and the fully grown hogs were shipped to out-of-state markets. He had just shipped a train carload of hogs to the Seattle market, which netted him $947. Alex Dow had a similar horse/hog operation near Arlee.[54]

Willis was also exploring the market for selling the cayuses to buyers in Cuba and horse meat canners in Oregon. Some of the horses from the reservation were probably purchased for transport and work, but apparently many were used for food for people and hogs.[55]

In August 1900 the Plains newspaper noted that Indians were selling bands of cayuses to Willis at his ranch near Plains and then spending their money in town.[56] That month, Willis accompanied ten railroad carloads of "choice" horses to eastern markets.[57] A week later, he returned to Plains after selling the horses in Billings and St. Paul.[58]

Most of Willis's purchases seemed to have been horses that tribal members drove to his ranch near Plains, but on July 16, 1901, he was given a permit for five days to purchase horses on the reservation.[59] In August of 1901 Willis received another permit for thirty days to purchase reservation horses. This permit also noted Willis could hire four Indians to assist in handling the horses.[60] According to a note in the Plains newspaper, Willis was buying reservation horses, breaking them, and shipping them on the railroad for British cavalry service in the Boer War in Africa. He had two men breaking them to lead and three riding the animals.[61] By September 1901 Willis and his crew had one hundred ready for shipment. According to the *Plainsman*, "The Indians are much pleased over their ability to sell their horses."[62]

A few of Willis's purchases got complicated. According to a newspaper report, an Indian woman named Melissa had horses to sell but could not leave the reservation due to the quarantine for the 1901 smallpox epidemic. She gave the horses to Joseph Pain, a mixed-blood, to sell to Willis for her. Pain sold her horses, but proceeded to drink up the sixty dollar payment in Plains. Melissa had Pain arrested for the theft.[63]

Late the next winter, in February 1902, Willis made another horse buying trip to fill out a shipment of horses.[64] Unfortunately for Willis, the Boer War ended in 1902, and he could not sell his last shipment to the British agents. In June 1902 Willis accompanied two railroad cars of horses to Minnesota to sell the horses for riding and farming work.[65]

Willis continued in the horse trade in 1903 and Agent Smead wrote Willis on April 15, 1903, that the new grazing tax introduced on the reservation should pressure more tribal members into selling their horses.[66] In July 1904 Willis shipped ninety-four head of reservation horses to Superior, Wisconsin.[67] About a week later, he shipped another consignment of reservation horses to Billings to be used by the Japanese army in their war against Russia.[68] Willis made at least one more shipment of Flathead horses to eastern markets in September 1904.[69]

There is no way to tell at this point how many reservation horses were sold to meat canning and hog farm operations, and how many were sold for riding and work animals. Smead's efforts to develop a market for reservation horses were remarkably successful. Especially in the year 1900, a large number of off-reservation buyers got permits from the Flathead agent to purchase horses on the reservation or to have the Missoula sheriff's department inspect the brands on horses being shipped off the reservation. For unknown reasons, the 1900 sales did not cause a dip in the number of horses recorded in the annual reports of the commissioner of Indian affairs. Many of the shipments mentioned in the sources were of good size. Table 3.1 shows some of the larger lots shipped in 1900, in addition to C. C. Willis's shipments. Horse sales reached their apex in 1900, but they continued at a vigorous pace until the end of Agent Smead's tenure in 1904. In 1903 Indian inspector Arthur M. Tinker estimated that 3,500 horses had been sold during the first nine months of the year.[70]

Table 3.1. Large Shipments of Horses from Flathead Reservation, 1900

Date	Size of shipment
March 20, 1900	Trainload of horses (about 400 head)[a]
April 13, 1900	1,800 cayuses[b]
May 11, 1900	800 ponies[c]
June 1, 1900	33 railroad carloads[d]
June 7, 1900	Allicott delivered 1,500 horses to Alex Dow[e]
June 29, 1900	100 railroad carloads[f]
June 29, 1900	Shipments total in the thousands of horses[g]
July 23, 1900	Alex Dow wants final 1,500 or 1,600 horses from Allicott under contract.[h]
August 10, 1900	1,000 cayuses[i]

a. "Will Inspect Horses," AS, Mar. 20, 1900, p. 16, col. 3.
b. *Inter Lake* (Kalispell, Mont.), Apr. 13, 1900, p. 5, col. 2.
c. *Plainsman*, May 11, 1900, p. 4, col. 4.
d. *Edwards' Fruit Grower & Farmer* (Missoula, Mont.), June 1, 1900, p. 8, col. 1.
e. Smead to CIA, June 7, 1900, 27,744/1900, NA CIA LR.
f. "A Trip to Selish," *Kalispell Bee*, June 29, 1900, p. 1, col. 5.
g. "Inspecting Horses," AS, June 29, 1900, p 12, col. 2.
h. "Indian Contract," AS, July 23, 1900, p. 12, col. 3.
i. *Plainsman*, Aug. 10, 1900, p. 4, col. 3.

The historical sources rarely mention tribal members being forced to sell their horses against their will. It was possible coercion occurred but was not noted in the documents. The only horse sale that was recorded in great detail was Allicott's autumn 1899 sale of up to 3,000 horses to Mr. W. W. White, who was acting as agent for Alex Dow, the Arlee trader. Allicott balked at completing the sale after delivering about half of the horses, maintaining that he had not understood the terms of the written contract. No coercion was charged in the original transaction, but Cyrus Beede, the Indian inspector who investigated the dispute, argued that Allicott should be forced to complete the sale of his horses to protect the range on the reservation.[71] The commissioner of Indian affairs agreed Allicott should deliver the remaining horses to Dow under the contract.[72]

An April 15, 1899, letter from Agent Smead to Angus P. McDonald, who was Duncan McDonald's half brother, recorded Smead threatening to have Angus P. removed from the reservation if he opposed Smead's efforts to sell reservation horse herds. Angus P. did not have any Salish or Kootenai blood, but he was later adopted into the tribes when formal enrollment was introduced.[73] On May 18, 1901, Smead encouraged Deaf Louis to sell his horses to F. E. Walters, a white horse buyer. Smead wanted A. L. Demers to do what he could to encourage Deaf Louis to make the sale, provided the buyer would pay Louis a fair price.[74]

As mentioned before, a number of the larger, more valuable horses from the reservation were purchased for the British cavalry for use in South Africa during the Boer War. Between 1899 and 1902, the British fought white Afrikaner settlers of Dutch descent for control of what became South Africa. On June 1, 1901, a Missoula newspaper noted that Frank C. Eldred was seeking to buy three carloads of reservation horses for the British war effort.[75] Breaking and selling horses for cavalry mounts was "an important industry" at Plains, Selish (Ravalli), and Arlee in September 1901.[76]

In November 1901 Arthur Larrivee and David Dowd from the reservation visited Missoula and claimed selling horses was the "chief industry" on the reservation at that time. Buyers for the British government had picked up four carloads of horses in the past few days.[77] By June 1902, however, the war ended and the British cavalry market dried up. As mentioned previously, by the end of the 1889 to 1904 period, the Russo-Japanese War broke out in the Far East, opening up a new customer for Flathead Reservation horses.[78]

To facilitate the market for reservation horses, on September 12, 1899, Agent Smead lobbied the Northern Pacific Railroad for reduced freight rates for Flathead horses shipped to eastern markets.[79] In April 1903 Smead was hoping to receive word of a special rate for shipping reservation horses in twenty-five railroad car lots.[80]

Another aspect of Agent Smead's efforts to "rationalize" the reservation stock industry was to import stallions that would increase the size and weight of reservation horses. Almost as soon as Smead became agent, he proposed a fine for owners of small-size stallions on the reservation range. The stallions would be castrated at the owner's expense. Pedigree stallions and those weighing over 1,250 pounds would be exempt.[81] The commissioner of Indian affairs did not respond to Smead's letter, but on June 1, 1901, Indian inspector W. J. McConnell recommended that the government furnish stallions to improve the horse herds rather than wagons of farming implements.[82] On February 24, 1903, Smead recommended that the government furnish tribal stockmen with good quality stallions to improve reservation herds. The stallions could be purchased from the proceeds of the new reservation grazing tax.[83] The commissioner of Indian affairs replied on March 5, 1903, that he would consider using the grazing tax money to purchase good quality stallions, if tribal members agreed to dispose of their inferior horses and ponies.[84] On May 2, 1903, Smead gave a permit to Westfield Importing Company to come on the reservation and sell stallions to tribal members. The prices charged needed to be reasonable and no higher than the prices charged white buyers.[85]

Several historical sources suggest Smead's efforts to reduce the horse herds on the reservation were successful in decreasing overgrazing and improving the open range for cattle raising. On June 29, 1900, a newspaper reported that reservation cattlemen were "rejoicing over the prospect of improved ranges for their stock."[86] Later, another newspaper noted upgraded range conditions resulting from the horse sales.[87] Alex Demers, a reservation trader, commented in June 1901, "The removal of so many horses from the ranges of the reservation has improved matters for the cattlemen."[88]

A side issue of the economics of horse culture on the Flathead Reservation was the number of tribal members who were involved in horse racing. Horse races had long been a part of Salish and Kootenai life. Blind Mose Chouteau remembered horse racing as a feature of tribal powwows at the beginning of the twentieth century. They took up three or four days of the celebration.[89] Tribal members were also prominent in Fourth of July horse racing in surrounding white communities. In 1899 a number of tribal members entered the races at Kalispell and won prize money from ten to sixty dollars per race. The tribal race winners included horses owned by Andrew Stinger, Angus McDonald, and Charles Allard.[90] The 1900 Fourth of July horse races in Kalispell featured those tribal horse owners and Joe Allard and an unnamed Kootenai Indian.[91] Some of the mixed-blood horse owners took racing very seriously. In May 1901 the Allard-Stinger stables hired A. Ewing, a "well know horse trainer," to train their horses.[92] In June 1901 Andrew Stinger raced a "range cayuse" from the reservation against some of the blooded horses being trained for the Missoula Fourth of July races. Stinger's horse won.[93] On June 30, 1903, Andrew Stinger raced his horse against one owned by Ben Cramer, a white man married to a tribal member, at the Kalispell race track. Each owner put up several hundred dollars to back their horse. Cramer's horse won the pot.[94]

Many tribal members took special pride in their horses, and some bought high-quality animals. In April 1903 Andrew Stinger paid $300 for a "fine team of matched grey draft horses." At the same time, Angus McDonald paid $400 for a 1,840-pound bay stallion.[95]

Another economic impact of horses on the reservation was the money paid by the Northern Pacific Railroad for Indian stock killed by trains. The total paid by the railroad was not clear in the documents. It was also not known if the amount paid fairly compensated the Indian owners for the stock killed by the trains. Mediating the settlements was a continuing problem for the Flathead agent.[96]

Between 1889 and 1904, horse sales were an important part of the reservation economy. Agent Smead's efforts to reduce the number of horses on the tribal range opened new opportunities for tribal members to sell horses for cash. This would have been an important income source for many full-blood Indian families.

Cattle and Cattle Exports

After the first recorded trainload shipment of cattle to off-reservation markets in 1888, the cattle industry continued growing through the 1889 to 1904 period. According to the estimates in the commissioner of Indian affairs annual reports, Flathead Reservation cattle herds grew from 13,250 head in 1889 to 28,000 in 1904.[97] Most of the cattle on the reservation ranges were owned by a few rich mixed-bloods such as Charles Allard and Michel Pablo, but many mixed-blood and full-blood families had small herds that shared the range. The industry was based on common open range with seasonal roundups. Between 1889 and 1904 the cattle industry was the backbone of the Flathead Reservation economy. Fall shipments of cattle from the reservation to off-reservation markets in Chicago and other cities were a principal source of income for Flathead stockmen. Little evidence has survived, but stockmen provided seasonal employment and income for many other mixed-blood and full-blood Indian families on the reservation.

No overall figures are available, but the cattle shipped to market from the reservation generated substantial revenue for the large stock owners. In January 1891 Charles Allard claimed one steer raised by Angus McDonald on the reservation weighed in at 1,274 pounds.[98] In August of that year Charles Allard and Michel Pablo shipped 400 head of cattle to a Chicago firm. They were paid $40 a head.[99] Malcolm McLeod accompanied Charles Allard Sr. and a trainload of cattle to Chicago in 1893.[100] Angus P. McDonald shipped three railroad cars of cattle to Chicago from Plains in September 1893.[101] In November 1893 another four trainloads were shipped from the reservation, but the individual sellers were not identified.[102] Agent Joseph Carter reported that $40,000 worth of reservation cattle were shipped to Chicago in 1894. One unnamed full-blood stockman netted $6,000 in 1894.[103] In August 1895 Charles Allard sold a trainload of reservation cattle in Chicago that averaged 1,653 pounds each.[104] Agent Carter predicted that 80–90 carloads of cattle would be shipped from the reservation in 1896, totaling 1,600 to 1,800 head. Another 500 head would be sold to traders on the reservation.[105] An October 1896 report estimated 60 carloads had been sent from the reservation that year.[106] A reservation trader estimated that 7,000 cattle had been shipped from the reservation in 1897.[107] Cattle shipments from the reservation continued through the end of this period in 1904, but much of the evidence described estimates or shipments from individual ranchers.

Most of the cattle on the reservation were owned by the large cattle owners—primarily mixed-bloods or white men who married into the tribes—but apparently, many other tribal members had smaller herds. In 1895 P. McCormick, an Indian inspector, figured there were about 20,000 cattle on the reservation, but half were owned by six or seven mixed-bloods.[108] The 1900 United States census found that most Flathead Reservation stockmen reported annual sales in 1899 of less than $1,000. Only nineteen had sales worth more than $1,000. Five sold more than $4,000 in stock, and one had $10,100 in livestock sales.[109] In July 1901 Frank C. Armstrong, a Department of the Interior special agent, found that about a quarter of the full-bloods on the reservation were farming and had some cattle. Between

St. Ignatius and the foot of Flathead Lake, he found forty full-blood Indians who were doing "fairly well" and had farms and cattle.[110] There was no way to tell how typical the case was, but in March 1898 the infant daughter of Philomene Peone inherited seven cattle and seven horses.[111]

In November 1902 Michel, a wealthy cattleman in Camas, was robbed of $22,000 in cash. According to Special Indian Agent Charles S. McNichols, he made the money raising cattle.[112] In January 1903 Charles S. McNichols compiled a list of the nineteen largest cattle owners on the reservation. Seven were white men married to Indian wives, seven were mixed-bloods, three were full-blood Indians, and two were Indians adopted from other tribes.[113]

The cattle industry on the reservation was based on open range but was supplemented by some winter feeding. In his last annual report in 1893, Agent Peter Ronan described semiannual roundups where calves were branded. All the stockmen took part.[114] According to a September 1904 newspaper article, a late summer roundup, where mature cattle were selected for market, was conducted jointly by the stockmen.[115]

As mentioned in the discussion of the reservation economy between 1882 and 1888, reservation cattlemen had developed a system of, at least, selective winter feeding. Putting up hay and feeding it to cattle during the winter greatly improved their survival during the coldest part of the year. The estimates in the annual reports of the commissioner of Indian affairs have the hay crop increasing from 6,040 tons in 1889 to 27,000 tons in 1904, an increase of nearly 450 percent.[116] On August 1, 1889, Agent Ronan wrote that Indian cattle owners were making strenuous efforts to harvest wild hay from marshy areas for winter feeding.[117] An 1891 traveler through the Mission Valley on the reservation found thousands of horses and cattle grazing on the open range in the valley. A few mixed-blood cattlemen had fenced off land to raise their stock separately from the common herd.[118] The Plains newspaper in July 1896 carried reports that the hay crop on the reservation that year was "immense," and two of the largest cattle owners were in Plains purchasing supplies for haying.[119] Many of the Indian farmers raised grain to feed as hay during the winter.[120] Much of the evidence about winter feeding of cattle on the reservation involved cattle losses due to hay running out before the new grass started to grow. In March 1897 the ranchers near Mud Creek had to turn their cattle out to rustle for themselves because hay supplies ran out.[121] The next year, a cold spring delayed the grass, and many cattle were suffering.[122] The shortage of hay in spring 1899 resulted in losses of 20 percent for some reservation ranchers.[123]

As mentioned previously, most of the large shipments of reservation cattle between 1889 and 1904 went to market in Chicago by way of the Northern Pacific Railroad. At least one shipment in September 1902, however, was shipped to market in Seattle.[124] Some of the reservation cattle were sold to buyers who came to Flathead and purchased directly from the ranchers. This may have been the principal marketing method for owners of smaller herds.

On June 13, 1899, Agent Smead gave permission for Peter Federsohn to buy cattle on the reservation for ten days.[125] Gaspard Deschamps was an active cattle buyer on the reservation in 1900 and 1901. On May 28, 1900, he got a permit to buy cattle for four days.[126] Another ten days were authorized in July 1900, and on May 20, 1901, he got a permit good for the entire 1901 season.[127] Frank Jette got permission to purchase reservation cattle on June 12, 1903.[128]

Other cattle were sold and butchered in Montana. Agent Carter mentioned this local market in his 1894 annual report.[129] John R. Daily, who operated a slaughterhouse and meat market in Missoula, was a frequent purchaser of reservation cattle.[130]

The reservation cattle owners fully supported Smead's plans to reduce reservation horse herds to make more room for cattle on the open range.[131] Most of Smead's agenda for reducing reservation horse herds involved developing the market so tribal members could sell their horses.

The second part of Smead's plan for the stock industry, however, was vigorously opposed by reservation cattlemen. This involved charging tribal members a one-dollar-per-year grazing fee for all horses and cattle tribal members owned over one hundred head. As early as August 27, 1897, W. J. McConnell, an Indian inspector, recommended a one-dollar-a-year grazing tax on all cattle and horses on the range in excess of fifty animals per owner.[132] Jame E. Jenkins, another Indian inspector, made a similar recommendation on March 15, 1902. Jenkins's tax would apply to stock in excess of one hundred head per person.[133] On January 5, 1903, another Indian inspector, Charles S. McNichols, submitted a report listing the herds of the largest cattle owners on the reservation. On February 2, 1903, the secretary of the interior authorized an annual grazing tax on herds of more than one hundred per family. The tax of one dollar per animal was to start on April 1, 1903.[134]

In February 1903 Agent Smead consulted with "some of my leading Indians" about the grazing tax. These leaders, presumably all full-bloods—had no problem with a grazing tax on the herds of white men, mixed-bloods, and Indians from other reservations. However, they were "seriously opposed to the full bloods who have rights here being taxed."[135]

The opposition to the grazing tax culminated in a spring 1903 protest delegation to Washington, D.C. The delegation included traditional chiefs, agency judges, and mixed-blood cattlemen.[136] The president and the commissioner of Indian affairs were not available, but the delegates were able to meet with the secretary of the interior. According to Duncan McDonald, one of the mixed-blood cattle owners, "The secretary of the interior would not yield an inch but simply settled down like a mired mule and wouldn't even answer us."[137]

Smead moved to implement the tax and threatened any stockmen who refused with removal from the reservation. William Irvine refused to pay, so on May 13, 1903, the commissioner of Indian affairs authorized Irvine's removal from the reservation.[138] Irvine capitulated and paid his grazing tax, and the removal order was canceled.[139] Joseph Morrigeau proved to be the most obstreperous opponent of the grazing tax. Morrigeau refused to pay the tax and refused to leave the reservation when police ordered him off the reservation.[140] In November 1903, soldiers were sent from Fort Missoula to remove Morrigeau.[141] After being forcibly removed, Morrigeau paid his grazing tax of $1,300 and was allowed to return home.[142] In order to undermine the opposition to the grazing tax, Smead pushed for a per capita payment. In January 1904 a $5 per capita payment was made to all tribal members from the money collected from the grazing tax.[143]

A perennial problem for the cattle industry—especially on an open range—was rustling. The historical records did not describe the problem in detail, but they did indicate it was a continuing irritant for Flathead Reservation cattlemen. In July 1897 a newspaper report on the recent roundup on the reservation mentioned that "nearly all the ranchmen report shortages in their stock." No explanation was given.[144]

The historical sources include several confusing accounts of an altercation between Angus P. McDonald, the prominent cattleman, and three other tribal members. Apparently, the fight was over cattle rustling.[145]

On May 18, 1901, Agent Smead wrote to the Montana Board of Stock Commissioners for help in gathering evidence to prosecute suspected cattle rustlers in the northern part of the reservation.[146] The reply from W. G. Preuitt, the commission secretary, said they could only provide limited help. Most of the money to pay an investigator would have to come from the local stockmen.[147] That fall, Preuitt offered $250 if Flathead and Missoula counties joined to hire a stock inspector. If Ravalli County joined the other two counties, Preuitt could provide a total of $600.[148] In August 1901 Arthur Larrivee and other mixed-blood cattlemen engaged in a fight with a group of six full-bloods, which may have involved rustling.[149]

In one case Isaac Bonaparte and his wife were arrested on the Nez Perce Reservation for stealing cattle on Flathead. They sold the cattle off the reservation before they left western Montana. According to Agent Smead, Bonaparte confessed to the theft.[150] In another case that was briefly mentioned in the record, in October 1902, Joe Blodgett Jr. was arrested and charged with shooting cattle belonging to another tribal member. Blodgett was acquitted after nine witnesses were examined by the United States commissioner.[151]

Father Leopold Van Gorp, in April 1904, accused two tribal members of stealing and slaughtering cattle belonging to the mission.[152] One of the thieves, Joseph Stychen, was arrested and sent before the federal grand jury in Helena for rustling in May 1904.[153] Apparently, he got a six-month sentence for the crime.[154]

As early as the fall of 1901, the reservation stockmen were looking to organize and hire a stock inspector to investigate rustling and protect their economic interests. On October 14, 1901, Agent Smead wrote to the Montana Board of Stock Commissioners for samples of bylaws and other information about starting the organization.[155] A few weeks later the Missoula newspaper carried reports that fifty reservation cattlemen met in St. Ignatius and organized a stockmen's association. The association members elected a temporary board of directors consisting of the chief of the Kootenais, a white man married into the tribe, and five mixed-blood tribal members. According to the reports, the fifty members owned 25,000 cattle and 20,000 horses.[156] On December 9, 1901, a permanent board was selected for the association consisting of Kakashe, the St. Ignatius judge; August Enstata, the Kootenai chief; and five mixed-blood cattlemen: Angus P. McDonald, T. G. Demers, Charles St. Peter, Joseph C. Allard, and Alex Matt. McDonald became president and Allard, secretary.[157]

When Agent Smead granted F. M. Rothrock of Wallace, Idaho, permission to purchase cattle on the reservation in November 1901, he included a provision that the buyer had to have his purchases inspected by the stock association. Smead expected the association to begin inspections in the near future.[158] On January 29, 1902, Smead gave J. S. Dupuis of Ronan permission to bring one hundred head of cattle onto the reservation. Smead noted that some of the Indians objected to outside cattle being brought onto the reservation and suggested Dupuis talk to two or three of the leading men around the agency to avoid possible problems.[159]

On April 7, 1902, Joseph Allard submitted rules for the cattlemen's association to Agent Smead for his approval. The rules levied a fee of 7.5 cents on member-owned cattle and 5 cents on horses. Members and nonmembers were not allowed to leave hides exposed for more than thirty days. One bull was to be provided for every twenty head of cattle put on the range. A stock inspector was to inspect the bulls. The association treasurer needed a $1,000 bond.[160] The 1902 annual meeting of the association was scheduled for May 15 at St. Ignatius. A number of new members were expected to join at the meeting.[161]

Stockmen maintained an informal system of brands on the reservation. Most of the brands were not registered with the state. New cattle owners were just required to make sure that they selected a brand that was not already being used on the reservation.[162]

Toward the end of this period, the reservation cattlemen unsuccessfully tried to keep sheep off the reservation range.[163] In January 1904 they circulated petitions on the reservation calling for all sheep to be removed.[164]

On July 7, 1903, W. B. Parsons, a Missoula physician, complained that 3,300 cattle on the reservation listed as belonging to mixed-blood cattlemen were actually owned by the Missoula Mercantile Company.[165] The Missoula Mercantile Company was part of A. B. Hammond's logging and commercial empire that dominated much of western Montana.[166] C. H. McLeod, who ran the mercantile for Hammond, denied owning any cattle grazing on the reservation. Agent Smead pointed out that the mercantile extended credit to reservation cattlemen and another Hammond business, the First National Bank of Missoula, held mortgages on reservation cattle.[167] Dr. Parsons repeated his charges that mixed-bloods and white men who grazed cattle on Flathead were fronting for the Missoula Mercantile Company.[168] The commissioner of Indian affairs declined to investigate the charges further.[169]

The Flathead Reservation buffalo herd represented a specialized part of the livestock business between 1889 and 1904. The buffalo, owned by Charles Allard and Michel Pablo, were butchered, sold, and exhibited as they became rarer nationally. In January 1891 Allard slaughtered a buffalo bull that dressed out to 700 pounds. He sold the front quarter for 50 cents a pound, the hind quarter for 35 cents a pound, and the head and hide for $150.[170]

In 1892 several proposals were floated to ship animals from the Pablo-Allard buffalo herd to Chicago for the 1893 world's fair. Frank R. Miles, who promoted numerous schemes in the 1890s, attracted the most publicity. Miles incorporated the Montana & Columbian Buffalo and Indian Exhibit Company to take Allard's buffalo and Indian people from the Flathead and other Montana reservations to Chicago.[171] In the fall of 1892 Miles returned to Montana with big plans for the exhibit and claimed to have rented a twenty-acre site near the world's fair grounds.[172] Allard began working with the buffalo so they could be handled by the cowboys.[173] As part of the preparations, Allard exhibited the buffalo at the foot of Flathead Lake in October 1893. Excursionists from Demersville could take a steamer across the lake, view the buffalo, and return for one dollar.[174]

Miles's plans for a Chicago exhibit alternated between hot and cold, but finally fell through.[175] Most of Miles's schemes during the 1890s either failed or were never carried out.[176] At the urging of Agent Peter Ronan, Allard tried to make arrangements to exhibit the buffalo in Chicago independent of Miles's plan. Unfortunately, it was too late, and no Flathead buffalo exhibit ever made it to Chicago.[177] Malcolm McLeod, one of Allard's cowboys, accused Miles of deliberately tying up the buffalo to keep Allard from exhibiting the buffalo at the fair.[178]

After the failure of the plans for a Chicago exhibit, Allard formed a Wild West show, which in the fall of 1893 performed in various Montana cities.[179] Admission to the Allard show in Butte in October 1893 was 60 cents for adults and 25 cents for children.[180] The headline event was Malcolm McLeod riding a buffalo.[181] According to one report, one thousand people attended the Missoula performance of the Wild West show, but the show seems to have disbanded after the Missoula engagement.[182]

In 1901 and 1902, Allard's son, Charles Allard Jr., organized another Wild West show to exhibit the buffalo. They performed in Missoula and other Montana cities in the spring and summer of 1901.[183] In the spring of 1902 the show was reorganized under a white promoter named George L. Hutchin.[184] The Great Buffalo and Wild West Show was incorporated with $50,000 capital stock. Allard Jr. was in charge of the buffalo in the show.[185] Unfortunately, the show went broke in the fall of 1902 and was disbanded in Marshalltown, Iowa.[186]

Despite the economic failure of efforts to organize a Wild West show based on the Flathead Reservation buffalo herd, buffalo were sold from the herd for slaughter and exhibit. In October 1897 two Allard buffalo got killed during transit through Missoula for sale to buyers in New York. The butchered meat was sold in Missoula for 30 cents a pound.[187] In December 1899, reservation buffalo were sold and butchered for Christmas dinners in Missoula, Kalispell, Helena, Butte, Anaconda, and Great Falls.[188] In December 1900 ten buffalo were purchased by Helena butchers for their holiday trade.[189] One Missoula butcher, Gaspard Deschamps, purchased several buffalo from the Allard herd in February 1902 and was selling the meat in Missoula.[190]

Most of the sales from the Flathead Reservation herd were either for exhibit or for establishing new herds. In June 1897 Michel Pablo sold 40 head to a Florida man for over $500 each.[191] Charles Conrad bought Allard's widow's share of the herd—about 25 head—in February 1900.[192] In April 1901 Charles Allard Jr. sold 20 buffalo to Buffalo Bill Cody for use in Cody's Wild West show.[193] Two buffalo were slaughtered in Plains in February 1902, and the hides and heads were prepared for shipment to New York City for exhibition in the natural history museum.[194] By February 1902 Agent Smead wrote that a quarter of the buffalo herd had been sold by the Charles Allard Sr. heirs.[195] Another 25 head were sold by the heirs to Yellowstone Park in the fall of 1902.[196] In November 1902 Buffalo Jones and Howard Eaton made a large purchase of a railroad carload of buffalo.[197]

Since much of the Flathead Reservation was excellent stock country, cattle raising grew between 1889 and 1904 to become the principal export industry on the reservation. The largest herds were owned by a few mixed-bloods and white men married into the tribes, but most families seemed to have either a small band of cattle or worked seasonally in the roundup and haying. Small sales of cattle provided important income for full-blood families who had previously supported themselves through hunting and gathering. The sales of horses, cattle, and buffalo supported many stock owners, cowboys, and other workers in the late nineteenth-century Flathead Reservation economy.

CHAPTER 4

Farming, Government Aid, and Wage Work, 1889–1904

Mixed-blood tribal members were the most involved and successful in the new economy, but many full-blood families had some horses and cattle and kept at least a small vegetable garden. The Flathead Agency provided some assistance for needy families, but most government aid was distributed as payment for labor or commodities used in agency operations. Casual labor and small sales of agricultural and craft products probably involved a number of tribal members but left only limited evidence in the written record. We do know that, while the Flathead Reservation tribes were not affluent between 1889 and 1904, they were self-supporting. This economic independence made it possible for the tribes to limit the powers of the Flathead Indian agent. The government never controlled the food supply or subsistence of the tribes.

Tribal Member Farming: 1889–1904

Farming activity on the Flathead Reservation continued to grow between 1889 and 1904. The holdings of a few rich mixed-blood rancher-farmers dominated the industry, but many or most tribal families had at least vegetable gardens for household support. According to the agents' estimates in the annual reports of the commissioner of Indian affairs, the acres under fence increased from 15,500 acres in 1889 to 50,000 acres in 1903, the last year for which estimates are available. That indicated a more than

300 percent increase. At the same time, acres cultivated rose from 8,900 in 1889 to 28,000 in 1904. The harvest figures for wheat, oats, barley, and vegetables varied greatly according to growing conditions. Since 1889 was an unusually good year, many later years had smaller harvests. The figures suggest the wheat harvest in 1904 was about twice that of 1889; the oat and barley crop was about the same in 1904 as in 1889; and the vegetable crop actually declined slightly by 1904.[1]

During the late nineteenth century, land ownership was determined by occupancy and use. New farmers were free to select any unused land to build their home and fence in a field. Each farmer and his or her family occupied a separate fenced holding. Boundaries were established by fencing, and conflicts were resolved by the chiefs or the agent. The boundaries were not aligned with any formal system of land survey, such as that established by the United States government off the reservation.

The principal exception to the pattern of individual family farms was the Kootenai village farm organized by Kootenai chief Eneas. The Kootenais had two hundred acres under fence and raised crops "in common." In 1885 Ronan estimated they raised one thousand bushels of wheat in addition to potatoes, turnips, cabbage, onions, carrots, parsnips, peas, and other vegetables.[2] The existence of a tribal farm worked in common had offended Agent Ronan's white American sensibilities. He commented in 1886, "This tribe or band have one large inclosure which they cultivate in common, a practice which should at once be broken up, and each head of a family placed in possession of an inclosure for himself, and taught self-reliance, by the cultivation of the soil for the exclusive benefit of himself and family."[3] Finally in December 1890, Ronan was authorized to hire a farmer to live in the Kootenai village and teach them how to farm like white men. Ronan hired Robert H. Irvine for the job. Irvine was a mixed-blood Kootenai-speaking farmer who lived at Crow Creek. Irvine moved to the Kootenai settlement to distribute agricultural aid and assist the Kootenais in "getting out rails, and to fence individual farms for families who may desire to cultivate the land."[4]

A partial, but probably temporary, exception to the single-family farm model was when Charlo and the Bitterroot Salish families arrived in the Jocko Valley in 1891. In 1892 Ronan turned over the government farm in Jocko to Charlo to fulfill a promise made by Gen. Henry Carrington. Charlo and four other families planted crops in the former agency fields during the 1892 season. Ronan was also able to get the remaining Bitterroot families "patches to cultivate inside the enclosures of other Indians who had more land under fence than they could cultivate."[5]

In general, farmland on the reservation between 1889 and 1904 was allocated by priority of claim. On December 11, 1902, Agent Smead wrote Sam Belmont in St. Ignatius that, unless another Indian had a prior claim to the land, Belmont could claim it and establish a farm.[6]

Agent Carter wrote in 1895, "They are not grouped into villages, but each head of a family has his definite, fenced, but not allotted, holding, and nearly all make more or less of an attempt at tilling the soil."[7] Agent Carter summarized the land tenure practices and handling of conflicting claims in his 1897 annual report. Carter emphasized the role of the Indian judges and downplayed the role of the "old chiefs":

> No allotments have been made, as they are extremely opposed to the survey and allotment of their reservation. Each is allowed practically all the land he can fence and cultivate, and their fields and fences are respected, and the occasional differences that arise in taking up and claiming lands are amicably adjusted by the judges of the Indian court, with the approval of the agent. Occasionally the jealousies of the old chiefs interfere somewhat and influence the decisions of the judges, but injustices are not tolerated and but little friction from this cause occurs.[8]

Since the agency local letter books have survived for 1898 to 1904, more details have survived about land tenure under Agent Smead. The traditional chiefs and judges probably also continued to play a role in assigning property rights, but only the agent's role was detailed in the surviving sources. On May 2, 1898, Antoine Parazo of St. Ignatius complained to Agent Smead. Smead had given Parazo permission to sell his farm and select another place "so long as it is not marked." The local chief or judge, however, wanted Parazo to pay for his new location.[9] In a comparable vein, Smead wrote Malcolm McLeod of Ronan on January 2, 1900, that he had "no objection for you [McLeod] to take a ranch for your own use and benefit but not for speculation."[10]

Agent Smead ordered Joseph Marion of Polson on October 22, 1903, to not fence in more than 160 acres of land per family member with rights on the reservation.[11] In one case in 1904 Moses Delaware complained that another tribal member tried to preempt a piece of land by plowing a furrow around the boundary without making improvements on the land. Smead replied that the claimant had to fence the land in order to claim it. Plowing a furrow around the boundary was not enough.[12]

Smead asserted the right of the agent to resolve disputes between tribal members over land. One example from Smead's correspondence was on August 28, 1899, when Smead wrote to Eli Morrigeau. Nicholi had complained to Smead that Morrigeau had built a fence that cut off Nicholi's access to his land. Smead decided that, if the charge was true, Morrigeau should put in a gate or open up the road.[13] Another case, from December 7, 1899, was a dispute between Ed Deschamps and Boston over a field and straw. Deschamps was given the chance to buy out Boston's share of the field for forty dollars. If he did not, then Boston could buy out Deschamps for the same price. If neither bought out the other, they were to share the field and straw equally.[14]

In March 1900 Antoine Parazo of Ronan was in conflict with "the Indians" about land he wanted to fence. Apparently Parazo wanted 160 acres, and "the Indians" were only willing to give him 50 to 60 acres in addition to the 20 acres he already had enclosed.[15]

The next month, Smead ordered Thomas Moss of Polson to desist from fencing and improving land that was also claimed by Ducharme.[16] In June 1900 Joseph Allard purchased some land from Mrs. Lacourse that was also claimed by Deschamps. Smead called a hearing so he could examine the competing claims.[17]

Smead, in August 1903, had Joseph Jones, the agency farmer at Ronan, investigate Eneas's claim to a farm that Eneas's late father had operated jointly with Eusta.[18] In September of 1903 Charles Allard complained to Smead that another cattleman, William Irvine, was fencing up all the good winter grazing from the common range in the Polson area.[19]

On December 27, 1903, Smead appealed to Chief Michael of Camas to investigate the competing claims of Big Semo and Louie Scullnah to Big Semo's late wife's ranch. The deceased woman was Scullnah's sister.[20]

In the preallotment period some Indian farms were rented, but there was no way to tell how common the practice was. On September 20, 1900, Smead informed Ed Deschamps of St. Ignatius that there was no legal way for nonmembers to come on the reservation and rent Indian farms.[21] Charlo's farm was rented in April 1901, but the source did not identify the renter.[22]

Agent Smead requested authority from the commissioner of Indian affairs on June 14, 1904, to allow Indian traders on the reservation to lease

Indian farms.[23] The commissioner of Indian affairs replied that, since the reservation was not allotted, all the land was owned in common by the Flathead tribes. Any leases would have to be approved by a "council speaking for the tribe," and presumably the rent money would go to the government to be spent for the benefit of the tribe, not the individual farmer.[24] One question that was only partially answered by the historical sources was: how many tribal families engaged in farming between 1889 and 1904? In particular, how many full-blood families were engaged in farming? Were only mixed-blood families farming? No surveys were conducted, but the historical sources suggest that most tribal families—mixed-blood and full-blood—were farming by the late nineteenth century. Many full-blood farmers, however, may have had little more than family vegetable gardens. Some of the mixed-blood families, on the other hand, had large enclosed fields growing grain in addition to vegetable gardens.

On August 7, 1890, Inspector Robert S. Gardner reported that farms on Flathead ranged from 10 or 12 acres to 160 acres. Some of the smaller operations, with only 6 or 8 acres in grain, used manually operated grain cradles rather than reapers or self-binders. Gardner concluded that "a large majority" of tribal members were engaged in farming and stock raising.[25] Another inspector, James H. Cisney, found on July 23, 1891, that almost every family had at least a large-sized garden, and many had large-sized fields.[26] P. McCormick, an Indian inspector, wrote on December 2, 1893, "Though many of the Indians, more especially the older ones, adhere to the traditional blanket, yet they all have houses fairly comfortable, with fields fenced with rails, and reasonably large (for Indians) farms. Some of the full bloods have as high as one hundred and sixty acres fenced, while others are content with a patch of ten or thirty."[27]

In his 1895 annual report Agent Carter claimed that "nearly all make more or less of an attempt at tilling the soil."[28] On a contrary note, Inspector C. C. Duncan concluded on October 10, 1896, "They cultivate but little land." Only six thousand acres on the reservation were, by Duncan's definition, "under proper Cultivation."[29]

The 1900 federal census gathered important information about farms and farmers on the reservation. It does not specifically address the question of what proportion of tribal families were engaged in farming or stock raising, but does suggest that most families had at least a small involvement. Table 4.1 gives the distribution of reservation farms by size. This table does not include farms of less than ten acres. Of farms of at least 10 acres in size,

Table 4.1. Size of Farms, Flathead Indian Reservation, 1900

Size	Number	Percent
10 and under 50 acres	6	4%
50 and under 100 acres	25	17%
100 and under 175 acres	72	48%
175 and under 260 acres	23	15%
260 and under 500 acres	13	9%
500 acres and over	11	7%
Total	150	100%

Source: U.S. Census Office, *Agriculture*, pt. 1: 100–101.

21 percent were from 10 to 99 acres. The majority of all farms were under 175 acres in size.[30] The average size of reservation farms was 186.4 acres, but a few large holdings raised the average.[31]

The census also reported the acreage on the reservation used for hay and forage for stock. Table 4.2 summarizes the result. About 50 percent of the acreage used for hay grew wild grass hay, and about 43 percent of the hay harvested in 1899 was wild grass hay.

Table 4.3 gives the degree of Indian blood for those individuals on the Flathead Reservation whose occupation in 1900 was given as farmer, farm laborer, or stockman. Twenty of the 150 individuals listed were white men who had married into the tribes. Fifty-two (or 35 percent) of the reservation farmers were full-blood Indians. Fifty-six (or 37 percent) were half Indian. The final 15 percent were less than half Indian—probably mostly one-quarter Indian.

Table 4.2. Hay and Forage, Flathead Indian Reservation, 1900

Type	Acres	Tons
Wild grasses	3,702	4,287
Alfalfa	15	60
Clover	12	12
Other cultivated grasses	2,738	3,918
Grain cut green for hay	808	1,176
Forage crops	170	410
Totals	7,445	9,863

Source: U.S. Census Office, *Agriculture*, pt. 2: 249.

Table 4.3. Farmers and Stockmen by Race, Flathead Indian Reservation, 1900

Degree of Indian Blood	Number	Percent
Full-blood	52	35
Half or more, but less than full-blood	56	37
Less than half	22	15
White	20	13
Total	150	100

Source: Calculated from U.S. Bureau of the Census, 12th Census of Population, 1900, National Archives Microfilm Publication T623, reel 913, Missoula County.

According to a 1902 census bulletin, wheat, oats, and wild hay were the principal crops grown on the reservation. Most of the wheat grown was ground into flour for home consumption or sale to neighbors and traders. On the reservation in 1900, "Most farms have small gardens in which are found potatoes, cabbages, onions, and sweet corn, and frequently small fruits. Orchards of bearing apple trees are quite common, and a few cherry, plum, and pear trees are also found."[32]

As mentioned previously, in 1901, Inspector F. C. Armstrong concluded that half the tribal population were French mixed-bloods and half full-blood Indian. Of the full-bloods, one quarter were farming and had some cattle. Another quarter of the full-bloods had small gardens and large herds of "cayuse ponies."[33]

The historical sources mention some full-blood Indians who farmed and raised cattle. According to Victor Vanderburg, Chief Charlo kept cattle and horses after moving to the Jocko Valley in 1891, but he did not farm as he had in the Bitterroot Valley.[34] Agent Peter Ronan petitioned the commissioner of Indian affairs on February 27, 1892, for help with the hospital expenses of Sabine Mary. Mary lived on a farm and cultivated the soil with the assistance of her children.[35] In October 1893 a newspaper correspondent described a "very productive" ranch in the Jocko Valley operated by two Indian women, an old woman and her daughter.[36] After a May 1902 trip to the Kootenai village, John Post, S.J., reported that Chief Augustine had a large field fenced and plowed and ready to seed. Another Kootenai, Ilimi, was plowing his field in leggings and Indian clothes.[37] Allicott, a full-blood Nez Perce who lived on Flathead Reservation, had an accident while operating his mowing machine cutting hay and injured his leg.[38]

Some farmers incorporated hunting into the agricultural cycle. In November 1890 Ronan wrote that many farmers went on their fall hunts after finishing the harvest. They usually returned in time for Christmas.[39] The *Anaconda Standard* noted on September 8, 1897, that a number of reservation farmers went hunting while the crops were growing and returned for the harvest.[40]

By the end of the nineteenth century, a small beginning had been made in irrigation on the reservation. According to the 1900 census, most of the farm locations in naturally irrigated river bottoms or nearby areas that could be irrigated with small private ditches were taken. The only other irrigation in 1900 was from two ditches the government built in the Jocko Valley — one five miles long and the other two and a half miles.[41] In 1902 Agent Smead claimed the reservation probably had 500,000 acres of agricultural land, but three quarters would require irrigation.[42]

The Flathead Reservation farmers between 1889 and 1904 were successful enough to meet family and local needs and also have a surplus to sell. Gen. Henry B. Carrington described the farms of the Bitterroot Salish Indians who had moved to the Jocko Valley before 1889. According to Carrington, "The *homes of the Flathead Indians* distributed through the Jocko Valley, are well built, by the Indians themselves, often having Curtained windows: the barns, & sheds for wagons, are Kept in good order: the fences compare with good fences anywhere: the ploughed ditches for irrigating purposes are well and effectively dispersed, and the whole valley indicates a substantial occupation, cultivation and development. Indians were seen hewing logs and splitting rails for further improvement."[43] Output from the farms varied according to weather, but in February 1890, Ronan wrote that many farmers had been in the habit of selling their surplus grain and vegetables for cash.[44]

Ronan was particularly proud of the progress the Kootenais were making with their new farmer in 1891. In April 1891 he wrote that the Kootenais had started thirty new farms that spring.[45] Kootenai chief Eneas and two teams hauled their 1891 crop all the way across the reservation to the Jocko Agency in October 1891. The Kootenai wheat crop was ground into flour.[46]

Father Hubert Post, S.J., in 1893 told about Joseph, an Indian farmer at the mission. Joseph had two sons to help him with the farm work, but he also hired a white man to work when the harvest was good.[47]

Agent Carter reported in 1896, that wheat and oats were the biggest crops on the reservation. The wheat was used by the farmers for flour, but the oats that were not fed to their stock were sold.[48] In July 1896 some unnamed reservation farmers were sending strawberries to Kalispell and selling them there.[49] A drought in 1896 stunted most of the crops except irrigated fruit.[50]

Duncan McDonald had a large apple orchard near Ravalli in the 1890s. In June 1897 a large thunderstorm dislodged boulders that caused heavy damage to his trees.[51] The orchard recovered enough to allow McDonald to send "some splendid specimens of apples" to the Missoula fair in October 1898.[52] By 1900 McDonald had an abundant crop of apples for export. According to one newspaper report, he sold 3,000 boxes of apples to eastern markets in 1900.[53] Agent Smead approached McDonald in August 1903 about exhibiting fruit at the 1904 St. Louis Exposition.[54]

Alphonse Clairmont was selling grain in March 1898 to pay the legal bill he owed to Joseph Dixon, the Missoula lawyer.[55] Eddie Clairmore traded wheat to the agency for a new wagon in April 1898. Agent Smead wanted to use the wheat to make flour for the Kootenais.[56] In October 1898 Indian farmers were bringing in "large quantities" of wheat and selling it in Missoula.[57]

Agent Smead wrote to the commissioner of Indian affairs in April 1899 that he could purchase 20,000 pounds of oats for the agency from reservation farmers.[58] The 1899 crop was good enough for reservation farmers to ship ten railroad carloads of wheat to the Bonner mills in December 1899.[59]

Louisa McDermott, the teacher at the government school at Jocko in 1899 and 1900, recorded that during the harvest and haying time around St. Ignatius, "one can not procure a team by any manner of means. The men and horses are all busy in the hay and harvest fields."[60] During the 1901 haying season, Mike Matt planned to put up 200 tons of hay.[61] The St. Ignatius Mission thrashed 1,300 bushels of grain for two Indian farmers, Louie and Chqaute, on September 17, 1902. They thrashed another 1,300 bushels for Felsman, a white man married to an Indian, on September 20, 1902.[62]

In another transaction Peter Matt sold wheat to Jon Haney of Ravalli in the fall of 1902. Matt was still trying to collect the money in April 1903.[63]

The 1903 harvest was so good that there was a scarcity of labor to bring it in.[64] Oliver Gebeau made a special request to keep his son, Joseph Gebeau, home from the Fort Shaw Indian School until September 20, 1903, to help harvest the oat crop.[65] In November 1903 Nine Pipes sold a railroad carload of hay to Missoula merchants.[66] The next year in August 1904, Ed Lameroux, a white man married to an Indian, put up 325 tons of hay.[67]

In September 1903 Inspector Arthur M. Tinker was very impressed by
the Flathead Reservation farmers:

> A large majority of them are good farmers for Indians and cultivate
> quite good sized farms, which usually produce good crops. It is esti-
> mated that more than 17,000 acres of land are now under cultivation,
> the work being done by Indian labor. The crop produced consists
> principally of wheat, oats, potatoes and vegetables; they also cut a large
> amount of hay which they feed to their cattle, the surplus which they
> bale and ship it, is [sic] estimated this year will be about 1,000 tons
> they sell to the whiteman off the reservation.
>
> They find ready sale for all the surplus products they produce at
> good prices. As this has been a favorable season, it is expected that the
> crop to be harvested will be large.
>
> Each year the number of acres of land cultivated has increased.[68]

The imposition of the federal policy of Indian allotment on the Flathead Reservation impacted tribal politics and the tribal economy. Allotment was forced on the reservation over the objections of the tribal chiefs,
however, the actual implementation of the policy after 1904 recognized the
authority of the chiefs to vote on enrollment and allotment of Indians from
other tribes on the Flathead Reservation. They also had a voice in selecting
the tribal representatives on the appraisal commission. A final impact was
ironic. Despite having no official legal voice in whether the reservation was
allotted, the chiefs led a bruising, but unsuccessful, fight against allotment
and the sale of "surplus" lands to white homesteaders after 1904.

Some of the arguments made by white proponents of allotment touted
the economic "benefits" of imposing a new form of land tenure on the
reservation. The principal economic impact of the policy was to transfer
tribal assets to white farmers at bargain prices. C. H. McLeod, of the Missoula Mercantile Company, wrote on January 2, 1904, that allotment would
"do more to stimulate business in Western Montana than any thing else
possibly can."[69]

Agent Smead and the other allotment proponents also argued that there
would be positive economic benefits for tribal farmers. According to supporters, one positive economic result of allotment would be to reduce the
concentration of agricultural land in the hands of a few rich mixed-bloods.
The large cattle operations relied on the open range, but they also enclosed

land for raising hay and grain for winter feeding. According to Indian inspector W. J. McConnell on June 1, 1901, "The great bulk of the most valuable land on this reservation is held in large tracts mostly by half and quarter breeds."[70] Special Indian Agent Charles S. McNichols compiled a list of the largest cattle owners on the reservation on January 5, 1903. The list also gave the number of acres each rancher had under fence. Eight had 500 acres or more under fence: Baptiste Jette (640 acres), Angus P. McDonald (1,800 acres), Joe Morrigeau (860 acres), Joseph Ashley (500 acres), Allen Sloan (1,500 acres), Ignace (640 acres), and Joe Finley (640 acres). Since allotment would limit holdings to 160 acres per family member, the result would be to reduce the holdings of the largest and richest cattlemen.[71]

Agent Smead developed the inequality argument in a February 27, 1900, report to the commissioner of Indian affairs:

> Land that will produce crops without irrigation and those on which water could be easily and cheaply carried have long since been claimed, and are in possession of white men and mixed bloods principally, many of whom have no rights on the reservation, and many others whose rights are in much doubt.
>
> Many of these people have large tracts inclosed, hundreds of acres in excess of what they would be entitled to providing they have rights to any at all, thus securing unto themselves large tracts of lands that should be in the possession of allottees.
>
> Under these circumstances, many young Indians, who above all others, should have farms, are without them.[72]

The other economic argument developed by Smead and other allotment proponents was that only formal surveys and allotment would assure reservation farmers that their improvements would not end up on someone else's land. Agent Smead used this argument in his first annual report on September 15, 1898.[73] He made the same argument to the commissioner of Indian affairs on April 23, 1903: "Many improvements are being made, new ranches located, houses, barns, ditches &c being constructed and it is only proper that persons making these improvements should know by surveys if they are on such sub-divisions as they will be able to hold when allotments are finally made."[74]

By 1904 farming on the Flathead Reservation was a significant industry. The returns were not distributed equally. Some mixed-bloods controlled large and lucrative operations, but most families seem to have had at least a garden and a small field of grain. Even more tribal members benefited from the part-time labor during harvesting and haying. The crops helped support the reservation tribes, despite the declining returns from hunting and gathering.

Government Aid, 1889–1904

The Flathead Agency provided supplemental economic assistance to tribal farmers, but mostly exchanged wagons and agricultural equipment for labor in support of agency operations. The quid pro quo may have been informal in the early years of the period under Agent Ronan. Agent Smead's ration books, however, have survived and clearly document the exchange of government assistance for labor during his tenure. The government did construct irrigation ditches, which played an important role in expanding farming on the reservation. Irrigation construction provided wages for tribal members, which will be discussed in the next section on wage labor. The Flathead Reservation tribes were largely economically self-supporting between 1889 and 1904. Government aid that was not used to pay for labor and supplies for the agency was limited to helping the old and infirm live a more comfortable life and helping new farmers develop their operations.

The agency did supply beef and other food supplies at councils called by the government. In June 1889 Agent Ronan and Special Agent Henry M. Marchant spoke at a council at the foot of Flathead Lake discussing the whiskey trade. Ronan ended his remarks with a reference to a beef and supplies of sugar, coffee, flour, and other food for a general feast after the meeting.[75] In September 1889 Ronan gave a steer and two hundred pounds of flour to feed a meeting after imploring the tribesmen to help arrest fugitive Indians accused of murdering white men.[76]

The only tribal members who regularly received rations were the old and infirm. In Agent Carter's 1894 annual report he wrote, "It has not been the practice to issue regular rations to the Indians of these tribes, but to confine issue of rations to the indigent, infirm and aged people."[77] On February 17, 1895, Indian inspector P. McCormick made a similar observation.[78] For example, on March 8, 1898, Agent Smead sent 1 shawl, 1 quilt, 1 blanket, 1 coat, 5.5 pounds of bacon, 20 pounds of flour, 3 pounds of coffee, and 4 pounds of sugar to relieve Egide and his wife, who were destitute.[79] On August 8, 1903, Agent Smead noted the government gave rations only to the "old and sick, and occasionally a family in distress from sickness or some other misfortune."[80] In April 1904 three widows, Marltin, Tellie, and Panarma, requested aid from the agency.[81]

The actual number of old and infirm rationers on the reservation was quite small. During the winter of 1890–91 Horatio L. Seward, a special agent, found only 8 percent of the tribal members were receiving rations.[82] On July 30, 1901, another special agent, Frank C. Armstrong, found only ninety old and infirm Indians drawing rations.[83] In September 1902 Agent Smead said two hundred persons were receiving support.[84]

Some Indians who were newly relocated on the reservation or just starting farms received temporary rations. The last of the Bitterroot Salish band under Chief Charlo arrived at the Jocko Agency in October 1891. No itemized list of assistance has been found, but Gen. Henry Carrington promised the Salish new houses in the Jocko, help starting farms, and provisions until the first harvest.[85]

The case of the Lower Kalispel settlement at Camas Prairie on the reservation illustrated the efforts and failure of the government support for newly established Flathead Reservation farmers. In April 1887 the Northwest Indian Commission met with the Lower Kalispels at Sand Point, Idaho. Part of the Lower Kalispel community, led by Chief Michel, agreed to move to the Flathead Reservation. In return, the new arrivals on the reservation were promised houses, assistance in establishing farms of not less than five acres per family, two milk cows, two work horses, wagons, plows, and other items. They were also promised subsistence for up to five years.[86] Unfortunately Congress never ratified the agreement despite repeated pleas from Agent Ronan. As a result, the promises were not fulfilled except for some emergency aid in 1889 and what assistance Ronan could provide from the regular Flathead Agency budget.[87] The Kalispels had to work to establish farms at Camas Prairie without most of the help promised by the government negotiators. In 1891 their crops were destroyed by crickets, and they received emergency subsistence supplies from the agency.[88]

When the Kalispels finally got established—without most of the promised assistance from the government—they refused to have anything to do with the Flathead Agency. In July 1901 Special Agent Frank C. Armstrong described the Kalispel community at Camas Prairie as prosperous and independent: "These people have very good good [sic] houses located around the valley, generally where small spring branches run from the mountains; have some very good fields, raise gardens, have some cattle, have large hay fields fenced, and are very good workers. They have a colony to themselves and do not allow the mixed bloods to settle among them."[89] Another special agent, Charles S. McNichols, was frustrated in his efforts to enroll the Camas Prairie Kalispels. McNichols stated the Camas Prairie Kalispel community was composed of both Chief Michel's band and other Kalispels who had previously lived on the Flathead Reservation: "All these not only refuse to be enrolled but refuse even to talk to me." According to McNichols, the Kalispels were "a peculiar, isolated lot and they claim that Government men have lied to them so often that they want nothing to do with any representative of the Government. . . . They allow no whites or mixed bloods to live among them. I am told they have never recognized the Agents, nor have they ever asked for any help or even medical assistance. Outside of drinking and gambling they are thrifty, industrious and entirely self-supporting, and conduct their own affairs."[90] In 1903, when the government imposed a grazing tax on tribal member cattle and horses, the Camas Prairie collected the tax from the stock owners in their area and distributed it locally "according to their own ideas."[91]

A significant limitation to the economic benefit from government assistance on the reservation was that most of the assistance was only available in the Jocko Valley. The Flathead Agency was located on the southern edge of the reservation, many miles from the tribal population centers in the Mission Valley to the north. The flour and sawmills and blacksmith and other agency employees were only available to tribal members "at considerable cost and inconvenience." Agent Ronan wrote on October 28, 1889, that, given the agency location, the expense of "transportation by wagons of lumber and wheat [from the agency] exceeds the value of the article itself."[92]

The problem of tribal member access to agency services was only addressed in 1894 and 1895 when a subagency was built at Spring Creek in the Mission Valley. In 1894 a sawmill was constructed at Spring Creek, and in 1895 a flour mill was added.[93] The Spring Creek subagency greatly improved tribal member access to agency services. Tribal members using the subagency still had to pay for the services in kind or cash. On January 15, 1900, Agent Smead reprimanded Robert Watson, who ran the subagency, for giving services on credit or before payment was received.[94] Later that year, on July 10, 1900, Smead informed the commissioner of Indian affairs that the subagency flour mill charged tribal members in kind. For every 60 pounds of clean wheat delivered to the mill, the grower received 30 pounds of flour and 10 pounds of bran, and the mill kept the flour and bran over that as the charge for grinding the wheat.[95]

Another government service—irrigation—was only provided to tribal farmers in the Jocko Valley. Before 1904 the government had constructed two irrigation ditches—one 5 miles long and the other 2.5 miles long. Both ditches were in the Jocko Valley on the south end of the reservation.[96]

One important thing about the role of government aid in the Flathead Reservation economy between 1889 and 1904 was that while the help was useful, it was not gratis. Tribal farmers were required to provide labor, goods, or money in exchange for the wagons, plows, and other implements they received from the agency. For example, Gen. Henry B. Carrington described the practice he found at the Jocko Agency in 1889: "The Indians were encouraged to work, by making it for their own interest to work. When they hauled logs to the sawmill, they took 'toll' in lumber. When they brought grain to the grist mill, they took 'toll' on flour. Blacksmithing, and various repairing, was so conducted that they exchanged equivalents, and were thus stimulated to persevere."[97] Similarly, in 1893, Father Hubert A. Post of St. Ignatius Mission wrote, "Our Indians do not receive rations, nay, not even tools, without some return or other. For example, does an Indian wish to get a wagon, a plough or some other article to be had at the agency, he betakes himself thither with his whole family and works at the Indian saw-mill as long as the agent wishes, that is to say, until his amount of work will compensate for the greater part of the value of the article he purchased."[98] On April 8, 1898, Agent Smead approved trading a wagon to Eddie Clairmore for seventy-five dollars worth of wheat.[99] In another exchange, on January 21, 1902, Smead approved giving Charley Moremon a wagon in exchange for twenty-three cords of wood delivered to the Spring Creek subagency.[100]

In 1904, when Agent Smead was relieved of his position as Flathead agent, the charges against him revolved around his handling of government assistance. Some of the aid was used to pay Canadian Cree Indians to get telephone poles out of the woods for a telephone line between the Arlee railroad station and the Spring Creek subagency to the north. Smead also used the rations to supplement the salary of the agency stableman. He traded the rations for large quantities of firewood, hay, and logs, which were not accounted for in the official government property records. Some of the firewood, hay, and lumber was used for agency operations, but some was used for the personal benefit of agency employees. Other rations paid Indians for washing and scrubbing in the homes of agency employees.[101]

Smead lost his position, but in the process two Flathead Agency ration books were sent to the Department of the Interior as inspection report enclosures. The ration books did not include the dates of specific transactions, but they made clear that rations were not gratis—they were used to pay for labor, hay, firewood, and other goods. A few examples will illustrate the economic exchanges involved:

1. In 1903 Ashbury Blodgett got a wagon, harness, a wood plane, and two bits. In exchange he delivered an unspecified amount of straw and 1,783 pounds of hay to the agency.[102]
2. Octave Couture received a wagon, harrow, sugar, coffee, bacon, a pipe, flour, and baking powder. He paid for the rations with 18,000 pounds of hay and work hauling freight.[103]
3. The Flathead Agency rented a house from Nine Pipes, and Nine Pipes received his rent in sugar, coffee, flour, and bacon.[104]
4. Frenchy, a Cree, provided firewood for the agency and was paid with sugar, coffee, two ax handles, flour, a crosscut saw, and bacon.[105]
5. Louie Chowtay received a wagon and other unitemized supplies in exchange for delivering poles to the agency.[106]
6. Joe Pierre paid for one set of harness and two collars with telegraph poles.[107]
7. Charley did unspecified work for the agency in exchange for bacon, sugar, coffee, and flour.[108]
8. Dan McLeod allowed the agency to use his team for four days and received oats and sugar in payment.[109]
9. Sapiel furnished thirty-seven logs, sawed wood, and did other work in exchange for bacon, sugar, coffee, and flour from the rations.[110]
10. Pascal furnished 16 3/4 cords of firewood for bacon, flour, and coffee.[111]
11. In 1899 Mack Couture got a harness in exchange for logs delivered to the sawmill.[112]
12. Dutch Lumpry worked for 6.5 days in exchange for sugar, baking powder, salt, coffee, flour, bacon, and one pair of shoes.[113]
13. Charley Gabe delivered logs and sawed wood for one pair of shoes, bacon, one pair of pants, a cooking stove, and one pair of boy's shoes.[114]
14. W. J. McClure got a cooking stove, furniture, sugar, coffee, bacon, baking powder, flour, and other supplies. He paid for these by labor on the jail building.[115]

15. Jerome sawed wood in exchange for bacon, flour, sugar, coffee, and baking powder.[116]
16. Benway hauled wood, presumably firewood, to pay for his bacon, candles, quilt, shawl, two skirts, a crosscut saw, soap, coffee, and other items.[117]
17. John Matt received shoes, ax handle, shawl, skirt, thread, and thimble in payment for hauling freight to the agency.[118]
18. Mrs. Gebeau did washing and ironing to pay for her bacon, rope, sugar, and other goods.[119]

On the Flathead Reservation between 1889 and 1904 government assistance was very limited and in most cases exchanged for goods and services needed for running the agency. The government helped tribal families, but obviously did not support them.

Wage Work and Casual Labor, 1889–1904

At the end of the nineteenth century a significant portion of tribal members worked for the Flathead Agency, the St. Ignatius Mission, or one of the mixed-blood ranchers. Most of the tribal wage earners were mixed-blood, but some were full-blood Indians. A much larger segment of the population probably earned money through seasonal or casual labor.

The salaries of agency employees were the best documented in the sources. While the administrative and skilled positions at the agency were usually held by white men, unskilled work and law and order were the domain of tribal members. The rosters of agency employees for 1889, 1897, and 1904 illustrate agency employment. The agency hired part-time and casual employees in addition to those on the formal lists.

For the fiscal year 1889–90, Alex Matt was the agency blacksmith, Robert Irvine was assistant miller, and four full-bloods served as agency judges: Joseph Kooto lay uch, Louison, Charloaine, and Joseph.[120] In 1890 fourteen Indian men were employed as agency policemen with Antoine Still tell kan as captain.[121] In 1897 Alex Matt was still blacksmith, Michel Revais was interpreter, Oliver Gebeau was assistant miller, and James Michel was teamster. Thirteen Indian men were employed as Indian policemen.[122] At the end of this period, in 1904, Michel Revais was interpreter, Dan McLeod was blacksmith, William Moss was teamster, and William Courtois was the additional farmer. Three Indian men were judges, and six were policemen under Capt. Pierre Joseph.[123]

The agency also provided seasonal and casual labor that was not included in the official register of employees. For example, in 1891 Agent Ronan hired Indians and mixed-bloods to build houses for the relocated Bitterroot Salish Indians moved to the Jocko Valley.[124] In 1892 Ronan hired Indian labor to dig an irrigation ditch in the Jocko Valley and deliver logs to the agency mill. Laborers were paid by the number of rods of ditch dug.[125] In July 1898 Agent Smead hired eight tribal members to work on the irrigation ditches for $1.50 per day.[126]

A hybrid form of agency employment was the work required of all reservation residents to maintain the roads. All able-bodied men on the reservation, except agency and St. Ignatius Mission employees, were required to contribute two days' labor annually on road maintenance on the reserve.[127] By October 1899 Agent Smead had increased the annual road work to five days or 2.5 days with a team. Any Indian who refused to fulfill his road work assignment was threatened with a term in the agency jail.[128]

As discussed previously, the Flathead Agency also provided considerable work for tribal members that was paid for in government ration goods. The bartering of labor for food, household goods, and agricultural equipment was in addition to the agency work that was paid for in cash.

Agency employees provided employment by hiring tribal members to perform domestic work. In about 1898 Mary Ann Topsseh Coombs got a job washing clothes for Peter Ronan's family at the Jocko Agency.[129] Gabriel Konomakan was working for Michel Revais, the agency interpreter, in November 1903.[130] And in 1904 Mrs. Oliver Gebeau did washing, ironing, and other work for agency employees.[131]

The St. Ignatius Mission also provided employment to tribal members and white men married to tribal members. The main account books for the mission have survived, but most of the wages paid to tribal members would have been recorded in other account books that are no longer available. One account book for the early 1890s recorded wages paid to Antoine, herder; Isaac Tellier, farmer; Adolph Barnaby, wood chopping; Louis, laborer; LaRose, splitting wood; Pierisch, herder; and others. Some entries only listed "wages for Boys." [132] According to an 1894 article in a Jesuit house organ, in 1890–91, tribal members were employed in making the bricks for the new church building.[133] Many other tribal members were hired by the mission for seasonal and occasional work, to be discussed in this section.

The rich mixed-blood cattlemen employed tribal members to work on their ranches and other work, but only limited documentation has survived.

The most extensive documentation of ranch employment on the reservation was the autobiography of Malcolm McLeod, who worked for Charles Allard Sr. in the 1890s. In 1891 McLeod went to work for Allard breaking horses, putting up hay, and doing other work as needed. In 1893 McLeod took a trainload of cattle to Chicago for Allard. Later that year, McLeod played a starring role in Allard's Wild West show in Butte and other Montana cities, riding a buffalo. McLeod worked for the Allard ranch until after Allard died in Chicago in July 1896.[134] In 1892 David Couture, a mixed-blood, was employed on the Charles Allard ranch for forty dollars a month.[135]

Reservation ranchers hired tribal members to work by the month on regular ranch operations, but they also hired extra hands for roundups, haying, harvest, and other seasonal work. For example, a newspaper reporter described an Indian threshing crew he saw in the Jocko Valley in September 1890. The crew might have included hired hands, but it could have been composed of members of an extended family.[136] Most of this employment was not documented in the historical records, but some accounts mention ranchers who owed workers for labor performed. In December 1899 Louis Courville owed John Carron $20 for cutting logs.[137] Two years later, Jim Grinder, an Indian from another reservation, was working for Michel Pablo.[138] Joe Gebeau claimed in September 1902 that John Battise Finley owed him $40 for work performed.[139] Thomas Dandy Jim was working for Benoit Nenema at the mouth of the Jocko in February 1904.[140] In January 1895 Agent Carter summarized the employment of tribal members in ranch work: "Each summer a number of adult Indians engage with the white farmers in the vicinity of the reserve doing general farm work. A still greater number are employed by the well to do mixed bloods and even by the full blooded Indians who have made considerable progress and are accumulating property; some assisting in general farm work, others in herding and range riding."[141]

Another poorly documented aspect of tribal member employment during the late nineteenth century was work for Indian traders. Two of the traders were tribal members: Telesphore Guillium Demers and Duncan McDonald. In 1889 Demers had a store at the arm of Flathead Lake.[142] Duncan McDonald operated a store, hotel, orchard, and other enterprises at Ravalli during this period.[143]

The traders hired tribal members for general work. In 1887 and 1888 Malcolm McLeod worked for Alexander L. Demers, who had the store in St. Ignatius. He was paid $15 a month. McLeod hauled hay, sawed wood, split firewood, and carried the wood to the kitchen, store, and Demers's dwelling house.[144] In July 1891 Alex Dow, the trader at Arlee, wanted to buy 25,000 board feet of lumber from tribal members. The Indians would harvest the logs, haul them to the agency sawmill, and after they were sawed into lumber, sell the lumber to Dow.[145] Mary Finley Nile's first job after leaving school at St. Ignatius was waiting tables at Duncan McDonald's restaurant at Ravalli. That would have been about 1895.[146]

Much of the work by tribal members in the late nineteenth century was irregular and sporadic. A few examples are given here. In November 1889 Father Jerome D'Aste paid Joe Barnaby $5 for bringing back Father Philip Canestrelli's wagon.[147] The estate of Peter Ronan in 1894 paid Maxime Matt $10 for driving cattle and $138 for feeding, branding, and care of cattle. It also paid Peter Calico $24 and Joel Matt $15 for rounding up cattle.[148] According to Agent Carter, in April 1896, Kootenai Indians camped near Kalispell supported themselves by fishing, sawing wood, and doing odd jobs for white residents of the town.[149] In June 1900 a party of white men were fishing in the Finley Creek area of the Jocko Valley when they lost their direction and had to hire an unnamed Indian to guide them back to their camp for $10. Then the guide was paid another $10 to find their missing horses and guide the party back to Arlee.[150] Father Jerome D'Aste was much taken aback in June 1901 when Ashbury Blodgett charged him a dollar for a ride from the Jocko Agency to Arlee.[151] In May 1902 the Great Buffalo and Wild West Show began with Charles Allard Jr. in charge of the buffalo and a number of unnamed tribal members performing.[152] The show went broke in September 1902.[153] While stationed at the Jocko Agency church on March 2, 1903, Father D'Aste paid an unnamed Indian $27 to erect a fence around the Jocko Church pasture.[154] In March 1904 Robert Watson, at the Ronan subagency, employed eight Indians for four days sawing lumber: John Vallie, Baptiste Merengo, Frank Chilten, Philip Sine lo, Charlie Vanderburg, Victor Thomem, and Albert Todd.[155] Finally, in 1904 Coert DuBois was contracted to survey the Flathead Reservation before it was allotted. He hired Boston Moran, a mixed-blood, to assist his survey crew.[156]

There was a continuing tug-of-war over allowing white men and Crees on the reservation to take jobs that could be done by tribal members. There is no way to tell how many white men and Crees were employed by tribal members on the reservation during this period, but there are numerous records of tribal ranchers requesting permits to hire white workers or newspaper notes of whites who worked on the reservation. Only a few examples will be given here. In 1893 Father Hubert Post wrote about an Indian farmer by the name of Joseph near the mission who hired a white man to assist him and his sons with the harvest.[157] In the summer of 1900 Willie Clark, a white man from Plains, worked for Angus McDonald on the reservation for several months.[158] Oliver Gebeau on the reservation employed an unnamed white man on his ranch near Evaro during the summer and fall of 1900.[159] In March 1902 Agent Smead gave Thomas McDonald a permit to employ Victor Feidler, a white man.[160] That same spring, Frank Norman complained to Agent Smead that Louis Clairmont Jr. owed him $32 for work done two years earlier.[161] John Bushman got a permit to employ a white man a few weeks later on May 29, 1902.[162] The next spring, 1903, R. Anderson got a permit to work for Zephyre Courville for two months.[163] Robert Delaithe of Plains was given permission on July 20, 1903, to work on haying for Arthur Larrivee on the reservation for seven weeks.[164] A few days later in July 1903 Joe Michand on the reservation hired ten Swedish men to work for $2 a day.[165] Alex Ashley got a permit on August 3, 1903, to employ an unnamed white man to help with haying.[166]

Some white people were hired for skilled jobs on the reservation. For example, in 1901 Caroline Tomfohr, a white woman who later married a mixed-blood tribal member, began working for Andrew Stinger as a cook and later seamstress.[167] George Breeden requested a permit on December 20, 1903, to work for Henry Burland as a blacksmith.[168] Another blacksmith, Milton Neff, moved to Plains in February 1904 after working for Angus P. McDonald on the reservation.[169]

Agent Smead tried to enforce a policy that tribal ranchers had to give hiring preference to Indian workers before he would give a permit for white men to work on the reservation. On July 13, 1899, Smead wrote Joe Marion in Ronan, "I desire that all the work on the reservation that is possible to be done by residents thereof should be done by the residents, however, if you are unable to get your work done by our own people, you may if you desire contract with those [white] people to do this work."[170] On October 31, 1903, he emphasized the need to permit as few outside workers as possible.[171]

In March 1902 the tribal judge at St. Ignatius, Baptiste Kakashe, had "an angry conversation" with Father Jerome D'Aste about the mission employing white men.[172] Kakashe apologized to D'Aste the next day.[173]

There were repeated reports of shortages of workers, especially during the haying season. In July 1900 Alex Dow was quoted that the shortage of labor for haying was retarding the harvest.[174] Duncan McDonald complained in August 1903 about the scarcity of labor for harvesting.[175]

Some observers complained about the work ethic of Indian workers. There is no way now to tell how much these reports were based on prejudice and how much on experience. For example, on September 3, 1903, an Indian Service employee in Ronan thought it was doubtful that he could get full-bloods to do the logging work he needed done.[176] Brother Cyprius-Celestin was stationed at St. Ignatius in 1903 and 1904 and claimed that many full-bloods refused to work like white men: "To work like white men seemed slavish to them. . . . To put aside money for bad days to come seemed foolish to them."[177] In a similar vein, B. H. Denison, an Indian trader at Arlee, complained on February 16, 1904, that Indian employees were expensive and not good workers.[178]

A number of Cree Indians worked on the reservation for a variety of employers. Those working for the St. Ignatius Mission were the best documented. On July 15, 1896, Father Jerome D'Aste noted that the Crees had been forced off the reservation, and the mission was having trouble hiring workers.[179] Agent Smead wrote to Rev. George de la Motte on November 9, 1898, defending his recent decision to expel the Crees from the reservation. Smead claimed the Crees working for the mission were doing work that should be done by local tribal members.[180] The overwhelming majority of tribal members who had wage labor recorded in the written record were mixed-bloods. There was probably a considerable amount of paid work by full-blood Indians that was not recorded. Most of the full-blood labor for money may have involved casual labor and small amounts of money paid for specific short-term jobs. There is no way now to tell how many full-bloods were involved in paid labor, but it could have been significant. The closest we came to a window on this "penny capitalism" was Father Jerome D'Aste's diaries for 1894 when he was stationed at the Jocko Church. D'Aste used his diary to keep track of his expenses.[181]

There were two workers whom D'Aste hired frequently in 1894 to do work around the church: LaRose and Louis. Apparently D'Aste paid his workers by the day or the job. He was careful to record in his diary the number of days worked. Two LaRoses were mentioned in the diary, so there is no way to tell which LaRose most of the references were to. LaRose first showed up on February 13, 1894, when D'Aste paid him and Anthony LaMus $2 to saw firewood. On March 28, 1894, D'Aste paid Dan LaRose an unspecified amount to fill in a ditch. On April 10, 1894, he paid Dan LaRose $2 for hauling rocks and wood. One of the LaRoses worked for D'Aste on April 12, 1894, but D'Aste noted he did "slow work." On May 15, 1894, D'Aste paid LaRose $1.50 in wages, and the next day Anthony LaRose "twice milked the cow." LaRose was paid another $1 on May 18, 1894, and on May 24, 1894, David LaRose drew $.50 in wages. Two days later, May 26, 1894, D'Aste paid LaRose $2 in cash and $2 in groceries. LaRose drew $.75 on June 3, 1894; $1.25 on June 7, 1894; $.60 on June 21, 1894; $1.50 on June 22, 1894; $.25 on June 23, 1894; $1 on June 30, 1894; $1 on July 3, 1894; and another $1 on July 11, 1894. On July 12, 1894, D'Aste paid LaRose $1.50 in credit at the store and $3.75 in cash. This settled the amount earned by LaRose, and LaRose quit working for D'Aste.

Louis was first paid $1 on June 6, 1894, for making a ditch. On June 14, 1894, D'Aste paid Louis $1 in cash and a sack of flour for two days' work. Louis worked for D'Aste on June 15, 1894, and on June 16, 1894, he dug a drain for a sink at the Sisters'. On June 20, 1894, Louis went after wire and returned D'Aste's horse for $1.50. Louis worked a half day on June 21, 1894, and all day on June 22 and 23, 1894. He was paid $5 in cash on June 22, 1894, and $.25 on June 27, 1894. On June 28, 1894, Louis worked half a day cutting ditches. When LaRose quit on July 12, 1894, D'Aste hired Louis and his wife, Frances, to milk the cow for $2 a week. A day later, Louis hauled two loads of wood from D'Aste's place to the Sisters'. On July 17, 1894, Louis worked half a day on the garden and chopped wood for the Sisters. D'Aste paid Louis $10 in advance on July 25, 1894, to help him buy a set of harness. On July 27, 1894, Louis got straw and put in glass at the Sisters'. Louis's last appearance in D'Aste's accounts was on August 4, 1894, when he brought boxes of drugs to Arlee and worked in the garden.

Some other workers appear in the diary for specific or short-term work. On January 16, 1894, D'Aste paid Michael and his team $.50 for a trip to Arlee. Two days later, D'Aste paid someone and their team $1.50 to haul freight from Mission to the Jocko Agency church. This could have been Michael. Michael was paid another $1 on January 25, 1894, for hauling goods. On February 13, 1894, D'Aste paid Michael $.50. Michael's final appearance in the diary was on May 23, 1894, when D'Aste paid him $3 for unspecified work.

On March 2, 1894, D'Aste paid Catherine $1 for washing. She got another $.50 on March 14, 1894.

D'Aste made a contract on June 11, 1894, for $40 with McLure to fence ten acres of land. McLure got $10 in credit at Dow's store on June 14, 1894.

He finished the fence on June 27, 1894, and got another $20 payment from D'Aste. D'Aste paid McLure his final $10 on July 2, 1894. Two other named payments were $2.50 in goods given Francois on August 19, 1894, for milking the cow and $1 to Martin on September 2, 1894, for hauling straw.

In addition, there were some payments for labor that did not name the workers. On January 19, 1894, D'Aste paid someone $1 for filling in a ditch and hauling bedsteads. He paid someone $.50 on February 4, 1894; $.50 on February 12, 1894; and another $.50 on February 14, 1894, for hauling firewood. On February 15, 1894, $.25 was paid to haul meat; on February 21, 1894, $3 to haul flour and coal oil; and on March 30, 1894, $1 to bring the Sisters from the railroad station. On April 7, 1894, D'Aste paid someone $5.50 to fill in a ditch.

Father Jerome D'Aste's 1894 diaries while at the Jocko Agency church describe an active and fluid small value economy. I would suggest they give us a rare glimpse into exchanges on the reservation based on wage work that was often short-term and informal. This part of the 1889–1904 reservation employment was usually not recorded in the documents, but gave many tribal members—including probably a number of full-bloods—an opportunity to earn small amounts of cash to spend at the traders' stores for necessities and incidental luxury purchases.

Working for money involved a significant portion of the tribal population between 1889 and 1904. Many tribal members supported themselves by regular or casual labor. The amounts many earned may have been small and erratic, but they allowed most tribal families to purchase some supplies and occasional extravagances from reservation traders.

Salish Chief Charlo. Montana Historical Society, Photograph Archives, Helena, 954-526.

Salish Chief Arlee. From Peter Ronan, *Historical Sketch of the Flathead-Indians from the Year 1813 to 1890* (Helena, Mont.: Journal Publishing, 1890), 78.

Pend d'Oreille Chief Michelle. Drawing by Gustavus Sohon. National Anthropological Archives, Smithsonian Institution, Washington, D.C., 08501400.

Kootenai Chief Eneas. Archives and Special Collections, Mansfield Library, University of Montana, Missoula, 81-284.

Peter Ronan, Flathead
Indian Agent, 1877–93,
Montana Historical Society,
Photograph Archives,
Helena, MMM 900-004.

W. H. Smead, Flathead
Indian Agent, 1898–1904.
Montana Historical Society,
Photograph Archives,
Helena, PAc 99-3667.

Charles Allard Sr., tribal member, cattleman, and businessman. Montana Historical Society, Photograph Archives, Helena, 940-336.

Duncan McDonald, tribal member, trader, and businessman. Montana Historical Society, Photograph Archives, Helena, 943-624.

Flathead Farm, 1884. Photograph by F. Jay Haynes. Montana Historical Society, Photograph Archives, Helena, H-1341.

Flathead Sawmill Crew, 1884. Photograph by F. Jay Haynes. Montana Historical Society, Photograph Archives, Helena, H-1334.

Flathead Indian Agency, 1884. Photograph by F. Jay Haynes. Montana
Historical Society, Photograph Archives, Helena, H-1271.

Alex Matt and view of irrigation canal built by him, ca. 1890. Photograph Sept. 1910. Flathead Irrigation Project Papers, box 1, F15, NA-8NS-75-97-221. U.S. National Archives, Denver, Colo.

Chief Martin Charlo and harvest, ca. 1910. Flathead Irrigation Project Papers, box 7, 222, NA-8NS-75-97-221. U.S. National Archives, Denver, Colo.

CHAPTER 5

Commercial Exchanges and Business Enterprises, 1889–1904

Most of the tribal income in the late nineteenth century was generated from exports of horses, cattle, and grain, as described previously. The boom in horse sales at the turn of the century must have been especially important for the full-blood families on the reservation. But there were other economic exchanges with the surrounding white economy that provided income for tribal members. A few tribal members operated businesses that served both Indians and non-Indians. The three most prominent tribal businessmen between 1889 and 1904 were Duncan McDonald, Charles Allard Sr., and Charles Allard Jr.

Between 1885 and 1891, Duncan McDonald operated a store, hotel, restaurant, and blacksmith shop at Ravalli. Given the growth of traffic from Ravalli north to the Upper Flathead Valley and the 1891 construction of the Great Northern Railroad, Duncan had plenty of business. A number of travelers recorded descriptions—frequently negative—of their dealings with McDonald's hotel and other businesses.[1] For example, on March 8, 1889, a young Oliver Vose and his family arrived at Ravalli and stayed at McDonald's hotel. It was cold and there was no heat in their room. Vose's two-year-old sister complained loudly. The Voses were able to get into McDonald's private living room to warm up, but the Voses felt McDonald and his family acted as if they did not want them there.[2] A few years later, Joseph Dixon, then a young novice lawyer, recorded a stay at McDonald's hotel in August 1891. The hotel was full to overflowing, and Dixon ended

123

up paying to sleep in "a log shanty" nearby.[3] Also in 1891 a journalist for the *Northwest Illustrated Monthly Magazine* complained: "Here you can witness the somewhat phenomenal feat of an ordinary-looking frame house with a capacity for accommodating ten or a dozen people being made to accommodate from forty to fifty persons, and some nights even more, for which each person is charged the modest sum of one dollar."[4] According to a Missoula newspaper correspondent in August 1891, McDonald was "a very wealthy man and his fortune is rapidly increasing."[5]

In the summer of 1891, during the construction rush for the Great Northern Railroad, McDonald was upset because the operator of the restaurant and boarding house established for the railroad employees at Ravalli was serving the traveling public. The Northern Pacific Railroad officials in July 1891 negotiated a compromise where the businesses on the railroad right-of-way would serve the public but agreed to not solicit or send out runners to advertise their competition to McDonald's businesses.[6]

On January 5, 1892, C. A. Stillinger and Arthur Larrivee announced their purchase of Charles Allard's stage line and McDonald's Ravalli businesses except the apple orchard.[7] Larrivee was a mixed-blood nephew of Charles Allard. After 1891 McDonald concentrated on his apple orchard and cattle raising.

Duncan McDonald's father, Angus McDonald, died on February 1, 1889. Duncan inherited 233 head of cattle as his share of the estate.[8] One especially large shipment of Duncan McDonald's cattle was on October 1904, when McDonald joined with the Dupuis brothers on the reservation to ship two trainloads of cattle to market in Chicago.[9]

McDonald's orchard produced some large crops of apples that were exported off the reservation. In 1895 he reported "an abundant crop."[10] Two conflicting newspaper accounts refer to an especially large apple harvest in 1900. One article referred to 1,500 boxes shipped to off-reservation markets and another mentioned 3,000 boxes.[11]

The other prominent tribal member businessmen between 1889 and 1904 were Charles Allard Sr. (who died in July 1896) and his son, Charles Allard Jr. The senior Charles Allard was best known for his stage line running from Ravalli to the Upper Flathead Valley and his buffalo exhibits.

The Allard stage line was the main transport from the Ravalli railroad station to Polson or Demersville before the Great Northern Railroad was constructed through the Upper Flathead Valley. The stage line did a bonanza business during 1891 as the Great Northern construction was underway.

The explosion of traffic in 1891 led to the introduction of a competing stage line run by a white man named T. M. Adams. The competition between the two lines led to a price war, which culminated in July 1891 in free rides for passengers. The rides included a free dinner at the Allard ranch.[12] Allard won the competition and bought out the Adams line in August 1891.[13]

The operation of the Allard line was frequently in the news between 1889 and 1891. On July 17, 1890, one passenger, John H. King, was injured in an accident on the line. He sued Allard for $5,000 in damages, but settled in October 1890, when Allard paid him $230.[14] Allard appointed a white man, Jesse Gawith, as his express agent in Demersville in November 1890.[15] Allard took delivery of a new stagecoach in January 1891, and in February traveled to Oregon to purchase horses for his stage line.[16] That same month of February 1891 Allard purchased a house in Demersville.[17] On April 3, 1891, a white female passenger complained to the Demersville newspaper that refined white women on Allard's stages were forced to sit next to lower-class white men.[18] Allard hired a new general manager, T. C. Willis, for the stage line office in Demersville in April 1891.[19] In November 1891 he purchased a livery stable in Demersville.[20] Finally, as noted previously, on January 5, 1892, the newspaper announced the sale of Allard's stage line and most of Duncan McDonald's Ravalli businesses to C. A. Stillinger and Arthur Larrivee, Allard's nephew.[21]

During the first half of the 1890s Allard worked to find ways to profit from his buffalo herd. As discussed in the section on cattle and buffalo raising, Allard Sr. established a short-lived Wild West show in 1893. The Wild West show closed after playing for several Montana cities in the summer of 1893. Plans to exhibit the buffalo in Chicago at the 1893 Chicago World's Fair failed to come together.

Several local showings of the buffalo were more successful. In September 1893 Allard advertised an excursion to Polson at the foot of the lake by steamer for one dollar per person to see the buffalo.[22] A year later, in September 1894, he organized another outing from Demersville by steamer. For one dollar, travelers got a boat ride from Demersville to Polson and back. Allard had part of his buffalo herd at Polson for the visitors to view.[23] One hundred and ten people turned out for the buffalo excursion.[24]

Allard had some other, less well-publicized business ventures. According to one report, Allard—one of the largest cattle owners on the reservation—opened a meat market at Ravalli in October 1889.[25] In February 1893 Allard took possession of a sawmill in settling a debt owed to him. He asked Agent

Ronan for permission to set up the sawmill on his ranch to manufacture lumber for sale on the reservation.[26] Allard received government permission, but there was no record of whether the lumber business was finally established. Between Allard's income from his cattle, buffalo, and other enterprises, he was very well-to-do. In October 1893 an envious newspaper reporter described Allard's personal carriage as "perhaps the most luxurious outfit that ever traveled overland." His rig was "a shiny, comfortably upholstered landau, drawn by glossy, well-groomed horses, whose harness glittered in the sunshine."[27]

After Charles Allard Sr. died in Chicago in July 1896, his son and namesake, Charles Allard Jr., carried on many of the family enterprises. As described previously, in 1901 and 1902, Allard was a partner in a Wild West show that featured the family buffalo herd. After touring various Montana cities and the Midwest, the show went broke in Iowa in the fall of 1902. Allard Jr. also continued to sell buffalo for slaughter and exhibition.

In January 1904 Allard Jr. and Oscar Sedman purchased the hotel, restaurant, and store at Polson, which had been operated for years by Henry Therriault.[28] Allard was in Missoula in July 1904 buying goods for his store.[29] Sedman sold his share of the business in November 1904.[30] C. H. McLeod of the Missoula Mercantile Company panned Allard as a merchant: "He is not a merchant and never will be." McLeod noted that Allard was "badly in debt" and in October 1904 still owed $6,000 on the purchase price for the Polson business.[31]

There was limited information about other tribal members who operated businesses between 1889 and 1904. For example, in the late 1880s, Elizabeth, a niece of Kootenai chief Eneas, and her husband, Francois "Savio" Gravelle, a Frenchman, operated a restaurant and hotel for travelers near the Kootenai village on Flathead Lake. One traveler, Oliver Vose, remembered the Savios in March 1889:

> That night we reached Savio's halfway house, just west of where Bigarm now stands. We arrived after dark at the little log cabin, where we were to stay the night. It did not look any too inviting, but we were pleasantly surprised when Mrs. Savio, an Indian woman, served us a good hot meal and showed us to our bunk beds, which were built double-deck along one side of the cabin. Everything, contrary to our expectations, was spick and span. Believe me we relished our breakfast the next morning, as we prepared for our last day's trip.[32]

In October 1890 S. W. Graham, a traveler, left an account of visiting the Savios and purchasing fresh milk from Mrs. Savio. Graham recorded that Mrs. Savio had a black eye, which he attributed to a domestic disagreement.[33]

Historical sources indicate the restaurant at Polson was operated by a mixed-blood woman in 1891. Mrs. Frank Nash remembered eating dinner in spring in a restaurant in Polson operated by Emily Brown Couture. [34] According to Agent Ronan in August 1891, Mrs. Couture and her husband, Maxime Couture, were operating the Polson restaurant and sought to open a store at the location. In 1895 Emily married William Irvine, a prominent reservation cattleman.[35]

Louisa McDermott, the teacher in the government school at Jocko in 1899 and 1900, told of a pop shop or small store run by Joe Barnaby in the Jocko Valley. According to McDermott:

> Joe Barnaby was a man of about thirty-five. He kept the pop shop, a kind of small store where the Indians could get soft drinks and be entertained. . . .
>
> He was a generous, kind-hearted fellow, burt [sic] very immoral, not a Catholic in practice at all. . . .
>
> . . . He kept his little store clean and tasty. The walls were decorated with pictures taken from the magazines that the chances of reservation life brought his way.[36]

Barnaby died in a railroad accident while returning from Missoula to Arlee in August 1900.[37]

On March 25, 1903, Agent Smead gave Frank Ducharme a permit to operate a small sawmill and sell lumber on the reservation.[38] No further details were found.

In addition to those Indians who operated businesses, there were frequent accounts of tribal members visiting surrounding towns, especially Missoula, Kalispell, and Plains, to patronize white-owned businesses in the city.

Newspaper accounts described the Salish, who sold their land in the Bitterroot Valley and spent the money in Missoula. A series of articles in the *Anaconda Standard* in April 1894 described a payout of $18,000 to Salish Indians for land sold in the Bitterroot Valley. The payments were made in Missoula, and the recipients purchased clothes, blankets, saddles, tobacco, plows, wagons, and harrows from Missoula merchants.[39] Big Sam's son used some of his money to pay off his father's six or seven-year-old debt to the Missoula Mercantile Company.[40] According to another article a week later, most of the Salish had used much of their land-sale money to purchase stock or equipment and improve their farms on the reservation. Some paid off long-standing debts to Bitterroot Valley merchants and purchased fancy clothes and blankets.[41]

In January 1896 another $8,800 was paid out at the Jocko Agency. Many of the recipients headed to Missoula the next day to purchase blankets, clothing, and supplies.[42] Two years later in April 1898, one Missoula merchant, Tyler Worden, complained that Agent Smead paid land sellers with purchase orders to Worden's competitor, the Missoula Mercantile Company, rather than cash.[43] Other Bitterroot land sellers came to Missoula in February 1903 to shop: "The merchants hail the coming of the Indian with delight, for the most of them are liberal buyers and it provides an opportunity to dispose of many odds and ends that might otherwise be a dead loss."[44]

Scattered accounts mention mixed-blood ranchers from the reservation visiting town to purchase supplies. Some visits were by white men married into the tribes. The Plains newspaper was especially likely to note the visits of reservation ranchers to local merchants. Wilkes Markle, who had married a tribal member, patronized Plains merchants in November 1895 and July 1896. Joseph Morrigeau was a Plains customer for haying supplies in July 1896.[45] A week later in July 1896 T. G. Demers, Oliver Courville, George Maillett, and Ed Lameroux were purchasing haying supplies at Plains.[46] Angus P. McDonald was shopping for provisions in Plains in May 1900.[47] Zephyre Courville purchased supplies and a new wagon in Plains in March 1902.[48] In July 1902 Angus P. McDonald was back in Plains to pick up a new buggy, "one of the best made."[49] The editor of the Plains newspaper noticed an unnamed reservation Indian in October 1902 had purchased an elegant range. The editor claimed most tribal families had sewing machines.[50] Ed Lameroux returned to Plains in July 1903 to purchase provisions and a new mowing machine.[51] T. G. Demers purchased a new harness and wagon during a July 1904 visit to Plains for the Fourth of July celebration.[52] On June 1, 1897, Plains merchant J. A. McGowan sued Alphonse and Oliver Courville from the reservation for over a thousand dollars in past-due bills.[53] McGowan collected $223.10 from the estate of Charles Allard Sr. for the balance owed on Allard's death in 1896.[54]

In the fall of 1897 one newspaper writer in Kalispell described the shopping habits of reservation Indian customers purchasing winter supplies.

They bargained for each item separately and were very particular in their purchases.[55] Kalispell newspapers noted a few shopping visits by tribal ranchers in 1901. In August 1901 Mike or Maxime Matt was shopping in Kalispell for supplies.[56] Another Kalispell newspaper noted in September 1901 that "a number" of reservation cattlemen were in town to purchase supplies for the annual roundup and hire additional workers.[57]

In Missoula in October 1898 one writer described an unnamed "civilized" Indian family from the reservation visiting Missoula. According to this report, the family dressed and acted like rural whites visiting the city.[58] In May 1901, reservation Indians were shopping in Missoula even while the reservation was under a smallpox quarantine.[59] One record was found of a July 1903 shopping trip to Missoula by Andrew Stinger to purchase machinery for haying.[60] An unnamed Indian from Ronan purchased a piano in Missoula in July 1904 for his daughter, who was attending an off-reservation school.[61] Reservation Indians were in Missoula in December 1904 spending their money from a per capita payment from the new reservation grazing fees.[62]

Toward the end of the 1889 to 1904 period some mixed-blood families from the reservation visited Missoula for Christmas shopping. In December 1901 A. Morrigeau and family were Missoula shoppers.[63] Between December 17, 1904, and December 21, 1904, Allen Sloan and daughter, Mrs. Octave Couture, Mrs. O. Dupuis, and Mrs. Sarah Ogden made Christmas shopping trips to Missoula.[64]

Joseph Dixon's files include correspondence from several tribal members who owed him money for legal work in Missoula. In February 1898 Mrs. Jessie Couture borrowed $25, using her horse as security, to pay Dixon for his work on her divorce.[65] Alphonse Clairmont promised in March 1898 to pay his bill for legal work after the roundup in July 1898.[66] Sam Pierre of Arlee hired Dixon in January 1899 to help collect payment from the Northern Pacific Railroad for a calf killed by a train.[67]

As mentioned previously, 1900 was the height of sales of Indian horses for the eastern market. Two of the notes in the Plains newspaper of Indians selling horses to buyers in Plains specifically noted that the Indian sellers spent the proceeds in Plains businesses. On May 11, 1900, the newspaper noted, "The transfer of the money to the Indians made business lively for our merchants for a few days."[68]

Another economic enterprise mentioned previously that engaged and enthused tribal members at the turn of the twentieth century was horse racing. One example was in September 1894, when Angus P. McDonald from the reservation ran a horse in the Kalispell horse races. Well over a thousand dollars changed hands when McDonald's horse won. According to the newspaper report, "A large crowd came up with McDonald from the reservation and when the old horse landed winner they fairly went wild with delight."[69] In the 1898 Fourth of July celebration at Kalispell, Pete Finley won $25 for second place in the quarter-mile race and two riders named Matt won fourth and sixth place in the pony race. Pete Finley also won the fat man's race.[70]

Flathead Reservation tribal members also took part in Montana's bounty program to kill coyotes and bears. Most of the bounties were collected by mixed-bloods, but some full-blood hunters also took part. A few examples will be given here. Angus McDonald turned in twenty-three coyote skins in Kalispell in September 1895.[71] Charles Allard Jr. cashed in forty coyote skins for $200 in October 1901.[72] A month later, Joseph Morrigeau brought in fifteen coyote pelts for $75.[73] Isaac Plant was active in 1903 and 1904. In December 1903 he brought in seventeen coyote hides and six in January 1904. In April 1904 he collected for four more coyotes.[74] Abraham Isaac turned in two coyotes in May 1904.[75] Malta got a bounty in June 1904 for a big brown bear he killed in the mountains near Arlee.[76] A few days later, Michael Peter was paid for three coyote hides.[77] Charles Gabe of Arlee got a bounty payment in July 1904 for two black bears.[78] Frank Lallassee cashed in two coyote hides later the same month.[79] In the fall of 1904 Alex Bigknife got a bounty for killing a grizzly bear in the Bitterroot. Another hunter in the same party, Victor Vanderburg, killed a black bear cub.[80] In August 1904 Molly Jones got a bounty for a coyote she killed and used the money to pay for her and her husband to go to the circus, which was then playing in Missoula.[81]

Another off-reservation commercial enterprise that included some tribal members was the sale of whiskey or other alcoholic beverages. Much of the evidence of the whiskey trade was indirect. References to Indians being drunk or fighting, as well as injuries or murders resulting from alcohol, were common in the historical sources. A few of the sources directly refer to tribal members purchasing alcohol. The willingness of white people to sell alcohol to Indian customers, despite the law, was frequently decried by tribal leaders. In June 1889 Kootenai chief Eneas complained that his young men "have acquired the habit and love the influence of whiskey, and in spite of your laws can procure all they can pay for."[82] According to

Henry B. Carrington, Chief Eneas and the tribal judges described selling whiskey to Indians as a business: "The white men sit up all night, with music and whiskey, and over the door it says, 'Licensed gambling saloon.' If the Indian gambles or drinks whiskey, they punish him. Why don't they punish the white man?"[83] One of Salish chief Charlo's objections to white schools was that "our children . . . will learn English in school. When they know English, they will go to the white towns and buy whiskey. The white man would not understand them if they spoke in Indian."[84]

Agent Ronan and the local authorities were frustrated in trying to prosecute saloon keepers who served Indian patrons. In 1889 Conrad Fisher and his wife, Lena Fisher, served Indian patrons at the South Missoula Beer Garden.[85] Ronan succeeded in getting the Fishers charged, but the case was dropped when the county attorney was unable to get a white jury to convict them.[86] When reporting on the Flathead Reservation in September 1889, Inspector William W. Junkin lamented, "It seems impossible to convict a white man on Indian testimony, and it is very discouraging to an Agent to have convincing testimony presented to him and find that it is not convicting testimony when presented to a white jury."[87]

In consequence, Indians from the reservation often openly patronized saloons or paid white men to buy liquor for them. In 1889 Ronan reported that a young man from the Bitterroot Salish band was part of a group patronizing a saloon in Deer Lodge County. The young man was killed in the resulting melee.[88] Ronan also complained that the Ramsdell brothers' trading post on the Tobacco Plains routinely served Indian customers.[89] Chief Eneas said in 1889 that his son Sam and two other young Kootenai men loaned a horse to a white man, Joe Morant, in exchange for whiskey. The party continued in Demersville, where the Kootenais had Jack Sheppard, another white man, buy more whiskey for them. Later during this visit, Sam was murdered, presumably by a white man living in the town.[90]

Ronan did succeed in getting Bernard Leopold of Missoula tried and convicted of selling whiskey to Felix and Adolph Barnaby of the reservation in February 1892. The Barnabys traveled to Arlee and attacked another mixed-blood tribal member in the ensuing party. Leopold was fined $500 by the court, but his prison sentence was for only two days in the penitentiary.[91]

Agent Carter got a Missoula drug store clerk named Frank Cyr charged with selling alcohol to tribal members in spring 1895. Cyr had even shipped alcohol to his customers on the reservation C.O.D.[92] In December 1899 three Indians—Lolo, Michael Stephens, and Ainsley—testified that they purchased whiskey from Michael Quinn, a white man. Lolo paid fifty cents for one bottle and a dollar for another.[93]

Not all of the attempted purchases of alcohol by Indians in Missoula were successful for the customers. In July 1895 Charlie Kickinghorse and Alex Packer, possibly Alex Parker, gave John Houston, a white man, $3.50 to buy whiskey for them. Houston kept the money and spent it for himself. Houston and his friend, A. Holland, were arrested for stealing the money, and Kickinghorse and Packer/Parker were held as witnesses.[94]

Many of the charges of selling whiskey to tribal members toward the end of the 1889–1904 period involved businesses in Plains, just off the reservation. On October 17, 1901, Agent Smead sent a telegram to the U.S. attorney in Helena asking for a warrant to arrest William Viloit, a Plains saloon keeper. According to Smead, Viloit sold whiskey to two Indians the day before.[95] But not all of the cases against Plainsmen selling liquor to Indians were successful. Three Indians purchased whiskey from a large, heavyset white man behind the Plains saloon owned by James Scott in January 1902. However, when the Indians were called before the U.S. commissioner, they either could not or would not identify James Scott as the man who sold them the alcohol.[96]

Chief Michel of the Camas Prairie Kalispels complained in July 1902 that his young men were buying whiskey at the saloons and drugstore in Plains.[97] Later that month, Agent Smead reported that he had secured the conviction of one Plains saloon keeper for selling alcohol to Indians, but he failed to get a conviction in a second case.[98] The business continued, and on December 7, 1904, J. A. McGowan, the Plains merchant, complained that one Plains saloon regularly and openly served Indian customers.[99]

Alcohol sales brought out the entrepreneurial instincts of some tribal members. They purchased alcohol from off-reservation businesses and bootlegged it for a profit on the reservation. Most, but not all, of the tribal bootlegger businessmen were mixed-bloods.

In December 1892 some of the Indian workers who were digging a new irrigation ditch in the Jocko Valley invested their wages buying alcohol in Missoula to bring onto the reservation. Several bottles of whiskey were found in the blanket of an Indian woman boarding the train for Arlee. The entire traveling party was arrested and jailed until they disclosed who sold them the alcohol. When they informed on their supplier, they were released, and the white man who sold the whiskey was arrested.[100] Benoit Nenema was arrested by the U.S. marshal in October 1900 for importing whiskey onto the reservation.[101] Pascale Antoine was sent to the U.S. District Court in Helena in January 1901 for selling whiskey on the reservation.[102] In June 1901 an anonymous letter writer accused Louie Camille of selling alcohol to Indians on the reservation and ordering more product from his off-reservation supplier.[103] Joseph Jangraw resold whiskey on the reservation in late 1901. Some of the whiskey he sold for cash, and some he exchanged with Alex Finley for a horse.[104]

In February 1903 Baptiste Nenema and Antle were arrested for smuggling whiskey onto the reservation. In a strange twist, M. H. Prideaux, a reservation trader, hired a white lawyer, Harry Parsons, to defend Nenema. Nenema was bound over to federal court and Prideaux and Alex Demers, another trader, posted Nenema's bond.[105] Two months later, Antoine Nenema was arrested and charged with bringing liquor onto the reservation. Nenema was released a few days later on a technicality.[106]

Louis Ashley was charged in November 1903 for smuggling whiskey onto the reservation for resale. Ashley was also represented by Attorney Parsons.[107] Ashley was found guilty and sentenced to sixty days in jail with a $100 fine.[108]

Adolph Barnaby was arrested on December 30, 1903, for bringing whiskey onto the reservation. He argued in court that he was not going to sell the whiskey but had bought the whiskey to share with his friends at a New Year's party.[109] Barnaby was indicted by the federal grand jury in September 1904.[110]

The final in this parade of alcohol entrepreneurs was Louis LaRose, who was arrested in May 1904 for bringing liquor onto the reservation. J. A. McGowan, the Plains merchant, and Alex Demers, the Indian trader, furnished his bond.[111] LaRose was also indicted by the federal grand jury in September 1904.[112]

Historical documents record tribal members in an assortment of other economic activities off the reservation between 1889 and 1904. In July 1889 a newspaper article noted that reservation Indians were patronizing a new flour mill operated in Missoula by Kennedy Dougan.[113] In October 1890 the *Weekly Missoulian* noted that M. Ignace of the reservation was a subscriber to the paper.[114] In one transaction, which may have been on the reservation, an unnamed Indian family camping near the shore of Flathead Lake in the summer of 1891 sold a bark canoe to two young white tourists.[115] An unnamed Indian farmer called for an off-reservation physician to attend a sick child in September 1895. The physician came part of the way before he heard the child was dead and then returned home. A conflict arose when he charged the farmer $75 for his travel.[116] In the summer of 1896 Antoine Ninepipe deposited money in a Missoula bank and received a certificate of deposit. The certificate was subsequently lost, and Ninepipe requested the bank stop payment on it.[117]

Agent Smead worked as a middleman in October 1899 for reservation Indians getting firewood and selling it in Missoula.[118] Later the same month an unnamed reservation Indian sold a Missoula physician a bear cub he had captured and tamed.[119] In July 1900 John Lomprey owed the Montana Marble Works money, presumably for a gravestone he purchased.[120] One of Ninepipe's sons put a horse in a Missoula stable during the summer of 1900 but did not have enough money to pay the bill, so he sold the horse to the stable owner. Later it turned out, the horse belonged to Ninepipe rather than his son.[121]

In February 1903 two Indian students named Peter and Abraham ran away from school on the reservation and traveled to Missoula to patronize a variety theater.[122] A crowd of tribal members traveled to Missoula in August 1904 to take in the circus and sideshow then in town.[123] Between 1889 and 1904, Flathead Reservation Indians may not have been the best patrons of off-reservation business, but their occasional business was enough to be a valuable part of the Kalispell, Plains, and Missoula economies.

Two types of on-reservation economic exchange were important for the 1889 to 1904 period. The first was tribal member purchases from reservation traders. The second group consisted of loans, purchases, and barter between tribal members. Traders furnished necessities and occasional luxuries to reservation residents by cash purchase, credit, and barter. The most active customers would have been the affluent mixed-bloods, but presumably the full-bloods and poorer mixed-bloods were occasional customers.

Unfortunately, almost no documentation has survived to describe the business exchanges between tribal members and the traders. Agent Smead did write letters to delinquent tribal members to help trader L. S. Jones of Ronan collect overdue accounts. On January 22, 1900, Smead contacted Antoine Parazo about his account at Jones's store.[124] Later that year, on June 20, 1900, Smead wrote to Basile Finley of Polson about $64.06 he owed Jones.[125] Smead mediated between Jones and Louis Camille of St. Ignatius about an overdue account in January and February 1902.[126] The agent also tried to help Jones collect an overdue bill owed by Isaac Ogden in 1902.[127] Finally, on October 6, 1902, Smead wrote to James Michael of Ronan about his account with Jones.[128]

One source suggests that small value purchases, loans, and exchanges may have been common between tribal members. As mentioned in the account of casual labor on the reservation, Father Jerome D'Aste used his diary as a running account book while he was in charge of the Jocko Church between October 1893 and August 1894.[129] D'Aste's largest purchases were for hay and firewood. On October 25, 1893, D'Aste arranged to pay Joe Blodgett $11 a ton for 8 tons of hay delivered.[130] D'Aste made payments for the hay over the next 7 months.[131] D'Aste purchased 11 logs of firewood from Martin in February 1894.[132] Part of the firewood purchase was paid off with 50 pounds of flour.[133] On March 29, 1894, D'Aste paid McLure $30 for firewood, and on April 18, 1894, McLure received another $45 payment.[134] D'Aste purchased 39 saw logs from Malta for $16 on May 19, 1894.[135]

Other purchases and sales were single events. On October 22, 1893, D'Aste sold 5 bushels of wheat to Antoine Felix for $2.50 on credit.[136] He got 10 pumpkins from Big Sam on October 28, 1893.[137] On January 10, 1894, he bought 10 sacks of potatoes from Charlo for $6.[138] Apparently, D'Aste paid Michael or some other Indian $.50 for deer meat on January 16, 1894.[139] He paid someone, possibly Joe Blodgett, $3 for potatoes on May 1, 1894.[140] Charlo sold D'Aste $1.20 worth of oats on May 17, 1894.[141] D'Aste agreed on June 24, 1894, to pay $1 a week for pasture for his horse.[142] On August 6, 1894, D'Aste paid someone $7 for a good load of hay.[143] He bought $1.75 worth of sugar for Charlo on August 28, 1894.[144]

In addition to purchases from neighboring Indians, D'Aste also gave money to tribal members. It was often not clear from the diaries which exchanges were gifts and which were loans. On January 18, 1894, D'Aste noted that he got back $3 of the $5 he had loaned to Mary Vandeburgh.[145] Louison received $2 from D'Aste on February 6, 1894.[146] He gave Michael $.25 on March 14, 1894;[147] Henriette $2 on May 5, 1894;[148] and Martin sKaltemiger $1 on May 14, 1894.[149] Joe La Mousse paid back $.60 on May 18, 1894,[150] and on May 22, 1894, John Peter paid back $2.[151] John Peter borrowed another $10 on June 5, 1894,[152] which he paid back on June 20, 1894.[153] D'Aste either loaned or gave John Lomprey $15 on July 21, 1894.[154]

Some of D'Aste's gifts or loans were in the form of goods rather than cash. On May 26, 1894, D'Aste gave Placid Cyril three bundles of shingles and some nails.[155] Sophie Kaluià got 100 pounds of flour and $2 in cash on June 2, 1894.[156] He gave Francoise 50 pounds of flour and Ignace Finley 100 pounds of flour on July 16, 1894.[157] Francoise also got 2 pounds of sugar the next day.[158]

Other D'Aste payments were obviously gifts. Here are a few examples. On July 18, 1889, he gave $2 to Deaf Louis.[159] That fall he gave Michel suKoe $.50 present.[160] D'Aste gave $2 alm on January 1, 1890, but he did not name the recipient.[161] That summer, on June 3, 1890, he gave Paul Guiznaiul $1 alm.[162] He let Lame Samuel have $5 on July 6, 1890, and another $5 the next day.[163] A few days later, on July 18, 1890, he gave Baptiste Kakashe, the chief, $5 alm.[164] A final example, on August 31, 1890, he "made a present" to Isaac Kiupè of the $5 he had given Isaac three days before.[165] There were also a few cases where Indians gave money to D'Aste as gifts. On November 24, 1901, he got $5 as a present from old Mary Saxa,[166] and on April 7, 1902, he got a $2 present from Arch McDonald.[167]

Father D'Aste's purchases and loans/gifts might have been more extensive than many tribal families, but they suggest that small value bartering and sales were not uncommon between Flathead Indian Reservation families. This sort of penny capitalism could have helped supplement the subsistence activities of many full-blood Indian families.

A final form of economic exchange on the reservation between 1889 and 1904 was theft. Jerome D'Aste's diary recorded a few thefts from the mission. On June 8, 1889, a saddle was stolen from the mission stable.[168] That fall Brother Campopiano's watch was stolen from the mill.[169] The mission complained in summer 1899 that some thieves were repeatedly stealing from and harassing the mission. Two unidentified young men were arrested for the crimes by Judge Joseph and locked up in the jail at the mission. The father of one of the prisoners then attacked Joseph.[170] Louis King led three other young men in a raid on the mission cellar to steal cider on October 6, 1902.[171] They were arrested by the tribal police and incarcerated in the agency jail.[172] In early June 1903 one of the students, Michael NKuto, ran off after pretending to be sick. To make his getaway, he broke into an Indian cabin and stole a bridle and a horse.[173]

While most of the thefts on the reservation between 1889 and 1904 involved horses, some other cases were in the records. In April 1891 someone stole a twenty-dollar gold piece from Red Owl or Louison, a tribal judge and cattle owner. Joseph Barnaby was arrested in Missoula for the crime.[174] Louie Pierre had a stove stolen from his home while he was off on a hunting trip in the fall of 1898.[175] On May 6, 1899, a saddle was stolen from an Indian at Arlee. Two Cree Indians were suspected of the theft.[176] Someone stole a pair of spurs from Joseph Allard in April 1901.[177]

The most famous theft on the reservation was the robbery of Michel in November 1902. Michel, a Kalispel Indian, was rumored to be the richest

Indian on the reservation, with large herds of cattle and horses. He kept $20,000 or more in cash in an old tin can. While Michel was away, some Indians stopped at his ranch and visited with the women of the household. While the women were distracted, the rest of the gang made off with the money. Despite a wide-ranging search and a $1,000 reward, the thieves were apparently never caught.[178] The robbery was even reported in the *New York Times*.[179]

Some cases of cattle theft were discussed in the section on the role cattle played in the reservation economy between 1889 and 1904. The most common form of theft during the period that made its way into the historical and legal records was horse theft. Horses were some of the most mobile and economically valuable resources available. Intertribal horse theft had ended by the late nineteenth century, but horses on the reservation owned by other tribal members were tempting targets.

In March 1894 Tsil Peh was arrested for stealing a horse belonging to Sam Cooley, a Northern Pacific Railroad employee who had lived at Arlee.[180] About a year later, Goosta attempted suicide in jail in Kalispell, where he was being held for horse stealing. A jury found him not guilty of the horse stealing charge in May 1895.[181] Two Indian policemen arrested an unnamed Indian camped south of Missoula in June 1895 for horse theft on the reservation.[182] Agent Carter and the Indian police lodged another accused Indian horse thief in the Missoula jail in August 1896.[183] Gravelle and Riley, two Indians from the reservation, were being held in the Kalispell jail for horse theft in March 1899.[184] The case against those two was dismissed because the crime occurred on the reservation.[185] In September 1899 another accused Indian horse thief from the reservation was arrested in Missoula by the Indian police.[186] Other cases of Indians charged with horse theft appeared sporadically in the historical record right through 1904.

Conclusion

Tribal members on the Flathead Reservation between 1889 and 1904 were economically active and productive. Tribal members continued traditional activities to the extent possible, but built new industries on the reservation as needed. For most tribal members, these changes were necessary, not preferred, but maintaining their economic independence and self-support were important goals.

CHAPTER 6

Turmoil and Progress, 1905–1910

The thirty years between 1875 and 1905 saw a far-ranging economic transformation on the Flathead Indian Reservation as access to traditional resources such as hunting and gathering steadily declined. In response to the growing scarcity of wild game and plant resources, the tribes expanded their cattle and horse herds, wage labor, and businesses. It was not a change that was probably desired by most tribal members, but it did allow them to maintain their economic independence and avoid general government rations.

The transition hit a land mine in 1904, when Congressman Joseph Dixon secured passage of a federal law imposing allotment on the Flathead Reservation. Two consequences of the allotment policy were immediate and affected the reservation during the 1905–10 period. First was the social and political turmoil surrounding tribal opposition to the allotment policy. Second was the redistribution of land and grazing assets as the open range was ended, and some large ranches may have been broken up and the land distributed to other tribal members.

It is reasonable to expect that the disruption to tribal society, as tribal leaders fought against allotment on the reservation, had economic consequences, but the historical evidence was not detailed enough to document its impact. The redistribution of land titles to give each tribal member an individual allotment may have reduced the preallotment landholdings of some of the rich mixed-blood families. As mentioned previously, the 1900 federal census found eleven farms on the reservation that enclosed more

138

than 500 acres each.[1] It is not known, however, if any of these eleven farms lost land as a result of allotment.

There was, however, considerable evidence that the end of the open range on the reservation, which resulted from allotment, impacted cattle- and horse-owning tribal members. The end of the open range forced many tribal members to sell their livestock—including buffalo.

Hunting, Fishing, and Gathering

Between 1905 and 1910 few Indian hunters were arrested for hunting off the reservation without state licenses. In October 1905 Abraham Isaac, Gabe Sapier, and Big Mouth Charley were convicted of hunting off the reservation without a license and fined.[2] A. M. Bliss, forest supervisor of the Lewis & Clark Forest Reserve, complained to Agent Bellew on November 20, 1905, that he had reports that Flathead Reservation hunters in the Clear- water and Swan River Valleys were violating state game laws.[3]

No cases of hunting without a state license appeared in the newspapers between 1906 and 1910. According to one newspaper article in 1905, many Indian hunters were checked by game wardens, but they had licenses and permits to leave the reservation.[4] Apparently by 1905 most Flathead Reser- vation tribal members hunting off the reservation felt it was less trouble to get a state license and permit from the agency than to fight with the game wardens.

In September 1905 E. Pain from the reservation was arrested and charged with setting a fish trap on the reservation. Fish traps were illegal off the reservation, but the court wrestled with whether they were illegal on the reservation.[5] Four years later, in August 1909, Agent Fred Morgan refused to give Joseph Pain of Dixon permission to use a fish trap on the reservation, because it was against state law.[6] About the same time, Morgan wrote that he was trying to get tribal members to observe state hunting laws.[7]

In October 1908 a Pend d'Oreille hunting party led by Antoine Scwi was drawn into a violent confrontation in the Swan Valley with Charles B. Peyton, a state game warden. The three men in the party had been careful to purchase state hunting licenses, and Yellow Mountain, an elderly man in the party who was not hunting, made a special effort to get written permis- sion for the trip from Agent Samuel Bellew at Flathead Agency. Some com- bination of Peyton's bigotry and cultural and language miscommunication led to a gun battle that left the four Pend d'Oreille men and Peyton dead.

Agent Bellew gathered evidence for the prosecution of Herman Rudolph, Peyton's deputy, for murder, but Missoula County officials dragged their feet until Rudolph disappeared. The lack of justice in the affair was a continuing grievance for tribal members.[8]

Tribal members continued to hunt big game during the 1905–10 period, but it was no longer the base of the reservation economy. Avoiding conflict with Montana state officials was a major concern, but hunting continued as a valuable part of tribal cultural life.

Gathering wild plants also continued in their seasons, but there was little mention in the historical sources. In July 1910 a Kalispell newspaper noted, "The Indians have all gone to the hills to pick huckleberries."[9]

To add insult to injury, in 1910 as the allotment and opening of the reservation was being forced on the tribes, Montana authorities moved to control Indian hunting on the reservation. The Montana attorney general declared in August 1910 that tribal members needed state licenses to hunt on the reservation. They would also have to observe all state fish and game regulations on the reservation.[10] This decision brought an immediate reaction from tribal leaders. On August 26, 1910, Charles Redeker of Polson relayed to the commissioner of Indian affairs a complaint from Kootenai chief Thomas Antiste.[11] The Flathead Reservation Indians would struggle for decades in the twentieth century to protect their hunting rights under the 1855 Hellgate Treaty.

Livestock and Open Range, 1905–1910

The economic engine that kept the Flathead Reservation residents self-supporting during the late nineteenth and early twentieth century was raising horses and cattle on the open range on the reservation. The 1905 and 1910 period saw the conclusion of efforts to reduce horse herds on the range. The effort started under Agent W. H. Smead to make more grass available for cattle. By 1906 and 1907, when the last of the large horse herds were liquidated, there was pressure from the end of the open range and the impending opening of the reservation to white homesteaders.

The sale and shipment of Flathead Reservation horses slowed down in the last five years before the 1910 opening but was still significant in 1906 and 1907. In 1905, newspaper accounts noted shipments of two railroad carloads to Michigan on May 2, 1905[12]; six carloads to Wisconsin on May 19, 1905[13]; and three more carloads to Wisconsin on May 25, 1905.[14] These shipments were in conjunction with the spring horse roundup.[15] Later in the summer and autumn of 1905, other shipments went out, mostly from Plains. In August 1905 two carloads went from Plains to Michigan, two carloads to Pennsylvania, two to Indiana, and another carload to Canada.[16] In late August 1905 a carload of horses was shipped from Ravalli to St. Paul.[17] In September 1905 two carloads of reservation horses went to North Dakota, and another two carloads went to Indiana from Plains.[18] Other shipments to eastern markets continued in 1906 and 1907, but they slowed down in spring 1908.

Agent Bellew reported in his 1905 annual report that 4,000 reservation horses were sold during 1904–5.[19] In July 1906 Bellew claimed 9,000 Flathead horses had been shipped to eastern markets in the past few years.[20] A newspaper report in September 1906 said 50,000 reservation horses had been sold in the previous seven years. This 1906 report found, "The result of the selling of the range horses from the reservation has been practically to divest the ranges of these animals," and the "demand has been so brisk that the supply was inadequate."[21] One horse buyer reported in the summer of 1906 that he found it difficult to find reservation horses to purchase.[22]

One case was found of horses shipped to the reservation in 1906. According to a newspaper report, an unnamed Indian family shipped a carload of horses from Washington State to Flathead in June 1906.[23] Some shipments were made to Canada, but Flathead horses no longer went to Africa and Japan. In January 1906 George Bellew, the Flathead Agency clerk, mentioned 1905 shipments to Canada for sale.[24] In June 1906 Ben Cramer, a white man married to a tribal member, shipped 150 reservation horses from Kalispell to British Columbia.[25] An Alberta rancher purchased 20 horses from Arthur Larrivee and shipped them from Plains to Canada in October 1906.[26] Charles Allard and Ben Cramer cooperated on a shipment of 50 horses that Cramer took to Alberta in May 1907.[27]

The years 1905 to 1907 saw the final liquidation of the large herd of horses owned by Allicott, a Nez Perce Indian living on the Flathead Reservation. Agent Smead's attempts to reduce Allicott's herd had led to a special government investigation in 1900. According to George Bellew, Allicott shipped 1,300 horses in 1905.[28] Another 500 Allicott horses were rounded up in May 1906 and sold at a public auction in Plains.[29]

In 1905, according to Agent Bellew, unbroken horses over 1,000 pounds sold for $20 to $30.[30] Bellew wrote one potential buyer from Ohio in 1906 that unbroken yearlings sold for $7.50 and broke saddle horses sold for from

$35 to $55.[31] A few months later in July 1906, Bellew wrote that the prices had risen to $15 to $25 per head.[32]

A specialized market for horses on the reservation was Charles Allard Jr. purchasing racing horses. In March 1906 Allard traveled east to purchase thoroughbred horses.[33] Allard shipped horses to Spokane in September 1906 to compete in a relay race.[34] His horses won the $1,500 prize in the interstate relay race in October 1906.[35] Allard also won first prize in the October 1908 relay race in Spokane.[36] In the spring of 1909 a horse buyer named Jerry Sullivan was on the reservation looking for "some fine horses" to buy.[37]

The Flathead Reservation cattle industry also went through wrenching change from 1905 to 1910 to adjust to the opening. Apparently, cattle prices were depressed at the beginning of the period. In his annual report for 1905 Bellew referred to low cattle prices during fall 1904 that complicated the collection of the grazing tax.[38] On February 1, 1906, Bellew complained that many of the largest tribal cattle owners were delinquent on their grazing taxes. Their cattle were heavily mortgaged, and the banks would not advance more money to the owners.[39] In the fall of 1906 Bellew wrote that cows on the reservation were getting $21.50 to $23 each, steers $37 to $40, and old bulls about $21.[40]

No references were found giving the total number of cattle shipped during the period, but some accounts claim "many" were shipped. A July 14, 1905, newspaper account mentioned that cattle buyers on the reservation had contracted for 1,300 head to be shipped to Spokane and various Montana destinations.[41] That August, Charles Allard reported 1905 had been "a great season on the reservation for the shipping of cattle and horses."[42]

A cattle buyer based in Plains estimated that more than 5,000 head of cattle had been sold to off-reservation buyers in the fall 1905 season. He noted shipments to Tacoma, Seattle, and Chicago.[43] Shipments to Tacoma of eleven carloads of reservation beef were noted in October 1905 and another eleven carloads in September 1906.[44] In September 1906 Angus McDonald shipped cattle to Omaha.[45] A newspaper report in August 1907 mentioned five to ten railroad carloads of cattle shipped daily from Plains. Most went to Spokane and points west.[46]

A surprising number of reservation cattle between 1905 and 1910 were sold to butchers in surrounding Montana communities. John R. Daily, a Missoula butcher, was one of the most frequent customers for reservation beef. He purchased two carloads of cattle in June 1905.[47] Daily returned for more cattle in September 1906, and for four more carloads in June 1907.[48] In October 1907 Daily got 400 more head of reservation cattle, which was enough to supply his butcher business for a month.[49]

In June 1905 John Wenger, a butcher from Anaconda, was purchasing cattle on Flathead.[50] That same month Lee W. Lewis of the Butte Butchering Company and Joe Ganger of Kalispell were also buying Flathead cattle.[51] G. F. Hibler, a butcher from Heron, purchased reservation cattle in November 1906.[52] In 1908 the W. B. Russell Meat Company of Plains sold reservation beef to local customers.[53] Zephyre Courville formed a joint venture with a white man named Cooper in 1909 to market meat from Courville's cattle to St. Regis and Plains customers.[54]

Given the impending loss of open-range grazing with the opening of the reservation, a number of prominent tribal cattle owners liquidated their herds between 1905 and 1910. Angus P. McDonald was negotiating in July 1905 to sell all 1,600 head of cattle he owned to the Hubert Cattle Company.[55] The deal fell through, however, at the last minute.[56] That fall in November 1905, Angus P. McDonald sold his herd to Arthur Larrivee on the reservation for $21 per head, not counting calves.[57]

Two newspaper reports in 1906 mentioned that Flathead Reservation stockmen were liquidating their cattle herds. In July 1906 a cattle buyer from Seattle reported, "I did not get many bargains on this account, [because the cattlemen were selling out,] for the Indians on the flathead reservation are good traders, and as many of them have considerable white blood in their veins, they are good business men and keep well informed as to the live stock market at all times."[58] Another report in September 1906 mentioned Angus P. McDonald, T. G. Demers, and Arthur Larrivee as tribal cattlemen who were liquidating their herds.[59] Agent Bellew wrote that cattle prices had improved in 1906, facilitating the reduction in herds.[60]

Mrs. J. B. Jette was planning to sell all her cattle on the reservation in 1907.[61] Duncan McDonald sold all of his cattle to Allen Forkner of Missoula in March 1910.[62]

A large number of Flathead Reservation cattle were shipped to open ranges on the Blackfeet Reservation and in Canada between 1905 and 1910. Most of these cattle were still owned by Flathead tribal members, but grazed on Canadian ranges. For example, In August 1905 Billy Irvine shipped twelve carloads of range cattle to Canada.[63] In Agent Bellew's 1905 annual report he estimated that most of the 5,000 cattle driven from the reservation that year went to Canada.[64] In June 1906, 2,000 reservation cattle were driven through Kalispell to ranges in Browning, the Sweet Grass Hills, and Alberta.[65] Bellew reported on February 7, 1907, that a "great number" of cattle had been driven to Canada in 1906.[66]

In 1908 Michel Pablo sold a large herd of cattle to an unnamed buyer in Browning. When the buyer went bankrupt, Pablo drove the cattle back to Flathead. Unfortunately, the cattle had become infected with scab or mange on Blackfeet and then introduced the disease on Flathead. As a consequence, all the cattle owners on the Flathead Reservation had to run their cattle through a disinfectant bath to eradicate the disease.[67]

Some of the reservation cattlemen reacted to the loss of the open range by upgrading the quality of their stock. In May 1908 William Irvine purchased several head of thoroughbred bulls from the Marcus Daly ranches in the Bitterroot Valley for breeding purposes.[68]

The occupation listings in the 1910 U.S. population census on the reservation suggested that, even though the mixed-bloods had the largest herds, many full-blood tribal members also had livestock. Of the 150 individuals listed as farmers or stockmen in the Indian census, 38 (or 25 percent) were full-blood; 55 (or 37 percent) were half or more Indian but less than full-blood; 34 (or 23 percent) were less than half Indian; and 23 (or 15 percent) were white.[69] In his 1910 annual report Agent Morgan wrote, "Practically every family on the reservation is engaged in the cattle business to a certain extent, and the herds vary from two or three cows to as high as a thousand head of cattle."[70]

Michel Pablo's buffalo herd was another important facet of the livestock industry on the Flathead Reservation between 1905 and 1910. The buffalo were a source of income, but the loss of the open range forced a liquidation of the herd. The roundup of the buffalo and their sale to Canada between 1907 and 1909 were major news. Reporters and photographers from around the United States and across Canada converged on the reservation to document the colorful events. The roundup was also a prominent event in the memories of many twentieth-century tribal elders.[71]

The economic impact of the sale of the buffalo herd was as important as the color the roundup added to reservation life. Michel Pablo had made occasional sales of small groups of buffalo in the early years of the twentieth century. In May 1905 Pablo sold 32 head of buffalo to George Miller for $16,000. They were shipped by rail to Oklahoma.[72]

After the United States government declined to purchase the buffalo, Pablo sold the entire herd to the Canadian government in the spring of

1907. According to newspaper reports, the Canadians paid $150,000 for an estimated 400 to 500 head.[73] The Canadian government paid Pablo $70,000 in September 1907 as the final payment for the purchase.[74]

Apparently, Pablo was responsible for the cost of the roundup to ship the buffalo from Ravalli, and the roundup proved much more challenging and expensive than expected. Pablo ended up hiring some seventy-five cowboys to collect the buffalo and drive them to the corrals. According to one account, the riders were paid $5 a day. Pablo also had to build substantial chutes and corrals to load the buffalo onto trains heading north. He built a twenty-six-mile-long wire wing-fence to guide the buffalo into a corral. In addition to the cowboys, Pablo hired other workers to operate the loading chutes and drive the captured bison in specially constructed wagons to Ravalli railroad station. Most of the cowboys and other workers were tribal members. In the end, over 700 buffalo were shipped to Canada, and the process took two years. Over 100 head of especially wild animals escaped into the hills and could not be captured.[75] The roundup and sale were a considerable stimulus to the reservation economy between 1907 and 1909.

With the opening of the reservation in 1910, the Montana attorney general declared the remaining outlaw buffalo wild game and under the control of Montana fish and game laws—not Pablo's personal property.[76] The commissioner of Indian affairs determined on December 5, 1910, however, that the remaining buffalo were Pablo's personal trust property.[77]

On the Precipice: Agriculture on the Flathead Indian Reservation, 1905–1910

The allotment and opening of the Flathead Reservation and the construction of the Flathead Irrigation Project imposed dramatic changes on the reservation farming economy between 1905 and 1910. During these five years, allotments were made and irrigation construction begun, but the impacts of these policies would only develop in the decades after 1910.

Land tenure on the reservation changed dramatically with the introduction of allotment. Before allotments were issued, tribal members were allowed to establish farms on any unoccupied land. Conflicts were adjusted by the chiefs and the agents as had been the custom since the late nineteenth century. With allotment, property lines were adjusted to the government land survey, and ownership was registered with the government.

Before allotment was completed at the end of this period, the agent was frequently called on to settle land disputes. For example, in March 1905 a Mr. C. F. Gates of Kalispell had a government trader's license but could not find unoccupied land at Polson for his store. Most of Polson was included in Baptiste Eneas's farm. Charles Allard had obtained a lease on Eneas's land for Allard's businesses in exchange for a promise to support Eneas in his old age. Gates brought his complaint to Agent Bellew, but no record was found of how the problem was resolved.[78]

At the end of March 1905 Bellew wrote Frank Ashley of St. Ignatius that tribal members were not permitted to rent their ranches to non-Indians.[79] Another case arose a few days later on April 3, 1905, when Frank Knowles wanted to rent his land to Helen Finley, a relative. Knowles was paralyzed and could not work his ranch.[80] Peter Michel and Jennie Lewis had conflicting claims to a field near Polson in April 1905. Bellew promised to settle the dispute during his next trip to Polson.[81] The same day, Bellew approved an agreement between Mrs. Napoleon Plouffe and Frank Carrier at St. Ignatius. Carrier would farm twenty-five acres of Plouffe's land, and in exchange Carrier would help build fences on the farm.[82] Just a few days later on May 2, 1905, William Dowd, a white trader at St. Ignatius, complained to Bellew about a complicated conflict with tribal member Joe Latattie. Dowd had rented Latattie's field and hired Latattie to cut firewood for him. Dowd wanted Bellew to adjudicate the disagreement.[83] Abraham Finley had a dispute with his son Louis in June 1905. Abraham had allowed Louis to work Abraham's land, and in exchange Louis was to support Abraham in his old age. Abraham complained that his son now claimed the land and would not support his father.[84] On July 3, 1905, Bellew was investigating the case of a white man who bought a ranch from Philip Cul-cow-wis-ka and failed to pay the amount due.[85]

The constant drumbeat of complaints and conflicts frustrated Agent Bellew. On July 12, 1905, Bellew wrote to J. R. Sears, the Ronan trader who farmed on the reservation, "I cannot be looking at these little matters all the time and if you cannot get along with the people up there I will be compelled to ask for your removal, lease or no lease."[86] Later that month, Bellew wrote James McKeever of St. Ignatius that he could not decide McKeever's land conflict on the evidence from one person. Bellew needed both parties to come to the agency and present their cases in the presence of the agent.[87]

Disputes over land continued under the old informal system of land tenure, but the agent was also called to adjudicate disputes over water rights.

Many of the early conflicts over water occurred on the semiarid Camas Prairie on the west end of the reserve. On April 21, 1905, Bellew wrote Joseph Morrigeau of Camas about his conflict with Oliver Courville over irrigation water. Bellew suggested that the ditch be enlarged enough to provide water for both parties.[88] The Courville-Morrigeau conflict continued well into 1906.[89]

Bellew granted Marcelene Plouffe permission to dig an irrigation ditch through the field of Deaf Louis to obtain water to irrigate Plouffe's crops. The stipulation was that the new ditch must not damage Louis's crops, and Bellew advised Plouffe to get Louis's consent before beginning the work.[90] The Hot Springs area in the western part of the reservation provided another water conflict in 1905. In August 1905 Mary Lameroux diverted the water from a creek that had been used by the T. G. Demers's family for domestic use.[91] This conflict was still an irritant in 1906.[92]

In August 1905 the Northern Pacific Railroad requested water from a tributary of Finley Creek in the Jocko Valley for use by their locomotives.[93] Railroad employees were digging a ditch through the field of Henry Matt to divert his irrigation water for use by the railroad.[94] Bellew objected to the railroad work and maintained that the Finley Creek tributary had only enough water to irrigate the field of Matt, the Indian farmer who was located on the creek. According to Bellew, the railroad engineer agreed and was willing to abandon the railroad's water claim.[95] On October 10, 1905, the railroad submitted a revised request for locomotive water to come from the main stream of Finley Creek.[96] The revised request was approved by the secretary of the interior on January 13, 1906.[97]

No written evidence has survived, but presumably some land and water conflicts were still settled by the chiefs, judges, and other leading men of the tribes. The informal system of assigning and adjudicating land tenure on the reservation that emerged in the late nineteenth century was superseded by the land boundaries under the allotment system. The ownership of allotted land became more and more convoluted in the twentieth century as inheritance complicated matters. In 1910, at the end of the period covered by this monograph, most allotments still had single owners and recognized boundaries. Some tribal farmers filed for water rights with Montana state courts in 1907 and 1908.[98]

Farming on the Flathead Reservation between 1905 and 1910 had both good and bad years. Many Indian farmers were established along waterways and had private irrigation ditches, especially watering family gardens, but there was also considerable dryland grain farming that was dependent on rain. Before 1910 the only other irrigation was the two ditches in the Jocko Valley constructed by the government in the nineteenth century.

The first year of the period was especially bountiful for reservation farmers. In June 1905 a Missoula newspaper reported that despite recent rains, rye grown on the reservation for hay was averaging six feet high, and winter wheat near Plains promised a "phenomenal" crop.[99] John Sloane, an agency employee, claimed that the 1905 crop of hay and grain was the best ever and that prices for reservation commodities were strong.[100] A week later the Daily Missoulian noted that the 1905 hay crop on the reservation was so large that reservation ranchers were recruiting white men in Missoula to help with the harvest.[101]

Reservation farmers were optimistic in 1906 and planted twice as much wheat and expanded their apple orchards.[102] The lack of early summer rains, however, cut back crop projections to 75 percent of normal.[103] Infestations of grasshoppers in the central Mission Valley further reduced the crops.[104] Heavy rains during the haying season destroyed 40 to 60 percent of the hay crop, sealing the bad weather for the 1906 season.[105]

Crop returns rebounded in 1907. Most of the accounts of farming success in 1907 involved grain, but one reference has been found of a crop of irrigated strawberries on the Henry Felsman farm near St. Ignatius. According to Father D'Aste, Felsman had a "monstrous" crop of strawberries in early July 1907.[106] That fall, in October 1907, a Missoula newspaper reported that the number of acres planted in wheat on the reservation was 20 percent greater in 1907 than it had been in 1906. The yield per acre was also almost 20 percent higher in 1907.[107] Another report at the end of October 1907 claimed 125,000 bushels of wheat had been threshed just in the Jocko Valley.[108] A competing newspaper wrote that Jocko Valley farmers had a good crop, but claimed only 40,000 bushels of grain for Jocko farmers.[109] Yet another Missoula newspaper had a report that the 1907 reservation crops were "immense" and the Indians had "more money than ever before."[110] In November 1907 the government flour mill burned, and Indian farmers lost about $3,000 worth of flour and grain stored in the building.[111]

Very little evidence was found about the 1908 harvest on the reservation. One report in the spring of 1908 claimed that Indian farmers were cultivating 50 percent more land than in 1907.[112]

The crops for 1909, however, were plentiful despite the limited access to irrigation. In April 1909 many Indian farmers were reported to be breaking new ground for crops.[113] In July 1909 a white man was in charge of putting up several hundred tons of hay for three tribal member farmers in the western portion of the reservation.[114] Reports in August 1909 claimed the crop that year was "the largest grain crop in the history of that country."[115] Even dryland farming produced a bountiful grain crop that year.[116] A November 1909 article put that year's grain crop on the reservation as the largest on record: "some of the stands of wheat were five feet tall and the heads were heavy."[117]

Rainfall on the reservation was not so generous in 1910. The dry weather led to a historic forest fire season in the northern Rocky Mountains. On August 6, 1910, Father D'Aste lamented, "The crops are very poor in the valley." One Indian farmer sowed 250 acres and "got only five bushels an acre."[118] At least some tribal farmers had a successful crop in 1910. In October 1910 a Ronan trader sold 25,000 bushels of wheat raised by reservation farmers, including Joe Matt, Frank Matt, Fred Roullier, and Joe Houle. It is not known whether the wheat was from the 1909 or 1910 season.[119]

Since most reservation farming between 1905 and 1910 was dryland grain dependent on the vagaries of rainfall, harvests varied greatly. Record returns alternated with drought. In good years, Indian farmers sold surplus grain. In bad years, most of the grain grown was needed to make flour or feed stock.

During good years, some sales of hay were made to the St. Ignatius Mission and Jocko Agency. On October 19, 1905, the mission purchased 1,300 pounds of hay from an Indian farmer for $4.50 for use at the Jocko.[120] On March 19, 1906, Father Louis Taelman paid an Indian woman $100 for an 18-ton stack of hay in the Mission Valley.[121] In 1906 Agent Samuel Bellew made at least two purchases from Indian farmers. He purchased 20 tons of hay from Octave Couture for $47.50 on August 4, 1906, and 6,000 pounds of wheat from Sam Pierre in November 1906.[122]

Some sources document reservation wheat being exported to off-reservation customers. In September 1905 a Missoula newspaper was celebrating the good harvest on the reservation and eagerly anticipated the Indian customers who would spend their money in Missoula.[123] One account claimed 60 railroad carloads of grain had been shipped from the reservation in 1905.[124] In June 1906, 50,000 bushels of wheat from the 1905 crop were shipped to Kalispell.[125] A white dealer from Polson was negotiating to sell 80,000 bushels of wheat to off-reservation buyers in September 1907.[126]

Despite varying rainfall, farming was a valuable economic resource for tribal members between 1905 and 1910. In 1910 Agent Fred Morgan estimated 30 percent of tribal members were living on and cultivating their allotments. The average area cultivated was only 20 acres, and only 300 Indians were cultivating more than a garden plot. Some mixed-bloods were farming 400 acres. The principal crops were wheat, oats, barley, timothy, clover, and native hay.[127]

Government Aid, 1905–1910

After Agent Smead was dismissed from office in 1904 over his management of government aid to Indian farmers, almost no documentation was found describing the aid distribution process between 1905 and 1910. Some aid must have still been given or bartered to tribal members after 1904, but the sources describing the transactions just dried up. The agency still operated several irrigation ditches in the Jocko Valley and provided gristmill, sawmill, and blacksmithing services at the Jocko Valley agency and the Ronan subagency.

The agency operated a threshing machine in the Jocko Valley in 1907. The farmers had to furnish part of the crew. They sold most of the grain to off-reservation buyers.[128]

When the government flour mill and sawmill were destroyed in a fire in Ronan in November 1907, tribal farmers lost an estimated $3,000 worth of flour and wheat that had been stored in the building.[129] Senator Joseph Dixon lobbied the commissioner of Indian affairs the same month to rebuild the mills as soon as possible.[130] They were not replaced until 1909.[131]

Government aid or rations were still given to the sick and indigent. In January 1907 a Missoula physician, W. B. Parsons, wrote Agent Bellew that two members of the Moss family near Arlee had pneumonia, and the father, William Moss, could barely cope with the ranch work and taking care of the sick. Parsons asked Bellew to help the family through the crisis.[132] In his 1910 annual report Agent Morgan noted that the thirty-eight Indians receiving subsistence rations on June 30, 1910, were "totally incapacitated to perform manual labor." Thirty were over 60 years of age, and eight were between 18 and 60 years old. On June 30, 1909, the number being helped had been larger, but Morgan had "rapidly" cut down the number during the last year.[133] Morgan's zeal in reducing the ration list was shown in November 1910 when he complained to the commissioner of Indian affairs that some of the elderly rationers would not agree to lease or sell their allotments to support themselves. Morgan wanted to be able to lease or sell the lands without the owners' consent. The commissioner of Indian affairs responded that, if the rationed allottees were incompetent, he could act for them. If they were competent but unwilling to lease or sell the land, Morgan could not force them.[134]

Working for Money and Prizes, 1905–1910

During this period some tribal members worked for money or competed for monetary prizes. Much of the employment was short-term, but some tribal members had regular jobs.

The Flathead Agency provided regular employment for some tribal members. On March 9, 1909, fifteen Indians had regular jobs at the agency. Most of those employed were judges on the Indian court or policemen, but the additional farmer, blacksmith, teamster, and interpreter were also Indian.[135] On July 8, 1907, Ignace Grandjo wrote Agent Bellew from the Helena jail. Grandjo apologized for his misconduct and proposed, "When I get out I will go and see you and if you want me to be a Police Man I will behave my Self and leave Whiskey alone."[136] In April 1910 Duncan McDonald was hired by the agency as a tribal judge to replace Louison.[137]

The agency also provided some short-term employment. In March 1909 Indians were given preference on contract excavation work on the new irrigation system.[138] H. N. Savage, the engineer in charge of the irrigation construction, was looking to hire fifty Indians with teams on Flathead.[139] Savage reported in July 1910 that "rapid progress" was being made and that the Indians hired were doing "good work" at excavating the ditches.[140] Since 1910 was a spectacular forest fire season, Agent Morgan pleaded in July 1910 for more money to hire Indians and others to fight fires on the reservation.[141]

The St. Ignatius Mission account books for 1905–10 have not survived, but some tribal members and white men married to Indians worked for the mission. Traders also hired Indians for specific jobs. According to B. H. Denison, the Arlee trader, in March 1905, he purchased cordwood, fencing, and saw logs from tribal members. As mentioned previously, Octave Couture provided cordwood, and Joe Laderoute and William Moss sold Denison poles for fencing.[142] In November 1905, however, Denison complained that he had an arrangement with Henry Matt to bale Denison's hay, but that Matt had not completed the job.[143]

Other tribal members traded time and effort for money between 1905 and 1910. In April 1905 William Matt wrestled Jack Curran in Missoula for prize money and bets.[144] William Dowd, a white man living at St. Ignatius, complained on May 2, 1905, that he had hired Joe Latattie to cut firewood for him, but that Latattie was refusing to deliver the wood.[145] Narcisse Delaware challenged some white high school boys in Missoula in May 1905 to a foot race for a $5 prize. Delaware lost but wanted a rematch when he was sober.[146] During June 1905, tribal members in St. Ignatius raised $1,000 in cash and ponies for prizes for the foot races, horse races, and athletic sports at the Fourth of July celebration at the mission.[147] Arthur Larrivee ran prize-winning horses at the Plains Fourth of July celebration in 1905.[148] Peter Magpie complained in July 1905 that Duncan McDonald had failed to pay him for five months labor.[149]

An official for the Montana State Fair in Helena tried to hire Indians in 1906 to perform at the fair. Agent Bellew replied that the Spokane fair had recruited ten lodges for their fair, which did not leave enough interested Indians to go to Helena.[150]

In November and December 1906 a Mr. A. Dexter from Oakland, California, tried to arrange a trip to Oakland for twenty-four young tribal members to put on an exhibit and play. The Indians were offered $30 a month plus subsistence and transportation.[151] Someone from Spokane wrote Agent Bellew accusing Dexter of being a con artist.[152] Bellew insisted he would only approve the trip if the young people had an adult accompany them and if Dexter would submit a bond to guarantee the funds for the return trip.[153]

Alphonse Courville, a tribal member, was working for Charles Allard in February 1907. The source did not identify the specific job.[154] In June 1907 the Kalispell Fourth of July committee was recruiting Indians for their holiday celebration. Seventy-five Indians in full costume were wanted to perform for three days for one dollar each day. They could also compete for $95 in prizes and sell any trinkets or curios they brought with them.[155] In addition, at the Kalispell Fourth of July horse races, Charles Allard's horses won or placed in four races. The combined purses for the four races was $800, but the article did not spell out how the purses were divided among the winners.[156]

In 1908 Sam Resurrection did fencing and other work for Michael Antony and Michael Stevens. He was to get a horse or cash as payment, but in March 1909 he was having trouble collecting his pay.[157] Between April and June 1910 Joseph Allard was employed taking the federal census on the reservation.[158] There is no way to tell how common it was between

1905 and 1910 for tribal members to work or compete for money, but by 1910 most tribal members must have operated at least partially in the western money economy.

Between 1905 and 1910 a substantial number of tribal members—mainly mixed-bloods—operated businesses. Charles Allard Jr. was the most prominent tribal businessman for the period. In August 1905 Allard sold his interest in a ferry he operated at Polson.[159] A year later, in August 1906, white men from Idaho sold some horses to Allard as they were traveling through Polson. Unfortunately, the horses turned out to have been stolen.[160] The Allard family home on Mud Creek burned down in March 1907. The house had been occupied by Charles senior's widow. Charles Jr. had his own ranch at the foot of Flathead Lake.[161] In February 1909 Charles was building a 36-foot by 90-foot livery and feed stable in Polson. His stage line accommodated traffic through the reservation and also catered to prospective homesteaders looking at land on the reserve.[162] Allard sold the stage line in January 1910 and the Polson livery in June 1910. The Polson livery was purchased by Alex McLeod of Ronan.[163]

Between 1905 and 1910 Telesphore G. Demers, the mixed-blood son of a prominent Frenchtown merchant, operated a hotel at the hot springs in the western part of the reservation.[164] Demers started work on a new hotel building in December 1908 that was supposed to have the capacity to house one hundred guests.[165] In March 1909 Demers was in Plains purchasing materials for the hotel expansion.[166] Demers traveled to Missoula in May 1909 to purchase furnishings for twenty-four bedrooms in the hotel.[167] A system of gasoline lights was added in May 1910.[168]

Another tribal member, Zephyre "Swift" Courville purchased a partial interest in a Plains meat market in November 1908.[169] In August 1909 Courville drove a bunch of his cattle from the reservation to Plains for sale in the Cooper & Courville meat market.[170] Apparently, they also had a meat market selling reservation beef in St. Regis.[171] The meat market was merged with a mercantile store in Plains in April 1910, and the combined enterprise built a new building. According to the newspaper report, Zephyre Courville was "a prominent cattleman of the reservation and by the shrewdness, and honest dealing, with his neighbors has amassed a small fortune."[172]

John Matt operated a business as a locator showing available land to prospective white homesteaders in 1909. Originally operating in partnership with a white man named Cutler, by the fall of 1910 he seemed to be in business by himself. He guided parties from Plains, Missoula, Kalispell, and Ravalli.[173] By November 5, 1910, John Matt had patented his allotment and become a United States citizen.[174]

Several members of the McLeod family operated businesses in Ronan and Polson. Richard McLeod operated a dance hall and pool hall in Ronan in 1910.[175] Hector McLeod had a livery barn in Ronan, and Alex McLeod had a livery barn in Polson in 1910.[176]

Other references to mixed-bloods operating businesses were scattered through the sources. Tony Cabell received permission to operate a ferry at Polson in April 1905.[177] In June 1905 C. E. Bisson requested a trader's license to operate a pool hall in Polson. Agent Bellew recommended against the application, and it was denied by the commissioner of Indian affairs in July 1905.[178] Mrs. Lameroux charged visitors to the hot springs on the reservation one dollar to camp at the springs in 1905.[179]

In October 1906 Peter Lucier and Baptist Couture applied for a license to operate a barbershop at Polson. They had learned the trade at Chemewa Indian School.[180] Mrs. Frank Lambert requested a permit in March 1907 to operate a restaurant in Polson.[181] Mrs. Alfred Normandin wanted a permit to open a candy store in May 1907.[182] In September 1907 Henry Burland applied to open a blacksmith shop at Polson.[183]

Mrs. Felix Dumontier inquired about getting a permit to operate a restaurant in St. Ignatius in April 1909.[184] Octave Couture purchased the butcher shop in Arlee from one of the Matts in June 1909.[185]

Andrew Stinger and one of the Morrigeaus built a new hotel in Ronan in the spring of 1910.[186] Andrew Vallee planned in September 1910 to log his ranch and sell the lumber.[187] Dave Couture was operating a ferry at Perma in October 1910.[188] In December 1910 the *Daily Missoulian* surveyed the lumber and firewood businesses on the reservation. The article mentioned Henry Raymond, Levi Allard, Louis Courville, Baptiste Marengo, John Vallie, and Phil Innias as dealers.[189]

Almost all of the tribal businessmen in the historical sources were mixed-bloods, but some full-bloods must have taken part in the informal economy. A couple of references have survived. Father Edward Griva visited the Kootenai camp in 1909 and mentioned that the Kootenais relied on fishing in Flathead Lake. When their catch exceeded their needs, they sold the surplus in Polson for money to spend.[190] During the Fourth of July celebration at Polson in 1910, Mose Auld and Phil Finley operated a soft drink stand near the Indian camp.[191]

White Men Working for Indians on the Reservation, 1905–1910

Tribal members hired white men, especially during haying and harvest season or when special skills were needed. White men needed to get permits to work on the reservation before it was opened for homesteaders. The requests usually identified the tribal member offering the job but often did not specify the work to be done.

D. D. Hull, the farmer stationed at Ronan, wrote Agent Bellew on January 16, 1905, conveying requests for permits for white men to work for Allen Sloan, Basile Finley, John Beauchene, and Camille Bisson. Except for one man hired to teach at Beauchene's school, the duties of the other white employees were not specified.[192] A few weeks later, Hull sent requests for white workers for E. Dubay and Louis Courville without details.[193] On February 1, 1905, Bellew sent a permit for a white man employed by Henry Burland.[194]

In July 1910 white workers were putting up hay for Oliver Courville, Charles Allard, and Indian Elemo on the reservation.[195] In 1906 James Dupuis hired James Howland, a white man, as a nurseryman and gardener. Unfortunately, Howland did not have the expertise he claimed, and he left Dupuis's employ.[196] Charles Eaton was working as an engineer operating a threshing machine on the reservation in October 1906.[197] In February 1907 Fred Therriault was working on the reservation as a well digger.[198] White carpenters were building barns on the reservation in February 1909 and October 1910.[199] Duncan McDonald requested a permit in March 1909 for his cousin, John McDonald, a white man, to work as a painter.[200] Finally, in December 1909 two white men completed stonework for Angus McDonald on the reservation.[201] There is no way to tell how extensive it was, but tribal members did employ white workers between 1905 and 1910.

Tribal Member Patronage of Off-Reservation Businesses, 1905–1910

The economic dealings of tribal members when off the reservation took several forms between 1905 and 1910. The incidents documented in the sources were probably only the tip of the iceberg, as small transactions in cash would have rarely left written records.

One type of exchange was turning in coyote or bear pelts for the state bounty. In January 1905 Big Pete from the reservation claimed the bounty for one coyote.[202] Victor Vanderburg cashed in one coyote pelt, and Moses Vanderburg brought two coyote pelts in February 1905.[203] The January 1905 bounty list also included a bear killed by an unnamed Indian from the reservation.[204] The $3.50 state bounty on bears was discontinued in March 1905, and this source of income for reservation hunters dried up.[205]

Another off-reservation economic activity for tribal members was paying court fines and posting bonds. A few of these cases made it into the newspapers. In January 1905 Joe Blodgett was fined $5 for sleeping on the sidewalk in Missoula.[206] Louis, John, and Henry Matt posted a $500 bond in June 1905 for Louis Matt, who was charged with shooting John Seymour on the reservation.[207] In August 1906 Isaac Plant offered to pay the fine for his nephew Michael Plant, who had gotten into trouble when he visited Missoula to attend the circus.[208] Jerome Vanderburg was fined $5 in September 1907 for drinking alcohol.[209] In October 1908 John Lempro was convicted of being drunk in Missoula. He was fined and released on a promise to send $5 to the court. He paid his fine as promised.[210] Alexander Cordier posted $500 bond in May 1909 for charges of taking liquor onto the reservation.[211] Marcial posted a $500 bond in May 1909 for Pierre Paul, who was charged with introducing whiskey on the reservation. He used money he had on deposit with George Beckwith in St. Ignatius as surety to have C. H. McLeod of the Missoula Mercantile sign the bond.[212] A few months later in July 1909, Henry Charoline, a relative of Marcial, needed bond for charges before the U.S. grand jury. Beckwith asked McLeod to arrange bail, and Beckwith would guarantee the money.[213]

William Q. Ranft, a Missoula attorney, tried to collect fees from Alphonse Clairmont and Dan McLeod for legal work getting their families enrolled.[214]

Most Christmas shopping must have been done with the traders on the reservation, but some families traveled to Missoula. Charles Allard was Christmas shopping in Missoula in December 1905.[215] In 1907 John Matt and his wife and other unidentified Indians were shopping in Missoula.[216] The newspapers noted in December 1908 that Eli Morrigeau, John Matt and family, Mrs. John Morrigeau, and Andrew Stinger were doing Christmas shopping in Missoula.[217]

Other shopping trips to Missoula and Plains were for general provisions, hunting supplies, and alcohol. In February 1905 Ed Lameroux and another Camas resident bought a wagonload of provisions in Plains.[218] That same month, $5,000 in payment to tribal members for Bitterroot land was spent on alcohol and "gee-gaws" in Missoula.[219] A day later, Three Heads purchased a big supply of groceries in Missoula that was shipped to Arlee.[220] Then an unnamed Indian rancher and his family purchased a wagon, two dogs, a new plow, a baby's high chair, and other provisions.[221] A crowd of reservation Indians attended a circus in Missoula in August 1905.[222]

Tribal elder Francois was shopping in Missoula in June 1906.[223] Rose Couture lost a roll of about $500 in bills somewhere in Missoula on October 10, 1906, during the Missoula fair.[224] Robert Demers purchased a wagonload of provisions in Plains in December 1907.[225] Mrs. Octave Couture shopped in Missoula in December 1908.[226] One September 1909 article in the Plains newspaper celebrated the completion of repairs on the road from the reservation to Plains. The improved road would induce many reservation people to shop in Plains rather than Kalispell.[227]

Other Cases of Capitalism and Trade, 1905–1910

Some other facets of the tribal economy between 1905 and 1910 were recorded in the written sources. Only limited detail of economic exchange on the reservation has survived, but business with traders and between tribal members was important.

In April 1905 C. H. McLeod was concerned whether the thirty-five Indians who had charge accounts at Ronan could pay their bills.[228] McLeod worried about a list of large accounts owed at the St. Ignatius store on October 6, 1905. Some of the credit had been given to white men who had married into the tribes, but others were tribal members. The largest overdue account was $1,560.74 owed by Nenami. Other bills were owed by McDonalds, Matts, and Joseph Allard.[229]

Red Thunder was jailed in Missoula in June 1907 for writing two bad checks. One was passed at a Missoula store, but the second was written to Alex Demers, the trader at Arlee.[230] Yet another economic exchange was a poker game at Arlee played by tribal members and Japanese section workers on the Northern Pacific Railroad. The three Japanese players pled guilty, and the cases against the eight Indian players were dismissed.[231]

More information has survived about mixed-blood Indians as stockholders and trustees of banks and other businesses. William Irvine, Charles Allard, and Mike Matt had stock in the First National Bank in Polson in June 1909.[232] William Irvine was proposed as a trustee for the bank.[233]

A second Polson bank in January 1910 included J. O. Dupuis and Charles Allard as investors.[234] Mike Matt was an investor in the First National Bank of Dayton in March 1910.[235] In April 1910 Mike Matt was a trustee in the Dayton Mercantile Company.[236]

Another specialized facet of the tribal economy between 1905 and 1910 that was partially documented in the written record was the whiskey trade. Most of the evidence about the whiskey trade was indirect, but the injuries and murders resulting from drunken rows were well documented in the sources.

Limited evidence was found about alcohol purchases as an economic activity. In March 1905 Lomay Matt ordered liquor from the Spokane Table Supply Company. The liquor was shipped by rail to the reservation but seized by the Indian police at the railroad station. The Spokane Table Supply Company pleaded that they did not know the address was on the reservation or that Matt was Indian. The U.S. attorney decided that since the liquor was seized on the railroad right-of-way, it was not yet on the reservation, and no prosecution could be made.[237] In April 1905 Agent Bellew complained that two saloon licenses had been issued for Dayton on the northern boundary of the reservation.[238] Bellew also protested to the Missoula County Commissioners against a liquor license issued for Evaro on the reservation's southern boundary.[239]

The Missoula superintendent of the Northern Pacific Railroad promised to stop the Japanese railroad workers on the reservation from selling liquor to Indians.[240] In February 1907 Bellew promised to bring charges against the Dayton liquor dealers if the town constable could find the evidence needed.[241] Bellew was investigating three cases in April 1908 of tribal members suspected of selling whiskey in Polson.[242] Two Chinese men working for the Beckwith Mercantile in St. Ignatius were arrested in February 1909 for selling whiskey to Indians.[243] A year later in March 1910, Sam Cone, a special United States officer, arrested a Polson druggist for selling Jamaica ginger to an Indian.[244] Charles Wilson, a black chimney sweep in Missoula, was charged in March 1910 with selling liquor to Indians.[245] Finally Pierre Paul pled guilty in federal district court in July 1910 to selling whiskey on the reservation.[246]

A number of tribal members were charged between 1905 and 1910 with bringing whiskey onto the reservation. Most of them were probably bootlegging the alcohol to other Indians. In April 1905 two tribal members were arrested for bringing liquor from Missoula. The charges were dismissed because they were on the railroad right-of-way, which was not technically part of the reservation.[247] Louie Tel Co Stair, Louie Hammer, Pa Las See, Louis Clairmont, Henry Clairmont, and Aeneas Grandjo were arrested in June 1907 for bringing liquor onto Flathead.[248] Benoit Nenema and his two sons, Baptiste and Francois, were arrested on the same charge in May 1908.[249] Special Agent Cone arrested Henry Clairmont, Julian Ashley, and James Raymond at Arlee on the same charge in August 1908. Michael Plant escaped but was captured at the end of the year.[250] Louis Clairmont was arrested again a few days later for bringing liquor on the reservation.[251] Antoine Finley and Peter Gingras were charged in 1909 with bringing liquor on the reservation.[252] Finally, in 1910 William Deschamps and Louis Carron were arrested for bringing liquor on the reservation.[253]

The remaining indirect evidence of the whiskey purchases by tribal members were the arrests for being drunk and the injuries and deaths resulting from drunken parties. Only a few of these cases will be mentioned here. In February 1905 four tribal members were tried in justice court for being drunk in Missoula: Big Pete, Keat Hee, Finley, and Betteu.[254] William, the son of Peter Paul, was arrested in March 1905 for threatening Baptiste Kakashe with a gun while William was drunk.[255] Three unidentified Indians were convicted and fined in May 1905 for being drunk in Plains.[256] Four more tribal members were convicted and fined in May 1905 for being drunk in Missoula.[257] On June 1, 1905, Joseph Arlee was found dead in St. Ignatius from whiskey.[258] Dave Finley shot Nazaire Courville at a drinking party near Ronan in June 1905.[259] Chief Michelle of the Camas Prairie Kalispels and four other Indians were charged with the murder of the wife of "rich Michelle" in a drinking party in Camas in October 1905.[260] Many other deaths and injuries between 1905 and 1910 were attributed to alcohol. One of the most gruesome cases was that of William Zingele in February 1907. He was probably drunk when killed by the railroad cars at Plains. Some pieces of the body were found at Thompson Falls.[261] The church buried the body because there was no proof he was drunk.[262]

The last economic exchange on the reservation between 1905 and 1910 was theft. Most of the thefts during this period involved stealing horses. In one of a few selected examples, on January 6, 1905, someone stole a horse, saddle, and bridle from the St. Ignatius Mission stable.[263] Two months later Alex Parker accused Antoine Finley of stealing one of Parker's horses.[264] Angus P. McDonald sued M. E. Quinn, presumably a white man, for stealing a horse and gear on the reservation.[265] Pete Finley and John Gingras

stole one of Kootenai chief Koostata's work horses in August 1905.[266] Finley
and Gingras were arrested, but they had already sold the horse to a white
livery stable owner in Kalispell before the arrests.[267] The livery stable owner
refused to return the horse without a court order. Koostata needed the horse
to put in his crop and did not have enough money to buy a replacement.[268]
In September 1905 two unnamed Kootenai Indians stole three horses from
a Cree camp in the Flathead Valley. The Kootenais were surprised when
the white men considered it a crime and arrested them.[269]

A few thefts did not involve horses. For example, in April 1905 Aneas
Grandjo was charged with assaulting his father-in-law and stealing his coat
with twenty dollars in it.[270]

In 1908 and 1909 the St. Ignatius Mission was the victim of a series of
burglaries. In March 1908 a thief stole forty pounds of alfalfa seed when
the planting crew took a break to have dinner. The same day another thief
stole the eggs set under a hen and a bucket to put them in.[271] On July
1, 1908, thieves stole an expensive saddle from the mission stable.[272] In
early October 1908 thieves broke into the new milk house and stole thirty
pounds of butter. They also took a good bucket to put the butter in.[273] On
October 3, 1909, a gang of young men led by James Buckman broke into
the mission cellar and stole gallons of cider. The agency police captured
many of the gang members, and Buckman was sentenced to seventy-five
days in the agency jail. He escaped soon after. One of the gang members,
Leo Barnaby, also broke into the local post office. Since that was a federal
offense, he was sent to Helena.[274] On the night of November 21, 1909, a
gun battle broke out between the thieves, led by Anthony Finley, and the
Indian police.[275] The agent and the clerk spent the nights of November 24,
1909, and November 25, 1909, on watch at the mission. The Missoula
sheriff arrived on November 25, 1909.[276] The incidents ended when the
mission hired a full-time private policeman, Captain White, on April 12,
1910.[277] Some of the thefts were perpetrated by disgruntled ex-students. The
thefts never generated much economic benefit for the burglars, but they
did undermine the sense of security and safety felt by the sisters and priests.

Conclusion

The Flathead Reservation economy between 1905 and 1910 was just beginning to deal with the disruption caused by allotment and opening the reservation. The impact was dramatic, but mostly occurred after 1910. Allotment

did force the end of open-range grazing on the reservation, which obliged the liquidation of the large horse, cattle, and buffalo herds. Montana state efforts to limit and control Indian hunting and the depleted big game populations reduced, but did not eliminate, the value of hunting to tribal members. Grain and garden farming varied according to rainfall and small-scale private irrigation except in the Jocko Valley. Government assistance may have been reduced during this period. Many tribal members worked for money and started businesses. The Flathead Reservation economy between 1905 and 1910 was positive and vibrant. The tribes continued to be self-supporting, proud, and entrepreneurial.

Afterword
The Post-1910 Economic Implications of Allotment on the Flathead Indian Reservation

The allotment policy on the reservation proved to be the genesis for many economic changes that impacted the tribes after 1910. Allotment on Flathead had direct and indirect consequences that would cascade through the twentieth and twenty-first centuries. The details of these economic impacts after 1910 are beyond the scope of this monograph but will be outlined here.

On April 25, 1904, President Theodore Roosevelt signed "An Act for the Survey and Allotment of Lands Now Embraced Within the Limits of the Flathead Indian Reservation, in the State of Montana, and the Sale and Disposal of All Surplus Lands After Allotment."[1] The passage of the Flathead Allotment Act was a critical political accomplishment of newly elected congressman Joseph M. Dixon.[2] At first, Dixon had tried to get tribal consent to allotment. On December 19, 1903, Dixon wrote to five prominent mixed-bloods on the reservation—Allen Sloan, Angus P. McDonald, Duncan McDonald, Michel Pablo, and Joseph Allard—to solicit comments on the proposed bill. Dixon was careful to point out that the recent U.S. Supreme Court decision in *Lone Wolf v. United States* meant the government no longer needed a treaty with the tribes to open the reservation.[3] He told Angus P. McDonald, "The only thing I wouldent want to hear you say is 'that we dont want it opened at all.'"[4]

Three of the mixed-blood leaders replied. Michel Pablo wrote that he was too busy taking care of his cattle to make suggestions relative to the bill.[5]

Duncan McDonald replied that he "never was in favor of Indian Reserves it is only building up nests for Indian Agents" and proposed having agents nominated by general councils of tribal members. Regarding allotment, McDonald lamented, "I have no suggestions to make only that I am dissatisfied and disgusted and have to take my medicine."[6]

The only tribal member to support allotment was Joseph Allard, who replied, "I am glad to hear of the allotment scheme. It could not take effect any too soon to suit me. But I fear that the Indians will not give their consent at first and perhaps that Congress will finally have to act direct. I have spoken to quiet [sic] a number of the leading members of the tribes and all they could say is that we don't want to open our reserve." Allard closed with a request to be considered for a job on one of the commissions the bill would establish to implement the allotment policy on Flathead.[7]

Failing to find a fig leaf of consent to the bill from the leading mixed-bloods, Dixon went back to the 1855 Hellgate Treaty and found the ultimate sleeper clause. Article 6 of the treaty allowed the president to allot individual lots of land to tribal members. The provision also referred to article 6 of the 1854 treaty with the Omaha Indians, which provided for dividing up the Omaha tribal lands into allotments and the sale of the "excess" or "surplus" lands to nonmembers.[8] Dixon welcomed the long-overlooked treaty provision as "a message from heaven almost in my arguments before the Indian Committee" which "apparently has silenced much of the opposition" to the Flathead Allotment Bill.[9] There was no specific indication in the official 1855 council proceedings that article 6 of the treaty was explained to the Indians attending or that the Indian negotiators agreed to its provisions.[10]

To compound the lack of tribal consent, the provisions of the Flathead Allotment Bill conspired to prevent the tribes from receiving full market value for the "surplus" lands. The act provided that, except for the timber land and state school land, the "surplus" land was to be "disposed of under the general provisions of the homestead, mineral, and town-site laws of the United States."[11] These federal laws were designed to distribute land to farmers, miners, and small businessmen. They were not meant to sell the land at market value. If the land had been sold at auction over a longer period to not flood the local market, the sale could have generated more money. The Bureau of Indian Affairs made an effort to dispose of the land at a low price because "it is clearly to the benefit of the Indians to have their country settled by progressive white people."[12]

The frenzy of white people registering for Flathead Reservation land in 1909 made it obvious that the land was sold at bargain prices. In all, 80,762 prospective homesteaders registered in Missoula and Kalispell for chances to get Flathead lands.[13] In 1910 the names of 6,000 of the 80,762 applicants were called at the Missoula and Kalispell land offices, but only a little over 1,000 of those 6,000 appeared to begin the process of filing for Flathead Reservation land.[14] On November 1, 1910, the remaining "surplus" lands were opened for general homesteading on a first-come, first-served basis.[15] The rush for land indicated most of the white homesteaders expected to get the land at a bargain price. Later in the twentieth century, the U.S. Court of Claims decided the tribes had received only $1,783,549 for $7,410,000 worth of land—24 cents on the dollar.[16]

As documented in the chapter describing the Flathead Reservation economy from 1889 to 1904, by 1905 the tribes were mostly self-supporting and relatively well-off. On September 20, 1903, Indian inspector Arthur M. Tinker described the economic status of the tribes:

> The Indians and mixed-bloods (of the latter class there are many) of this reservation are said to be generally industrious and seem to be quite progressive. From all indications they appear to be in good financial condition. No supplies or rations are issued except to a few aged and infirm . . .
>
> A large majority of them are good farmers for Indians and cultivate quite good sized farms, which annually produce good crops.[17]

Research by Harvard-trained economist Ronald Trosper indicated that the allotment of the reservation accounted for virtually all of the difference between the 1969 per capita income of tribal members and the average per capita income for all United States residents that year.[18] This would suggest that poverty on the Flathead Reservation during the late twentieth century was largely the consequence of the forced sale of tribal assets through allotment.

Much of the economic consequence of allotment on the reservation would not surface until after 1910, but tribal leaders expressed their outrage and opposition repeatedly after 1904. The government refused to listen to tribal views and proceeded to impose enrollment, allotment, appraisals, and land sales on the tribes. The political and social turmoil of the frustrating fight to be heard could have impacted the tribal economy between 1905 and 1910, but the historical evidence did not have enough detail to document the effect.

As discussed in the preceding chapter, the evidence did show that the loss of open-range grazing on the reservation forced many tribal ranchers to sell off their livestock herds. The other immediate impact of allotment might have been the breaking up of the large ranches or farms, making more land available to tribal members who lacked land. This equity argument was made by some government agents, as mentioned previously, but no evidence has been found to prove or disprove it.

There is evidence that many of the allotments issued to tribal members were valuable agricultural land. Economist Ronald Trosper located data indicating that white irrigators on the Flathead Irrigation Project produced more crops per acre than did Indian irrigators. However, the Indian farms had fewer workers and less equipment and capital improvements than the white farms. When Trosper controlled for the lower labor and capital inputs of Indian farmers, he found that the Indian farmers were as productive or more productive than the white farmers. This meant that the land farmed by Indian farmers was as fertile as that farmed by white farmers on the Flathead Project.[19]

As mentioned before, the sale of "surplus" tribal land to white farmers for less than its fair market value reduced the assets and future income of tribal members. According to the U.S. Court of Claims, the tribes received only 24 percent of the value of the land.[20]

Other land sales that resulted from the allotment policy were the sales of tribal member allotments after patents were issued by the Bureau of Indian Affairs. Hopefully future researchers will determine exactly how much land was lost by tribal members through sales. The Flathead Agency conducted sales of inherited land, which discouraged families from keeping land within the family.[21] It would also be important to find out how many tribal members were selling their land willingly. Coercion and blackmail might have been involved in some sales. Another question to be researched would be whether tribal land sellers got full value for their land.

One development spawned from Flathead allotment was the Flathead Irrigation Project. The project was authorized by a 1908 congressional act pushed by Joseph Dixon. The original act provided for using tribal money to reimburse the government for construction costs of the irrigation project. Tribal members vigorously opposed using tribal money to build an irrigation system that largely benefited white homesteaders. In 1916 the tribal money was returned to the tribes, and the construction costs were made liens on the irrigated land. Water users—Indian and white—argued that they could not afford to pay the construction costs of the project from their increased production. A 1948 compromise used profits from electric power sales on the reservation to reimburse the construction costs. In the twenty-first century, water users still argued over who should operate the project and how the century-old system could be rebuilt and modernized. The irrigation project also fought long legal battles over the preexisting irrigation rights of many tribal farmers.[22]

Only a month after the Flathead Allotment bill became law on April 25, 1904, white businessmen came rushing in with plans to claim possession of the Flathead Lake dam site near Polson. On May 25, 1904, a group of white businessmen led by Frank R. Miles filed a claim for the water rights at the dam site. A month later, on June 29, 1904, another group, led by Jeremiah Miller, filed a competing claim on the site.[23] The federal government reserved the dam site, which prevented corporations from appropriating the site as private property. After years of battle, the government finally decided the dam site belonged to the tribes and that rentals would go to the tribes. When the Montana Power Company got the license to build the dam in the 1930s, they were obliged to provide the irrigation system a block of power at reduced rates, which helped pay for the irrigation construction costs. Rentals and ownership of the dam at the foot of Flathead Lake continued to roil tribal politics throughout the rest of the twentieth century. In the twenty-first century, the tribes took over ownership and operation of the dam.[24]

A final spin-off from the allotment policy was the ownership and development of the Camas hot springs on the reservation. Dixon secured legislation reserving the hot springs, and in the 1930s the tribes developed the area as a public recreation site.[25] One Kalispell newspaper expressed fears that a tribal member might get an allotment covering the hot springs and wanted "to save the springs for the benefit of the white settlers."[26] In the twenty-first century, the hot springs are tribal property, but they have only limited commercial development.

Economic development on the Flathead Reservation after 1910 is beyond the scope of this monograph. The twentieth century was full of challenges and travails for the Salish and Kootenai tribes, but their success in moving from a hunting and gathering economy to a ranching and farming economy between 1875 and 1910 suggested they could meet the new challenges.

Appendix A
Flathead Reservation Chiefs, 1875–1910

Chief Arlee, Salish/Nez Perce (ca. 1815–1889)

As a young man Arlee was an exceptionally brave warrior, and he became second chief of the Salish at the death of Chief Ambrose in 1871. He was part Nez Perce but lived all his life with the Salish. After moving from the Bitterroot Valley to the Flathead Reservation in 1873, he was a frequent critic of the operation of the Flathead Agency and the St. Ignatius Mission. Despite his unhappiness, he cooperated with Flathead Agent Peter Ronan in keeping peace on the reservation and was a prominent speaker at church celebrations. Almost all we know about his views was recorded by his opponents, but he was obviously a capable, opinionated person who would not agree to let white men run tribal affairs.[1]

Arlee became well known as a warrior, but only a few examples of his bravery were recorded. In 1835 Arlee had a horse shot out from under him while leading the attack on a retreating party of Blackfeet who had just killed three Hawaiian Hudson's Bay Company employees at Evaro. According to Duncan McDonald, Arlee was "in many big battles which took place between the various western tribes."[2]

In addition to his war exploits, Arlee was a successful farmer and rancher in the Bitterroot Valley. In 1860 or 1861 Arlee traded 3 and 3/4 bushels of wheat to Thomas W. Harris, a white man living in the Bitterroot Valley, in exchange for $18 in merchandise at the local store. On February 20, 1864, Arlee sold Harris a two-year-old steer.[3]

Arlee was elected second chief of the Bitterroot Salish in 1871. According to Duncan McDonald, the younger Salish were worried that, since Charlo did not drink or gamble, they needed a second chief who would be less severe: "So the young gamblers elected Arlee as second Chief. But Arelee [sic] fooled the gamblers & wets. & reformed. change to a good sober temperate man he was more severe one than Charlo."[4]

Angus McDonald described the twenty-year-old Arlee as "a bold, well proportioned youth," but in later years Arlee was corpulent. In 1877 Bishop James O'Connor described Arlee: "He wore a white Kossuth hat and a blue blanket, and an eagle's wing hung at his girdle. Obesity had taken all grace from his figure, but I thought I had never seen a finer head or face than his. I could hardly take my eyes off him." Peter Ronan's wife, Mary, described Arlee as "a fat and pompous monarch." In 1887 he was five feet, four inches tall and weighed over two hundred pounds.[5]

In 1872, when Congressman James Garfield came to the Bitterroot Valley to negotiate with the Salish, Arlee and Adolph agreed to leave, but Charlo refused. Arlee worried that the government would take the Jocko Valley from the Salish just as they had the Bitterroot Valley, but he finally signed.[6] Arlee and five related families moved from the Bitterroot Valley to the Jocko Valley on the Flathead Indian Reservation in 1873. Later that year, Flathead Agent Daniel Shanahan had the federal government recognize Arlee as head chief of all the Salish.[7] With the support of Agent Charles Medary, Arlee organized a police force among the Salish in 1875, which was under Arlee's control.[8]

Between 1875 and 1877 Arlee was involved in a bitter fight with Flathead Indian agent Charles S. Medary. Arlee's opposition to Medary had some support from Chief Michelle of the Pend d'Oreilles, and considerable financial and legal support from T. J. Demers, a white Frenchtown merchant who had married into the tribes. Arlee's complaints about Flathead Agency management under Medary were aired in Montana Territory newspapers and a federal grand jury. Arlee made so much trouble for Medary that the commissioner of Indian affairs asked for Medary's resignation. Basically Arlee and his allies were able to run the agent out of town.[9]

Arlee frequently criticized the Jesuit missionaries at St. Ignatius Mission, but also took a leading role in church festivals. In 1875 missionary Philip Rappagliosi, S.J., visited Arlee in the Jocko Valley and tried to mollify Arlee's anger at the mission. Rappagliosi never really explained Arlee's complaints and believed Arlee was motivated only by an irrational pique. Whatever the basis of Arlee's feelings, Rappagliosi claimed he won Arlee "back completely," and Arlee came to St. Ignatius for the next Easter feast.[10] In July 1883 Arlee complained to U.S. Indian inspector S. S. Benedict about the management of the St. Ignatius Mission school and said, "he wants his people to be taught something besides how to pray." Ronan argued in two letters, November 24, 1883, and December 26, 1883, that Arlee was just a general complainer motivated by greed.[11]

That fall Arlee repeated his complaints about the mission school to Senator G. G. Vest and his party, who were visiting Flathead Agency. Vest concluded Arlee was upset because his son had been put to work on the harvest while a student at the school. Ronan made the same argument in his letter of November 24, 1883.[12] In 1887 Arlee wrote the "Supretenant of indian Afares" complaining about the Flathead Agency and St. Ignatius Mission that "we have a Cotholic Skool here 23 years and none of my children Can read or write yet. we want a skoole here. we dont want any Priests they are no good."[13]

But even as Arlee complained about the missionaries, he was an active speaker and participant in church celebrations. According to an oral tradition, on Christmas Day 1876 Arlee was on the buffalo plains and led a Christian religious service to celebrate the occasion.[14] A Helena newspaper story about the 1882 St. Ignatius Day celebration reported that after the school program was completed, Arlee spoke to the assembled crowd in Salish. He welcomed Archbishop Charles Seghers to the mission, condemned the young Indians for drinking and fighting, and led the crowd in the rosary. Arlee also spoke at the 1884 St. Ignatius Day celebration, but then his speech was that the school exhibition was "all very good but that he was very hungry, and that it was time to go and eat."[15]

Arlee's relations with Agent Peter Ronan could also be contradictory: including both support and complaints about how Ronan ran the agency. On July 11, 1877, Ronan reported that Arlee swore that he and his people would defend the white people against the hostile Nez Perces. During the fall of 1881 Arlee was said to have told Gen. John Gibbon that his opinion of Ronan was positive: "As the agent of the government we respect him; as a friend, an advisor and a neighbor, we love him, and I trust I may never live to see the appointment of his successor."[16] In 1882 a Colonel Warrington visited the Flathead Reservation and Arlee's house. Warrington recollected that Arlee had a log cabin with a fenced yard that also enclosed a tepee and estimated that Arlee was worth some twenty thousand dollars. The cabin contained "a rusty stove, with an old tin coffee-pot on it, a deal table, a chair, a pile of blankets down in one corner, for a bed" and a picture of President James Garfield on the wall.[17]

Arlee could be very diplomatic in his personal relations. On one occasion he informed Ronan's young daughter, Mary, that she had been given the Indian name of "Red Hair," but little Mary objected. Arlee then declared that the girl's Indian name would be "Pretty Hair," which met with her approval.[18]

In August 1882 Arlee played a prominent role in the negotiations between the Flathead Reservation tribes and Joseph McCammon for the sale of the right-of-way for the Northern Pacific Railroad through the reservation. Arlee wanted the railroad to head down the Clark's Fork River and bypass the reservation, but McCammon said he was not able to change the route. Arlee countered by asking for a million dollars for the right-of-way. A shocked McCammon argued that the whole reservation was not worth that much. McCammon finally conceded that the reservation might be worth a million dollars to the tribes, but refused to offer more than $16,000 plus reimbursement for the timber used by the railroad. The chiefs got McCammon to promise to use his influence to get the Upper Flathead Valley added to the reservation. With this concession, the chiefs finally agreed to let the railroad have use of the land—but not to outright sell the right-of-way land—and they signed the agreement. The written agreement, however, had language transferring full title to the right-of-way land to the railroad. McCammon did submit a request to the Department of Interior to enlarge the reservation, but by 1883 the tribes decided they could not risk any boundary changes and dropped the idea.[19]

On June 21, 1882, Koonsa Finley murdered Frank Marengo on the reservation during a drinking party. After sobering up, Koonsa went to Chief Michelle and confessed. Arlee and Michelle took Koonsa's horses and put him in the tribal jail as punishment for the murder. To Ronan's disgust, the U.S. District Court dismissed federal murder charges against Koonsa, because he had already been tried for the crime under tribal law and prosecution in federal court would be double jeopardy, which was prohibited under the U.S. Constitution.[20]

This case was the opening volley in a long-running battle between Arlee and Ronan over control of law and order on the reservation. Arlee's testimony in the federal case against Koonsa in late 1882 was published in a local newspaper. Arlee defended traditional Indian justice dispensed by the chiefs, which did not allow for long terms in the territorial prison in Deer Lodge or hanging. Arlee also claimed that the white men who sold the liquor shared responsibility for the murder: "When an Indian is drunk and kills another Indian we don't consider that he did anything. The Indian never had whiskey before the white man came here, and we blame the white people who gave him the liquor."[21]

Ronan and Arlee cooperated in arranging a series of foot and horse races by tribal members during the summer of 1883 to entertain a group of Northern Pacific Railroad officials who were visiting the Jocko Valley. The white visitors paid for the prizes for the winners.[22]

On December 4, 1883, Inspector C. H. Howard reported to the secretary of interior about complaints by Indians on the Flathead Reservation. Most of the complaints seem to have come from Arlee. Arlee's criticisms indicated Agent Ronan had stolen agency cattle and ran his personal cattle with the stock of white men trespassing on the reservation. But when Howard questioned Peter Finley, whom Arlee claimed originally made the allegations, Finley denied the charges.[23] According to Ronan's January 15, 1884, letter, Arlee later recanted and claimed the charges against Ronan were based on hearsay.[24] Tribal members Louison and Thomas McDonald supported Ronan's rebuttal to the charges.

In December 1885 Arlee joined other tribal leaders and Agent Ronan to defuse a hazardous situation that developed from the killing of an intoxicated Indian by the white trader and the white postmaster at Arlee station. The crisis brought the Missoula County sheriff and an armed white posse on the reservation. The sheriff wanted to arrest the surviving Indian involved in the altercation, Big Jim, and take him to Missoula. Some tribal members wanted to keep Big Jim on the reservation to try him under tribal law. Arlee supported allowing the sheriff to take Big Jim to Missoula to avoid conflict with the whites. The final decision by the assembled tribal members was to let the sheriff take Big Jim to be tried by the white justice system. In the end the two white men were released by the court on the basis of self-defense, and Big Jim was released for lack of evidence.[25]

In the final years of his life, Arlee opposed the Flathead Agency–sponsored courts and police established in 1885, which undermined the authority of the traditional chiefs on the reservation. In an April 29, 1887, speech on the reservation before the Northwest Indian Commission, Arlee said, "We don't want any judges or policemen. We want the chiefs to rule the people." Arlee charged that the judges had a sick man and a pregnant woman whipped and the woman had a miscarriage.[26]

Ronan wrote on January 1, 1887, about his efforts to arrest a member of Arlee's household who had been accused of adultery.[27] Arlee's refusal to acknowledge the authority of the agency court and police led to an impasse where Ronan would no longer deal with Arlee on tribal business. Ronan also charged that Arlee had received money from the government and grown personally rich and greedy. The characterization of Arlee as personally greedy was also made by Agent Medary during their battles in the middle 1870s. Unfortunately we do not have Chief Arlee's side of the argument to balance the charges against him.

Arlee did become well-to-do on the reservation. On March 19, 1878, Ronan reported that Arlee, his son, and his daughter together owned 2 hogs, 100 cattle, and 100 horses.[28] In his August 1885 annual report Ronan credited Arlee as having 160 acres under fence and an 1884 crop of 800 bushels of wheat and oats.[29] In his August 17, 1885, testimony, Ronan listed Arlee as having 100 horses and 150 cattle.[30]

In early 1889 the conflict between Arlee and the agency-sanctioned tribal court flared up again. Arlee made two trips to the offices of the *Weekly Missoulian* to complain about "merciless" whippings administered by the tribal judges to both men and women: "Recently, it is claimed, men and women have been beaten cruelly and out of all reason." During his second visit, Arlee's "right hand man" claimed "an Indian who had broke jail was hung up by his hands and kept there for forty-eight hours. An Indian woman who is supposed to have deserted her husband was given 120 lashes and is now lying in a precarious condition and her recovery is extremely doubtful." Arlee wanted offenders to be punished "just as white people are punished; no more and no less."[31] In letters to the commissioner of Indian affairs on May 1, 1889, and June 17, 1889, and a May 14, 1889, article in the *Helena Independent*, Ronan argued that Arlee's only supporters were murderers and rapists, particularly Larra Finley, who made "sensational and lying complains against the cruelty of the Indian police."[32]

On August 8, 1889, Arlee died at his house in the Jocko Valley of dropsy at about seventy-four years of age. On his deathbed Arlee was surrounded by his relatives, tribal leaders, and Agent Ronan and other agency employees. He had recently been visited by Bishop John Brondel and Father Jerome D'Aste, S.J., who gave him the last rites of the Roman Catholic Church. According to Mary Ronan, his funeral was "a grand occasion and Indians gathered from far and wide to attend." His funeral was at the Jocko Church and his burial in the Jocko Cemetery. One account said over a half a dozen fat steers were roasted for the funeral feast.[33]

Much of the surviving evidence about Chief Arlee's life is contradictory and incomplete. He was a dynamic but enigmatic figure in Flathead Reservation history.

Chief Charlo (Little-Claw-of-a-Grizzly-Bear), Salish (1830–1910)

Charlo succeeded his father, Victor, as chief of the Bitterroot Salish tribe in 1870. He continued Victor's policies of allying with the white men against the Blackfeet, Sioux, and other Plains tribes, and protecting the tribe's right to their homeland in the Bitterroot Valley. As the buffalo declined, he worked hard to expand the tribe's farms and stock herds to maintain its economic independence.

In his July 11, 1877, letter, Flathead Indian agent Peter Ronan reported that Charlo refused to join the Nez Perces in fighting the white settlers.[34] Charlo said he and his tribe would protect the Bitterroot whites if needed, but otherwise would not attack the Nez Perces. Charlo wanted peace with the white people, but insisted that a correct interpretation of the 1855 Hellgate Treaty entitled the Salish to a reservation in the Bitterroot Valley.[35]

Father Lawrence Palladino, S.J., characterized Charlo as

a man of a quiet yet firm disposition, a true representative of his race and a thorough Indian. . . . His conduct during the Nez Percés outbreak gained him the admiration of all, and proved once more the loyal friendship for the whites on the part of the Flat Heads. . . . But while friendly toward the whites, he surely is not in love with their ways. . . . Charlot is a sincere and practical Christian.[36]

Between 1877, when Ronan began his term, and 1889, Charlo worked to develop his farm and encouraged other tribal members to do the same. In 1877 a newspaper reporter described his farm:

Charlos, the Flathead chief, has a home in their [the Bitterroot Flathead settlement's] midst. His dwelling is a two-story log house with four rooms, and his farm which covers over a pretty little park before his house, encloses seven or eight acres, upon which there is a good growing crop of wheat.[37]

In 1889 the Bitterroot Salish and their white neighbors suffered through a record drought, and the resulting poverty forced Charlo and the Salish to agree to remove to the Jocko Valley.

Between January and March 1884, Charlo, four other Bitterroot Salish leaders, interpreter Michel Revais, and Ronan visited Washington, D.C.[38] The government tried to induce the Salish to move to the Flathead Reservation, but Charlo insisted he only wanted to secure the tribe's right to remain in the Bitterroot Valley. Their time in Washington was well documented in Ronan's surviving writings and correspondence. While in Washington, Charlo had a successful operation to remove cataracts from his eyes.

In the Bitterroot Valley during the 1880s, Charlo and the other Salish maintained a delicate balance trying to protect their rights while also maintaining peace with their white neighbors. Ronan's November 1, 1881, letter described Charlo's efforts to get justice for the murder of Cayuse Pierre in a drunken brawl with two white men in Stevensville.[39]

Ronan's letters gave only brief glimpses of the 1889 negotiations between Henry B. Carrington and the Salish, where drought and poverty finally forced Charlo and the Salish to agree to leave the Bitterroot Valley. The letters do detail the further impoverishment of the Salish between 1889 and 1891 resulting from the delay in the removal that Carrington promised would happen in the spring of 1890.[40]

After the removal in 1891 Ronan had trouble getting the government to fund the promises Carrington had made to Charlo and the other Salish. In his March 10, 1892, letter, Ronan described turning the agency farm over to Charlo in lieu of the late Chief Arlee's farm, which Carrington had promised.[41] Ronan's November 30, 1892, letter related the difficulties the Salish had in getting the government to pay them for the Bitterroot allotments as they were sold.[42]

On the reservation, Charlo worked hard to preserve the tribal culture and ways and was worried about the negative impact schooling would have on Salish youth. An Ursuline nun working at the Jocko Agency school during the early 1890s described dealing with Charlo:

The chief was an Indian to the core. Although he had always been on good terms with the whites, he detested their ways. "Our children," he objected, "will learn English in school. When they know English, they will go to the white towns and buy whiskey. The white man would not understand them if they spoke in Indian. In the school the hair of our children will be cut. We do not wish to see them with short hair. Only the white man was made by God to wear his hair short. God made the Indian with long hair. Our children will become like whites in other ways in school and, when they grow up they will fly away like birds and leave their parents." . . . The chief protested up to the very day we opened [the Jocko school]. Nevertheless, he sent his own son, little Victor.[43]

Charlo joined the other tribal leaders on the reservation in fighting to protect the reservation land base from white encroachment. During the early twentieth century he fought vigorously to prevent the reservation from being allotted and "surplus" land sold to white settlers. He died in the Jocko in 1910 just as the government was completing the forced allotment and opening of the reservation without tribal consent.[44]

Chief Eneas Big Knife, Kootenai (1828–1900)

Eneas, the chief of the Dayton Creek or Ksanka Kootenai for thirty-five years, was born in 1828 to an Iroquois father, Big Knife, and a Kootenai mother, Suzette or Ahn-Akah.[45] The historical evidence suggested he was a remarkable man, and Flathead Indian agent Peter Ronan obviously came to respect him highly over their years working together. During the 1880s and early 1890s, the reservation Kootenai faced white aggression in the Upper Flathead Valley, but somehow the Kootenais under Eneas's leadership were able to avoid war and continue the struggle to protect their interests and rights. The government often failed to fulfill its promises to protect Kootenai property and rights, but the small band avoided the destruction and death that could have resulted from open warfare.

As a young man, Eneas was a leading warrior and a war chief. He took part in repeated battles with the Blackfeet, Cree, and other tribes.[46] At six feet, four inches tall, Eneas was an imposing figure.[47] According to Flathead Agent Charles Hutchins, Eneas became head chief on January 1, 1865, after his predecessor, Battiste, was killed by the Blackfeet while returning from the buffalo country. Eneas was only thirty-seven years old then. In 1866 Flathead agent Augustus Chapman requested funds to build a house for Eneas and his family.[48]

In his first annual report on August 13, 1877, Flathead Indian agent Peter Ronan wrote that Eneas was "better respected and has more influence among his people than any other chief on the reservation." Ronan was especially impressed that Eneas used his salary as chief to purchase a mowing and reaping machine and a set of blacksmith's tools for the use of his tribe. Eneas was "a good man, kind and generous, and spends all the money he receives from Government in relieving the wants of his poor and struggling people."[49] In his August 12, 1879, report, Ronan commended Eneas for working to induce the Kootenais to turn to farming to replace the declining game and gathering resources in western Montana.[50] By 1879 the Kootenais had enclosed several farms.

By August 1885 Eneas and the Kootenais had 200 acres fenced and "about 1,000 bushels of wheat [were] raised in common, besides potatoes, turnips, cabbage, onions, carrots, parsnips, peas, &c."[51] But farming in common offended Ronan's Euro-American cultural values, and in August 15, 1886, Ronan proposed that a farmer be employed to show the Kootenais how to set up individual family farms like white people had.[52]

In 1883, when Joseph McCammon came to Montana to negotiate for the sale of the right-of-way for the Northern Pacific Railroad to cross the reservation, Eneas emphasized the importance of the reservation to the tribes. Eneas questioned selling part of the reservation because: "It is a small country; it is valuable to us; we support ourselves by it; there is no end to these lands supporting us; they will do it for generations."[53]

Due to their location on the northern boundary of the reservation, the Kootenais were particularly affected by problems with the survey of the reservation boundary. Eneas and the Kootenais thought the northern line followed a ridge of hills that provided a well-defined natural boundary. The official survey placed the line several miles south of the hills. In the twentieth century the U.S. Court of Claims decided the official boundary had been in error but still placed the line south of the boundary preferred by the Kootenais. This change in the northern boundary made it harder to keep white-owned cattle off the reservation and also cut off hay and pasture land used for years by the Kootenais. Some of the white cattle owners paid Eneas for grazing, but trespassing cattle and loss of land caused problems for Eneas and his tribe for the rest of the nineteenth century.[54]

During the late 1880s and early 1890s, the Kootenais continued to exercise their right to seasonally hunt, fish, and gather plants in the Upper Flathead Valley. Most of the Kootenai-white interactions were peaceful, but some were complicated by language and cultural differences, alcohol, and white aggression. In 1888 two reservation Kootenai were lynched for murdering two white men at the head of Flathead Lake in 1887. After the lynching, an armed mob of white men invaded the reservation and confronted Eneas and the Kootenais. Eneas kept calm and was able to defuse the crisis, and no further violence broke out. Eneas did not object to the punishment of Kootenai murderers, but he felt they should at least receive a fair trial.[55]

In 1889 Eneas kept up his efforts to get justice while avoiding open warfare. Two white men killed a Kootenai Indian in an altercation that probably involved alcohol. Eneas threatened to kill the two guilty whites but made clear that other white people would not be harmed.[56]

In a June 8, 1889, council with Ronan and a special agent of the U.S. Justice Department about the whiskey problem, Eneas emphasized his work to punish Kootenais guilty of violence resulting from alcohol use. Traditional Kootenai practice had the chief use the whip to punish lawbreakers, but white officials opposed whipping because it offended nineteenth-century white sensibilities. Eneas complained that without the whip, he could not control tribal members who got drunk and committed adultery or other crimes. He pointed out that the Kootenais did not have good jails, so he had no alternative punishment available. One account quotes Delima Demers Clifford, a tribal member, as seeing Eneas drinking alcohol on New Year's Eve 1887. But even if Eneas was not a teetotaler, he vigorously opposed the violence and other crimes that sometimes resulted from drinking.[57]

Eneas's struggle to get justice for the Kootenais while keeping the peace struck a personal note in August 1889 when his son, Samuel, was murdered by white people in Demersville. Eneas traveled to Demersville to find out what happened. The white people fed the Kootenais but refused to help bring the murderer to justice. The Demersville whites fumed and ranted that Eneas's visit had been an invasion. Ronan put Eneas's side of the story in writing, sent it to Washington, D.C., and had it published in a Helena newspaper and the commissioner of Indian affairs' annual report.[58] In December, Ronan tried to get the case before a grand jury, but the jury adjourned before he was able to get Eneas and the Indian witnesses to the courthouse. No one was ever punished for the murder.[59]

In July 1890 U.S. Army troops and a posse of white men surrounded the Kootenai camp and demanded that Eneas surrender Kootenai Indians accused of murdering white men. Eneas offered to cooperate, but he asked why white men who killed Kootenai were not also punished. According to newspaper reports, Missoula County sheriff William Houston held Eneas hostage until the accused Indian murderers were surrendered, but Ronan's letters suggested Eneas decided himself to help the sheriff. Ronan wrote that Eneas did not object to Indian murderers being punished but wanted equal justice for white people who murdered Indians.[60] Father Jerome D'Aste, S.J., recorded the hostage version of Eneas's role in his diary.[61] One newspaper account noted that "it is largely due to his [Eneas's] aid that Pascale and other Indian criminals have been apprehended."[62] Two Kootenai Indians were convicted in a Montana court of murder and hung in Missoula in December 1890.

In January 1891 Robert H. Irvine, a mixed-blood tribal member chosen by Eneas, was finally appointed as Kootenai farmer and moved to Dayton Creek to begin work. That October Eneas and the Kootenais brought several wagonloads of wheat to the agency to be ground into flour. The trip of sixty miles to the agency took six days and a ferry crossing the Flathead River at the foot of Flathead Lake. According to Ronan, Eneas was "much elated at the acchievement [sic]."[63] That summer Eneas and the reservation Kootenai extended an invitation to the Bonners Ferry Kootenai to settle with them at Dayton Creek.[64]

In August 1891 Ronan traveled to the Kootenai camp and laid out off-reservation allotments for land just north of the official reservation boundary. The land had been used for years by the Kootenais, who believed it was on the reservation. Unfortunately, by December of that year, white homesteaders were already jumping the Kootenai allotments. Ronan was able to get the government to remove the first white trespassers, but others persisted in harassing the Kootenai farmers.[65]

In one particularly egregious example of white belligerence, Clarence Proctor actually built a fence around the improvements of a Kootenai farmer and claimed the right to the land in the enclosure, including the Kootenai farm.[66] In another case Eugene McCarthy, a white settler who had worked on the erroneous boundary survey, claimed the land of a Kootenai farmer, Jean Jan Graw (Gingras), which contained a house, barn, and enclosed field that the Kootenais had occupied for twelve years. Eneas was crippled by rheumatism and hindered by language problems, but he tried to explain to McCarthy that the land belonged to the Kootenai farmer as a result of years of occupancy and a government allotment. McCarthy then proceeded to Demersville and filed charges against Eneas, claiming that

Eneas had personally threatened him. Ronan put up a bond for Eneas to appear in court on the charge since Eneas was too sick to travel just then. Apparently the charges were later dropped as the case dragged on in the courts.[67] The restraint shown by Eneas and the aggrieved Kootenai farmers was remarkable. No open conflict flared, but white trespassers continued over the years to encroach on the Kootenai claims, and after Ronan died in 1893, no one else seemed to pressure the government to act. Finally in the early twentieth century the Kootenais had lost possession of almost all of the allotments, and the government pressured the Kootenai allottees to relinquish their claims in return for small payments from the white trespassers.

On February 1, 1894, Eneas, most reservation tribal leaders, and many tribal members signed a petition asking for a resurvey of the northern boundary of the reservation, but Agent Joseph Carter panned it as a "matter worthy of little attention." The commissioner of Indian affairs refused to consider a resurvey.[68] In 1895 Eneas returned Goosta, a Kootenai Indian accused of horse stealing, to jail after he escaped.[69] Eneas was again called upon to defend the tribe in 1898 when Missoula County tried to tax most of the mixed-bloods and adopted tribal members on the reservation. When Eneas claimed jurisdiction over the reservation and tribal members, the Missoula deputy county treasurer replied: "What I want to tell that old Indian is that he may go to h—. . . . Tell him that this is not his country, but that it belongs to the government at Washington." Fortunately, despite the racist hostility of the county officials, the government won most of the court cases against the taxes.[70]

In much of the late 1890s Eneas was confined to his bed and not able to exercise his authority as chief. Father Augustine Dimier, S.J., complained that Eneas's disability permitted gambling and other sins to reinfect Kootenai life.[71] Eneas died in 1900.[72]

Chief Michelle, Pend d'Oreille (1805–1897)

Chief Michelle of the Upper Pend d'Oreille Indians actively worked to maintain peace with the white settlers and supported the missionaries at St. Ignatius Mission. Most accounts suggest he was less active and influential in tribal affairs than his predecessor Alexander. He was spokesman for decisions reached by the tribal community, often after long hours of collective deliberation.[73]

According to information that probably came from Michel Revais, the Pend d'Oreille Flathead Agency interpreter, Michelle was elected Pend d'Oreille chief in 1868. Michelle had previously been only a minor chief, but two more senior subchiefs, Andre and Pierre, declined the office. Little has been recorded about his life before 1868.[74]

The one event before 1868 that has been documented was the 1864 lynching of Michelle's son by white miners at Hell Gate, near present-day Missoula. A white miner named Ward had been killed near Hell Gate by an Indian in the fall of 1863. Michelle's son was accused of the murder but maintained his innocence. According to an account given by Michelle in the early 1880s, Michelle asked his son to "sacrifice his life for the good of his people" and "go bravely to death" to avoid war with the whites. His son was lynched and later evidence indicted the murder had been committed by an Indian from another tribe.[75]

Michelle was known for his Christian piety and loyalty to the missionaries. In 1882 he delivered a speech at the St. Ignatius Day celebrations, but the topic was not recorded. According to Duncan McDonald, Michelle "punishes severely to this day any member of his tribe who refuses to believe in his creed." McDonald also reported that sometime around 1870, Chief Michelle used traditional Indian medicine to attract buffalo to a Pend d'Oreille hunting camp on the Plains. He may have valued the power of both Christianity and traditional Pend d'Oreille religious beliefs.[76]

Michelle suffered a tragic accident in late April 1872 when he was thrown from his horse and dislocated his hip. The agency doctor and Father Anthony Ravalli were not able to reset the joint, and Michelle was crippled for the rest of his life.[77]

In December 1873 Michelle recounted the recent history of conflict between the Pend d'Oreilles and the Crow Indians. The Crows had killed four Pend d'Oreilles during the summer of 1873, including Michelle's father-in-law Cow-ackan. During spring 1873 the Crows killed two more Pend d'Oreilles and wounded three women and a boy. One of the women was not expected to survive. The Crows stole thirty-one Pend d'Oreille horses and a mule from a hunting camp in the Little Blackfoot in the fall of 1872. Ten years before, in 1863, the Crows stole eighty Pend d'Oreille horses and blamed it on the Snakes, igniting a war between the Pend d'Oreilles and the Snakes. Michelle complained: "When we go to the Crow country we always go in peace but the Crows always attack us first."[78]

Michelle swore out a statement on May 2, 1874, before a justice of the peace complaining about Flathead agent Daniel Shanahan. The statement was forwarded to Washington, D.C., by T. J. Demers, a white Frenchtown merchant who had married into the tribes. Michelle accused Shanahan of stealing tribal annuities and of trying to force off the reservation five white men who had tribal member wives and mixed-blood children. Michelle also complained that Shanahan had stopped the treaty payments to the St. Ignatius Mission schools. Other treaty promises of services to the tribes had never been fulfilled. Michelle wanted Shanahan removed as agent and asked that "the choice of an agent for them [the Flathead Reservation tribes] be left to the Indians themselves and that they by Election or otherwise with the approval of the reverend fathers of the mission—shall name who shall be agent for them."[79]

During 1874 Chiefs Michelle and Arlee demanded that the agency employees cut their hay and grain. Agent Peter Whaley asked the commissioner of Indian affairs for instructions because while Michelle was poor and crippled, Arlee was well-to-do and, according to Whaley, did not need the help.[80] In his September 12, 1874, annual report, Whaley reported that, while on the annual buffalo hunt, the Pend d'Oreilles stole horses from other tribes and refused to return them. Since Michelle was crippled, he could no longer accompany the buffalo hunters and was unable to stop the raids. Michelle was "powerless to exact obedience to his commands." Whaley wanted the government to promote the second chief, Andre, to head the Pend d'Oreilles, because Andre "appears to have the confidence of his people and to influence them according to his will."[81]

Michelle's dealings with Flathead agent Charles S. Medary between 1875 and 1877 were also stormy. Michelle supported Chief Arlee's complaints against Medary about the operation of the agency. In December, Michelle, Arlee, and Duncan McDonald, a mixed-blood trader on the reservation, traveled to Deer Lodge to present their complaints to the United States grand jury. Most of the indictments referred to the failure of the government to fulfill promises made in the 1855 Hellgate Treaty and 1872 agreement between Congressman James Garfield and the Bitterroot Salish. During the 1870s Michelle lived on a farm near the agency in the Jocko Valley while most of the Pend d'Oreilles lived near the St. Ignatius Mission in the Lower Flathead Valley. Since Michelle did not live among his tribe and could not accompany them on the buffalo hunts, in 1875 Medary wrote that Andre was "chief in all but drawing a salary from the Government." Medary did claim in September 1876 that he had convinced Michelle to give up the practice of whipping women who were guilty of adultery.[82]

Michelle's relations with Flathead agent Peter Ronan, 1877–93, were much more cordial. In his July 11, 1877, letter during the Nez Perce War crisis, Ronan wrote that Michelle joined the other reservation chiefs in promising to maintain peace with the whites. Michelle personally assured the Ronan family of protection during the scare and offered to guard the agency.[83]

In his August 13, 1877, annual report, Ronan wrote that Michelle had lost influence among the Pend d'Oreilles because he lived at the agency, some twenty miles from most of the tribe, and could no longer travel on the buffalo hunts. Ronan concluded that Michelle "has in a great measure lost control, a fact which he is well aware of himself, as he came to consult in regard to removing from the agency and going back among his people, with a view of regaining his lost influence."[84] On March 19, 1878, Michelle lived in the Jocko Valley and had twenty-six cattle and nineteen horses.[85]

Ronan forwarded a report to the commissioner of Indian affairs on July 29, 1878, about a July 14, 1878, council with Chief Michelle about recent violence committed by some Nez Perce refugees returning from exile in Canada. Michelle informed Ronan of a message he had received from Sitting Bull threatening the Pend d'Oreilles if they did not join the fight against the whites. Michelle replied that the Pend d'Oreilles were friends of the whites and traditional enemies of the Sioux. He assured Sitting Bull: "We are not well armed, and have nearly forgotten the modes of war; but a mouse though small, if trodden upon will turn and bite. Tell your chief if he comes we will give him battle, and die by our homes." When asked to provide scouts to watch for possible war parties coming west across the mountains, Michelle agreed, but only if the scouts were given supplies, arms, and pay and were under his and Ronan's control.[86]

In November 1878 Michelle demonstrated his personal diplomatic skills when he bestowed his Indian name, Plenty Grizzly Bear, on the Ronans' newborn son. Michelle then had no Indian name until the Lower Kalispels granted him permission to take the Indian name of their recently deceased chief, Man Who Regrets His Country. The name transfers were formally announced at the 1878 Christmas celebrations at St. Ignatius Mission.[87]

Koonsa Finley committed murder on June 21, 1882, but after sobering up, he went to Chief Michelle and confessed. Michelle and Arlee took Finley's horses and put him in the tribal jail for a short term. When Ronan came to arrest Finley and transport him to Missoula, Michelle argued that he was chief and had already decided the case. Ronan countered that Finley had committed an offense against the United States government and so fell under the jurisdiction of the agent and the federal courts. Finley was tried for murder in the United States court in Deer Lodge but was released because he had already been tried and punished under tribal law. This frustrated Ronan's efforts to try Finley in a white court, where he could have been sentenced to the penitentiary at Deer Lodge or hung.[88]

During the September 1882 negotiations between Joseph McCammon of the U.S. Interior Department and the Flathead Reservation tribes for the Northern Pacific Railroad right-of-way, Michelle supported selling the right-of-way. When McCammon replied to Chief Arlee's request for $1,000,000 for the right-of-way by stating that the whole reservation was not worth that much, Michelle was offended: "Now I do not agree with you." McCammon explained that he did not mean the reservation was not worth a million dollars to the Indians. Michelle countered that the government's offer of $15,000 was too low, as after the railroad was completed, it would make that much in a day. Michelle offered to exchange the right-of-way for an extension of the reservation boundary to include the Upper Flathead Valley. During the negotiations Michelle emphasized that the tribes were not selling the land, just the use of the right-of-way:

MICHELLE: . . . it is borrowing this strip of land.
COMMISSIONER: It is the use of it.
MICHELLE: I don't want you, after you get away, to let the white people suppose you have bought the reservation, and let the white people squat on it. That is the way I think. It is like the railroad borrowing the strip of land.
COMMISSIONER: It is just buying the use of the strip of land.

The written agreement, however, said the tribes "do hereby surrender and relinquish to the United States, all the right, title, and interest which they now have" to the right-of-way land.[89]

When Senator G. G. Vest of Missouri and Montana delegate Martin Maginnis visited the reservation in September 1883, tribal members met for two days ahead of time to discuss the issues and select Michelle to be their spokesman for the collective decisions. Tribal members decided they did not want to run the risk of being cheated in moving the boundary of the reservation north to the Canadian border, so they opposed any boundary changes. The Bitterroot Salish were welcome to move to the reservation, but the tribes categorically rejected allotment:

> SENATOR VEST: Don't you think it would be better to have more money and cattle and less land?
>
> MICHELLE: If I had good and plenty land and few cattle and a little money I would be glad. The reverse would not please me, because my children are cultivating the land more and so get money.

When asked if the St. Ignatius schoolchildren were happy, Michelle replied: "Yes; because their fathers send the children to learn, and therefore they will be happy if they are taught to read and write." Michelle also wanted the white people to stop selling liquor and playing cards to the Indians.[90]

The Northwest Indian Commission negotiated with the Flathead Reservation tribes in April 1887, and Michelle declared that the Lower Pend d'Oreilles or Kalispel Indians and Spokane Indians would be welcome on the reservation. The proposed agreement also "set apart" two sections of land for the use of the Jesuits and Sisters at the St. Ignatius schools "for educational and religious purposes, as long as they are used for said purposes and no longer." Michelle made sure during the negotiations that the land was being lent and not sold to the missionaries.[91]

By the middle of the 1880s Michelle had moved to a ranch on Mud Creek, sixteen miles north of the mission. In 1885 he had 160 acres under fence, and in 1884 he raised 250 bushels of wheat and oats. In 1885 he had twenty horses and fifteen cattle. In 1887 he purchased $31 worth of fruit trees for his ranch.[92]

Sometime during the summer or autumn of 1888 Chief Michelle's nephew and family were murdered while hunting in the Sun River area. Evidence found at the scene suggested that the murderers were either white men or Cree mixed-bloods. Despite Ronan's efforts to publicize the case and get the local white authorities to investigate, no one was ever charged with the crime.[93]

The white Montana justice authorities showed much more interest in pursuing Indian people who were accused of murdering white people. During August 1890 Missoula County sheriff William Houston arrested Chief Eneas of the Kootenais and Chief Michelle and held them hostage until local Indian people and the Indian police delivered up tribal members wanted for murdering white men. Baptiste Kakashe and a party of armed Pend d'Oreilles tried to force the white posse to release Michelle, but in order to avoid conflict, Michelle refused to go. Michelle was released after Pierre Paul was captured by the Indian police and a white posse. Ronan gave most of the credit to the Indian police, but the Montana newspapers played up the role of the sheriff and posse.[94]

On May 11, 1897, Chief Michelle died at his home on Mud Creek at the age of ninety-two. He was buried at St. Ignatius Mission.[95]

Appendix B
Flathead Reservation Indian Agents, 1875–1910

Charles S. Medary (1841–1901)

As part of President Ulysses S. Grant's Peace Policy, Indian agents in the 1870s were nominated by church missionary societies. Charles Ewing of the Bureau of Catholic Indian Missions nominated agents for Catholic reservations such as the Flathead. Ewing had recommended Charles S. Medary for the job because: "He is a member of one of the oldest & most influential families of Ohio, nearly if not quite all of who are converts to the [Roman Catholic] Church."[1]

Biographical information is sparse, but Charles Stuart Medary was the son of Samuel Medary, a newspaperman who had been territorial governor of Minnesota and later Kansas during the 1850s. Samuel and the Democratic Ohio newspaper he edited opposed the Civil War, antagonizing many Ohioans. In 1863 a mob attacked the paper and wrecked his printing press.[2] Charles was born in October 1841 in Ohio.[3] Despite sharing many of his father's views about President Abraham Lincoln and the Civil War, Charles joined the Union army in 1861 and rose to the rank of first lieutenant. He left the army in 1870.[4] In 1875, when he was appointed agent, he was living in New York State and had a wife and child who joined him at Flathead Agency in September 1875.[5] The government provided a house at the agency for the agent and his family.

Medary's twenty-three-month tenure as Flathead Indian agent between July 1, 1875, and June 1, 1877, was the most thoroughly documented period of his life in the historical record. He entered the position with self-confidence and a determination to impose his will on the situation. Unfortunately, however, he lacked the diplomatic skills needed to succeed. Medary proceeded to make enemies of prominent tribal leaders and an influential white businessman and politician in neighboring Frenchtown, Montana.

On arriving at the Flathead Agency in 1875, Medary "found the Agency in a horrible condition." He concluded he would "have a good many changes to make which will keep me busy for some time to come."[6] Only a month after taking charge of the agency, Medary was already caught up in a controversy that demonstrated the independence of the tribal leaders and the perils of politics in the western Montana white community. On August 6, 1875, Montana governor B. F. Potts wrote Medary complaining that parties of Pend d'Oreilles and Salish Indians were leaving the reservation to hunt without U.S. Army escorts. On August 14, 1875, Medary replied that he was powerless to enforce the Indian Department order to keep Indian people confined to the reservation: "They insist on having the right under the Stevens Treaty, to leave the reservation at pleasure."[7]

The imbroglio that finally sank Medary as Flathead Indian agent was his conflict with T. J. Demers, a Frenchtown merchant whose wife was Pend d'Oreille, and Chief Arlee over who should be entitled to live on the reservation and avoid Missoula County taxes. In August 1875 the Missoula County commissioners requested that Medary remove all non-Indians and their property from the reservation so they could be taxed to help the county avoid bankruptcy. T. J. Demers was chairman of the Missoula County commissioners.[8] In August 1876 Medary accused Demers of illegally having cattle on the Flathead Reservation and asked the U.S. District Attorney to bring suit against him. At the same time during 1876 while Medary was riling his relations with Demers, he was also involved in a long-running battle with Chief Arlee over the $5,000 annual payment to the Bitterroot Salish, who had removed to the Jocko under the 1872 agreement with Congressman James Garfield.[9]

By the end of 1876 Medary had alienated some of the most vocal and influential tribal leaders on the reservation and a very important business and political leader in the western Montana white community.[10] His enemies entangled him in various legal actions that embarrassed him and ruined him financially. Finally. the commissioner of Indian affairs decided it was not worth the trouble to keep Medary as agent and asked for his resignation. He left Montana in defeat in 1877.[11]

After leaving Montana in 1873, Medary spent many years as an aquaculturist raising carp in New Jersey. He remained involved in Democratic Party politics and died in New York City in 1901.[12]

Peter Ronan (1839–1893)

Despite sharing the cultural prejudices of late nineteenth-century white Americans, Agent Peter Ronan was diplomatic enough to get along with most tribal leaders and community members. Ronan and the Salish and Kootenai chiefs and headmen shared some goals and were able to cooperate to reach these common objectives. In areas where they disagreed, Ronan seems to have moved slowly and generally avoided confrontations with tribal members when possible. Apparently, Ronan was able to treat Indian people with respect.

In 1883 Indian inspector S. S. Benedict recorded the complaints of Chief Arlee and Duncan McDonald about the St. Ignatius Mission schools and the Flathead Agency and then went on to conclude: "Agent Ronan is quite popular with these Indians. They speak in high terms of his honesty, and fair treatment."[13] A short magazine article commenting on Ronan's reappointment in 1890 observed: "The Indians in his charge all like and respect him . . . He has no hobbies about the treatment of Indians and does not expect to make white men of them in a single generation." This article, probably written by journalist E. V. Smalley, summarized Ronan's low-pressure approach: "He never tries to boss them except when necessary to preserve order and keep things moving in the right way."[14] In 1895 Inspector P. McCormick noted that Ronan had been more popular with the tribal members than his successor, Joseph Carter, because Ronan humored the Indians more than Carter did.[15] Despite Ronan's ability to respect Indian people and work with tribal leaders, he accepted the white American ideology of the superiority of "civilized" over "savage" life and saw his mission as helping the Salish and Kootenai people progress beyond their "uncivilized" and "savage" traditional lifestyles.[16]

By 1890 Ronan's influence had grown to the point that he used the government-paid police force to suppress an "outbreak" of Indian dancing and gambling. Details are sketchy, but Ronan discharged some of the police for failing to enforce his orders.[17] As agent, Ronan frequently argued in favor of tribal requests and interests in his correspondence with the Office of Indian Affairs. Ronan's defense of tribal members might not have met twenty-first-century standards, but one anti-Indian newspaper correspondent in 1889 accused him of being "not only an eager champion of the aborigines" but of being "activated by a prejudice against those of his own color."[18]

The two areas where Ronan and most tribal members had complimentary goals were (1) developing agriculture and ranching on the reservation to take up the economic slack caused by the loss of the buffalo and the decline of other wild game, root, and berry resources; and (2) keeping the peace on the reservation and not giving the U.S. Army or the Missoula County sheriff excuses to intervene in reservation affairs.

A continuing aggravation for the chiefs and Ronan was the problem of uneven justice in late nineteenth-century Montana. Cases of Indians accused of murdering white men were pursued vigorously by the white justice officials and the courts, but those involving Indian people murdered by whites were largely ignored. Four Indians convicted of murdering white men, mainly on Indian testimony, were hung in Missoula on December 20, 1890. The murderers of Chief Eneas's son in Demersville and Chief Michelle's relatives in eastern Montana about the same time were never caught or punished. Ronan wrote to Washington, D.C., frequently about the problem, but his calls for equal justice were not answered.[19]

In 1885 Ronan supported allotment on the reservation and thought he could convince the tribes to go along.[20] In 1887 however, when the commissioner of Indian affairs suggested that the new allotment act be applied to Flathead, Ronan demurred because of tribal complaints about boundary surveys that had worked against their interests and asked for "ample time to the Agent and his employes to induce the Indians to take allotments in sev[e]ralty, and to pursuade [sic] them to forget their prejudices against the word 'Survey.'"[21] Five years later, in 1892, Ronan again recommended that allotment not be forced on the Flathead Reservation tribes: "I do not believe it would be wise to negotiate with them for the cession of any surplus lands, or to attempt at present to have the lands surveyed and allotted."[22]

Ronan may have personally believed in the allotment policy, but his opposition to forcing allotment on the reservation delayed it for twenty years from about 1890 to 1910. Federal policy changes during the early twentieth century progressively weakened the trust protection of the allotments, but since the protection of the allotment patents expired after twenty-five years under the policy, an 1890 allotment would have resulted in even fewer restrictions on the sale of tribal member lands during the 1910s and 1920s. Since the reservation was not opened until 1910, it meant that the trust protection was set to expire during the 1930s, when government policy changed and continued the trust status indefinitely.

Peter Ronan was born on June 1, 1839, at Antogomish, Nova Scotia, Canada.[23] He attended a village school in Nova Scotia before his family moved to Rhode Island when he was thirteen years old. At fourteen he was apprenticed at a print shop in Rhode Island. When he was seventeen he became foreman of the book and job printing office of M. B. Young, Providence, Rhode Island. Between 1854 and 1860, he worked as a compositor for a Dubuque, Iowa, newspaper. For two years following the Pike's Peak gold rush, he prospected in the Rocky Mountains, and then he returned to Kansas to work as a partner in a Democratic newspaper. After being caught up in the political turmoil surrounding the Civil War, in 1863, Ronan headed to Alder Gulch or Virginia City in what became Montana. Ronan spent several years in mining before starting a series of newspapers in Virginia City and Helena with various partners, including Martin Maginnis, who was later to become his political patron. Ronan's newspaper was burned out by the Helena fires of 1872 and 1874, and he returned to mining. He was undersheriff of Lewis and Clark County when he was appointed as Flathead Indian agent in 1877. His twin interests in mining and journalism continued as he speculated in various mining ventures during his years at the Jocko Agency and exhibited his journalistic skills in his voluminous correspondence as agent.

Ronan had a reputation for honesty, and in 1890 the *Northwest Illustrated Monthly Magazine* noted, "The Major has served a long time at the [Flathead] agency and is one of the few Indian agents who have made no money."[24] When Ronan died at the Jocko Agency on August 20, 1893, he left assets in Missoula County appraised at $5,402.88, mostly in cattle, real estate, and various mining claims.[25] But most of these assets had been purchased with borrowed money. The probate court allowed a $1,500 family allowance for the widow and her children. On June 8, 1896, the estate still had outstanding debts of $5,251.83. Most of the money was owed to Ronan's friends from his mining days. In 1896, $4,017.90 was owed to Henry Bratnober, who made a fortune from the Drum Lummon Mine at Marysville, near Helena, and was a hunting partner with Ronan in 1890.[26] Ronan's second large debt was $2,208.33, owed to William A. Clark, the famous Butte

Copper King and Montana politician. In 1867 William and his brother, Joseph, ran a mail line between Missoula and Walla Walla, Washington, which traversed the Flathead Reservation.[27] When the Ronan estate was finally settled in 1907, interest had increased the debts to $7,211.83 with only $277.33 in cash available. The outstanding debts were settled for less than four cents on the dollar. Clearly Ronan had not grown personally rich from his position, and his death left his family in straightened circumstances.

Joseph T. Carter (1862–1947)

Joseph T. Carter was born in Iowa in February 1862 to Michael and Catherine Carter, Canadians originally from Nova Scotia. In 1880 he was working as a gardener and living in Cicero, Illinois, with his parents.[28] Carter was a cousin of Peter Ronan, his predecessor as Flathead Indian agent. He moved to Montana in 1885 to work in the bookkeeping department of the Missoula Mercantile Company.[29] In January 1886 he moved to Butte to keep the books for Andrew B. Hammond's Montana Improvement Company.[30] In 1890 he was working in Thompson Falls.[31] By 1893 he was Flathead Agency clerk, and he was appointed agent when Ronan died that year. Carter, in turn, nominated Ronan's eldest son, Vincent, as clerk to help support Ronan's surviving family.[32]

The letters supporting Carter for agent in 1893 include Thomas P. Smith, the special Indian agent who had interim charge of the Flathead Agency; Marcus Daly, of Butte; W. A. Clark, of Butte; Martin Maginnis, of Washington, D.C.; S. T. Hauser, of Helena; and other prominent Democrats. Most of the letters endorsed Carter's competence, but emphasized his willingness to help support Ronan's widow and young children. Vincent Ronan, the eldest son, was about twenty years old, but the youngest Ronan child was only two years old in 1893. Ronan's death threatened his family with impoverishment unless they could continue living at the Flathead Agency.[33]

When he took over charge of the Flathead Agency in October 1893, Carter stated that he was going to continue with the policies and personnel left by Ronan. The sources, however, suggest tribal leaders were considerably less happy with Carter's handling of the agency than they had been with Ronan. Ronan had built up considerable personal influence and respect with tribal members that Carter lacked.[34] In 1895 P. McCormick, an Indian inspector, reported that Carter was stricter with the Indians than Ronan had been:

Agent Carter is not as popular with the Indians as his predecessor Maj. Ronan, because he does not humor them as he did, and requires them to work. He issues nothing to a young Indian unless he earns it by working on his [the Indian's] ranch. The Indians protested to me, that is the old non progressive element, against Agent Carter, but received but little comfort, as I cordially endorse his methods.[35]

According to tribal member Henry Matt, Carter taught members

how to farm, and would take up the pick and shovel himself and show the Indian how the work should be done, and they would then take hold and work themselves. He encouraged and showed them how to plant their gardens and raise a little wheat, and when Mr. Indian would bring his little handfull of wheat to the mill to get it ground into the staff of life Major Carter would compliment him on doing so well and encourage him to keep on trying.[36]

On August 21, 1895, Carter married Mary E. Ronan, Peter Ronan's daughter. Carter was thirty-three years old and his wife was twenty years old.[37]

Carter's comparative lack of diplomacy and influence with tribal leaders was particularly emphasized by a series of events in March 1895. In early March 1895, tribal members of the Salish and Pend d'Oreille tribes on the Flathead Indian Reservation held a pre-Lenten dance in the Jocko Valley. Since it was a traditional Indian dance with Indian music, and not a fiddle dance as conducted by the whites and mixed-bloods, it was illegal under the agency code of Indian offenses. Agent Carter sent a party of agency Indian police to the gathering to order it dispersed. A former agency Indian judge, Louison, was at the dance and spoke to encourage the Indians to cease dancing and go home to prepare for Lent the next day.[38]

Louison was later arrested by the Indian police under orders of Agent Carter and charged with having encouraged the dancers to keep on dancing despite Carter's order to cease. Louison was locked up in the tribal jail at the Jocko Agency. According to Duncan McDonald, Louison's arrest resulted from a mistranslation of Louison's remarks that made them appear seditious. Carter wrote the commissioner of Indian affairs on March 4, 1895, requesting authority to remove Louison from the Flathead Reservation because his father was Nez Perce. Carter charged that Louison was "non-progressive" and encouraged traditional Indian customs and ceremonies.[39]

While Louison was being held in the agency jail, a crowd of Indian men attempted to break him out. Carter rounded up enough supporters, Indian and white, to stop the attempted release and arrest the three leaders. One source gave the names of the three as Nicolas, Voissant, and Pierrilot; another identified them as Swasah, Nicolla, and Louis Coull-Coullee. Carter's group loaded up the three prisoners and attempted to drive them to confinement in the Missoula County jail. Before they were out of the valley, however, Chief Charlo asked a group of his followers to prevent the removal of the three prisoners to Missoula. An opposition group, led by Big Pierre, confronted Carter and the Indian police escorting the prisoners. Carter bluffed his way through this obstruction by claiming that U.S. Army troops were on their way to enforce his order. Carter delivered the three prisoners to the county jail.[40]

By March 22, 1895, Big Pierre and the other three accused were in custody and brought before the United States commissioner in Missoula. Big Pierre, Swasah, and Nicolla were bound over to the United States grand jury and Louis Coull-Coullee was discharged, apparently because he had been arrested by mistake.[41]

The three remaining prisoners were taken before the U.S. grand jury in Helena in early May 1895, where they were indicted. U.S. attorney Leslie, however, could not find any specific law that they had broken and so could not draw up the charges. Carter appealed to the Indian Office in Washington, D.C., for legal help but did not seem to have received a reply.[42] Finally, in mid-May 1895, the charges against Swasah and Nicolla were dismissed, and they were released in Helena to make their own way back to the reservation. Big Pierre was indicted but not tried due to scheduling problems. He was sent back to the reservation and apparently returned to the agency jail.[43]

Carter applied in 1897 for reappointment as Flathead agent, but Republicans had won the 1896 election for president, and the administration selected W. H. Smead, a loyal Republican, for the position. Carter did get a letter of support from Thomas Sherman, a Jesuit priest and son of the famous Civil War general. Sherman asked President William McKinley to not replace Carter, a Catholic, with a non-Catholic agent. Carter was also endorsed by William H. Dewitt and Elbert D. Weed, two former Montana U.S. attorneys who had served in Republican administrations.[44]

After leaving Jocko Agency in 1898, Mary Ronan and her younger children moved to Missoula, and Carter and his wife moved to Butte. Between

1898 and 1906 he was the junior partner in the Butte architectural firm of Link & Carter. Link & Carter designed a number of important buildings such as a Baptist church in Billings, a hotel at Gregson Springs, the new library at Deer Lodge, and the Montana building at the 1904 Louisiana Purchase Exposition in St. Louis.[45]

In 1908 Carter moved to San Francisco, California, and opened an architectural firm there. In San Francisco, he supervised some of the rebuilding after the earthquake and fire in the city. In 1923 he moved to Los Angeles due to failing health. He worked as an architect in Los Angeles until 1929 and died in that city in 1931.[46] His widow, Mary Ronan Carter, died in San Francisco in 1947.[47]

William Henry Smead (1862–1948)

W. H. Smead, Flathead Indian agent between 1898 and 1904, was an energetic entrepreneur who was constantly looking for new business and management opportunities. Throughout most of his life, he had multiple enterprises going at the same time. His efforts to reorder the Flathead Indian Reservation generated intense opposition among tribal members. The allotment policy he, and later Joseph M. Dixon, imposed on the tribes impacted the tribal community and economy for generations to come.

Smead was born in Wisconsin in 1862 and attended the University of Illinois. After working briefly for an Illinois bank, Smead headed west in 1884. He settled in Dillon, Montana, and organized the Dillon Lumber & Grain Company. From Dillon, he branched out into the lumbering business in Kalispell and other western Montana locations.[48] In 1891 he relocated to Missoula and incorporated the State Lumber Company. He was also one of the incorporators of the Kalispell Lumber and Water Company in 1891.[49]

Smead also threw himself into Missoula County Republican politics. Smead was nominated as the Republican candidate for Montana state senator from Missoula in September 1894. In November 1894 Smead won election to the Montana Senate in a three-way race.[50] One of Smead's first actions on arriving in Helena for the 1895 session of the Montana legislature was to propose a senate joint memorial supporting the allotment and opening of the Flathead Indian Reservation. The argument for the opening was that white people wanted the land and resources of the reservation. It did not speak of obtaining tribal consent.[51] Smead's Flathead Reservation memorial was immediately praised by the *Daily Missoulian*, the local Republican newspaper.[52] The Missoula Democratic newspaper, however, panned the memorial as a scheme by a Missoula corporation to gain control of the reservation's resources.[53]

On February 3, 1895, the *Daily Missoulian* editorialized in support of Smead's memorial and the allotment of the Flathead Reservation. The newspaper argued it was only "just and right" to set aside land for the tribal members, but "it occurs to us that 160 acres for each individual Indian now on the reservation is land enough for them. The government for several years yet would have to care for them through an agent as now. But this, we believe, would eventually be the best thing for the Indian." And of course, opening the reservation would provide thousands of acres of agricultural land for white settlers and expand the local economy. No mention was made of what the Indian people might think of the allotment proposal.[54] On February 15, 1895, news reached Missoula that Smead's Flathead Reservation memorial had passed the Montana House of Representatives and would be sent to Washington, D.C.[55]

The Missoula delegation returned from Helena in March 1893 to widespread acclamation for their work. According to one report, Smead "looked a little sleepy for a day or two" on his return, but "it is noticed that his fingers have an involuntary, nervous, sliding movement at times, and his right hand reaches out unconsciously as if scooping in a pot."[56]

But Smead still had political ambitions, and in 1896 his friends were pushing him forward as a Republican candidate for Montana governor. The boom for Governor Smead seems to have died out quickly.[57] Meanwhile Smead was busy scaling timber being sold by the state.[58] In the 1897 legislative session Smead introduced a bill to provide money to erect and furnish buildings at the state university in Missoula.[59] In February 1897 Smead voted in favor of a bill granting an eight-hour workday for all employees on public works projects, but the bill was defeated.[60]

In 1897, when the new Republican administration of President William McKinley was looking to fill political patronage jobs, Smead applied for the Flathead Indian agent position. According to one account, Smead wanted either the Flathead Agency or a consulship someplace in Mexico.[61] Smead's principal competition for the Flathead Agency job was Missoula attorney Gust Moser. Moser had worked for the Missoula Mercantile Company before entering private practice. When Smead got the Flathead Agency, Moser was appointed supervisor of the Lewis and Clark Forest Preserve.[62]

Smead was also actively opposed by the Roman Catholic Church, because he was seen as unsympathetic to the work of the St. Ignatius Mission.[63] Several sources indicate that Smead was a member of the American Protective Association, an anti-Catholic secret society that was politically powerful in late nineteenth-century America.[64] Smead supported the establishment of a government boarding school at the agency, which resulted in competition with the St. Ignatius Mission schools for students. Smead's use of pressure and even physical force to recruit students for government schools was opposed by many tribal members. The missionaries also had influential friends in the nation's capital and the Bureau of Catholic Indian Missions to lobby for them.

As Flathead Indian agent, Smead was more confrontational than his predecessors had been over the last twenty years. Smead was anxious to impose nineteenth-century white American ideals of business and social order on the Salish and Kootenai tribal community on the reservation. One of his first moves was to increase the agent's control over law and order on the reservation. Officially law and order had been controlled by the agent since 1885, when the United States government established a paid Indian police and court system. But whereas Agents Peter Ronan and Joseph Carter had appointed older, more influential community leaders as police and judges, Smead wanted younger men who could be more easily controlled by the agent. These changes reduced the political influence of the traditional chiefs.

Despite being a product of the Missoula County Republican Party, Smead was surprisingly vigorous in defending tribal members when the Missoula County government attempted to tax mixed-blood cattlemen on the reservation. At the same time, however, he did not seem anxious to protect the rights of off-reservation Kootenai Indian allotment holders on Dayton Creek from white trespassers. He did publicly support the right of tribal members to travel freely off the reservation, but only after the commissioner of Indian affairs pointed out the provision in the 1855 Hellgate Treaty protecting tribal off-reservation hunting rights.

Smead's efforts to "rationalize" the livestock industry on the reservation won both support and vigorous complaints from tribal members. His efforts to reduce the herds of small Indian ponies on the reservation rangelands was applauded by the rich mixed-blood cattlemen. When he moved to impose a grazing tax on resident-owned herds of horses and cattle, he stirred up vehement resistance from tribal cattle barons.

Between 1898 and 1904, tribal leaders vigorously opposed allotment and the sale of reservation land to white men. As time went on, more tribal members must have become aware of Smead's political and lobbying efforts to impose the allotment policy on the reservation.

While agent, Smead continued some of his other personal business activities. According to one account, he was still investing in mining properties.[65] Smead was widely believed to have a financial interest in at least one reservation tradership. The surviving evidence is patchy, but on February 20, 1901, the Missoula newspapers reported that M. H. Prideaux was Alex Demer's new partner in his St. Ignatius store.[66] The missionaries at St. Ignatius believed Prideaux was a front to allow Smead to illegally purchase an interest in the store. In any event, Prideaux was Smead's nephew.[67] Finally on March 28, 1902, Prideaux forced Demers out and took over the entire business.[68] During the 1901 smallpox epidemic on the reservation, there were complaints that Smead had quarantined the reservation to keep tribal members from dealing with off-reservation businesses. Indians would then be forced to patronize stores on the reservation that were allegedly partly owned by Smead. Smead denied he had any financial motivation or interest in the quarantine.[69]

Smead was popular among the agency employees. When he was reappointed agent in 1902, the employees threw a surprise party for him at the agency. As a token of esteem, Smead was given a $200 diamond ring.[70] As Smead's tenure at Jocko Agency progressed, he antagonized more and more powerful interests. By 1904 it was reported that he was afraid to travel around the reservation unless heavily armed.[71]

In April 1904 Special U.S. Indian Agent S. L. Taggart began an investigation into a series of thirty-one charges against Smead filed by Harry H. Parsons. The accusations covered a wide range of alleged misconduct by Smead, but the early newspaper reports emphasized complaints that Smead colluded with W. Q. Ranft to charge mixed-bloods for enrollment.[72] Harry H. Parsons was a prominent Missoula attorney who was also active in local Republican politics. The conflict between Smead and Parsons evolved into a personal feud that festered for years.[73]

At the conclusion of the investigation, Indian inspector C. F. Nesler and Special Indian Agent Charles S. McNichols submitted their report to the secretary of the interior on June 21, 1904. They considered each of the thirty-one charges filed by Parsons and found Smead innocent of most of them. Some other charges were true, but not "serious offences." They found Smead guilty of five of Parsons's charges but concluded that they were "not of sufficient gravity, considered alone to warrant summary action. . . . while they do not show dishonesty they exhibit an inclination to traffic in a petty way on improper lines." The investigation concluded there was "an organized conspiracy between Attorney Parsons and certain mixed bloods of the reservation to secure Agent Smead's removal."[74]

In the course of their investigation, however, the inspectors learned of irregular methods Smead employed in the construction of a telephone line from the Arlee railroad station to St. Ignatius and Ronan. Despite the project being turned down by the commissioner of Indian affairs, Smead used rations and agency labor to build the line without official approval. Tribal members and Canadian Cree Indians were paid in rations to get the telephone poles out of the woods. The labor of agency employees was used to set the poles and string the wire. The inspectors felt the telephone line was needed but concluded its construction was "grossly irregular." Smead had also used rations to supplement employee salaries and pay for firewood, hay, saw logs, and work around the agency. Smead used the agency saw-mill to saw lumber for reservation traders. Despite Indian Office policies requiring labor in exchange for rations given to able-bodied Indians, the inspectors recommended Smead's immediate dismissal as Flathead Indian agent.[75] On July 1, 1904, Samuel Bellew succeeded Smead as Flathead Indian agent.[76]

In 1905 Smead published a book advertising the *Flathead Reservation: Land of the Flatheads: A Sketch of the Flathead Reservation, Montana*.[77] Smead also began giving lectures on the resources and land on the reserva-tion.[78] Soon after in July 1905, Smead announced that he had joined with Elmer E. Hershey, a Missoula lawyer who had previously worked in the Mis-soula land office, to form the Flathead Reservation Homestead Agency. For a five dollar membership fee, they promised timely and detailed news about the progress and procedures for getting land on the Flathead Reservation. Each member also received a copy of Smead's book. Members were to get assistance in selecting good land on the reservation when it was opened.[79]

Smead's Flathead Reservation Homestead Agency was competing with the Flathead Reservation Information Agency founded by W. Q. Ranft. The Information Agency also charged a five dollar membership fee and prom-ised members access to detailed information on every forty-acre tract on the reservation.[80] On December 18, 1905, Smead and his partner announced the receipt of ten large land ledgers, which the Flathead Reservation Homestead Agency would use to record soil and irrigation information on every forty-acre reservation subdivision. The information would be available for members to use in selecting land on the reservation.[81]

In the fall of 1906 Smead brought disbarment proceedings against S. G. Murray and H. H. Parsons. Smead alleged that Murray and Parsons had attempted to defraud Smead on a mortgage on a piece of Missoula property.[82] The disbarment case became sensationalized when it was learned that an area mining company had hired a Pinkerton detective to infiltrate the Murray and Parsons law office. The detective, W. A. Dunn, had posed as a law student in order to gain entrance to the law office, go through their trash, and make daily reports about conversations he overheard.[83] The case became very contentious, with conflicting testimony and raw emotions.[84] Smead's personal bitterness toward Parsons led to the exchange of physical blows on a Missoula street following a hearing in the case. The fisticuffs were exchanged on February 6, 1907.[85] The disbarment case was dismissed by the Montana Supreme Court on June 4, 1907.[86]

When registration for Flathead Indian Reservation lands opened in Missoula in July 1909, thousands of white people came through Missoula to file for the land drawing. Smead and other Missoula notaries did a brisk business collecting notary fees from the applicants. The rush to apply indicated that land seekers understood that the price set on the land was well below its real value.[87] In 1910 the W. H. Smead Company worked as land locators providing advice to prospective settlers on the quality of the different tracts available. They had offices in Kalispell and Missoula.[88] Smead subdivided a tract near Ronan in April 1911 into city lots to create the Smead addition to the town.[89] In 1915, when the villa sites around Flathead Lake were auctioned off, Smead was the largest purchaser. He bought properties both for himself and his company's clients.[90]

In 1920 and 1921 Smead headed the Smead-Simons Building Corporation that built the Wilma Theater Building in downtown Missoula.[91] The new building was dedicated in May 1921.[92] Complications developed in the funding, however, which led to an extended legal conflict over control of the building. The primary funding apparently came from the Minneapolis Trust Company.[93]

Smead relocated to Rexburg, Idaho, in 1922, where he opened a sawmill and engaged in the lumber business. He died in Rexburg in 1948.[94]

Samuel Bellew (1843–1921)

Samuel Bellew, the Flathead Reservation Indian agent between 1904 and 1908, was born in New York State in 1843. He was already sixty-one years old in 1904 when he took office at Jocko Agency.[95]

Samuel Bellew was a Civil War veteran who later reenlisted and served in the regular army. He was commissary sergeant at Fort Missoula and was stationed at Fort Missoula in 1877 during the Nez Perce War, and he remained at Missoula for almost ten years. In 1884 he was transferred from Fort Missoula to Fort Snelling, Minn., and later to Fort Niagara, New York. He retired from the army in 1891 and returned to Missoula with his family to live.[96]

Samuel Bellew's first wife, Mary, was born in England and died in 1895. The couple had three children, including a son named George and a daughter named Zoe. Bellew married Lizzie or Sarah Ralls in Missoula in 1899.[97]

Back in Missoula in the 1890s and 1900s, Samuel Bellew was active in a number of veteran, social, and political organizations. Bellew was post commander for the Missoula division of the Grand Army of the Republic, an organization of Civil War veterans.[98] He was also secretary of the Masonic Lodge in Missoula and secretary of the Odd Fellows in Missoula, two social and fraternal organizations.[99]

Most relevant to Bellew getting the Flathead agent position was his prominence in Missoula County Republican circles. Bellew was chairman of the Missoula Republican Municipal Convention in 1892 and of the Republican Missoula County Central Committee in 1902.[100]

As a reward for his work in the Missoula County Republican Party, Bellew served in a series of local government positions. In 1892 Bellew was deputy clerk of the district court. Five years later, in 1897, Bellew was elected to the Missoula school board; in 1899 he was a deputy county clerk; in 1901 he was registration agent for the municipal election; in January 1904 he became deputy postmaster for Missoula; in May 1904 he got a position in the Missoula Clerk and Recorder's Office.[101]

On August 1, 1904, he assumed his duties as Flathead Indian agent when he was sixty-one years old.[102] The priests at St. Ignatius Mission and some government inspectors complained that Bellew took too relaxed an approach to his job as agent. For example, on June 4, 1906, the house diarist at St. Ignatius Mission wrote, "Many drunken people and gamblers are following the horse round up. At last our sleeping Agent awoke, and sent here some Policemen."[103] Father Louis Taelman complained to Bellew on May 13, 1907, that the failure of the agency police to return runaway students to the school was undermining discipline, and that "the boys believe they can run away with impunity, because nothing is done."[104] Later that year, on August 16, 1907, Taelman complained to the Bureau of Catholic Indian Missions in Washington, D.C.: "What we need here, is a good agent with a *strong hand*. Our present Agent is a good man in his private capacity, but as a public official, he lacks strength & backbone."[105] Father Jerome D'Aste lamented to Bellew on February 10, 1908, that he "never saw our Indians of this Reservation so immoral as they are now."[106] Taelman complained to Bellew on September 18, 1908, that "this Reservation is becoming more and more a nest of prostitution."[107]

Two government inspectors complained to the commissioner of Indian affairs about Bellew's laxness. On August 25, 1906, John Rankin, the special allotting agent working on the reservation, protested that he had "seen more drunken Indians in and around St. Ignatius Mission Since I have been here, than during all the years I have been in the service."[108] Father D'Aste noted on June 5, 1907, that there was a big Indian meeting at St. Ignatius with Reuben Perry, a supervisor for the U.S. Indian Service attending. According to D'Aste, "the Indians asked Agent Bellew to resign."[109] A few days later in his report to the commissioner of Indian affairs on June 10, 1907, Perry complained, "Many unsatisfactory conditions exist on this reservation and so long as the Agent remains passive and inactive in the handling of affairs there will be no marked improvement. He does not seem to realize the responsibility of his position; the Judges and old Indians say that he allows the reservation to run itself and to a large extent this seems to be true."[110]

Bellew was not reappointed when his term expired in 1908.[111] He died in Missoula in 1921.[112]

In the late 1890s and early 1900s, Bellew's two younger children, George P. and Zoe, were regular members of an "outing club." The club spent the hot summer months camped on the shore of Flathead Lake.[113]

In the summer of 1903 Charles Allard Jr., from the reservation, joined the camping circle and also took a prominent role in a September 1903 grand ball and supper the group held in Missoula. The camp was called "Kamp Kootenai" in 1903.[114] George Bellew visited Allard on the reservation in January 1904.[115]

George Bellew was chief clerk at the Flathead Agency in 1905 and 1906. He resigned from the agency to work for a mining company in the Bitterroot Valley owned by his future brother-in-law.[116]

In 1907 George Bellew was employed for ninety dollars a month to scale logs from a reservation timber sale on Finley Point. However, Reuben Perry, an Indian Office supervisor, investigated and found George had only visited the logging camp for two short visits and was not scaling the logs cut. George admitted the dereliction to Perry and claimed he had left the logging camp "to obtain medical treatment."[117] There was evidence in 1908 suggesting that George Bellew was a cocaine addict.[118]

In 1909 George was charged with cashing bogus checks.[119] George Bellew drowned in November 1909 while bathing in the Lolo hot springs.[120]

Fred C. Morgan (1871–1958)

Fred C. Morgan was born in New York in 1871.[121] Morgan came to Missoula about 1892 at twenty-one years of age.[122] In February 1894 Morgan had his picture taken dressed in "full Indian war costume." At that time he was a carrier for the *Anaconda Standard* newspaper in Missoula.[123]

Twelve years later, in 1906, Morgan was a Republican candidate for the Montana State House of Representatives, and was elected as one of the Missoula County representatives in the 1907 legislature.[124] As a freshman representative, Morgan was assigned to the standing committee on affairs of cities.[125] In 1907 the state legislature selected the United States senators from Montana, and on January 15, 1907, Morgan voted with the majority to give the office to Joseph M. Dixon.[126] During the session Morgan introduced bills to amend the act creating Sanders County, to limit the liabilities of incorporated cities and towns for damages from personal injuries on sidewalks and streets, and to provide for temporary floors and safe scaffoldings in buildings during construction. He also supported a memorial to the United States Congress to allot and open the Blackfeet Reservation. On February 22, 1907, he signed a resolution complaining about the heat and poor air circulation in the house chambers.[127]

A few days after the legislature adjourned on March 7, 1907, he was appointed mayor of Missoula but occupied the office for only two months until the next municipal election.[128] In Evaro in 1907 and 1908, Morgan scaled Flathead Reservation timber purchased by Edward Donlan, a Missoula businessman and politician.[129] According to one newspaper report,

Morgan got to know elderly Indians on the reservation and took their portraits with his camera.[130]

In November 1908 Morgan was named as the new Flathead Indian agent
to succeed Samuel Bellew.[131] M. K. Sniffen, an agent for the Indian Rights
Association, identified Senator Joseph Dixon as Morgan's political patron
in securing the agent appointment.[132]

He took office at Jocko on December 1, 1908.[133] Morgan was thirty-seven
years old when he took charge and was twenty-eight years younger than his
predecessor. He approached the work with a reformist zeal that impressed
the St. Ignatius Mission priests and government inspectors. Particular attention was paid to combatting the whiskey trade and Indian custom marriages.
Morgan found a ready ally in a young priest, Father Louis Taelman, S.J.
After just a month in office, Taelman wrote Morgan, "we all realize the
happy change for the better, which has already become apparent since You
stepped into Office."[134] Thomas Downs, the special Indian agent working
on the Flathead enrollment effused, "Owing to his efforts order and discipline are rapidly taking place."[135]

Morgan ran the Flathead Agency between 1908 and 1917. During this
period the reservation was opened to white homesteaders, and government
policies used forced patents and other means to reduce tribal assets, especially landholdings. This was the nadir of Flathead Reservation history. The
Flathead Agency was moved from the Jocko Valley to Dixon, Montana,
in 1915.[136] Morgan found some tribal members he could work with, but
many Indians emphatically opposed these policies. Duncan McDonald was
chairman of the agency-recognized Flathead Business Committee. The
business committee tried to mollify some of the more negative aspects of
federal Indian policy during the 1910s, but they were later supplanted by the
first Flathead Tribal Council composed of more radical agency opponents.
This pre–Indian Reorganization Act council fought for radical changes in
federal Indian policy during the late 1910s and 1920s.[137]

In the 1910 U.S. Census, Morgan was single and living at the Jocko
Agency in a residence with two agency clerks and a housekeeper.[138] He was
Flathead Reservation agent between 1908 and 1910 and Flathead Reservation superintendent after 1910, for a total of nine years. In March 1917 he
was promoted to the Colville Agency in Washington State.[139] By 1922 he
was superintendent of the Mescalero Agency in Arizona.[140]

Morgan married a divorced lawyer, Eva E. Waterhouse Bean, in Nevada,
Missouri, in 1925, and retired from the Indian Service. The couple moved

to her family home in Saco, Maine.[141] Fred Morgan retired at the age of fifty-four years old. In the 1930 census for Saco, he was listed as having no occupation, and his wife was an attorney at law. Eva Morgan was a leader in the Daughters of the American Revolution. She campaigned for the adoption of the Star-Spangled Banner as the official national anthem in 1931 and was a prominent speaker for women's clubs and other organizations.

Fred Morgan died at Saco, Maine, on January 12, 1958, after thirty-three years of retirement. His wife died later the same year.[142]

Notes

Abbreviations

ARCIA	Annual Report, Commissioner of Indian Affairs
AS	*Anaconda Standard* (Anaconda, Mont.)
BCIM Papers	St. Ignatius File, Bureau of Catholic Indian Missions Papers, Marquette University Archives, Milwaukee, Wis.
CIA	Commissioner of Indian Affairs
CIA LR NA 234	U.S. Office of Indian Affairs, "Letters Received by the Office of Indian Affairs, 1824–1880," National Archives Microfilm Publication M234
DM	*Daily Missoulian* (Missoula, Mont.)
FH Agency Papers LR	Flathead Agency Papers, letters received, 8NS-075-96-323, National Archives, Denver, Colo.
FH Agency Papers LS	Flathead Agency Papers, letters sent, local copy books, 8NS-075-96-318, National Archives, Denver, Colo.
MHS	Montana Historical Society, Helena, Mont.
NA CIA CCF	Records of the Commissioner of Indian Affairs, RG 75, Central Classified Files, National Archives, Washington, D.C.
NA CIA LR	Letters received, Records of the Commissioner of Indian Affairs, RG 75, National Archives, Washington, D.C.
NA CIA LS	Letters sent, Records of the Commissioner of Indian Affairs, RG 75, National Archives, Washington, D.C.
NAmf	National Archives Microfilm Publication
NAmf M1070	U.S. Department of the Interior, "Reports of Inspection of the Field Jurisdictions of the Office of Indian Affairs, 1873–1900,"

	National Archives Microfilm Publication M1070, reel 11, Flathead Agency
NNW	*New North-west* (Deer Lodge, Mont.)
PNTMC	Robert C. Carriker and Eleanor R. Carriker, eds., "The Pacific Northwest Tribes Missions Collection of the Oregon Province Archives of the Society of Jesus" (Wilmington, Del.: Scholarly Resources, 1987).
Ronan letters, vol. 1	Peter Ronan, *"A Great Many of Us Have Good Farms": Agent Peter Ronan Reports on the Flathead Indian Reservation, Montana, 1877–1887*, ed. Robert J. Bigart (Pablo, Mont.: Salish Kootenai College Press, 2014).
Ronan letters, vol. 2	Peter Ronan, *Justice to Be Accorded to the Indians: Agent Peter Ronan Reports on the Flathead Indian Reservation, Montana, 1888–1893* (Pablo, Mont.: Salish Kootenai College Press, 2014).
SecInt	Secretary of the Interior
WM	*Weekly Missoulian* (Missoula, Mont.)

Introduction

1. Thomas R. Wessel, "Historical Report on the Blackfeet Reservation in Northern Montana," U.S. Indian Claims Commission, Docket No. 279-D, 1975, 28–93.

2. Hoxie, *Parading Through History*, 36–41, 266–94.

3. Rzeczkowski, *Uniting the Tribes*, 129–53.

4. Peltier, *A Brief History*, 52–68; Woodworth-Ney, *Mapping Identity*, 105–14; Seltice, *Saga of the Coeur d'Alene*, 158–61, 189–91, 229–37.

5. Fowler, *Arapahoe Politics*, 84–89.

6. Fowler, *Tribal Sovereignty*, 13–14, 18, 31–34, 42; Berthrong, *The Cheyenne and Arapaho Ordeal*, 58–77.

7. Foster, *Being Comanche*, 75–99.

8. Meyer, *The White Earth Tragedy*, 72–88.

9. Harmon, *Indians in the Making*, 113–20.

10. Stern, *The Klamath Tribe*, 57–73.

11. Beck, *The Struggle for Self-Determination*, 46–62.

Chapter 1

1. Bigart and McDonald, *Duncan McDonald*, 32.

2. "A Hunt," WM, Jan. 13, 1875, p. 2, col. 5.

3. Peter Whaley to CIA, June 1, 1875, BCIM Papers.

4. Peter Whaley to CIA, June 1, 1875, BCIM Papers.

5. Chas. S. Medary to CIA, Oct. 1, 1875, BCIM Papers.

6. Medary to CIA, Aug. 16, 1875, CIA LR NA 234, r. 502, f. 641.

7. Blackfeet Agent to Comd'g Officer, Fort Shaw, M.T., October 8, 1875, General Letters Sent, June 1875–June 1915, vol. 1, Blackfeet Agency Papers, RG 75, National Archives, Rocky Mountain Region, Denver, Colo.

8. John S. Wood, Blackfeet Agency, to Commanding Officer, Fort Shaw, Mont., Oct. 20, 1875, Copies of General Letters Sent, 1875–1915, vol. 1, pp. 96–98, Blackfeet Agency Papers, RG 75, National Archives, Rocky Mountain Region, Denver, Colo.; "The Country North," *Helena Daily Herald*, Oct. 26, 1875, p. 1, col. 2–3.

9. Chas. S. Medary to CIA, Nov. 1, 1875, BCIM Papers; "Short Stops," *Helena Independent* (daily), Nov. 4, 1875, p. 3, col. 2.

10. "Short Stops," *Helena Independent* (daily), Nov. 4, 1875, p. 3, col. 2; "Indian Troubles," *Helena Independent* (daily), Nov. 5, 1875, p. 3, col. 3.

11. "Indian Horse Thieves," *Helena Daily Herald*, Feb. 25, 1876, p. 3, col. 2; "X. Beidler on the War Path," *Fort Benton Record*, Feb. 26, 1876, p. 3, col. 1.

12. "Indian Horse Thieves," *Helena Daily Herald*, Feb. 25, 1876, p. 3, col. 2; "Local News," WM, Mar. 8, 1876, p. 3, col. 1; "Horse Thief in Limbo," *Helena Daily Herald*, Mar. 18, 1876, p. 3, col. 2; "The County Jail," *Helena Daily Herald*, Apr. 11, 1876, p. 3, col. 3.

13. NNW, Mar. 3, 1876, p. 3, col. 3.

14. "Wayside Notes," *Helena Independent* (daily), June 10, 1876, p. 3, col. 2–3.

15. "Sale of Arms and Ammunition to Indians," NNW, Sept. 8, 1876, p. 2, col. 4.

16. WM, Sept. 13, 1876, p. 3, col. 2.

17. "Indians in State Celebrate Yule Fifty-First Time," DM, Dec. 23, 1937, p. 1, col. 5 and p. 6, col. 3; "Missionary Work Among the Indians," *Helena Independent* (daily), Feb. 23, 1877, p. 3, col. 3.

18. WM, Mar. 9, 1877, p. 3, col. 2.

19. Ronan to Maginnis, Aug. 21, 1877, Ronan letters, v. 1: 27.

20. W. T. Sherman, General, to Geo. W. McCrary, Secretary of War, September 3, 1877, in Sheridan and Sherman, *Reports of Inspection*, 44.

21. Ronan to CIA, Jan. 15, 1878, Ronan letters, v. 1: 42–43.

22. Ronan to CIA, Jan. 16, 1878, Ronan letters, v. 1: 43–47.

23. Ronan to CIA, May 1, 1878, Ronan letters, v. 1: 62–64.

24. Ronan to CIA, Aug. 12, 1878, Ronan letters, v. 1: 75–78.

25. Ronan to CIA, Aug. 20, 1878, Ronan letters, v. 1: 78–80.

26. Ronan to CIA, Aug. 20, 1878, Ronan letters, v. 1: 78–80.

27. WM, Oct. 4, 1878, p. 3, col. 3.

28. Ronan to CIA, Nov. 27, 1878, Ronan letters, v. 1: 86–87.

29. Garcia, *Tough Trip Through Paradise*, 139–53.

30. Ronan to CIA, Feb. 24, 1879, Ronan letters, v. 1: 97–99.

31. Ronan to CIA, Mar. 3, 1879, Ronan letters, v. 1: 99–100.

32. Ronan to CIA, Mar. 29, 1879, Ronan letters, v. 1: 101–2.

33. Ronan to CIA, May 6, 1879, Ronan letters, v. 1: 103–4.

34. *Helena Daily Herald*, June 25, 1879, p. 3, col. 1; *Helena Independent* (daily), June 25, 1879, p. 3, col. 1.

35. "The Flatheads," *Helena Independent* (daily), July 29, 1879, p. 3, col. 1; *Helena Daily Herald*, July 29, 1879, p. 3, col. 1.

36. "Helena Letter," *Bozeman Avant Courier*, Oct. 30, 1879, p. 3, col. 5–6.

37. "Indian Ponies Stolen," *Helena Weekly Independent*, Oct. 30, 1879, p. 5, col. 3.

38. *Helena Independent* (daily), Feb. 10, 1880, p. 3, col. 3; Ruger, "Report of Col. Thos. H. Ruger," 1880, 76–78.

39. WM, May 14, 1880, p. 3, col. 3; WM, May 21, 1880, p. 3, col. 3.

40. NNW, Apr. 8, 1881, p. 3, col. 3; "Missoula County," Apr. 8, 1881, p. 3, col. 6; Bigart, *Life and Death at St. Mary's Mission*, 239–40.

41. "Savage Visitors," *Helena Daily Herald*, June 13, 1881, p. 3, col. 4; *Rocky Mountain Husbandman* (White Sulphur Springs, Mont.), June 30, 1881, p. 3, col. 2; NNW, Aug. 12, 1881, p. 3, col. 3.

42. Bigart, *Getting Good Crops*, 181.

43. "Indian Difficulty," *Helena Independent* (daily), July 13, 1879, p. 3, col. 3; "The Murders Near Lincoln," NNW, July 18, 1879, p. 3, col. 2; "The Lincoln Indian Affair," NNW, Aug. 8, 1879, p. 3, col. 2.

44. *Helena Independent* (daily), Oct. 25, 1879, p. 3, col. 3.

45. WM, Jan. 30, 1880, p. 3, col. 2.

46. Elsie F. Nicholas, "As Missoula Was in 'The Good Old Days,'" DM, Jan. 28, 1923, editorial section, p. 1, col. 6, and p. 3, col. 1–4.

47. "Down the Benton Road," *Helena Independent* (daily), July 15, 1881, p. 3, col. 4.

48. Ronan letters, v. 1: 159–63.

49. "A Big Trout," *Helena Daily Herald*, Nov. 1, 1879, p. 3, col. 3.

50. "A Big Trout," *Helena Daily Herald*, Sept. 6, 1881, p. 3, col. 2.

51. ARCIA, 1875–81; Whaley to CIA, Jan. 10, 1875, CIA LR NA 234, r. 503, f. 183.

52. Ronan to CIA, Aug. 12, 1878, Ronan letters, v. 1: 75–78.

53. Ronan to CIA, Jan. 1881, Ronan letters, v. 1: 145–46; "Missoula County Items," *Helena Independent* (daily), Mar. 2, 1881, p. 3, col. 3.

54. John F. Finnerty, "Joys of the Jacko," *The Times* (Chicago, Ill.), Aug. 9, 1881, p. 6, col. 4–5.

55. Capt. C. C. Rawn, Missoula, to Acting Asst. Adjutant General, Fort Shaw, M.T., July 16, 1877, Rothermich, "Early Days at Fort Missoula," 387.

56. Ronan to CIA, Aug. 13, 1877, Ronan letters, v. 1: 20–24.

57. *Benton Record* (Ft. Benton, Mont.), Sept. 14, 1877, p. 3, col. 1.

58. Ronan to CIA, Mar. 19, 1878, Ronan letters, v. 1: 50–58.

59. Ronan to CIA, Mar. 29, 1879, Ronan letters, v. 1: 101–2.

60. "Helena Letter," *Bozeman Avant Courier*, Oct. 30, 1879, p. 3, col. 5–6.

61. "Estray," WM, Feb. 6, 1880, p. 3, col. 4.

62. ARCIA, 1875–81.

63. Bigart, *Getting Good Crops*, 90–94.

64. Martin Maginnis to CIA, undated (recd. Jan. 20, 1876), CIA LR NA 234, r. 505, f. 169; Medary to CIA, Jan. 28, 1876, CIA LR NA 234, r. 505, f. 194; Medary to CIA, Feb. 11, 1876, CIA LR NA 234, r. 505, f. 204.

65. J. F. McAlear, "William Irvine, Picturesque Character of West . . . ," DM, Mar. 26, 1939, p. 4, col. 3–4.

66. Ronan to CIA, Mar. 19, 1878, Ronan letters, v. 1: 50–58.

67. "Journey to the West Side," *Helena Independent* (daily), Aug. 9, 1878, p. 2, col. 2–3.

68. Ronan to CIA, Aug. 26, 1878, Ronan letters, v. 1: 82–83.

69. Ronan to CIA, Mar. 3, 1879, Ronan letters, v. 1: 97–99.

70. Ronan to CIA, May 7, 1879, Ronan letters, v. 1: 104–6.

71. Ronan to CIA, Sept. 17, 1880, Ronan letters, v. 1: 142–43.

72. Ronan to CIA, Nov. 1, 1881, Ronan letters, v. 1: 170–72.

73. Dave Couture, "Route of the DeMers Drive," in Whealdon, *"I Will Be Meat,"* 193–95; Arthur Larivee, et. al., "Add to Jack Demers Article," in Whealdon, *"I Will Be Meat,"* 217–21.

74. *Rocky Mountain Husbandman* (White Sulphur Springs, Mont.), Sept. 22, 1881, p. 3, col. 2.

75. ARCIA, 1875–81.

76. Peter Whaley to CIA, Jan. 10, 1875, CIA LR NA 234, r. 503, f. 183.

77. Peter Whaley to CIA, May 1, 1875, BCIM Papers.

78. Peter Whaley to CIA, June 1, 1875, BCIM Papers.

79. Charles S. Medary to CIA, Aug. 16, 1875, CIA LR NA 234, r. 502, f. 641.

80. Charles S. Medary to CIA, Sept. 13, 1875, ARCIA (1875), 304–7.

81. Chas. S. Medary to CIA, Oct. 1, 1875, BCIM Papers.

82. Glover, *Diary of Eli Sheldon Glover*, 14.

83. WM, Mar. 30, 1877, p. 3, col. 2.

84. Ronan to CIA, Dec. 14, 1878, Ronan letters, v. 1: 87–88.

85. *Rocky Mountain Husbandman* (Diamond City, Mont.), July 12, 1877, p. 2, col. 1.

86. Ronan to CIA, Aug. 13, 1877, Ronan letters, v. 1: 20–24.

87. Ronan to CIA, May 1, 1878, Ronan letters, v. 1: 62–64.

88. WM, June 14, 1878, p. 3, col. 2.

89. "Journey to the West Side," *Helena Independent* (daily), Aug. 9, 1878, p. 2, col. 2–3.

90. Ronan to CIA, Aug. 12, 1878, Ronan letters, v. 1: 75–78.

91. Ronan to CIA, Dec. 30, 1878, Ronan letters, v. 1: 89–93.

92. Ronan to CIA, Feb. 24, 1879, Ronan letters, vol. 1: 97.

93. "Visit to the Flathead Agency," *Rocky Mountain Husbandman* (Diamond City, Mont.), May 1, 1879, p. 2, col. 3–4.

94. Ronan to CIA, May 6, 1879, Ronan letters, v. 1: 103–4.

95. Ronan to CIA, May 7, 1879, Ronan letters, v. 1: 104–6.

96. Ronan to CIA, Aug. 15, 1879, Ronan letters, v. 1: 114–15.

97. Ronan to CIA, Nov. 5, 1879, Ronan letters, v. 1: 122–23.

98. Ronan to CIA, Aug. 20, 1880, Ronan letters, v. 1: 140–42.

99. Ronan to CIA, Jan. 1, 1881, Ronan letters, v. 1: 145–46.

100. Ronan to CIA, June. 1, 1881, Ronan letters, v. 1: 155–56.

101. Ronan to CIA, Aug. 1, 1881, Ronan letters, v. 1: 158–59.

102. Ronan to CIA, Aug. 15, 1881, Ronan letters, v. 1: 159–63.

103. Ronan to CIA, July 11, 1877, Ronan letters, v. 1: 15–19; Capt. C. C. Rawn, Missoula, to Acting Asst. Adjutant General, Fort Shaw, M.T., July 16, 1877, in Rothermich, "Early Days at Fort Missoula," 387.

104. Ronan, *Girl from the Gulches*, 177–78, 196–98.

105. WM, Feb. 8, 1878, p. 3, col. 4; WM, Apr. 25, 1879, p. 3, col. 2.

106. Duncan MacDonald to T. D. Duncan, undated, Samuel E. Johns Papers, SC 165, microfilm, Toole Archives, Mansfield Library, University of Montana, Missoula, vol. 1, pp. 35–36.

107. Garcia, *Tough Trip Through Paradise*, 168–72, 189.

108. Stone, *Following Old Trails*, 143–49.

109. Ronan to CIA, Aug. 26, 1879, Ronan letters, v. 1: 117; Ronan to CIA, Dec. 18, 1880, Ronan letters, v. 1: 143–44.

110. Medary to CIA, Feb. 11, 1876, CIA LR NA 234, r. 505, f. 204.

111. WM, Feb. 8, 1878, p. 3, col. 4.

112. "Premiums," WM, Oct. 18, 1878, p. 3, col. 3–5.

113. Garcia, *Tough Trip Through Paradise*, 139–253, 296–325.

114. [Account book for W. H. H. Dickinson store, Missoula, Mont., 1879–80], Box 1, folder 7, Financial Records, 1879–80, W. H. H. Dickinson Papers, LC 23, Toole Archives, Mansfield Library, University of Montana, Missoula, pp. 305, 339.

115. WM, Sept. 12, 1879, p. 3, col. 3.

116. "County Fair," WM Sept. 12, 1879, p. 3, col. 5.

117. "Savage Visitors," *Helena Daily Herald*, June 13, 1881, p. 3, col. 4.

118. Ronan to CIA, Aug. 15, 1881, Ronan letters, v. 1: 159–63.

119. "Bitter Root Items," WM, Sept. 16, 1881, p. 3, col. 4.

120. Ronan to CIA, Nov. 1, 1881, Ronan letters, v. 1: 170–72.

121. Ledger, 1881, Charles H. McLeod Papers, MS 1, Toole Archives, Mansfield Library, University of Montana, Missoula, vol. 52.

122. WM, May 17, 1876, p. 3, col. 2.

123. WM, Oct. 25, 1876, p. 3, col. 2.

124. WM, June 28, 1876, p. 3, col. 2; Chief Clerk, Dept. of Int., to CIA, Jan. 26, 1877, CIA LR NA 234, r. 507, f. 730.

125. Ronan to CIA, Aug. 26, 1878, Ronan letters, v. 1, pp. 82–83.

126. Duncan MacDonald to T. D. Duncan, undated, Samuel E. Johns Papers, SC 165, microfilm, Toole Archives, Mansfield Library, University of Montana, Missoula, vol. 1, pp. 35–36.

127. Ronan to CIA, Dec. 29, 1879, Ronan letters, v. 1: 128–29.

128. "From Missoula County," *Helena Weekly Herald*, Jan. 6, 1881, p. 8, col. 3; "Former Prices," DM, Nov. 21, 1911, p. 10, col. 2; WM, Nov. 11, 1881, p. 3, col. 2; WM, Dec. 16, 1881, p. 3, col. 1.

129. WM, July 19, 1876, p. 3, col. 6; WM, Sept. 13, 1876, p. 3, col. 4; Ronan to CIA, Dec. 14, 1878, Ronan letters, v. 1: 87–88.

130. Ronan to CIA, Dec. 29, 1879, Ronan letters, v. 1: 128–29.

131. "Ferry Notice!" WM, July 29, 1881, p. 3, col. 4; Ronan to CIA, Aug. 1, 1882, Ronan letters, v. 1: 186–87.

132. Ronan to CIA, Dec. 29, 1879, Ronan letters, v. 1: 128–29.

133. Ronan to CIA, Aug. 20, 1881, Ronan letters, v. 1: 163–64.

134. Chas. S. Medary to CIA, Oct. 1, 1875, BCIM Papers.

135. WM, Feb. 8, 1878, p. 3, col. 4.

136. "Drunken Indians," NNW, June 21, 1878, p. 3, col. 1.

137. NNW, Mar. 28, 1879, p. 3, c.2.

138. WM, Apr. 25, 1879, p. 3, col. 2.

139. Ronan to CIA, May 7, 1879, Ronan letters, v. 1: 104–6.

140. "Indian Difficulty," Helena Independent (daily), July 13, 1879, p. 3, col. 3; "The Murders Near Lincoln," NNW, July 18, 1879, p. 3, col. 2; "An Indian Row," NNW, July 18, 1879, p. 3, col. 2; "The Lincoln Murders," NNW, Aug. 1, 1879, p. 3, col. 1; "The Lincoln Indian Affair," NNW, Aug. 8, 1879, p. 3, col. 2.

141. "Our Abiding Place," WM, Mar. 12, 1880, p. 2, col. 3–5.

142. "Missoula County," NNW, Apr. 8, 1881, p. 3, col. 6.

143. Ronan to CIA, Aug. 1, 1881, Ronan letters, v. 1: 158–59.

144. WM, Aug. 19, 1881, p. 3, col. 2; WM, Aug. 26, 1881, p. 3, col. 1.

145. Bigart and Woodcock, In the Name of the Salish, 12–13.

146. "Maj. Whaley Not Removed," WM, Jan. 13, 1875, p. 3, col. 3.

147. Peter Whaley to CIA, Mar. 17, 1875, CIA LR NA 234, r. 503, f. 278.

148. Peter Whaley to CIA, May 1, 1875, BCIM Papers.

149. Taft, Atty. Gen., to SecInt, Jan. 8, 1876 [sic, 1877], CIA LR NA 234, r. 508, f. 382; Duncan McDonald, "From Jocko Reservation," NNW, Feb. 9, 1877, p. 2, col. 8.

150. Ronan to CIA, Aug. 13, 1877, Ronan letters, v. 1: 20–24.

151. Ronan to CIA, Aug. 20, 1877, Ronan letters, v. 1: 24–27.

152. Ronan to CIA, Jan. 15, 1878, Ronan letters, v. 1: 42–43; Ronan to CIA, Apr. 1, 1878, Ronan letters, v. 1: 59–60.

153. "Proposals for Flathead Agency," Helena Independent (daily), Oct. 7, 1877, p. 3, col. 4.

154. Ronan to CIA, Dec. 24, 1877, Ronan letters, v. 1: 33–34.

155. Ronan to CIA, July 5, 1878, Ronan letters, v. 1: 64–66.

156. Ronan to CIA, Aug. 12, 1878, Ronan letters, v. 1: 75–78.

157. Ronan to CIA, Aug. 20, 1878, Ronan letters, v. 1: 78–80.

158. Ronan to CIA, Nov. 27, 1878, Ronan letters, v. 1: 86–87.

159. "Visit to the Flathead Agency," Rocky Mountain Husbandman (Diamond City, Mont.), May 1, 1879, p. 2, col. 3–4.

160. WM, May 21, 1880, p. 3, col. 3.

161. Ronan to CIA, Aug. 20, 1880, Ronan letters, v. 1: 140–42.

162. Ronan to CIA, Sept. 17, 1880, Ronan letters, v. 1: 142–43.

163. Ronan to CIA, June 1, 1881, Ronan letters, v. 1: 155–56.

164. Ronan to CIA, May 1, 1881, Ronan letters, v. 1: 153.

165. John F. Finnerty, "Joys of the Jacko," *The Times* (Chicago, Ill.), Aug. 9, 1881, p. 6, col. 4–5.

166. Ronan to CIA, Sept. 16, 1881, Ronan letters, v. 1: 168–69.

167. Ronan to CIA, Nov. 1, 1881, Ronan letters, v. 1: 170–72.

168. Turney-High, *The Flathead Indians*, 54–55.

169. John S. Wood, Blackfeet Agency, to Commanding Officer, Fort Shaw, Mont., Oct. 20, 1875, Copies of General Letters Sent, 1875–1915, vol. 1, pp. 96–98, Blackfeet Agency Papers, RG 75, National Archives, Rocky Mountain Region, Denver, Colo.

170. "Indian Horse Thieves," *Helena Daily Herald*, Feb. 25, 1876, p. 3, col. 2; "X. Beidler on the War Path," *Fort Benton Record*, Feb. 26, 1876, p. 3, col. 1.

171. WM, June 28, 1876, p. 3, col. 3; WM, Aug. 16, 1876, p 3, col. 1.

172. Chas. S. Medary to CIA, Sept. 1, 1876, ARCIA (1876), 492–94.

173. Bud Ainsworth, "Neptune Lynch Family Were First White Settlers in Plains Valley . . ." *Rocky Mountain Husbandman* (Great Falls, Mont.), Aug. 4, 1932, p. 1, col. 1–3; Ronan letters, v. 1: 31–33.

174. Mrs. E. L. Willis, "Laughlin One of First Missoulian Subscribers," DM, Aug. 29, 1937, Progress Edition, *Missoulian* Section, p. 9, col. 3–8.

175. "Sun River Items," *Benton Record* (Ft. Benton, Mont.), Oct. 12, 1877, p. 3, col. 1.

176. Ronan, *Girl from the Gulches*, 179.

177. Indian Depredation Claim #1836, RG 75, NA; WM, Apr. 12, 1878, p. 3, col. 3; Ronan letters, v. 1: 125–27, 166–67.

178. "Arrest of the Murderer of George Moutour," WM, Apr. 19, 1878, p. 3, col. 2.

179. WM, June 7, 1878, p. 3, col. 3 (two items).

180. Ronan to CIA, Mar. 3, 1879, Ronan letters, v. 1: 97–99.

181. "The Murders Near Lincoln," NNW, July 18, 1879, p. 3, col. 2.

182. WM, Aug. 19, 1881, p. 3, col. 2.

Chapter 2

1. Ronan to CIA, Jan. 3, 1882, Ronan letters, vol. 1: 175.

2. Ronan to CIA, Jan. 16, 1882, Ronan letters, vol. 1: 175–76.

3. Martin Maginnis to CIA, Mar. 21, 1882, Ronan letters, vol. 1: 183–85.

4. "Indian Interference," *Helena Daily Herald*, Jan. 10, 1882, p. 3, col. 3.

5. "Railroad Obstruction," NNW, Mar. 17, 1882, p. 3, col. 1.

6. WM, Jan. 13, 1882, p. 3, col. 2.

7. Ronan to CIA, Feb. 1, 1882, Ronan letters, vol. 1: 176–78; WM, Feb. 24, 1882, p. 3, col. 1.

8. "The Northern Pacific and the Indians," *Helena Independent* (daily), July 9, 1882, p. 2, col. 1–2.

9. "The Flathead Reservation," *Helena Independent* (daily), July 12, 1882, p. 3, col. 2; "Right of Way Across the Flathead Reservation" *Helena Daily Herald*, July 13, 1882, p. 2, col. 1.

10. "Railroad Contracts," *Helena Daily Herald*, July 10, 1882, p. 3, col. 1.

11. WM, July 14, 1882, p. 3, col. 3.

12. "The Reservation Hindrance," NNW, July 28, 1882, p. 2, c 2; WM, July 28, 1882, p. 2, col. 1.

13. CIA to Ronan, July 19, 1882, telegram, land, letter book 99, p. 83, NA CIA LS.

14. U.S. President, "Message," 1883, 11, 14.

15. Jos. K. McCammon to CIA, Nov. 21, 1882, Ronan letters, vol. 1: 196–98.

16. Ronan to CIA, Oct. 1, 1883, Ronan letters, vol. 1: 223–26.

17. U.S. President, "Message," 1883, 16, 19; WM, Sept. 8, 1882 p. 2, col. 1.

18. "They Have Bad Records," AS, Dec. 3, 1899, p. 14, col. 2.

19. "The Flathead Right-of-Way Treaty," *Helena Daily Herald*, Sept. 7, 1882, p. 2, col. 2; "Commissioner M'Cammon in the Capital," *Helena Daily Herald*, Sept. 7, 1882, p. 3, col. 3.

20. "Western Montana News," *Helena Independent* (daily), Sept. 14, 1882, p. 3, col. 1.

21. Ronan to CIA, Oct. 1, 1882, Ronan letters, vol. 1: 192–93.

22. WM, Oct. 20, 1882, p. 3, col. 2.

23. Ronan to CIA, Dec. 1, 1882, Ronan letters, vol. 1: 198–99.

24. Ronan to CIA, Aug. 13, 1883, Ronan letters, vol. 1: 215–18.

25. SecInt to CIA, May 19, 1883, Ronan letters, vol. 1: 209–10.

26. S. S. Benedict to SecInt, July 10, 1883, NAmf M1070, 3093/83.

27. S. S. Benedict to SecInt, July 10, 1883, NAmf M1070, 3093/83.

28. Robert S. Gardner to SecInt, Jan. 30, 1885, NAmf M1070, 585/1885; "Great Joy on the Reservation," *Missoula County Times*, Jan. 14, 1885, p. 3, col. 2.

29. Ronan to CIA, June 11, 1884, Ronan letters, vol. 1: 263–65.

30. Ronan to CIA, Aug. 30, 1884, Ronan letters, vol. 1: 275–80.

31. "Railroad Racket," WM, Sept. 5, 1884, p. 2, col. 2.

32. Ronan to CIA, Sept. 12, 1884, Ronan letters, vol. 1: 281–83.

33. "Indian Reservation Jollification," *Livingston Enterprise*, Nov. 22, 1884, p. 1, col. 3–4.

34. Ronan to CIA, Nov. 1, 1882, Ronan letters, vol. 1: 194–95.

35. NNW, Apr. 20, 1883, p. 3, col. 3.

36. Ronan to CIA, Oct. 14, 1885, Ronan letters, vol. 1: 327–29.

37. "Indians Recalled," p. 5, col. 3.

38. WM, Oct. 23, 1885, p. 3, col. 2.

39. "About Flathead Indians," Oct. 27, 1885, Ronan letters, vol. 1: 329–32.

40. Geo. B. Pearsons to SecInt, Nov. 11, 1886, NAmf M1070, 6543/1886.

41. "The Flathead Treaty," May 28, 1887, Ronan letters, vol. 1: 389–91.

42. Bigart, *A Pretty Village*, 269.

43. Staveley Hill, *From Home to Home*, 369, 372.

44. "Notes of the Yellowstone Trip," Oct. 5, 1883, Ronan letters, vol. 1: 226.

45. Smalley, "The Kalispel Country," 447–55.

46. WM, Nov. 6, 1885, p. 3, col. 2.

47. Olga W. Johnson, "Bull River Homesteader," *Spokesman-Review* (Spokane, Wash.), July 6, 1958, *Inland Empire Magazine*, p. 5, 13.

48. ARCIA (1882–88).

49. *Helena Daily Herald*, June 28, 1882, p. 3, col. 1.

50. Smalley, "The New North-West," 865.

51. WM, Oct. 27, 1882, p. 3, col. 1.

52. Ronan to CIA, May 2, 1883, Ronan letters, vol. 1: 206–9; WM, Apr. 20, 1883, p. 3, col. 2.

53. WM, July 6, 1883, p. 3, col. 3.

54. "From St. Paul to Portland," *New-York Times*, Sept. 23, 1883, p. 6, col. 5–6.

55. Ronan to CIA, Oct. 1, 1883, Ronan letters, vol. 1: 223–26.

56. *Missoula County Times*, May 28, 1884, p. 2, col. 3.

57. Ronan to CIA, Aug. 30, 1884, Ronan letters, vol. 1: 275–80.

58. Ronan to CIA, Feb. 12, 1885, Ronan letters, vol. 1: 306–10.

59. WM, May 8, 1885, p. 3, col. 4.

60. "Flathead Agency," WM, July 24, 1885, p. 2, col. 2–3.

61. Ronan to CIA, Aug. 1885, Ronan letters, vol. 1: 316–21.

62. "Estrays," WM, Aug. 14, 1885, p. 3, col. 4.

63. "Estray Horse," WM, July 30, 1886, p. 3, col. 5.

64. "Another Indian Offense," NNW, Dec. 3, 1886, p. 3, col. 6.

65. H. McDonald Clark, "Charlie Young Still Going Strong at 85," *Great Falls Tribune*, Feb. 13, 1955, Montana Parade, pp. 10–12.

66. Palladino, *Indian and White*, 160–61.

67. "An Indian Horse Thief," *Butte Semi-Weekly Miner*, May 18, 1887, p. 4, col. 5; "An Indian Clubbed to Death," *Butte Semi-Weekly Miner*, May 21, 1887, p. 2, col. 4.

68. McLeod, *A Cowboy's Life*, 13.

69. ARCIA (1882–88).

70. ARCIA (1882–88).

71. Smalley, "The New North-West," 863–72.

72. Ingersoll, "The Last Remnant of Frontier," 131–44.

73. White, "Garfield!: An Incident," 10–11.

74. Ronan to CIA, Aug. 13, 1883, Ronan letters, vol. 1: 215–18.

75. Dana, "Among the Kalispel," p. 2, col. 2–3.

76. Ronan to CIA, Aug. 20, 1883, Ronan letters, vol. 1: 219–22; "The Flatheads Object," *Helena Independent*, Aug. 25, 1883, p. 5, col. 3.

77. Ronan to CIA, Oct. 1, 1883, Ronan letters, vol. 1: 223–26.

78. Ronan to CIA, June 11, 1884, Ronan letters, vol. 1: 263–65.

79. Ronan to CIA, Aug. 30, 1884, Ronan letters, vol. 1: 275–80.

80. F. Jay Haynes photos H-1338 and H-1341, MHS Photograph Archives, Helena, Mont.

81. Wheeler, W. F., "A Journey to the West Side," 4–5.

82. "St. Ignatius News," *Butte Semi-Weekly Miner*, Dec. 15, 1886, p. 1, col. 6.

83. WM, Feb. 24, 1888, p. 3, col. 1; "For Sale: 500 Head of Cattle," WM, Feb. 24, 1888, p. 3, col. 4.

84. *Missoula Gazette*, Aug. 18, 1888, p. 3, col. 2.

85. E. D. Bannister to SecInt, Oct. 20, 1888, NAmf M1070, 5261/1888.

86. *Weekly Missoulian*, May 1, 1885, p. 3, col. 1; "Raising Buffaloes," *Missoula County Times*, June 8, 1887, p. 3, col. 2.

87. "The Latest—A Buffalo for Christmas," WM, Dec. 19, 1888, p. 3, col. 2; *Missoula Gazette* (weekly), Dec. 29, 1888, p. 3, col. 2.

88. ARCIA (1882–88).

89. Ronan to CIA, Feb. 1, 1882, Ronan letters, vol. 1: 176–78.

90. Smalley, "The New North-West," 863–72.

91. Ronan to T. C. Power, July 27, 1882, Ronan letters, vol. 1: 185–86, Ronan to T. C. Power, Sept. 25, 1882, Ronan letters, vol. 1: 191–92.

92. Peter Ronan to Thos. C. Power, Aug. 29, 1883, Aug. 25 and 30, 1884, Thomas C. Power Paper, MS 55, MHS Archives, Helena, Montana.

93. Ingersoll, "The Last Remnant of Frontier," 140.

94. U.S. President, "Message," 1883, 24.

95. [DeRouge], "Mission of St. Ignatius," 206–12.

96. S. S. Benedict to SecInt, July 10, 1883, NAmf M1070, 3093/83.

97. WM, Aug. 10, 1883, p. 3, col. 4; War Dept. to CIA, August 23, 1883, LR 15,679/1883, NA CIA LR; War Dept. to CIA, Sept. 6, 1883, LR 16,640/1883, NA CIA LR.

98. Ronan to CIA, Dec. 26, 1883, Ronan letters, vol. 1: 234–36.

99. "Arlee," WM, Aug. 22, 1884, p. 2, col. 3.

100. Robert S. Gardner to SecInt, Jan. 30, 1885, NAmf M1070, 585/1885.

101. Wheeler, W. F., "A Journey to the West Side," 4–5.

102. Ronan to CIA, Aug. 1885, Ronan letters, vol. 1: 316–21.

103. Ronan to CIA, Oct. 14, 1885, Ronan letters, vol. 1: 327–29.

104. Ronan to CIA, Mar. 29, 1886, Ronan letters, vol. 1: 351–53.

105. Ronan to CIA, Apr. 30, 1886, Ronan letters, vol. 1: 354–56; Ronan to CIA, Sept. 1, 1886, Ronan letters, vol. 1: 365–66.

106. Ronan to CIA, June 3, 1886, Ronan letters, vol. 1: 359–60.

107. Ronan to CIA, Aug. 15, 1886, Ronan letters, vol. 1: 360–64.

108. Geo. B. Pearsons to SecInt, Nov. 11, 1886, NAmf M1070, 6543/1886.

109. Ronan to CIA, Dec. 1, 1886, Ronan letters, vol. 1: 372–73.

110. A. L. Demers to T. M. Sweeney, Aug. 2, 1886, Thomas C. Power Papers, MS 55, MHS Archives, Helena; A. L. Demers to T. C. Power & Co., Sept. 6, 1888, Thomas C. Power Papers, MS 55, MHS Archives, Helena.

111. Ronan to CIA, Aug. 27, 1887, Ronan letters, vol. 1: 401–8.

112. E. D. Bannister to SecInt, Oct. 20, 1888, NAmf M1070, 5261/1888.

113. Ronan to CIA, Mar. 27, 1884, Ronan letters, vol. 1: 256–59.

114. WM, Jan. 23, 1885, p. 3, col. 1.

115. Ronan to CIA, Mar. 2, 1886, Ronan letters, vol. 1: 348–49.

116. Ronan to CIA, Jan. 23, 1888, Ronan letters, vol. 2: 2–3.

117. Ronan to CIA, Aug. 7, 1888, Ronan letters, vol. 2: 14–15.

118. Smalley, "The New North-West," 863–72.

119. Ronan to Thos. C. Power, Sept. 25, 1882, box 117, folder 1, Thomas C. Power Papers, MS 55, MHS Archives, Helena.

120. Ronan to CIA, Aug. 12, 1884, Ronan letters, vol. 1: 268–72.

121. Ronan to CIA, Aug. 15, 1886, Ronan letters, vol. 1: 360–64.

122. Ronan to CIA, Mar. 29, 1886, Ronan letters, vol. 1: 351–53.

123. Ronan to CIA, Nov. 1, 1882, Ronan letters, vol. 1: 194–95.

124. S. S. Benedict to SecInt, July 10, 1883, NAmf M1070, 3093/83.

125. Ronan to CIA, Nov. 24, 1883, Ronan letters, vol. 1: 232–36.

126. Ronan to CIA, Apr. 30, 1886, Ronan letters, vol. 1: 354–56.

127. Ronan to CIA, Jan. 15, 1884, Ronan letters, vol. 1: 238–43; R. M. Baird to CIA, Feb. 18, 1884, Ronan letters, vol. 1: 252–53.

128. Bigart, A Pretty Village, 106–9, 212–17, and 227–30.

129. Ronan to CIA, Dec. 1, 1882, Ronan letters, vol. 1: 198–99.

130. Ronan to CIA, Aug. 13, 1883, Ronan letters, vol. 1: 215–18.

131. Bigart and McDonald, Duncan McDonald, 49–52.

132. Bigart and McDonald, Duncan McDonald, 55–61.

133. Ronan to CIA, Jan. 15, 1889, Ronan letters, vol. 2: 31.

134. U.S. Interior Department, Official Register (1887), vol. 1: 550–51.

135. U.S. Interior Department, Official Register (1881), vol. 1: 572.

136. "Flathead Reservation," WM, May 8, 1885, p. 2, col. 4.

137. Ronan to CIA, Oct. 6, 1882, Ronan letters, vol. 1: 193–94.

138. Ronan to CIA, July 26, 1883, Ronan letters, vol. 1: 214–15.

139. Peter Ronan to T. C. Power, Jan. 14, 1884, box 117, folder 1, Thomas C. Power Papers, MS 55, MHS Archives, Helena.

140. Photograph H-1334, MHS Photographic Archives, Helena, Montana.

141. Ronan to CIA, Mar. 2, 1886, Ronan letters, vol. 1: 348–49.

142. Ronan to CIA, Dec. 28, 1886, Ronan letters, vol. 1: 376–77.

143. St. Ignatius Mission account book, reel 6, frames 377–78, 383, 408, 411–12, 429, and 430, PNTMC.

144. Smalley, "Among the Flathead Indians," 515.

145. Howlett, "His Mystery," WM, Mar. 27, 1885, p. 1, col. 5–7.

146. "Arlee," WM, Aug. 22, 1884, p. 2, col. 3.

147. U.S. Attorney-General, Annual Report, 134; Dept. of Justice to CIA, Feb. 11, 1886, 4,717/1886, NA CIA LR.

148. C. H. Howard to SecInt, Dec. 4, 1883, NAmf M1070, 5061/83.

149. WM, Jan. 18, 1884, p. 3, col. 3.

150. McLeod, A Cowboy's Life, 12–13.

151. Staveley Hill, From Home to Home, 369, 372.

152. "Travel Stains," WM, Oct. 19, 1883, p. 2, col. 1.

153. Smalley, "The Kalispel Country," 447–55.

154. Manning, "Traveling in Montana," 8–10.

155. Smalley, "Recollections of the Northwest," 16–17.

156. Ingersoll, "The Last Remnant of Frontier," 138–39.

157. Ronan to CIA, Aug. 1, 1882, Ronan letters, vol. 1, pp. 186–87; CIA to Ronan, Sept. 18, 1882, letter press, vol. 37, part 1, pp. 171–74, civilization, NA CIA LS.

158. Staveley Hill, *From Home to Home*, 375.

159. C. H. Howard to SecInt, Dec. 4, 1883, NAmf M1070, 5061/83; Ronan to CIA, Dec. 26, 1883, Ronan letters, vol. 1, pp. 234–36.

160. Stout, *Montana*, vol. 3: 1277, "C. A. Stillinger"; "Around the Town," DM, Feb. 28, 1923, p. 2, col. 3.

161. "The Indian Troubles," WM, Dec. 25, 1885, p. 2, col. 1.

162. *Missoula County Times*, June 8, 1887, p. 3, col. 3.

163. Bigart and McDonald, *Duncan McDonald*, 63–68.

164. Ronan to CIA, Oct. 23, 1886, Ronan letters, vol. 1: 369–71.

165. A. L. Demers to T. M. Sweeney, Aug. 12, 1886, box 17, folder 20, Thomas C. Power Papers, MS 55, MHS Archives, Helena; A. L. Demers to T. C. Power & Co., Sept. 6, 1888, box 19 folder 17, Thomas C. Power Papers, MS 55, MHS Archives, Helena.

166. "Selish," WM, Apr. 18, 1884, p. 2, col. 3.

167. Ronan to CIA, July 28, 1884, Ronan letters, v01.1: 265–67.

168. S. S. Benedict to SecInt, July 10, 1883, NAmf M1070, 3093/83.

169. WM, July 7, 1882, p. 3, col. 2.

170. WM, Dec. 8, 1882, p. 3, col. 2.

171. *Rocky Mountain Husbandman* (White Sulphur Springs, Mont.), Feb. 23, 1882, p. 3, col. 1.

172. Smalley, "The New North-West," 864.

173. "Tyson D Duncan," Samuel E. Johns Papers, SC 165, microfilm, Toole Archives, Mansfield Library, University of Montana, Missoula, vol. 3: 16–23.

174. "Arlee," WM, Aug. 22, 1884, p. 2, col. 3.

175. WM, May 1, 1885, p. 3, col. 1.

176. "School News," WM, Oct. 23, 1885, p. 2, col. 4.

177. Ronan to CIA, Dec. 17, 1885, Ronan letters, vol. 1: 343–46; "Bad Indians," WM, Dec. 18, 1885, p. 3, col. 4.

178. WM, Dec. 25, 1885, p. 3, col. 4.

179. "St. Ignatius Mission," *Catholic Sentinel for the Northwest* (Portland, Ore.), May 20, 1886, p. 1, col. 1–5.

180. WM, May 28, 1886, p. 3, col. 4.

181. "The Latest—A Buffalo for Christmas," WM, Dec. 19, 1888, p. 3, col. 2; *Missoula Gazette* (weekly), Dec. 29, 1888, p. 3, col. 2.

182. Jerome D'Aste, S.J., diaries, Dec. 29, 1888, PNTMC, reel 29, fr. 573.

183. William Flynn, "Story of How Major Ronan Quelled Trouble Between Indians and Section Crew . . . ," *Mineral Independent* (Superior, Mont.), Dec. 14, 1933, p. 3, col. 1–6; J. H. Mitchell, Washington, D.C., to CIA, Mar. 12, 1885, LR 5,369/1885, NA CIA LR; Ronan to CIA, Mar 13, 1885, Ronan letters, vol. 1: 313–14.

184. WM, June 30, 1882, p. 2, col. 1; WM, June 30, 1882, p. 3, col. 3; Dec. 1, 1882, Ronan letters, vol. 1: 198–99.

185. WM, Sept. 8, 1882, p. 3, col. 2.

186. "A Whisky Seller to Indians Sold," *Helena Daily Herald*, Sept. 13, 1882, p. 3, col. 2.

187. WM, Jan. 26, 1883, p. 3, col. 2; "An Exhibit of the Receipts and Expenditures of Missoula County, Montana Territory, from March 1, 1882, to March 1, 1883," WM, Mar. 30, 1883, p. 4, col. 1–4; Ronan to Mr. Eastman, Feb. 1, 1883, Ronan letters, vol. 1: 202–3.

188. NNW, May 20, 1887, p. 2, col. 7; "An Indian Clubbed to Death," *Butte Semi-Weekly Miner*, May 21, 1887, p. 2, col. 4.

189. Ruger, "Report of Col. Thomas H. Ruger," 1883, 122–23; WM, Aug. 10, 1883, p. 3, col. 2; WM, Aug. 10, 1883, p. 3, col. 4; Ronan to CIA, Aug. 13, 1883, Ronan letters, vol. 1: 215–18.

190. "Flathead Reservation," WM, May 8, 1885, p. 2, col. 4.

191. Inspector C. H. Howard, Washington, D.C., to SecInt, Jan. 19, 1884, LR 1,465/1884, NA CIA LR.

192. "Assaults, Mishaps Etc.," *Missoula County Times*, Oct. 21, 1885, p. 3, col. 5.

193. "Indians and Whisky," *Butte Semi-Weekly Miner*, Oct. 9, 1886, p. 1, col. 8.

194. Ruger, "Report of Col. Thomas H. Ruger," 1883, 120; WM, Apr. 20, 1883, p. 3, col. 2.

195. WM, Oct. 26, 1883, p. 3, col. 3–4.

196. WM, Nov. 2, 1883, p. 3, col. 2.

197. "An Indian Horse Thief," *Butte Semi-Weekly Miner*, May 18, 1887, p. 4, col. 5.

198. "An Indian Clubbed to Death," *Butte Semi-Weekly Miner*, May 21, 1887, p. 2, col. 4.

199. "They Captured Him," NNW, Oct. 7, 1887, p. 3, col. 4; *Missoula County Times*, Oct. 12, 1887, p. 3, col. 3.

Chapter 3

1. Jerome D'Aste, S.J., diaries, Sept. 21 and 25, 1890, Bigart, *Zealous in All Virtues*, 59–60.

2. Jerome D'Aste, S.J., diaries, Oct. 4, 1902, PNTMC, reel 30, fr. 19.

3. Ronan to CIA, Nov. 20, 1889, Ronan letters, vol. 2: 103–4.

4. Bigart and Woodcock, *In the Name of the Salish*, 12.

5. J. S. Booth, "Game Warden Booth's Trip After Indians on the Thompson River," *Weekly Plainsman*, Mar. 28, 1896, p. 1, col. 5; DM, Apr. 15, 1896, p. 1, col. 5.

6. Carter to CIA, Apr. 16, 1896, 15,291/1896, NA CIA LR.

7. CIA to Carter, May 1, 1896, land, letter book 331, pp. 420–24, NA CIA LS.

8. J. B. Weber, Forest Supervisor, Hamilton, to Smead, Aug. 25, 1903, FH Agency Papers LR.

9. SecInt to CIA, Oct. 21, 1903, 68,273/1903, NA CIA LR.

10. Brownell, "The Genesis of Wildlife," 13–43.

11. "The Pesky Red-Skins," WM, Mar. 5, 1890, p. 3, col. 3; "Flathead Lake News," WM, Mar. 19, 1890, p. 4, col. 5.

12. "Game Laws Violated," *Inter Lake* (Kalispell, Mont.), Mar. 31, 1893, p. 2, col. 2; "To Fight the Game Law," AS, Apr. 13, 1893, p. 6, col. 1.

13. "Missoula Mention," AS, Dec. 14, 1894, p. 6, col. 1.

14. *Inter Lake* (Kalispell, Mont.), Feb. 7, 1896, p. 8, col. 2.

15. "Indian in Hard Luck," AS, Apr. 9, 1897, p. 1, col. 6.

16. Walcheck, "Montana Wildlife 170 Years Ago," 15–30; Koch, "Big Game in Montana," 357–70.

17. Koch, "Big Game in Montana" 368.

18. Lippincott, "Grandeur in an American Forest," 24–28.

19. "Game Law a Dead Letter," AS, Oct. 28, 1900, p. 14, col. 1–3.

20. "Alex Bigknife Loses His Gun," *Missoulian* (daily), Sept. 5, 1903, p. 8, col. 2.

21. W. F. Scott, Mont. Fish & Game Warden, Helena, to Smead, Sept. 8, 1903, FH Agency Papers LR.

22. "Indians Contest State Law," *Missoulian* (daily), Sept. 13, 1903, p. 1, col. 4; p. 8, col. 3.

23. Henderson, "The Flathead Indians," 1–3.

24. Mariam L. Clayton, "Smead Landing Early Cedar Mill Location," *Sanders County Ledger* (Thompson Falls, Mont.), June 2, 1966, p. 1, col. 5–7; p. 2, col. 5–7.

25. "Autumn Sport on Flathead Lake," *Atlanta Constitution* (Atlanta, Ga.), May 19, 1895, p. 24, col. 4–6.

26. Justice Court Dockets, Feb. 1888–July 1900, Missoula County Records, MS 310, Toole Archives, Mansfield Library, University of Montana, Missoula, series II, vol. 138, p. 14, and vol. 153, p. 168.

27. McKeogh, "The New Scholasticate," 71–85.

28. Morton J. Elrod, "Four Stories About Flathead Indians," Morton J. Elrod Papers, MS UM 4, Toole Archives, Mansfield Library, University of Montana, Missoula, box 14, folder 9.

29. Smead to Henry Fingado, Chatauqua, Mont., May 7, 1903, FH Agency Papers LS.

30. Mariam L. Clayton, "Smead Landing Early Cedar Mill Location," *Sanders County Ledger* (Thompson Falls, Mont.), June 2, 1966, p. 1, col. 5–7; p. 2, col. 5–7.

31. Jerome D'Aste, S.J., diaries, June 2, 1901, PNTMC, reel 29, fr. 973–74.

32. Dan Longpre, "People and Places in the Frenchtown Valley," Frenchtown Historical Society Collection, OH 47–9, Toole Archives, Mansfield Library, University of Montana, Missoula.

33. ARCIA (1889–1904).

34. "It's Time to Make a Kick," *Inter Lake* (Demersville, Mont.), Feb. 6, 1891, p. 3, col. 3–4.

35. *Missoula Gazette* (daily), Jan. 6, 1892, p. 4, col. 2.

36. *Flathead Herald-Journal* (Kalispell, Mont.), Sept. 8, 1893, p. 8, col. 1.

37. Special Agent M. D. Shelby to CIA, July 31, 1897, 32,290/1897, NA CIA LR.

38. Mr. C. W. Howe, Missoula, to Smead, Feb. 9, 1898, FH Agency Papers LR.

39. Smead to Lackery, Indian, May 8, 1898, FH Agency Papers LS.

40. Smead to Judge Joseph Standing Bear, St. Ignatius, May 20, 1898, FH Agency Papers LS.

41. Smead to John Peter, Missoula, July 5, 1898, FH Agency Papers LS.

42. Smead to Charles Allard, Ronan, Nov. 12, 1898, FH Agency Papers LS; Smead to George Guardepe, Mission, Nov. 26, 1898, FH Agency Papers LS.

43. Smead to Horatio Cook, Columbia Falls, Aug. 23, 1899, FH Agency Papers LS.

44. Smead to (no addressee), June 13, 1900, FH Agency Papers LS; J. H. Corrall, Missoula Feed Corral, to Smead, Mar. 25, 1901, FH Agency Papers LR.

45. Olin D. Wheeler, *Indianland and Wonderland*, 27.

46. "The Flathead Indians," *Silver Occident* (Missoula, Mont.), May 16, 1896, p. 3, col. 5.

47. Carter to CIA, Aug. 20, 1897, ARCIA (1897), pp. 166–70.

48. "Indians and Horses," AS, Nov. 2, 1895, p. 10, col. 3–4.

49. "The Nez Perce Cayuses," AS, Nov. 14, 1895, p. 10, col. 3–4.

50. Carter to CIA, Jan. 29, 1896, 4,996/1896, NA CIA LR.

51. Carter to CIA, Aug. 20, 1897, ARCIA (1897), pp. 166–70.

52. Smead to U.S. Indian Agent, Pendleton, Ore., Feb. 21, 1899, FH Agency Papers LS.

53. Cyrus Beede to CIA, Aug. 14, 1900, 40,931/1900, NA CIA LR.

54. Cyrus Beede to SecInt, Aug. 25, 1900, NAmf M1070, 6597/1900.

55. "They Spoil the Range," AS, Feb. 27, 1900, p. 16, col. 2.

56. *Plainsman*, Aug. 17, 1900, p. 4, col. 4.

57. *Plainsman*, Aug. 31, 1900, p. 1, col. 5.

58. *Plainsman*, Sept. 7, 1900, p. 1, col. 6.

59. Smead to C. C. Willis, Plains, July 16, 1901, FH Agency Papers LS.

60. Smead to C. C. Willis, Plains, Aug. 23, 1901, FH Agency Papers LS.

61. *Plainsman*, Aug. 23, 1901 p. 4, col. 5.

62. *Plainsman*, Sept. 20, 1901, p. 4, col. 4.

63. "Pain Held to Grand Jury," AS, Nov. 27, 1901, p. 14, col. 5; "Indian Confidence Game," *Missoulian* (daily), Nov. 27, 1901, p. 5, col. 5.

64. *Plainsman*, Feb. 14, 1902, p. 4, col. 3.

65. "Picked from the Plainsman," *Missoula Democrat*, June 19, 1902, p. 8, col. 4–5.

66. Smead to Mr. C. C. Willis, Plains, Apr. 15, 1903, FH Agency Papers LS.

67. *Missoulian* (daily), July 5, 1904, p. 3, col. 5.

68. "Jap Agents in Local Horse Market," *Missoulian* (daily), July 14, 1904, p. 3, col. 2.

69. "Montana Range Horses Shipped to the East," AS, Sept. 11, 1904, p. 13, col. 4.

70. Report from Inspector Arthur M. Tinker to Secretary of the Interior, Sept. 20, 1903, Office of the Secretary of the Interior, RG 48, National Archives, Washington, D.C., #9007/1903.

71. Cyrus S. Beede, Flathead Agency, to CIA, Aug. 14, 1900, 40,931/1900, NA CIA LR.

72. CIA to Smead, Sept. 22, 1900, land, letter book 452, pp. 210–12, NA CIA LS.

73. Smead to Angus P. McDonald, Dayton, Apr, 15, 1899, FH Agency Papers LS.

74. Smead to A. L. Demers, St. Ignatius, May 18, 1901, FH Agency Papers LS; Smead to Deaf Louie, St. Ignatius, May 18, 1901, FH Agency Papers LS.

75. *Missoulian* (daily), June 1, 1901, p. 4, col. 3.

76. "Demand for Horses Is Exceedingly Large," AS, Sept. 9, 1901, p. 10, col. 3.

77. *Missoulian* (daily), Nov. 2, 1901, p. 8, col. 3.

78. "Japanese Want Our Horses," *Missoulian* (daily), July 9, 1904, p. 3, col. 3.

79. Smead to Mr. S. L. Moore, General Freight Agent, St. Paul, Minn., Sept. 12, 1899, FH Agency Papers LS; Smead to Mr. H. F. Ruger, General Agent, Helena, Sept. 12, 1899, FH Agency Papers LS.

80. Smead to Mr. C. C. Willis, Plains, Apr. 15, 1903, FH Agency Papers LS.

81. Smead to CIA, Feb. 10, 1898, 7,976/1898, NA CIA LR.

82. Report from W. J. McConnell to Secretary of the Interior, June 1, 1901, Interior Department Inspection Reports, RG 48, National Archives, Washington, D.C., #4584/1901.

83. Smead to CIA, Feb. 24, 1903, 13,682/1903, NA CIA LR.

84. CIA to Smead, Mar. 5, 1903, land, letter book 589, pp. 179–81, NA CIA LS.

85. Smead to no addressee, May 2, 1903, FH Agency Papers LS.

86. "Inspecting Horses," AS, June 29, 1900, p 12, col. 2.

87. *Plainsman*, Aug. 17, 1900, p. 4, col. 4.

88. "Missoula Valley Looks Fine," AS, June 28, 1901, p. 12, col. 2.

89. Matt, "Blind Mose Remembers," 6–7.

90. "The Horse Races," *Inter Lake* (Kalispell, Mont.), July 7, 1899, p. 5, col. 3.

91. "Had a Good Time," *Kalispell Bee*, July 6, 1900, p. 3, col. 3–4; "The Fourth in Kalispell," *Inter Lake* (Kalispell, Mont.), July 6, 1900, p. 5, col. 2–3.

92. "Missoula Notes," AS, May 30, 1901, p. 16, col. 4.

93. "The Cayuse Won," *Missoulian* (daily), June 29, 1901, p. 1, col. 5.

94. "Tuesday's Races," *Inter Lake* (Kalispell, Mont.), July 3, 1903, p. 5, col. 4.

95. *Plainsman*, Apr. 17, 1903, p. 4, col. 5.

96. Smead to Jos. Sepay, Ravalli, Apr. 9, 1900, FH Agency Papers LS; Smead to J. F. Fulton, Claim Agent, Northern Pacific Railroad, St. Paul, May 16, 1904, FH Agency Papers LS.

97. ARCIA (1889–1904).

98. WM, Jan. 14, 1891, p. 4, col. 2.

99. *Missoula Gazette* (daily), Aug. 8, 1891, p. 4, col. 2.

100. McLeod, *A Cowboy's Life*, 22.

101. *Evening Missoulian*, Sept. 8, 1893, p. 4, col. 1.

102. *Montana Populist* (Missoula, Mont.), Nov. 16, 1893, p. 3, col. 1.

103. Carter to CIA, Aug. 20, 1895, ARCIA (1895), pp. 189–92.

104. *Evening Republican* (Missoula, Mont.), Aug. 19, 1895, p. 4, col. 1.

105. Carter to CIA, Aug. 27, 1896, ARCIA (1896), pp. 184–88.

106. "No M'Kinley Votes," AS, Oct. 15, 1896, p. 10, col. 1.

107. "A Cattle Shipment," AS, Oct. 26, 1897, p. 10, col. 1.

108. P. McCormick to Secretary of the Interior, Feb. 17, 1895, NAmf M1070, 1627/95.

109. U.S. Census Office, *Census Bulletin*.

110. Interior Department to CIA, Aug. 5, 1901, 42,669/1901, NA CIA LR.

111. Smead to Mrs. Philomene Peone, DeSmet, Idaho, Mar. 14, 1898, FH Agency Papers LS.

112. Charles S. McNichols, Jocko, Mont., to CIA, Dec. 31, 1902, 822/1903, NA CIA LR.

113. Chas. S. McNichols, Jocko, Mont., to CIA, Jan. 5, 1903, 1,789/1903, enclosure no. 1 of 6,311/1903, NA CIA LR.

114. Ronan to CIA, August 5, 1893, Ronan letters, vol. 2: 371–79.

115. "Big General Roundup of Cattle and Horses," AS, Sept. 18, 1904, p. 2, col. 4.

116. ARCIA (1889–1904).

117. Ronan to CIA, August 1, 1889, Ronan letters, vol. 2: 60–61.

118. [Smalley?], "The Fertile Flathead Country," 46–48.

119. *Weekly Plainsman*, July 4, 1896, p. 1, col. 3; *Weekly Plainsman*, July 11, 1896, p. 1, col. 3.

120. "Heard on the Side," AS, Aug. 9, 1896, p. 10, col. 1.

121. "Cattle on the Jocko," AS, Mar. 24, 1897, p. 10, col. 1.

122. "Feed Is Short," AS, May 11, 1898, p. 10, col. 1.

123. "A Heavy Loss of Stock," AS, Apr. 29, 1899, p. 12, col. 2.

124. *Plainsman*, Sept. 5, 1902, p. 4, col. 4.

125. Smead to To Whom It May Concern, June 13, 1899, FH Agency Papers LS.

126. Smead to Gaspard Deschamps, May 28, 1900, FH Agency Papers LS.

127. Smead to Gaspard Deschamps, July 18, 1900, FH Agency Papers LS; Smead to Gaspard Deschamps, Missoula, May 20, 1901, FH Agency Papers LS.

128. Smead to Frank Jette, Kalispell, June 12, 1903, FH Agency Papers LS.

129. Carter to CIA, Aug. 20, 1894, ARCIA (1894), 173–77.

130. "Cattle in Healthy Condition," AS, Sept. 29, 1900, p. 12, col. 2; John R. Daily, Missoula, to Smead, Mar. 21, 1901, FH Agency Papers LR; *Plainsman*, June 7, 1901, p. 4, col. 4.

131. "Inspecting Horses," AS, June 29, 1900, p 12, col. 2.

132. W. J. McConnell to SecInt, Aug. 27, 1897, NAmf M1070, 6566/97.

133. Report from Inspector Jame E. Jenkins to Secretary of the Interior, Mar. 15, 1902, Office of the Secretary of the Interior, RG 48, National Archives, Washington, D.C., #2828/1902.

134. CIA to Smead, Feb. 2, 1903, letter book 582, pp. 68–71, land, NA CIA LS.

135. Smead to CIA, Feb. 24, 1903, 13,682/1903, NA CIA LR.

136. Charlot, et. al., to SecInt, Apr. 4, 1903, Sisters of Providence, "St. Ignatius," 154.

137. "The Tax Levy Must Be Paid," *Missoulian* (daily), Apr. 10, 1903, p. 3, col. 1; "They'll Have to Pay It," AS, May 4, 1903, p. 10, col. 1.

138. CIA to Smead, May 13, 1903, letter book 603, pp. 105–6, land, NA CIA LS.

139. Smead to CIA, June 1, 1903, 34,876/1903, NA CIA LR.

140. Smead to CIA, Oct. 22, 1903, 68,996/1903, NA CIA LR; Smead to CIA, Nov. 20, 1903, telegram, 75,236/1903, NA CIA LR.

141. "Soldiers Leave for Reservation," AS, Nov. 27, 1903, p. 12, col. 1–2.

142. "It Was a Wierdly [sic] Garbled Account," AS, Nov. 29, 1903, p. 12, col. 1–2; Smead to CIA, Nov. 29, 1903, telegram, 77,120/1903, NA CIA LR.

143. "Stock Tax Collected," Missoulian (daily), Dec. 20, 1903, p. 8, col. 2.

144. "Shortages of Stock," AS, July 7, 1897, p. 10, col. 2.

145. "In a Desperate Fight," AS, Aug. 24, 1899, p. 12, col. 2; "Was All in Fun," AS, Aug. 31, 1899, p. 10, col. 2.

146. Smead to W. G. Preuitt, Helena, May 18, 1901, FH Agency Papers LS.

147. Wm. Preuitt, Montana Board of Stock Commissioners, to Smead, May 27, 1901, FH Agency Papers LR.

148. W. G. Preuitt, Sec, Mont. Board of Stock Commissioners, to Smead, Sept. 12, 1901, FH Agency Papers LR.

149. "Reds on War Path," Missoulian (daily), Aug. 6, 1901, p 1, col. 2.

150. Smead to Stranahan Agent, North Lapwai, Idaho, telegram, Aug. 31, 1901, FH Agency Papers LS; Smead to Major C. T. Stranahan, Spaulding, Idaho, Sept. 5, 1901, FH Agency Papers LS; Smead to Maj. C. T. Stranahan, Spaulding, Idaho, Sept. 10, 1901, FH Agency Papers LS; Smead to David Dowd, St. Ignatius, Sept. 10, 1901, FH Agency Papers LS.

151. "Charged with Stealing Cattle," AS, Oct. 31, 1902, p. 16, col. 3–4; "Acquitted of Cattle Stealing," AS, Nov. 2, 1902, p. 14, col. 7.

152. L. Van Gorp, St. Ignatius, to Smead, Apr. 29, 1904, FH Agency Papers LR.

153. "Stychen Held to Grand Jury," Missoulian (daily), May 12, 1904, p. 6, col. 5.

154. Jerome D'Aste, S.J., diaries, Nov. 23, 1904, PNTMC, reel 30, fr. 98.

155. Smead to Mr. W. G. Preuitt, Helena, Oct. 14, 1901, FH Agency Papers LS.

156. "Stockmen Organize," Missoulian (daily), Nov. 17, 1901, p. 8, col. 3–4; Missoulian (daily), Nov. 17, 1901, p. 6, col. 4.

157. "Permanent Organization," Fruit Grower and Farmer (Missoula, Mont.), Dec. 6, 1901 (i.e., Dec. 13, 1901), p. 3, col. 3.

158. Smead to F. M. Rothrock, Wallace, Idaho, Nov. 22, 1901, FH Agency Papers LS.

159. Smead to J. S. Dupuis, Ronan, Jan. 29, 1902, FH Agency Papers LS.

160. Joseph Allard, St. Ignatius, to Smead, Apr. 7, 1902, FH Agency Papers LR.

161. "Meeting of Flathead Stockmen," AS, Apr. 24, 1902, p 14, col. 5.

162. Smead to CIA, May 19, 1900, 24,870/1900, NA CIA LR; Smead to Frank McLeod, Mar. 7, 1902, FH Agency Papers LS.

163. Ki Ki Shee, St. Ignatius, to Smead, Nov. 9, 1903, FH Agency Papers LR; Smead to Henry Felsman, St. Ignatius, Nov. 10, 1903, FH Agency Papers LS.

164. "Eight Petitions Being Circulated," AS, Jan. 21, 1904, p. 12, col. 3.

165. W. B. Parsons, M.D., Missoula, to CIA, July 7, 1903, 42,944/1903, NA CIA LR.

166. Gordon, When Money Grew on Trees, 13–14, 160–61.

167. Smead to CIA, Aug. 24, 1903, 55,135/1903, NA CIA LR.

168. Dr. W. B. Parsons, Missoula, to CIA, Dec. 20, 1903, 82,847/1903, NA CIA LR.

169. CIA to W. B. Parsons, Jan. 2, 1904, letter book 644, pp. 105–6, land, NA CIA LS.

170. Inter Lake (Demersville, Mont.), Jan. 16, 1891, p. 3, col. 1.

171. "A Novel Exhibit," *Missoula Gazette* (daily), May 18, 1892, p. 1, col. 3.

172. "Miles' Buffalo Exhibit," *Kalispell Graphic*, Aug. 24, 1892, p. 3, col. 1–2; "Interesting Interview," *Inter Lake* (Kalispell, Mont.), Sept. 2, 1892, p. 2, col. 2–3.

173. *Morning Missoulian*, Aug. 27, 1892, p. 5, col. 1.

174. "Buffalo Exhibit," *Kalispell Graphic*, Sept. 21, 1892, p. 2, col. 4.

175. "Not Declared Off," *Inter Lake* (Kalispell, Mont.), Mar. 3, 1893, p. 1, col. 6–7; "Buffalo and Indians," *Inter Lake* (Kalispell, Mont.), Mar. 31, 1893, p. 1, col. 6.

176. Ronan to CIA, Mar. 25, 1892, Ronan letters, vol. 2: 295–98.

177. *Evening Missoulian*, Apr. 20, 1893, p. 4, col. 1.

178. McLeod, *A Cowboy's Life*, 22, 25.

179. "A Fortune in Buffalo," *Evening Missoulian*, Sept. 26, 1893, p. 4, col. 1.

180. "The Buffalo Are Here," AS, Oct. 8, 1893, p. 6, col. 4–6.

181. "Looked Like Old Times," AS, Oct. 9, 1893, p. 5, col. 1–2; McLeod, *A Cowboy's Life*, 22–29.

182. "A New Buffalo," AS, Nov. 1, 1893, p. 6, col. 3.

183. "The Wild West Show," *Missoulian* (daily), May 20, 1901, p. 4, col. 4; "Buffaloes Home Again," AS, June 16, 1901, p. 26, col. 4.

184. "Buffalo and Wild Indians," *Missoulian* (daily), May 4, 1902, p. 1, col. 6.

185. "Wild West Show," *Missoulian* (daily), May 8, 1902, p. 3, col. 3.

186. "Show Is Buffaloed," *Missoulian* (daily), Sept. 13, 1902, p. 8, col. 3; "Show People Return," AS, Sept. 14, 1902, p 14, col. 2.

187. DM, Oct. 15, 1897, p. 4, col. 1–2.

188. "For Christmas Dinners," AS, Dec. 20, 1899, p. 12, col. 4; "A Christmas Buffalo," *Inter Lake* (Kalispell, Mont.), Dec. 22, 1899, p. 5, col. 3; "Bunch of Buffalo," *Daily Democrat-Messenger* (Missoula, Mont.), Dec. 20, 1899, p. 1, col. 5; "Buffalo Killed," AS, Dec. 21, 1899, p. 1, col. 3.

189. "Missoula Notes," AS, Dec. 15, 1900, p. 16, col. 4.

190. *Missoulian* (daily), Feb. 11, 1902, p. 4, col. 6.

191. "High Priced Buffalo," AS, June 20, 1897, p. 10, col. 2.

192. "Bought Some Buffalo," *Inter Lake* (Kalispell, Mont.), Feb. 9, 1900, p. 5, col. 2.

193. *Kalispell Bee*, Apr. 17, 1901, p. 4, col. 1.

194. "Buys Buffaloes," AS, Feb. 12, 1902, p. 14, col. 4; *Plainsman*, Feb. 14, 1902, p. 1, col. 6.

195. Smead to C. Hart Merriam, Chief, Biological Survey, Washington, D.C., Feb. 18, 1902, FH Agency Papers LS.

196. "Buffalo for the Park," *Missoulian* (daily), Oct. 2, 1902, p. 1, col. 6.

197. "Buffalo Jones Buys More Buffaloes," AS, Nov. 14, 1902, p. 14, col. 4.

Chapter 4

1. ARCIA (1889–1904).

2. Ronan to CIA, Aug. 1885, Ronan letters, vol. 1: 319.

3. Ronan to CIA, Aug. 15, 1886, Ronan letters, vol. 1: 363.

4. Ronan to CIA, Oct. 31, 1890, Ronan letters, vol. 2: 168–70.

5. Ronan to CIA, Mar. 10, 1892, and June 1, 1892, Ronan letters, vol. 2: 288, 304–7.

6. Smead to Sam Belmont, St. Ignatius, Dec. 11, 1902, FH Agency Papers LS.

7. Carter to CIA, Aug. 20, 1895, ARCIA (1895), 189–92.

8. Carter to CIA, Aug. 20, 1897, ARCIA (1897), 166–70.

9. Antwin Parazo, St. Ignatius, to Smead, May 2, 1898, FH Agency Papers LR.

10. Smead to M. W. McLeod, Ronan, Jan. 2, 1900, FH Agency Papers LS.

11. Smead to Joseph Marion, Polson, Oct. 22, 1903, FH Agency Papers LS.

12. Smead to Moses Delaware, Ronan, Jan. 27, 1904, FH Agency Papers LS.

13. Smead to Eli Morrigeau, Aug. 28, 1899, FH Agency Papers LS.

14. Smead to no addressee, Dec. 7, 1899, FH Agency Papers LS.

15. Antoine Parzo, Ronan Spring, to Smead, Mar. 10, 1900, FH Agency Papers LR; Joseph Jones, Ronan, to Smead, Mar. 20, 1900, FH Agency Papers LR.

16. Smead to Thomas Moss, Polson, Apr. 5, 1900, FH Agency Papers LS.

17. Smead to Joe Deschamps, St. Ignatius, June 7, 1900, FH Agency Papers LS.

18. Smead to Joseph Jones, Ronan, Aug. 27, 1903, FH Agency Papers LS.

19. Chas. Allard, Polson to Smead, Sept. 19, 1903, FH Agency Papers LR.

20. Smead to Chief Michael, Camas, Dec. 27, 1903, FH Agency Papers LS.

21. Smead to Ed Deschamps, St. Ignatius, Sept. 20, 1900, FH Agency Papers LS.

22. Smead to Chas. Russell, Missoula, Apr. 29, 1901, FH Agency Papers LS.

23. Smead to CIA, June 14, 1904, 40,262/1904, NA CIA LR.

24. CIA to Smead, June 22, 1904, letter book 684, pp. 313–14, land, NA CIA LS.

25. Robert S. Gardner to Secretary of the Interior, Aug. 7, 1890, NAmf M1070, 5223/90.

26. James H. Cisney to Secretary of the Interior, July 23, 1891, NAmf M1070, 5803/91.

27. P. McCormick to Secretary of the Interior, Dec. 2, 1893, NAmf M1070, 9040/93.

28. Carter to CIA, Aug. 20, 1895, ARCIA (1895), 189–92.

29. C. C. Duncan to Secretary of the Interior, Oct. 10, 1896, NAmf M1070, 6805/96.

30. U.S. Census Office, Census Bulletin.

31. U.S. Census Office, Agriculture, pt. 1: 100–101.

32. U.S. Census Office, Census Bulletin.

33. Interior Department to CIA, Aug. 5, 1901, 42,669/1901, NA CIA LR.

34. Dusenberry, "Samples of Pend d'Oreille," 116–18.

35. Ronan to CIA, February 27, 1892, Ronan letters, vol. 2: 280–81.

36. "At the Reservation," AS, Nov. 1, 1893, p. 6, col. 1–2.

37. John Post, S.J., St. Ignatius, to Smead, May 8, 1902, FH Agency Papers LR.

38. "He Will Be Laid Up for Quite a Time," AS, Aug. 19, 1903, p. 12, col. 5; "Is a Son of Indian Chief," Missoulian (daily), Aug. 19, 1903, p. 8, col. 2.

39. Ronan to CIA, November 22, 1890, Ronan letters, vol. 2: 173–74.

40. "Hunting Fever," AS, Sept. 8, 1897, p. 10, col. 2.

41. U.S. Census Office, Census Bulletin.

42. Smead to Mr. L. G. Powers, Chief Statistician, Washington, D.C., Jan. 14, 1902, FH Agency Papers LS.

43. Henry B. Carrington, Arlee, Mont., to CIA, Oct. 28, 1889, 31,413/1889 NA CIA LR.

44. Ronan to CIA, February 1, 1890, Ronan letters, vol. 2: 119–20.

45. Ronan to CIA, Apr. 1, 1891, Ronan letters, vol. 2: 200–201.

46. Ronan to CIA, telegram, October 25, 1891, Ronan letters, vol. 2: 248; Ronan to CIA, November 2, 1891, Ronan letters, vol. 2: 253–54.

47. Post, "A Model Indian Mission," 723–24.

48. "Indian Farmer," AS, May 8, 1896, p. 10, col. 1.

49. Inter Lake (Kalispell, Mont.), July 14, 1896, p. 4, col. 1.

50. Carter to CIA, Aug. 27, 1896, ARCIA (1896), 184–88; "With the Flatheads," AS, Oct. 1, 1896, p. 10, col. 1.

51. "An Electrical Storm," AS, June 25, 1897, p. 10, col. 2.

52. "Western Montana Fair," AS, Oct. 6, 1898, p. 12, col. 2.

53. Kalispell Bee, Oct. 19, 1900, p. 3, col. 1.

54. Smead to Duncan McDonald, Ravalli, Aug. 31, 1903, FH Agency Papers LS.

55. Alphonse Clairmont, Ronan, to Joseph Dixon, Mar. 25, 1898, Joseph Dixon Papers, Toole Archives, Mansfield Library, University of Montana, Missoula.

56. Smead to C. W. Patten, Ronan, Apr. 8, 1898, FH Agency Papers LS.

57. "Missoula Notes," AS, Nov. 2, 1898, p. 12, col. 4.

58. Smead to CIA, Apr. 3, 1899, 16,085/1899, NA CIA LR.

59. "Good Wheat," AS, Dec. 17, 1899, p. 43, col. 3.

60. McDermott, "Ethnology and Folklore," 15–16.

61. Flathead Herald-Journal (Kalispell, Mont.), Aug. 1, 1901, p. 8, col. 2.

62. St. Ignatius Mission House Diary, Sept. 17, 1902, PNTMC, reel 3, fr. 223; St. Ignatius Mission House Diary, Sept. 20, 1902, PNTMC, reel 3, fr. 223.

63. Smead to Mr. Jon Haney, Ravalli, Apr. 18, 1903, FH Agency Papers LS.

64. "Conditions Around Selish," AS, Aug. 19, 1903, p. 12, col. 3.

65. Smead to Mr. F. C. Campbell, Supt Fort Shaw, Mont., Aug 23, 1903, FH Agency Papers LS.

66. AS, Nov. 19, 1903, p. 12, col. 3.

67. Plainsman, Aug. 19, 1904, p. 4, col. 4.

68. Report from Inspector Arthur M. Tinker to SecInt, Sept. 20, 1903, Office of the Secretary of the Interior, RG 48, National Archives, Washington, D.C., #9007/1903.

69. C. H. McLeod to Joseph M. Dixon, Jan. 2, 1904 (filed under Apr. 4, 1904), Joseph M. Dixon Papers, Toole Archives, Mansfield Library, University of Montana, Missoula.

70. Report from W. J. McConnell to SecInt, June 1, 1901, Inspection Report File, Office of the Secretary of the Interior Records, RG 48, National Archives, Washington, D.C., #4584/1901.

71. Chas. S. McNichols, Jocko, Mont., to CIA, Jan. 5, 1903, NA CIA LR 1,789/1903, enclosure no. 1 of 6,311/1903.

72. Smead to CIA, Feb. 27, 1900, 10,894/1900, NA CIA LR.

73. Smead to CIA, Sept. 15, 1898, ARCIA (1898), 190–92.

74. Smead to CIA, Apr. 23, 1903, 27,201/1903, NA CIA LR.

75. Ronan to CIA, June 12, 1889, Ronan letters, vol. 2: 42–45.

76. Jerome D'Aste, S.J., diaries, Sept. 12, 1889, in Bigart, A Pretty Village, 304.

77. Carter to CIA, Aug. 20, 1894, ARCIA (1894), 173–77.

78. P. McCormick to Secretary of the Interior, Feb. 17, 1895, NAmf M1070, 1627/95.

79. Smead to Rev. J. Daste, S.J., St. Ignatius, Mar. 8, 1898, FH Agency Papers LS.

80. Smead to CIA, Aug. 8, 1903, 51,714/1903, NA CIA LR.

81. Geo. A. Buck, Plains, to Smead, Apr. 15, 1904, FH Agency Papers LR.

82. U.S. Census Office, Report on Indians, 363–65.

83. Armstrong, "Condition of Reservation Indians," 35–40.

84. "Progressive Red Men," Kalispell Bee, Sept. 23, 1902, p. 5, col. 2.

85. Ronan to CIA, August 27, 1891, Ronan letters, vol. 2: 229–31; Ronan to CIA, November 2, 1891, Ronan letters, vol. 2: 253–54; Ronan to CIA, Mar. 4, 1892, Ronan letters, vol. 2: 281–82; Ronan to CIA, July 4, 1892, Ronan letters vol. 2: 309.

86. "Reduction of Indian Reservations," 40–46, 56–60.

87. Ronan to CIA, September 9, 1889, Ronan letters, vol. 2: 83–85; Ronan to CIA, August 14, 1890, Ronan letters, vol. 2: 148–57.

88. James H. Chisney to SecInt, July 23, 1891, NAmf M1070, 5803/91; Ronan to CIA, September 1, 1891, Ronan letters, vol. 2: 235–42.

89. Armstrong, "Condition of Reservation Indians," 35–40.

90. Charles S. McNichols, Jocko, Mont., to CIA, Dec. 31, 1902, 822/1903, NA CIA LR.

91. Chas. S. McNichols, Jocko, Mont., to CIA, Aug. 14, 1903, 53,262/1903, NA CIA LR.

92. Ronan to CIA, Oct. 28, 1889, Ronan letters, vol. 2: 99–101.

93. "Among the Flatheads," AS, Jan. 1, 1894, p. 6, col. 2; Carter to CIA, Aug. 20, 1894, ARCIA (1894), 173–77; "On the Reservation," AS, Nov. 3, 1895, p. 12, col. 1; Carter to CIA, Aug. 20, 1895, ARCIA (1895), pp. 189–92.

94. Smead to Robert Watson, Ronan, Jan. 15, 1900, FH Agency Papers LS.

95. Smead to CIA, July 10, 1900, 33,833/1900, NA CIA LR.

96. U.S. Census Office, Census Bulletin; Ronan to CIA, Aug. 5, 1893, Ronan letters, vol. 2: 371–79.

97. Henry B. Carrington, "The Exodus of the Flathead Indians," Carrington Family Papers, Sterling Library, Yale University, New Haven, Conn., ch. 6, p. 7.

98. Post, "A Model Indian Mission," 723–24.

99. Smead to C. W. Patten, Ronan, Apr. 8, 1898, FH Agency Papers LS.

100. Smead to Joseph Jones, Ronan, Jan. 21, 1902, FH Agency Papers LS.

101. Inspection report from C. F. Nesler and Chas. M. McNichols, June 21, 1904, 6655/1904, Interior Department Inspection Report File, RG 48, National Archives, Washington, D.C.

102. Inspection report, exhibit Q, p. 2.

103. Inspection report, exhibit Q, pp. 5, 48.
104. Inspection report, exhibit Q, p. 10.
105. Inspection report, exhibit Q, p. 12.
106. Inspection report, exhibit Q, p. 13.
107. Inspection report, exhibit Q, p. 16.
108. Inspection report, exhibit Q, p. 20.
109. Inspection report, exhibit Q, p. 22.
110. Inspection report, exhibit Q, p. 24.
111. Inspection report, exhibit Q, p. 28.
112. Inspection report, exhibit R., pp. 6–7.
113. Inspection report, exhibit R, pp. 24–25.
114. Inspection report, exhibit R, pp. 28–29.
115. Inspection report, exhibit R, pp. 30–31.
116. Inspection report, exhibit R, pp. 44–45.
117. Inspection report, exhibit R, pp. 52–53.
118. Inspection report, exhibit R, p. 65.
119. Inspection report, exhibit R, p. 108.
120. Rosters of Agency Employees, 1889–90, vol. 19, entry 978, Commissioner of Indian Affairs, RG 75, National Archives, Washington, D.C.
121. Roster of Indian Police, 1890–91, vol. 9, entry 982, Commissioner of Indian Affairs, RG 75, National Archives, Washington, D.C.
122. ARCIA (1897), 517.
123. ARCIA (1904), 637.
124. Ronan to CIA, Nov. 27, 1891, Ronan letters, vol. 2: 257–58.
125. Ronan to CIA, Nov. 29, 1892, Ronan letters, vol. 2: 339; Ronan to CIA, Dec. 2, 1892, Ronan letters, vol. 2: 345.
126. Smead to CIA, Aug. 1, 1898, 36,009/1898, NA CIA LR.
127. Ronan to CIA, February 3, 1892, Ronan letters, vol. 2: 277–78; CIA to Ronan, Mar. 3, 1892, letter book 232, land, p. 164, NA CIA LS.
128. Smead to Dave Couture, Ronan, Oct. 31, 1899, FH Agency Papers LS.
129. Matt, "Mary Ann Topsseh Coombs," 8–9.
130. L. Van Gorp, St. Ignatius, to Smead, Nov. 1, 1903 (filed under Sept. 30, 1903), FH Agency Papers LR.
131. Report from Inspectors C. F. Nessler and Chas. M. McNichols to Secretary of the Interior, June 21, 1904, Office of the Secretary of the Interior, RG 48, National Archives, Washington, D.C., #6655/1904, exhibit E, p. 128.
132. St. Ignatius Mission Account Books, PNTMC, reel 6, fr. 251, 259, 262, 266, 283.
133. "Rocky Mountain Mission," 192–95.
134. McLeod, A Cowboy's Life, 21–32.
135. Josephine Agnes Couture v. David Couture, Sept. 23, 1892, divorce, case 729, District Court Records, Missoula County Courthouse, Missoula, Mont.
136. "Among the Reds," Missoula Weekly Gazette, Sept. 10, 1890, p. 12, col. 3–4.
137. Smead to Louis Courville, Ronan, Dec. 20, 1899, FH Agency Papers LS.

138. Smead to Mr. F. Soues, Gov. Agent, Clinton, B.C., Dec. 3, 1901, FH Agency Papers LS.

139. Smead to John Battise Finley, St. Ignatius, Sept. 9, 1902, FH Agency Papers LS.

140. L. Van Gorp, St. Ignatius, to Smead, Flathead Agency Papers, Feb. 11, 1904, FH Agency Papers LR.

141. Carter to CIA, Jan. 25, 1895, 5,294/1895, NA CIA LR.

142. U.S. Senate, "In the Senate of the United States," Senate Report No. 2707, 50th Congress, 2d Sess. (1889), serial 2623.

143. Bigart and McDonald, *Duncan McDonald*, 63–106.

144. McLeod, *A Cowboy's Life*, 12–13.

145. Ronan to CIA, July 9, 1891, Ronan letters, vol. 2: 214–15.

146. Mildred Chaffin, "Smallpox Epidemic Recalled," *Missoulian*, May 21, 1967, p. 11-A.

147. Jerome D'Aste, S.J., diaries, Nov. 23, 1889, PNTMC, reel 29, fr. 594; Jerome D'Aste, S.J., diaries, Nov. 24, 1889, PNTMC, reel 29, fr. 594.

148. Estate of Peter Ronan, Probate file 339 (1893), Clerk of District Court, Missoula County Courthouse, Missoula, Mont., #20 Annual Account of Administratrix, June 14, 1895.

149. Carter to CIA, Apr. 10, 1896, 14,317/1896, NA CIA LR.

150. "They Went for Fish," *Edwards' Fruit Grower & Farmer* (Missoula, Mont.), June 15, 1900, p. 2, col. 4.

151. Jerome D'Aste, S.J., diaries, June 3, 1901, PNTMC, reel 29, fr. 974.

152. "Buffalo and Wild Indians," *Missoulian* (daily), May 4, 1902, p. 1, col. 6.

153. "Show People Return," AS, Sept. 14, 1902, p 14, col. 2.

154. Jerome D'Aste, S.J., diaries, Mar. 2, 1903, PNTMC, reel 30, fr. 31.

155. Robert Watson, Ronan, to Smead, Mar. 23, 1904, FH Agency Papers LR.

156. DuBois, *Trail Blazers*, 41–44.

157. Post, "A Model Indian Mission," 723–24.

158. *Plainsman*, July 13, 1900, p. 4, col. 3.

159. "A Terrible Death," *Daily Democrat-Messenger* (Missoula, Mont.), Dec. 3, 1900, p 1, col. 4.

160. Smead to Thos. McDonald, St. Ignatius Mar. 11, 1902, FH Agency Papers LS.

161. Smead to Louis Clairmont, Jr., Ronan, May 9, 1902, FH Agency Papers LS.

162. Smead (by Holland) to Alexander LaFle . . . [rest of name illegible], May 29, 1902, FH Agency Papers LS.

163. Smead to Zephrya [*sic*] Courville, Camas, May 28, 1903, FH Agency Papers LS.

164. Smead to Robert Delaithe, Plains, July 20, 1903, FH Agency Papers LS.

165. Jerome D'Aste, S.J., diaries, July 26, 1903, PNTMC, reel 30, fr. 45.

166. Smead to no name, Aug. 3, 1903, FH Agency Papers LS.

167. Ida S. Patterson, "Polson's No. 1 Woman Recalls Early Days," DM, Oct. 30, 1949, p. 6.

168. Geo. L. Breeden, Ronan, to Smead, Dec. 20, 1903, FH Agency Papers LR.

169. *Plainsman*, Feb. 19, 1904, p. 4, col. 5.

170. Smead to Joe Marion, Ronan, July 13, 1899, FH Agency Papers LS.

171. Smead to D. D. Hull, Ronan, Oct. 31, 1903, FH Agency Papers LS.

172. Jerome D'Aste, S.J., diaries, Mar. 9, 1902, PNTMC, reel 29, fr. 1005.

173. Jerome D'Aste, S.J., diaries, Mar. 11, 1902, PNTMC, reel 29, fr. 1005.

174. "Shipment of Horses," AS, July 19, 1900, p. 12, col. 5.

175. "Conditions Around Selish," AS, Aug. 19, 1903, p. 12, col. 3.

176. Jos. Jones, Ronan, Indian Service, to Smead, Sept. 3, 1903, FH Agency Papers LR.

177. Bro. Cyprius-Celestin, F.I.C. (Celestin Tregret), "Seven Years Among the Western Indians," unpublished manuscript, Oregon Province Archives, Gonzaga University, Spokane, Wash., p. 56.

178. Smead to CIA, June 14, 1904, 40,262/1904, enclosure, NA CIA LR.

179. Jerome D'Aste, S.J., diaries, July 15, 1896, PNTMC, reel 29, fr. 811.

180. Smead to Rev. Geo. de la Motte, St. Ignatius, Nov. 9, 1898, FH Agency Papers LS.

181. The following 1894 expense examples have been abstracted from Jerome D'Aste, S.J., diaries, 1894, in Bigart, *Zealous in All Virtues*, 257–306. A few unpublished references are from PNTMC, reel 29.

Chapter 5

1. Bigart and McDonald, *Duncan McDonald*, 63–106.

2. "Flathead Had to Import Its Potatoes in Pioneer Days," DM, Mar. 1, 1936, p. 7, col. 1–3.

3. Dixon, "Young Joe Dixon," 12–19.

4. [Smalley?], "The Fertile Flathead Country," 46–48.

5. "Ravalli and Arlee," *Missoula Gazette* (daily), Aug. 12, 1891, p. 4, col. 1.

6. Ronan to CIA, June 10, 1891, Ronan letters, vol. 2: 209–10; Ronan to CIA, July 14, 1891, Ronan letters, vol. 2: 217–18.

7. "Stage Line Change," *Missoula Gazette* (daily), Jan. 5, 1892, p. 1, col. 6; *Missoula Weekly Gazette*, Nov. 26, 1890, p. 3, col. 1.

8. Bigart and McDonald, *Duncan McDonald*, 77.

9. "Montana Cattle Go East," *Missoulian* (daily), Oct. 4, 1904, p. 8, col. 4.

10. *Evening Republican* (Missoula, Mont.), Sept. 9, 1895, p. 1, col. 4.

11. *Plainsman*, Aug. 10, 1900, p. 4, col. 4; *Kalispell Bee*, Oct. 19, 1900, p. 3, col. 1.

12. "Tales of Montana's Early Days: The Allard Stage Line," AS, Nov. 26, 1899, p. 19, col. 1–7; "A Fierce War," WM, July 15, 1891, p. 4, col. 1; *Missoula Weekly Gazette*, June 10, 1891, p. 3, col. 2.

13. WM, Aug. 12, 1891, p. 4, col. 2.

14. John H. King v. Charles Allard, damages, Sept. 18, 1890, case 131, District Court Records, Missoula County Courthouse, Missoula, Mont.; *Inter Lake* (Demersville, Mont.), Oct. 17, 1890, p. 3, col. 1.

15. *Inter Lake* (Demersville, Mont.), Nov. 14, 1890, p. 3, col. 3.

16. *Inter Lake* (Demersville, Mont.), Jan. 16, 1891, p. 3, col. 3; *Missoula Gazette* (daily), Feb. 18, 1891, p. 8. col. 1.

17. *Inter Lake* (Demersville, Mont.), Feb. 20, 1891, p. 3, col. 1.

18. *Inter Lake* (Demersville, Mont.), Apr. 3, 1891, p. 3, col. 3.

19. *Inter Lake* (Demersville, Mont.), Apr. 24, 1891, p. 3, col. 2.

20. *Inter Lake* (Demersville, Mont.), Nov. 27, 1891, p. 3, col. 2.

21. "Stage Line Change," *Missoula Gazette* (daily), Jan. 5, 1892, p. 1, col. 6.

22. "Buffalo Excursion," *Inter Lake* (Kalispell, Mont.), Sept. 1, 1893, p. 3, col. 3.

23. "Buffalo Excursion," *Inter Lake* (Kalispell, Mont.), Sept. 7, 1894, p. 4, col. 2.

24. *Inter Lake* (Kalispell, Mont.), Sept. 14, 1894, p. 4, col. 2.

25. WM, Oct. 30, 1889, p. 4, col. 3.

26. Ronan to CIA, February 27, 1893, Ronan letters, vol. 2: 354–56.

27. "Many Birds of Passage," AS, Oct. 8, 1893, p. 8, col. 1.

28. "Polson Property Is Sold," AS, Jan. 28, 1904, p. 14, col. 5.

29. *Missoulian* (daily), July 10, 1904, p. 3, col. 5.

30. *Missoulian* (daily), Nov. 12, 1904, p. 3, col. 5.

31. C. H. McLeod to Geo. H. Beckwith, Sept. 24, 1904, and C. H. McLeod to Geo. H. Beckwith, Oct. 10, 1904, col. H. McLeod Papers, Toole Archives, Mansfield Library, University of Montana, Missoula.

32. "Flathead Had to Import Its Potatoes in Pioneer Days," DM, Mar. 1, 1936, p. 7, col. 1–3; Bigart and Woodcock, "St. Ignatius Mission, Montana," 163.

33. S. W. Graham, "A Readable Letter," *Inter Lake* (Demersville, Mont.), Oct. 31, 1890, p. 3, col. 3–5.

34. "Polson Woman Tells of State's Infancy," DM, May 10, 1930, p. 3, col. 1.

35. Ronan to CIA, August 25, 1891, Ronan letters, vol. 2: 224–25.

36. McDermott, "Ethnology and Folklore," 29.

37. "Joe Barnaby Killed," AS, Aug. 22, 1900, p. 12, col. 2.

38. Smead to Frank Ducharme, Mar. 25, 1903, FH Agency Papers LS.

39. "It Was a Red Picnic," AS, Apr. 7, 1894, p. 6, col. 3.

40. "Lesson for Some Whites," AS, Apr. 9, 1894, p. 6, col. 2.

41. "He's Happy Now," AS, Apr. 18, 1894, p. 6, col. 1.

42. "One Honest Indian," AS, Jan. 15, 1896, p. 10, col. 1; AS, Jan. 16, 1896, p. 10, col. 1.

43. M. L. Crouch, Attorney, Missoula, to Smead, Apr. 20, 1898, FH Agency Papers LR.

44. "Missoula Full of Noble Red Men on a Purchasing Tour," *Missoulian* (daily), Feb. 20, 1903, p. 8, col. 3–4.

45. *Plainsman*, Nov. 23, 1895, p. 3, col. 5; *Weekly Plainsman*, July 11, 1896, p. 1, col. 3.

46. *Weekly Plainsman*, July 18, 1896, p. 1, col. 4.

47. *Plainsman*, May 11, 1900, p. 4, col. 4.

48. *Plainsman*, Mar. 28, 1902, p. 4, col. 4.

49. *Plainsman*, July 11, 1902, p. 4, col. 3.

50. *Plainsman*, Oct. 3, 1902, p. 4, col. 5.

51. *Plainsman*, July 17, 1903, p. 4, col. 4.

52. *Plainsman*, July 8, 1904, p. 4, col. 4–5.

53. J. A. McGowan v. Alphonse Courville, debt, June 1, 1897, case 1505, District Court Records, Missoula County Courthouse, Missoula, Mont.

54. "District Court," AS, Mar. 14, 1899, p. 12, col. 3.

55. "Side Notes," *Inter Lake* (Kalispell, Mont.), Nov. 5, 1897, p. 5, col. 3–4.

56. *Flathead Herald-Journal* (Kalispell, Mont.), Aug. 1, 1901, p. 8, col. 2.

57. "Cattle Roundup," *Kalispell Bee*, Sept. 21, 1901, p. 3, col. 2.

58. "In Every Quarter," AS, Oct. 21, 1896, p. 10, col. 1.

59. *Daily Democrat-Messenger* (Missoula, Mont.), May 4, 1901, p. 1, col. 5.

60. *Missoulian* (daily), July 11, 1903, p. 8, col. 1.

61. "Reservation Indian Buys a Piano," *Missoulian* (daily), July 22, 1904, p. 8, col. 2.

62. "The Noble Red Man Spending Money," AS, Dec. 14, 1904, p. 2, col. 4–5.

63. *Missoulian* (daily), Dec. 20, 1901, p. 8, col. 2.

64. DM, Dec. 17, 1904, p. 3, col. 6; DM, Dec. 20, 1904, p. 7, col. 2; DM, Dec. 21, 1904, p. 3, col. 2.

65. Mrs. Jessie Couture, St. Ignatius, to Joseph Dixon, Jan. 21, 1898, Joseph Dixon Papers, Toole Archives, Mansfield Library, University of Montana, Missoula; Mrs. Jessie Couture, St. Ignatius, to Joseph Dixon, Feb. 15, 1898, Joseph Dixon Papers, Toole Archives, Mansfield Library, University of Montana, Missoula.

66. Alphonse Clairmont, Ronan, to Joseph Dixon, Mar. 25, 1898, Joseph Dixon Papers, Toole Archives, Mansfield Library, University of Montana, Missoula.

67. Sam Pierre, Arlee, to Joseph Dixon, Jan. 15, 1899, Joseph Dixon Papers, Toole Archives, Mansfield Library, University of Montana, Missoula; Sam Pierre, Arlee, to Joseph Dixon, Jan. 21, 1899, Joseph Dixon Papers, Toole Archives, Mansfield Library, University of Montana, Missoula.

68. *Plainsman*, May 11, 1900, p. 4, col. 4; *Plainsman*, Aug. 17, 1900, p. 4, col. 4.

69. "Exciting Horse Race," *Kalispell Graphic*, Sept. 5, 1894, p. 2, col. 2.

70. "The Celebration," *Inter Lake* (Kalispell, Mont.), July 6 [i.e., 8], 1898, p. 5, col. 3–4.

71. *Kalispell Graphic*, Sept. 18, 1895, p. 3, col. 1.

72. "Got Forty Bounties," *Edwards' Fruit Grower & Farmer* (Missoula, Mont.), Oct. 4, 1901, p. 3, col. 5.

73. *Edwards' Fruit Grower & Farmer* (Missoula, Mont.), Nov. 8, 1901, p. 5, col. 3.

74. "Bounty Report for December," WM, Jan. 8, 1904, p. 5, col. 3; *Missoulian* (daily), Jan. 31, 1904, p. 9, c 6; "Missoula Notes," AS, Apr. 27, 1904, p. 12, col. 4.

75. "Bounty Inspector Worden Busy," AS, May 29, 1904, p. 14, col. 5.

76. "Malta's Eye Is Keen," *Missoulian* (daily), June 15, 1904, p. 3, col. 1.

77. *Missoulian* (daily), June 17, 1904, p. 3, col. 5.

78. "Charles Gabe of Arlee Kills Two Black Bear," AS, July 14, 1904, p. 12, col. 6.

79. *Missoulian* (daily), July 23, 1904, p. 3, col. 5.

80. "Big Knife Maintains Reputation," *Missoulian* (daily), Oct. 12, 1904, p. 7, col. 1.

81. *Missoulian* (daily), Aug. 11, 1904, p. 3, col. 6.

82. Ronan to CIA, June 12, 1889, Ronan letters, vol. 2: 42–45.

83. U.S. President, "Message," 1890, 21–22.

84. Menager, "Reminiscences of a Missionary Sister," 59–61.

85. WM, Aug. 14, 1889, p. 4, col. 4; Ronan to CIA, Dec. 2, 1889, Ronan letters, vol. 2: 111–12.

86. Ronan to CIA, February 1, 1890, Ronan letters, vol. 2: 119–20.

87. William W. Junkin to SecInt, Sept. 11, 1889, NAmf M1070, 5552/89.

88. Ronan to CIA, August 20, 1889, Ronan letters, vol. 2: 68–74.

89. Ronan to CIA, September 1, 1889, Ronan letters, vol. 2: 75–79.

90. Ronan to CIA, September 9, 1889, Ronan letters, vol. 2: 80–83.

91. Ronan to CIA, June 1, 1892, Ronan letters, vol. 2: 304–7.

92. Carter to CIA, May 7, 1895, 20,517/1895, NA CIA LR.

93. "Quinn Is Bound Over," AS, Dec. 15, 1899, p. 12, col. 2.

94. AS, July 6, 1895, p. 6, col. 2; DM, July 6, 1895, p. 4, col. 1.

95. Smead to Rodgers, US Attorney, Helena, telegram, Oct. 17, 1901, FH Agency Papers LS.

96. "James Scott Not Guilty," *Plainsman*, Jan. 24, 1902, p. 4, col. 1.

97. John Post, S.J., St. Ignatius, to Smead, July 23, 1902, FH Agency Papers LR.

98. Smead to CIA, July 29, 1902, 45,976/1902, NA CIA LR.

99. J. A. McGowan, Plains, to Bellew, Dec. 7, 1904, FH Agency Papers LR.

100. Ronan to CIA, January 4, 1893, Ronan letters, vol. 2: 349–50.

101. Jerome D'Aste, S.J., diaries, Oct. 24, 1900, PNTMC, reel 29, fr. 950.

102. *Daily Democrat-Messenger* (Missoula, Mont.), Jan. 9, 1901, p. 4, col. 1; *Edwards' Fruit Grower & Farmer* (Missoula, Mont.), Jan. 25, 1901, p. 2, col. 5.

103. Anonymous, St. Ignatius, to Smead, June 30, 1901, FH Agency Papers LR.

104. "Gangraw, the Whisky Seller, Caused Death of Sac Arlee," *Missoulian* (daily), Jan. 19, 1902, p. 1, col. 1–2; "For Giving Indians Whiskey," AS, Jan. 26, 1902, p. 13, col. 2.

105. "Clever Capture of Indians with Bottles of Firewater," *Missoulian* (daily), Feb. 14, 1903, p. 1, col. 3–4; "Baptiste Nenema Pleads Not Guilty," AS, Feb. 19, 1903, p. 14, col. 3; "Reds Causing Trouble," AS, Feb. 21, 1903, p. 14, col. 5.

106. "Taking Liquor Onto Reservation," AS, Apr. 26, 1903, p. 16, col. 4; "He Had the Goods But Was Innocent," AS, Apr. 28, 1903, p. 14, col. 3.

107. "Indian Is Charged with Selling Whiskey," AS, Nov. 4, 1903, p. 10, col. 1; "Indian Is Bound Over," AS, Nov. 5, 1903, p. 10, col. 4; "Ashley Bound Over," *Missoulian* (daily), Nov. 5, 1903, p. 3, col. 3.

108. Carl Rasch, U.S. Attorney, Helena, to Smead, May 19, 1904, FH Agency Papers LR.

109. "Barnaby Given a Hearing," AS, Jan. 20, 1904, p. 12, col. 3–4.

110. "Indians Before Grand Jury," *Missoulian* (daily), Sept. 29, 1904, p. 6, col. 2.

111. "LaRose Free on Bonds," *Missoulian* (daily), May 12, 1904, p. 3, col. 2.

112. "Indians Before Grand Jury," *Missoulian* (daily), Sept. 29, 1904, p. 6, col. 2.

113. "On a Trip," *Missoula Gazette* (weekly), July 17, 1889, p. 3, col. 3.

114. WM, Oct. 1, 1890, p. 4, col. 3.

115. Ollason, "Canoeing on the Flathead," 161–63; and 187–88.

116. Carter to CIA, Oct. 17, 1895, 45,176/1895, NA CIA LR.

117. Smead to Hon. J. M. Keith, Missoula, Mar. 15, 1898, FH Agency Papers LS.

118. Smead to A. M. Stevens & Co., Missoula, Oct. 14, 1899, FH Agency Papers LS.

119. *Daily Democrat-Messenger* (Missoula, Mont.), Oct. 31, 1899, p. 4, col. 2.

120. Smead to Montana Marble Works, Helena, July 17, 1900, FH Agency Papers LS.

121. J. H. Carroll, Missoula Feed Corral, to Smead, Mar. 25, 1901, FH Agency Papers LR.

122. "Peter and Abraham," *Missoulian* (daily), Feb. 21, 1903, p. 3, col. 1.

123. "Gaudily Attired and Joyously Happy," *Missoulian* (daily), Aug. 11, 1904, p. 3, col. 2.

124. Smead to Antine Parazo, Ronan, Jan. 22, 1900, FH Agency Papers LS.

125. Smead to Bazil Finley, Polson, June 20, 1900, FH Agency Papers LS.

126. Smead to Louis Camelle, St. Ignatius, Jan. 17, 1902, FH Agency Papers LS; Smead to Louie Camille, St. Ignatius, Feb. 7, 1902, FH Agency Papers LS.

127. Smead to Isaac Ogden, Ronan, July 15, 1902, FH Agency Papers LS; Smead (by Holland) to Angus McDonald, Sr. Ronan, Sept. 7, 1902, FH Agency Papers LS.

128. Smead to James Michael, Ronan, Oct. 6, 1902, FH Agency Papers LS.

129. Almost all the 1893 and 1894 references to Father D'Aste's diaries in this section were published in Bigart, *Zealous in All Virtues*, 216–87.

130. Jerome D'Aste, S.J., diaries, Oct. 25, 1893, PNTMC, reel 29, fr. 716; Jerome D'Aste, S.J., diaries, Oct. 27, 1893, PNTMC, reel 29, fr. 716.

131. Jerome D'Aste, S.J., diaries, May 1, 1894, PNTMC, reel 29, fr. 734.

132. Jerome D'Aste, S.J., diaries, Feb. 8, 1894, PNTMC, reel 29, fr. 725–26; Jerome D'Aste, S.J., diaries, Feb. 9, 1894, PNTMC, reel 29, fr. 726.

133. Jerome D'Aste, S.J., diaries, Feb. 25, 1894, PNTMC, reel 29, fr. 727.

134. Jerome D'Aste, S.J., diaries, Mar. 29, 1894, PNTMC, reel 29, fr. 730; Jerome D'Aste, S.J., diaries, Apr. 18, 1894, PNTMC, reel 29, fr. 733.

135. Jerome D'Aste, S.J., diaries, May 19, 1894, PNTMC, reel 29, fr. 735.

136. Jerome D'Aste, S.J., diaries, Oct. 22, 1893, PNTMC, reel 29, fr. 716.

137. Jerome D'Aste, S.J., diaries, Oct. 28, 1893, PNTMC, reel 29, fr. 716.

138. Jerome D'Aste, S.J., diaries, Jan. 10, 1894, PNTMC, reel 29, fr. 722.

139. Jerome D'Aste, S.J., diaries, Jan. 16, 1894, PNTMC, reel 29, fr. 723.

140. Jerome D'Aste, S.J., diaries, May 1, 1894, PNTMC, reel 29, fr. 734.

141. Jerome D'Aste, S.J., diaries, May 17, 1894, PNTMC, reel 29, fr. 735.

142. Jerome D'Aste, S.J., diaries, June 24, 1894, PNTMC, reel 29, fr. 738.

143. Jerome D'Aste, S.J., diaries, Aug. 6, 1894, PNTMC, reel 29, fr. 745.

144. Jerome D'Aste, S.J., diaries, Aug. 28, 1894, PNTMC, reel 29, fr. 747.

145. Jerome D'Aste, S.J., diaries, Jan. 18, 1894, PNTMC, reel 29, fr. 723.

146. Jerome D'Aste, S.J., diaries, Feb. 6, 1894, PNTMC, reel 29, fr. 725.

147. Jerome D'Aste, S.J., diaries, Mar. 14, 1894, PNTMC, reel 29, fr. 729.

148. Jerome D'Aste, S.J., diaries, May 5, 1894, PNTMC, reel 29, fr. 734.

149. Jerome D'Aste, S.J., diaries, May 14, 1894, PNTMC, reel 29, fr. 735.

150. Jerome D'Aste, S.J., diaries, May 18, 1894, PNTMC, reel 29, fr. 735.

151. Jerome D'Aste, S.J., diaries, May 22, 1894, PNTMC, reel 29, fr. 735.

152. Jerome D'Aste, S.J., diaries, June 5, 1894, PNTMC, reel 29, fr. 737.

153. Jerome D'Aste, S.J., diaries, June 20, 1894, PNTMC, reel 29, fr. 738.

154. Jerome D'Aste, S.J., diaries, July 21, 1894, PNTMC, reel 29, fr. 743.

155. Jerome D'Aste, S.J., diaries, May 26, 1894, PNTMC, reel 29, fr. 736.

156. Jerome D'Aste, S.J., diaries, June 2, 1894, PNTMC, reel 29, fr. 736.

157. Jerome D'Aste, S.J., diaries, July 16, 1894, PNTMC, reel 29, fr. 743.

158. Jerome D'Aste, S.J., diaries, July 17, 1894, PNTMC, reel 29, fr. 743.

159. Jerome D'Aste, S.J., diaries, July 18, 1889, PNTMC, reel 29, fr. 586.

160. Jerome D'Aste, S.J., diaries, Nov. 4, 1889, PNTMC, reel 29, fr. 593.

161. Jerome D'Aste, S.J., diaries, Jan. 1, 1890, PNTMC, reel 29, fr. 598.

162. Jerome D'Aste, S.J., diaries, June 3, 1890, PNTMC, reel 29, fr. 609.

163. Jerome D'Aste, S.J., diaries, July 6, 1890, PNTMC, reel 29, fr. 612; Jerome D'Aste, S.J., diaries, July 7, 1890, PNTMC, reel 29, fr. 612.

164. Jerome D'Aste, S.J., diaries, July 18, 1890, Bigart, *Zealous in All Virtues*, 47.

165. Jerome D'Aste, S.J., diaries, Aug. 28, 1890, and Aug. 31, 1890, Bigart, *Zealous in All Virtues*, 58.

166. Jerome D'Aste, S.J., diaries, Nov. 24, 1901, PNTMC, reel 29, fr. 992.

167. Jerome D'Aste, S.J., diaries, Apr. 7, 1902, PNTMC, reel 29, fr. 1008–09.

168. Jerome D'Aste, S.J., diaries, June 8, 1889, in Bigart, *A Pretty Village*, 294–95.

169. Jerome D'Aste, S.J., diaries, Aug. 19, 1889, in Bigart, *A Pretty Village*, 301.

170. Smead to Judge Joseph, St. Ignatius, July 31, 1899, FH Agency Papers LS; Joseph the Judge, St. Ignatius, to Smead, Oct. 13, 1899, FH Agency Papers LR.

171. St. Ignatius Mission House Diary, Oct. 6, 1902, PNTMC, reel 3, fr. 223; Jerome D'Aste, S.J., diaries, Oct. 6, 1902, PNTMC, reel 30, fr. 19.

172. Jerome D'Aste, S.J., diaries, Oct. 16, 1902, PNTMC, reel 30, fr. 20.

173. St. Ignatius Mission House Diary, June 5, 1903, PNTMC, reel 3, fr. 229; Jerome D'Aste, S.J., diaries, June 8, 1903, PNTMC, reel 30, fr. 40.

174. WM, Apr. 29, 1891, p. 3, col. 3; WM, Apr. 29, 1891, p. 4, col. 3.

175. Smead to Joseph Standing Bear, Judge, St. Ignatius, Oct. 20, 1898, FH Agency Papers LS.

176. Smead to Sheriff Curran, Missoula, May 7, 1899, FH Agency Papers LS.

177. Smead to Joseph Allard, St. Ignatius, Apr. 11, 1901, FH Agency Papers LS.

178. Smead to Prescott, Sheriff, Missoula, telegram, Nov. 3, 1902, FH Agency Papers LS; Smead to Sheriff, Spokane, Nov. 10, 1902, FH Agency Papers LS; "Supposed Leader of the Gang That Robbed Michel Is Caught," AS, June 1, 1903, p. 12, col. 1–2.

179. "Indian Robbed of $22,000," *New York Times*, Nov. 4, 1902, p. 1, col. 3.

180. *Evening Missoulian*, Mar. 14, 1894, p. 4, col. 2; "He Is a Very Bad One," AS, Mar. 15, 1894, p. 6, col. 1–2.

181. "Very Near a Good Indian," *Kalispell Graphic*, Mar. 13, 1895, p. 3, col. 1; "Court Proceedings," *Inter Lake* (Kalispell, Mont.), May 17, 1895, p. 3, col. 4–5.

182. DM, June 28, 1895, p. 4, col. 2.

183. DM, Aug. 28, 1896, p. 4, col. 2–3.

184. *Inter Lake* (Kalispell, Mont.), Mar. 17, 1899, p. 5, col. 2.

185. "District Court," *Flathead Herald-Journal* (Kalispell, Mont.), Mar. 30, 1899, p. 1, col. 4.

186. "The Sheriff's Visitor," AS, Sept. 18, 1899, p. 10, col. 5.

Chapter 6

1. U.S. Census Office, *Agriculture*, pt. 1: 100–101.

2. "Guilty of Violating Game Law," DM, Oct. 14, 1905, p. 3, col. 3; "Jail Looks Good to Charley," DM, Oct. 15, 1905, p. 7, col. 1.

3. A. M. Bliss, Forest Supervisor, Ovando, to Bellew, Nov. 20, 1905, FH Agency Papers LR.

4. "Jail Looks Good to Charley," DM, Oct. 15, 1905, p. 7, col. 1.

5. DM, Sept. 14, 1905, p. 2, col. 4; "Will Decide Question," DM, Sept. 15, 1905, p. 2, col. 3.

6. Morgan to Joseph Pain, Dixon, Aug. 23, 1909, FH Agency Papers LS.

7. Morgan to William McCormick, Game Warden, Missoula, Aug. 25, 1909, FH Agency Papers LS.

8. Salish–Pend d'Oreille Culture Committee, "The Swan Massacre," 62–93.

9. "Big Arm," *Kalispell Journal*, July 21, 1910, p. 5, col. 1–2.

10. "Reservation Ceased with Proclamation," *Lake Shore Sentinel* (Polson, Mont.), Aug. 19, 1910, p. 1, col. 2.

11. File 71,147/1910 Flathead 302, NA CIA CCF.

12. DM, May 2, 1905, p. 3, col. 3–4.

13. "Buying Flathead Ponies," DM, May 19, 1905, p. 2, col. 7.

14. "Missoula Notes," AS, May 25, 1905, p 14, col. 3.

15. "Will Begin Round-up," DM, May 6, 1905, p 6, col. 2.

16. "Range Horses Being Shipped," *Plainsman*, Aug. 18, 1905, p. 2, col. 2.

17. DM, Aug. 31, 1905, p. 2, col. 4.

18. *Plainsman*, Sept. 15, 1905, p. 3, col. 1 (two items).

19. Bellew to CIA, Aug. 26, 1905, ARCIA (1905), 242.

20. "Indians' Days Are Numbered," DM, July 25, 1906, p. 3, col. 3–6.

21. "Indians Preparing for Big Hunt," DM, Sept. 9, 1906, p. 6, col. 4.

22. "Buying Horses," *Sanders County Signal* (Plains, Mont.), July 19, 1906, p. 1, col. 4.

23. "Thompson Tales," *Plainsman*, June 29, 1906, p. 5, col. 3.

24. "Horse Shipments Heavy from the Reservation," AS, Jan. 12, 1906, p. 11, col. 1.

25. "Horses for Canadians," *Kalispell Bee*, June 8, 1906, p. 1, col. 6.

26. *Plainsman*, Oct. 12, 1906, p. 2, col. 4.

27. *Inter Lake* (Kalispell, Mont.), May 24, 1907, p. 5, col. 2.

28. "Horse Shipments Heavy from the Reservation," AS, Jan. 12, 1906, p. 11, col. 1.

29. "Public Auction," *Sanders County Signal* (Plains, Mont.), May 23, 1907, p. 4, col. 2–3; *Plainsman*, May 24, 1907, p. 3, col. 3.

30. Bellew to Mr. L. B. Seybold, Dell, Mont., Aug. 9, 1905, FH Agency Papers LS.

31. Bellew to J. B. McIntyre, Columbus, Ohio, Apr. 21, 1906, FH Agency Papers LS.

32. Bellew to Mr. Geo. F. Fromey, Culbertson Valley Co., Mont., July 23, 1906, FH Agency Papers LS; "Indians Preparing for Big Hunt," DM, Sept. 9, 1906, p. 6, col. 4.

33. "Going East to Buy Blooded Stock," DM, Mar. 2, 1906, p. 2, col. 1.

34. *Sanders County Signal* (Plains, Mont.), Sept. 27, 1906, p. 1, col. 5.

35. "Great Relay Rider Comes to Town," DM, Oct. 8, 1906, p. 9, col. 1.

36. *Plainsman*, Oct. 15, 1908, p. 3, col. 2.

37. *Plainsman*, May 6, 1909, p. 3, col. 3.

38. Bellew to CIA, Aug. 26, 1905, ARCIA (1905), 242.

39. Bellew to CIA, Feb. 1, 1906, 11,422/1906, NA CIA LR.

40. Bellew to Mr. E. B. Ryan, Billings, Oct. 24, 1906, FH Agency Papers LS.

41. "Indians to Soon Have Plenty of Hard Cash," AS, July 14, 1905, p. 12, col. 2.

42. "Great Season on the Flathead Reservation," AS, Aug. 27, 1905, p. 13, col. 5.

43. "Exceeds 5000 Head," *Plainsman*, Sept. 15, 1905, p. 3, col. 2.

44. "Eleven Cars of Beef," *Plainsman*, Oct. 27, 1905, p. 3, col. 3; *Plainsman*, Sept. 28, 1906, p. 3, col. 2.

45. *Sanders County Signal* (Plains, Mont.), Sept. 27, 1906, p. 1, col. 5.

46. "Plains Is Booming Says Woodworth," DM, Aug. 16, 1907, p. 8, col. 2.

47. *Plainsman*, June 16, 1905, p. 3, col. 1.

48. DM, Sept. 4, 1906, p. 2, col. 5; *Sanders County Signal* (Plains, Mont.), June 13, 1907, p. 1, col. 2.

49. "Four Hundred Head a Month," *Missoula Herald*, Oct. 21, 1907, p. 2, col. 2.

50. *Plainsman*, June 16, 1905, p. 3, col. 1.

51. "May Buy Fat Cattle on Flathead," DM, June 23, 1905, p. 2, col. 2; *Flathead Herald-Journal* (Kalispell, Mont.), June 29, 1905, p. 8, col. 2.

52. *Plainsman*, Nov. 30, 1906, p. 1, col. 1.

53. *Sanders County Signal* (Plains, Mont.), Apr. 9, 1908, p. 1, col. 2.

54. *Sanders County Signal* (Plains, Mont.), Apr. 24, 1909, p. 4, col. 2; *Sanders County Signal* (Plains, Mont.), Aug. 21, 1909, p. 3, col. 2.

55. *Plainsman*, July 14, 1905, p. 3, col. 2.

56. *Plainsman*, July 21, 1905, p. 3, col. 2.

57. *Plainsman*, Nov. 10. 1905, p. 3, col. 1.

58. "Good Business Men," *Sanders County Signal* (Plains, Mont.), July 26, 1906, p. 1, col. 3.

59. "Stockmen to Retire from the Business," AS, Sept. 10, 1906, p. 10, col. 2.

60. Bellew to CIA, Feb. 7, 1907, 14579/1907, NA CIA LR.

61. D. D. Hull, Ronan, to Bellew, Feb. 18, 1907, FH Agency Papers LR.

62. "M'Donald Disposes of All His Cattle," *Missoula Herald*, Mar. 16, 1910, p. 2, col. 3.

63. *Kalispell Bee*, Aug. 22, 1905, p 8, col. 2.

64. Bellew to CIA, Aug. 26, 1905, ARCIA (1905), 242.

65. "Shipping Many Cattle," *Inter Lake* (Kalispell, Mont.), June 29, 1906, p. 5, col. 4.

66. Bellew to CIA, Feb. 7, 1907, 14,579/1907, NA CIA LR.

67. Chas Allard, Polson, to Morgan, Jan. 27, 1909, FH Agency Papers LR; St. Ignatius Mission House Diary, Mar. 2, 1909, PNTMC, reel 3, fr. 305; "Cattle Are Scabby," *Kalispell Bee*, Apr. 6, 1909, p. 1, col. 6.

68. *Sanders County Signal* (Plains, Mont.), May 28, 1908, p. 1, col. 3.

69. U.S. Bureau of the Census, 13th Census, 1910 [Population Schedules], National Archives Microfilm Publication T624, Montana, reel 832 (Flathead County), reel 834 (Missoula County), and reel 835 (Sanders County).

70. Morgan to CIA, Annual Report, Sept. 10, 1910, U.S. Bureau of Indian Affairs, "Superintendents' Annual Narrative and Statistical Reports from Field Jurisdictions of the Bureau of Indian Affairs, 1907–1938," NAmf M1011, reel 42, p. 3.

71. See for example the elders interviewed for the Montana Writers Project in the 1930s in Whealdon, "*I Will Be Meat*," 91–98 and 125–38. For one example of publicity on the roundup see MacTavish, "The Last Great Round-Up," 482–91 and 25–35.

72. "Buffaloes in East Cause Trouble," DM, May 12, 1905, p. 3, col. 3–4.

73. "Buffalo Herd Sold to Canada," DM, Apr. 26, 1907, p. 8, col. 4; "Canada Buys Buffaloes," *Washington Post*, Apr. 26, 1907, p. 3, col. 2.

74. "Final Payment Is Made on the Allard Buffalo," DM, Sept. 10, 1907, p. 8, col. 3.

75. Whealdon, "*I Will Be Meat*," 91–98 and 149–38.

76. "Buffaloes Given Protection," *Missoula Herald*, Oct. 28, 1910, p. 1, col. 5; "Pablo Cannot Kill Buffaloes," *Missoula Herald*, Oct. 29, 1910, p. 1, col. 1–2; "No Slaughter of Bison Now," DM, Oct. 31, 1910, p 1, col. 6; p. 6, col. 2.

77. CIA to Morgan, Dec. 5, 1910, file 92,843/1910 Flathead 170, NA CIA CCF.

78. Bellew to Mr. C. F. Gates, Kalispell, Mar. 5, 1905, FH Agency Papers LS; C. F. Gates, Kalispell, to Bellew, Mar. 15, 1905, FH Agency Papers LR.

79. Bellew to Frank Ashley, St. Ignatius, Mar. 29, 1905, FH Agency Papers LS.

80. J. Daste, St. Ignatius, to Bellew, Apr. 3, 1905, FH Agency Papers LR.

81. Bellew to Peter Michel, Polson, Apr. 21, 1905, FH Agency Papers LS.

82. Bellew to Mrs. Napoleon Plouffe, St. Ignatius, Apr. 21, 1905, FH Agency Papers LS.

83. Wm. Dowd, St. Ignatius, to Bellew, May 2, 1905, FH Agency Papers LR.

84. J. Daste, St. Ignatius, to Bellew, June 26, 1905, FH Agency Papers LR.

85. Bellew to John Boe, Dayton, July 3, 1905, FH Agency Papers LS.

86. Bellew to Mr. J. R. Sears, Ronan, July 12, 1905, FH Agency Papers LS.

87. Bellew to Jas. McKeever, St. Ignatius, July 25, 1905, FH Agency Papers LS.

88. Bellew to Jos. Morrigeau, Camas, Apr. 21, 1905, FH Agency Papers LS.

89. Bellew to Oliver Courville, Camas, Mar. 28, 1906, FH Agency Papers LS.

90. Bellew to Marcelline Pluffe, St. Ignatius, June 3, 1905, FH Agency Papers LS.

91. Bellew to Mary Lamaroux, Warm Springs, Aug. 24, 1905, FH Agency Papers LS.

92. T. G. Demers, Camas, to Bellew, June 10, 1906, FH Agency Papers LR; Bellew to Mrs. Mary Lamoreaux, Camas, and Susan Maillette, Camas, Aug. 13, 1906, FH Agency Papers LS.

93. Britton and Gray to CIA, Aug. 21, 1905, 67,133/1905, NA CIA LR.

94. Bellew to Supt. Rocky Mountain Division, Northern Pacific Railroad, Missoula, Sept. 7, 1905, FH Agency Papers LS.

95. Bellew to CIA, Sept. 27, 1905, 78,421/1905, NA CIA LR.

96. Britton & Gray, Washington, D.C., to CIA, Oct. 10, 1905, 81,398/1905, NA CIA LR.

97. Secretary of Interior to CIA, Jan. 13, 1906, 4,060/1906, NA CIA LR.

98. "Indians File Water Right," *Missoula Herald*, Nov. 22, 1907, p. 1, col. 7; Bellew to E. F. Tabor, Project Engineer, St. Ignatius, Nov. 18, 1908, FH Agency Papers LS.

99. "Rye Being Harvested on Reservation," DM, June 6, 1905, p. 2, col. 7.

100. "Abundance of Hay on Reservation," DM, July 15, 1905, p. 2, col. 1.

101. "Men Are Scarce," DM, July 21, 1905, p. 2, col. 7.

102. "Allotment to Begin Monday," DM, June 1, 1906, p. 2, col. 1.

103. "Indians' Days Are Numbered," DM, July 25, 1906, p. 3, col. 3–6.

104. "Plague of Grasshoppers on Indian Reservation," AS, July 26, 1906, p. 11. col. 2.

105. "Rain Has Damaged Hay Crop," DM, Nov. 21, 1906, p. 2, col. 1.

106. Jerome D'Aste, S.J., diaries, July 9, 1907, PNTMC, reel 30, fr. 213.

107. "Caught on the Run About Town," DM, Oct. 11, 1907, p. 10, col. 2.

108. "Caught on the Run About Town," DM, Oct. 27, 1907, p. 12, col. 2.

109. "Indians as Farmers on the Reservation," AS, Nov. 1, 1907, p. 4, col. 1.

110. "Indians Have Lots of Money," *Missoula Herald*, Nov. 2, 1907, p. 1, col. 2.

111. "Fire Destroys Many Buildings at Ronan," WM, Nov. 8, 1907, p. 7, col. 5.

112. "Indians Doing Spring Work," AS, Apr. 12, 1908, p. 3, col. 3.

113. "Preparing for Rush of Settlers," DM, Apr. 23, 1909, p. 7, col. 1–2.

114. "Reservation Items," *Plainsman*, July 29, 1909, p. 4, col. 4.

115. *Kalispell Journal*, Aug. 9, 1909, p. 8, col.1.

116. "Great Crops," DM, Aug. 17, 1909, p. 12, col. 2.

117. "Indian Wheat Crop Turned into Flour," *Kalispell Journal*, Nov. 11, 1909, p. 1, col. 2.

118. Jerome D'Aste, S.J., diaries, Aug. 6, 1910, PNTMC, reel 30, fr. 330.

119. "Fine Wheat Crop on Flathead," DM, Oct. 19, 1910, p. 3, col. 2.

120. St. Ignatius Mission House Diary, Oct. 19, 1905, PNTMC, reel 3, fr. 258.

121. St. Ignatius Mission House Diary, Mar. 19, 1906, PNTMC, reel 3, fr. 270.

122. Bellew to Octave Couture, Arlee, Aug. 4, 1906, FH Agency Papers LS; Bellew to D. D. Hull, Ronan, Nov. 27, 1906, FH Agency Papers LS.

123. "These Red Men Are Industrious," DM, Sept. 5, 1905, p. 2, col. 1.

124. "Great Change on the Reservation," DM, June 8, 1906, p. 3, col. 1.

125. *Inter Lake* (Kalispell, Mont.), June 15, 1906, p. 5, col. 3.

126. *Kalispell Bee*, Sept. 10, 1907, p. 3, col. 1.

127. Fred C. Morgan to CIA, Sept. 10, 1910, U.S. Bureau of Indian Affairs, "Superintendents' Annual Narrative and Statistical Reports from Field Jurisdictions of the Bureau of Indian Affairs, 1907–1938," NAmf M1011, reel 42, pp. 1–2.

128. "Indians as Farmers on the Reservation," AS, Nov. 1, 1907, p. 4, col. 1.

129. "Fire Destroys Many Buildings at Ronan," WM, Nov. 8, 1907, p. 7, col. 5; "Fire at Ronan," *Missoula Herald*, Nov. 5, 1907, p. 4, col. 4.

130. Jos. M. Dixon, U.S. Senate, to Mr. F. T. Sterling, Missoula, Nov. 16, 1907, FH Agency Papers LR.

131. Fred C. Morgan to CIA, July 20, 1909, ARCIA (1909), 29–31.

132. W. B Parsons, Missoula, to Bellew, Jan. 15, 1907, FH Agency Papers LR.

133. Fred C. Morgan to CIA, Sept. 10, 1910, U.S. Bureau of Indian Affairs, "Superintendents' Annual Narrative and Statistical Reports from Field Jurisdictions of the Bureau of Indian Affairs, 1907–1938," NAmf M1011, reel 42, p. 8.

134. File 90,270/1910 Flathead 320, NA CIA CCF.

135. Morgan to no name, Mar. 9, 1909, FH Agency Papers LS.

136. Ignace Grandjo, Helena County Jail, to Belew, July 8, 1907, FH Agency Papers LR.

137. "New Tribal Judge Named," DM, Apr. 17, 1910, p. 7, col. 2–3.

138. "Lots of Indians," WM, Mar. 19, 1909, p. 5, col. 4.

139. "Engineer Savage Visits Missoula," AS, Mar. 26, 1909, p. 2, col. 1–3.

140. "Indians Working on Great Ditches," AS, July 12, 1910, p. 11, col. 2.

141. File 57,496/1910 Flathead 339, NA CIA CCF.

142. B. H. Denison, Arlee, to Bellew, Mar. 14, 1905, FH Agency Papers LR.

143. B. H. Denison, Arlee, to Bellew, Nov. 27, 1905, FH Agency Papers LR.

144. "Will Matt Defeats Jack Curran," DM, Apr. 22, 1905, p. 8, col. 2–3.

145. Wm. Dowd, St. Ignatius, to Bellew, May 2, 1905, FH Agency Papers LR.

146. DM, May 18, 1905, p. 6, col. 5–6.

147. "Indians to Gather at Mission," DM, June 28, 1905, p 2, col. 2.

148. *Plainsman*, July 7, 1905, p. 3, col. 1.

149. Peter Mag Pie, Dixon, to Bellew, July 18, 1905, FH Agency Papers LR.

150. Bellew to Jno. W. Pace, Sec., Montana State Fair, Helena, Sept. 3, 1906, FH Agency Papers LS.

151. Susie Ogden, Dixon, to Bellew, Dec. 11, 1906, FH Agency Papers LR.

152. W. M. ____ [torn page], Spokane, Wash., to Indian Agent, Nov. 5, 1906, FH Agency Papers LR.

153. Bellew to Suzie Ogden, Dec. 20, 1906, FH Agency Papers LS.

154. D. D. Hull, Ronan, to Bellew, Feb. 2, 1907, FH Agency Papers LR.

155. "Bring Along the Tribes," *Kalispell Bee*, June 7, 1907, p. 1, col. 3–4.

156. "The Races," *Kalispell Journal*, July 11, 1907, p. 1, col. 6–7.

157. Sam Reserarection, Arlee, to Major, Mar. 29, 1909, FH Agency Papers LR.

158. "Uncle Samuel Is Counting Noses," *Lake Shore Sentinel* (Polson, Mont.), Apr. 15, 1910, p 1, col. 1; "Census About Completed," *Flathead Courier* (Polson, Mont.), June 2, 1910, p. 1, col. 3.

159. *Kalispell Bee*, Aug. 11, 1905, p. 8, col. 1.

160. "Arrested by Reed," *Kalispell Bee*, Aug. 3, 1906, p. 1, col. 5–6.

161. "Allard House Well Known Since the Coaching Days," DM, Mar. 22, 1907, p. 6, c 4–6.

162. "Polson News," *Kalispell Bee*, Feb. 2, 1909, p. 4, c.3; "Polson Livery," *Kalispell Journal*, June 28, 1909, p. 5, col. 2; "Reserve Is Busy," DM, June 29, 1909, p. 12, col. 2.

163. *Kalispell Bee*, Jan. 28, 1910, p. 3, col. 1; *Flathead Courier* (Polson, Mont.), June 2, 1910, p. 8, col. 3.

164. "Springs Are Popular," *Kalispell Bee*, July 4, 1905, p. 7, col. 3.

165. *Sanders County Signal* (Plains, Mont.), Dec. 10, 1908, p. 1, col. 4.

166. *Plainsman*, Mar. 18, 1909, p. 4, col. 1.

167. *Sanders County Signal* (Plains, Mont.), May 22, 1909, p. 2, col. 5; *Plainsman*, June 3, 1909, p. 3, c 3.

168. "Camas News," *Plainsman*, June 2, 1910, p. 5, col. 3.

169. *Sanders County Signal* (Plains, Mont.), Nov. 26, 1908, p. 1, col. 3.

170. *Sanders County Signal* (Plains, Mont.), Aug. 21, 1909, p. 3, col. 2.

171. *Plainsman*, July 1, 1909, p. 3, col. 3.

172. "Have Faith in Plains," *Sanders County Democrat* (Plains, Mont.), Apr. 29, 1910, p. 3, col. 5.

173. *Plainsman*, July 8, 1909, p. 3, col. 4; *Missoula Herald*, Dec. 3, 1909, p. 6, col. 5; "Homeseekers Attention," *Daily Inter Lake* (Kalispell, Mont.), Aug. 31, 1910, p. 8, col. 4; "John Matt," DM, Sept. 16, 1910, p. 10, col. 6; "John Matt: Locator Flathead Indian Lands," *Daily Inter Lake* (Kalispell, Mont.), Oct. 14, 1910, p. 7, col. 5–6.

174. "Fullfledged Citizen," *Missoula Herald*, Nov. 5, 1910, p. 1, col. 1.

175. "Ronan Items," *Lake Shore Sentinel* (Polson, Mont.), Apr. 8, 1910, p. 2, col. 1–2; "Ronan Items," *Lake Shore Sentinel* (Polson, Mont.), May 20, 1910, p 4, col. 3.

176. "Ronan Items," *Lake Shore Sentinel* (Polson, Mont.), Apr. 15, 1910, p 3, col. 3; "McCloud Livery," *Flathead Courier* (Polson, Mont.), July 7, 1910, p 7, col. 3.

177. Bellew to Tony Cabell, St. Ignatius, Apr. 21, 1905, FH Agency Papers LS.

178. Bellew to CIA, June 10, 1905, 45,658/1905, NA CIA LR; Bellew to Mr. Bisson, Kalispell, June 22, 1905, FH Agency Papers LS.

179. "Lightning Bugs," *Kalispell Bee*, June 16, 1905, p. 1, col. 2.

180. Peter Lucier, St. Ignatius, to Bellew, Oct. 21, 1906, FH Agency Papers LR.

181. D. D. Hull, Additional Farmer, Ronan, to Bellew, Mar. 3, 1907, FH Agency Papers LR.

182. Mrs. Alfred Normandin, St. Ignatius, to Bellew, May 18, 1907, FH Agency Papers LR.

183. D. D. Hull, Additional Farmer, Ronan, to Bellew, Sept. 7, 1907, FH Agency Papers LR.

184. Mrs. Felix Dumontier, St. Ignatius, to Morgan, Apr. 25, 1909, FH Agency Papers LR.

185. "Arlee News Notes," DM, June 16, 1909, p. 6, col. 7.

186. "Says Ronan Is Booming," *Missoula Herald*, Apr. 2, 1910, p. 1, col. 6–7; p. 8, col. 3.

187. "Camas News," *Plainsman*, Sept. 15, 1910, p. 4, col. 3–4.

188. *Sanders County Democrat* (Plains, Mont.), Oct. 28, 1910, p. 3, col. 5.

189. "Lumber and Fuel on Flathead," DM, Dec. 5, 1910, p. 2, col. 3.

190. Edward M. Griva, S.J., "History of the 50 Years of My Missionary Life Among Indians and Whites from July 1894 till the end of September 1944," PNTMC, reel 32, p. 56.

191. *Flathead Courier* (Polson, Mont.), June 30, 1910, p. 8, col. 4.

192. D. D. Hull, Ronan, to Bellew, Jan. 16, 1905, FH Agency Papers LR.

193. D. D. Hull, Ronan, to Bellew, Jan. 31, 1905, FH Agency Papers LR.

194. Bellew to D. D. Hull, Ronan, Feb. 1, 1905, FH Agency Papers LS.

195. "Camas News," *Plainsman*, July 21, 1910, p. 4, col. 3–6; "Big Arm," *Kalispell Journal*, July 21, 1910, p. 5, col. 1–2.

196. James Dupuis, Polson, to Bellew, July 26, 1906, FH Agency Papers LR.

197. DM, Oct. 30, 1906, p. 2, col. 1.

198. D. D. Hull, Ronan, to Bellew, Feb. 13, 1907, FH Agency Papers LR.

199. Wm. Bell, Jr., Polson, to Morgan, Feb. 15, 1909, FH Agency Papers LR; "Camas News," *Plainsman*, Oct. 6, 1910, p. 4, col. 3–4.

200. Duncan McDonald, Ravalli, to Morgan, Mar. 31, 1909, FH Agency Papers LR.

201. "Rollins," *Kalispell Journal*, Dec. 2, 1909, p. 5, col. 1.

202. "Missoula Notes," AS, Jan. 26, 1905, p. 12, col. 5.

203. DM, Feb. 23, 1905, p. 6, col. 2; DM, Mar. 1, 1905, p. 2, col. 4.

204. "January Varmints on Bounty List," DM, Feb. 3, 1905, p. 3, col. 2.

205. "New Bounty Law Is Not Liked," DM, Mar. 10, 1905, p. 6, col. 1.

206. "Police Court Troubles," DM, Jan. 28, 1905, p. 3, col. 1.

207. "Must Answer in Court for Shooting Seymour," AS, June 10, 1905, p. 14, col. 1.

208. Bellew to Davis Graham, Sheriff, Missoula, Aug. 3, 1906, FH Agency Papers LS.

209. "Flathead and Drink," *Missoula Herald*, Sept. 21, 1907, p. 1, col. 4.

210. "Honest Injun Comes Across with His Fine," DM, Oct. 30, 1908, p. 2, col. 1.

211. "Charged with Taking Liquor Onto Reservation," AS, May 7, 1909, p 5, col. 6.

212. C. H. McLeod to Geo. H. Beckwith, May 11, 1909, col. H. McLeod Papers, Toole Archives, Mansfield Library, University of Montana, Missoula.

213. Geo. H. Beckwith to C. H. McLeod, July 28, 1909, col. H. McLeod Papers, Toole Archives, Mansfield Library, University of Montana, Missoula.

214. Bellew to William Q. Ranft, Missoula, Mar. 3, 1906, FH Agency Papers LS; William Q. Ranft, Missoula, to Bellew, Mar. 6, 1906, FH Agency Papers LR; W. B. Parsons, M.D., Missoula, Mont., to CIA, Mar. 15, 1906, 25,140/1906, NA CIA LR.

215. DM, Dec. 16, 1905, p. 7, col. 2.

216. *Missoula Herald*, Dec. 21, 1907, p. 4, col. 2; "Caught on the Run About Town," DM, Dec. 19, 1907, p. 10, col. 3.

217. DM, Dec. 22, 1908, p. 2, col. 4; DM, Dec. 22, 1908, p. 2, col. 3; DM, Dec. 23, 1908, p. 2, col. 4; DM, Dec. 25, 1908, p. 2, col. 4.

218. *Plainsman*, Feb. 24, 1905, p. 4, col. 4.

219. "Indians Spend Coin for Gee-Gaws," DM, Mar. 1, 1905, p. 6, col. 2.

220. DM, Mar. 2, 1905, p. 2, col. 4.

221. "Money Well Spent by Indian," DM, Mar. 3, 1905, p. 6, col. 4.

222. "Indians in Town to See Circus," DM, Aug. 10, 1905, p. 7, col. 1.

223. DM, June 7, 1906, p. 3, col. 3–4.

224. "Woman Loses a Big Roll of Money," DM, Oct. 11, 1906, p. 2, col. 3.

225. *Plainsman*, Dec. 19, 1907, p. 5, col. 2.

226. *Missoula Herald*, Dec. 10, 1908, p. 8, col. 2.

227. "A Good Road to the Reservation Now," *Plainsman*, Sept. 9, 1909, p. 2, col. 4.

228. C. H. McLeod to Geo. H. Beckwith, Apr. 12, 1905, col. H. McLeod Papers, Toole Archives, Mansfield Library, University of Montana, Missoula.

229. C. H. McLeod to Geo. H. Beckwith, Oct. 6, 1905, col. H. McLeod Papers, Toole Archives, Mansfield Library, University of Montana, Missoula.

230. "Red Thunder Jailed for Fraud," DM, June 16, 1907, p. 12, col. 3.

231. "Eleven Caught in Poker Game in Arlee Bunkhouse," AS, Nov. 8, 1909, p. 2, col. 6; "Japs Plead Guilty, Indians Are Freed," DM, Nov. 11, 1909, p. 10, col. 3.

232. "A Strong Institution," *Kalispell Journal*, June 3, 1909, p 4, col. 3.

233. "Polson Bank Gets Charter," *Kalispell Journal*, June 17, 1909, p. 4, col. 2.

234. "Polson Banking Center," *Kalispell Bee*, Jan. 28, 1910, p. 1, col. 1.

235. "Two New Banks," *Kalispell Journal*, Mar. 31, 1910, p. 1, col. 2.

236. "Dayton Mercantile Company," *Kalispell Bee*, Apr. 19, 1910, p. 4, col. 2.

237. Michael & Co., Proprietors, Spokane Table Supply Co., Spokane, Wash., to Bellew, Mar. 28, 1905, FH Agency Papers LR; C. M Rasch, U.S. Attorney, Helena, to Bellew, Mar. 30, 1905, FH Agency Papers LR.

238. Bellew to Mrs. Scott, Dayton, Apr. 8, 1905, FH Agency Papers LS.

239. Bellew to Board of County Commissioners, Missoula, Aug. 31, 1905, FH Agency Papers LS.

240. [Illegible name], Supt., Northern Pacific Railroad, Missoula, to Bellew, Jan. 18, 1907, FH Agency Papers LR.

241. Bellew to Thomas Reed, Constable, Dayton, Feb. 2, 1907, FH Agency Papers LS.

242. U.S. Indian Agent, Flathead Agency, to D. D. Hull, Ronan, Apr. 16, 1908, FH Agency Papers LR.

243. Jerome D'Aste, S.J., diaries, Feb. 21, 1909, PNTMC, reel 30, fr. 281.

244. "Sam Cone Arrests Druggist," DM, Mar. 25, 1910, p. 6, col. 2.

245. "Indians Are in Trouble Three Are Under Bonds," AS, Apr. 1, 1910, p. 9, col. 5.

246. "Indian Murderer Is Found Guilty," DM, July 23, 1910, p. 4, col. 4.

247. "Capture Liquor on Reservation," DM, Apr. 26, 1905, p. 5, col. 3; "They Had the Whiskey But Were Off Reserve," AS, May 23, 1905, p. 12, col. 4.

248. "Red Men in Custody of Deputy Marshal," DM, June 2, 1907, p. 12, col. 4; "Nakazumi and Booze Get Into the Court," DM, June 13, 1907, p. 8, col. 2; "Indian Is Well Loaded Wet Goods for Friends," AS, June 14, 1907, p. 13, col. 2; "Aeneas Grandjo Is Held for Handling Fire Water," DM, June 14, 1907, p. 6, col. 3.

249. "Indians Put In Jail for Carrying Liquor," AS, Mar. 26, 1908, p. 5, col. 4.

250. "Many Arrests Made by Sam Cone," DM, Aug. 18, 1908, p. 8, col. 5–6; "Michael Plant Caught; Grand Jury Wants Him," AS, Jan. 2, 1909, p. 5, col. 6.

251. "One More Is Arrested for Carrying Liquor," AS, Aug. 20, 1908, p. 5, col. 4.

252. "Indian Is Charged with Murder," DM, Feb. 19, 1909, p. 8, col. 4; "Two Indians Face Commissioner," DM, June 19, 1909, p. 6, col. 5.

253. "Consumptive Indian Sent to Jail," DM, Jan. 7, 1910, p. 7, col. 2; "Indians Are in Trouble Three Are Under Bonds," AS, Apr. 1, 1910, p. 9, col. 5.

254. "Remorseful Reds Punished," DM, Feb. 28, 1905, p. 8, col. 3.

255. Jerome D'Aste, S.J., diaries, Mar. 21, 1905, PNTMC, reel 30, fr. 111–12; Jerome D'Aste, S.J., diaries, Mar. 23, 1905, PNTMC, reel 30, fr. 112.

256. *Plainsman*, May 19, 1905, p. 1, col. 1.

257. "In the Police Court," AS, May 23, 1905, p. 12, col. 3; "Justice Court Troubles," DM, May 23, 1905, p. 5, col. 5.

258. St. Ignatius Mission House Diary, June 1, 1905, PNTMC, reel 3, fr. 253.

259. "Shooting Scrape Near Ronan," DM, June 13, 1905, p. 8, col. 2.

260. "Woman Is Killed in Drunken Orgy," DM, Oct. 24, 1905, p. 8, col. 2.

261. St. Ignatius Mission House Diary, Feb. 25, 1907, PNTMC, reel 3, fr. 281; Jerome D'Aste, S.J., diaries, Feb. 28, 1907, PNTMC, reel 30, fr. 198.

262. Jerome D'Aste, S.J., diaries, Mar. 1, 1907, PNTMC, reel 30, fr. 198.

263. Jerome D'Aste, S.J., diaries, Jan. 8, 1905, PNTMC, reel 30, fr. 104.

264. Bellew to Davis Graham, Sheriff, Missoula, Mar. 1, 1905, FH Agency Papers LS.

265. "Wants Value of Horse and Damages Besides," AS, July 18, 1905, p. 12, col. 3.

266. Bellew to Sheriff of Flathead County, Kalispell, Aug. 8, 1905, FH Agency Papers LS.

267. "Two Prisoners Captured," DM, Aug. 17, 1905, p. 3, col. 2.

268. Bellew to Mr. Schlestine, Livery Stable Owner, Kalispell, Feb. 26, 1906, FH Agency Papers, LS; Chief Koos-ta-ta, Dayton, to Bellew, Mar. 9, 1906, FH Agency Papers LR.

269. "Not Considered a Crime," *Kalispell Bee*, Sept. 15, 1905, p. 1, col. 5.

270. "Back to Reservation," AS, Apr. 2, 1905, p. 12, col. 3.

271. Jerome D'Aste, S.J., diaries, Mar. 27, 1908, PNTMC, reel 30, fr. 242; St. Ignatius Mission House Diary, Mar. 27, 1908, PNTMC, reel 3, fr. 294.

272. Jerome D'Aste, S.J., diaries, July 1, 1908, PNTMC, reel 30, fr. 254.

273. Jerome D'Aste, S.J., diaries, Oct. 6, 1908, PNTMC, reel 30, fr. 264.

274. St. Ignatius Mission House Diary, Oct. 3, 1909, PNTMC, reel 3, fr. 313; Jerome D'Aste, S.J., diaries, Oct. 4, 1909, PNTMC, reel 30, fr. 303; Jerome D'Aste, S.J., diaries, Oct. 16, 1909, PNTMC, reel 30, fr. 304.

275. Jerome D'Aste, S.J., diaries, Nov. 21, 1909, PNTMC, reel 30, fr. 308.

276. Jerome D'Aste, S.J., diaries, Nov. 23, 1909, PNTMC, reel 30, fr. 308; Jerome D'Aste, S.J., diaries Nov. 24, 1909, PNTMC, reel 30, fr. 308–09; St. Ignatius Mission House Diary, Nov. 25, 1909, PNTMC, reel 3, fr. 315.

277. St. Ignatius Mission House Diary, Apr. 12, 1910, PNTMC, reel 3, fr. 319; Jerome D'Aste, S.J., diaries, Apr. 12, 1910, PNTMC, reel 30, fr. 322.

Afterword

1. "The Flathead Bill Is Signed by President," AS, Apr. 26, 1904, p. 1, col. 6; U.S. Statutes at Large, vol. 33 (1903–5), 302–8.

2. Karlin, *Joseph M. Dixon*, 54–59.

3. Dixon to Duncan McDonald, Dec. 19, 1903 (filed under Dec. 29, 1903), Joseph Dixon Papers, MS 55, Toole Archives, Mansfield Library, University of Montana, Missoula.

4. Dixon to Angus P. McDonald, Dec. 19, 1903, Joseph Dixon Papers, MS 55, Toole Archives, Mansfield Library, University of Montana, Missoula.

5. Michel Pablo to Dixon, Dec. 1903, Joseph Dixon Papers, MS 55, Toole Archives, Mansfield Library, University of Montana, Missoula.

6. D. McDonald to Dixon, Dec. 29, 1903, Joseph Dixon Papers, MS 55, Toole Archives, Mansfield Library, University of Montana, Missoula.

7. Joseph Allard to Dixon, Jan. 2, 1904, Joseph Dixon Papers, MS 55, Toole Archives, Mansfield Library, University of Montana, Missoula.

8. Bigart and Woodcock, *In the Name of the Salish*, 9–16; "Treaty with the Omaha, 1854," in Kappler, *Indian Affairs*, vol. 2: 612–13.

9. Dixon to J. M. Keith, Feb. 28, 1904, Joseph Dixon Papers, MS 55, Toole Archives, Mansfield Library, University of Montana, Missoula.

10. Bigart and Woodcock, *In the Name of the Salish*, 19–65.

11. U.S. Statutes at Large, vol. 33 (1903–5), 302–8.

12. CIA to John Matt, Mar. 4, 1908, file 10,691/1908 Flathead 304, NA CIA CCF.

13. "Big Rush Begins for Indian Lands," AS, July 15, 1909, p. 1, col. 7; p. 6, col. 4.; "Like a Circus Day in Busy Missoula," AS, Aug. 4, 1909, p. 5, col. 5; "Land Drawing for Applicants," AS, Aug. 8, 1909, p. 1, col. 4; p. 3, col. 1.

14. "Last Name Called in Land Drawing," *Daily Inter Lake* (Kalispell, Mont.), June 1, 1910, p. 1, col. 4–5; "Last of Three Thousand for Reservation Lands," AS, June 9, 1910, p. 6, col. 4; "Flathead Opening Is Closed," DM, Sept. 30, 1910, p. 2, col. 1.

15. "One Big Time Expected Today," DM, Nov. 1, 1910, p. 1, col. 1; p. 6, col. 3–4.

16. Confederated Salish and Kootenai Tribes v. United States, U.S. Court of Claims Docket 50233, paragraph 10, decision Jan. 22, 1971.

17. Arthur M. Tinker to Secretary of the Interior, Sept. 20, 1903, Interior Department Inspection Reports, 9,007/1903, RG 48, National Archives, Washington, D.C.

18. Trosper, "The Economic Impact," 347–48.

19. Trosper, "The Economic Impact," 183–96.

20. Confederated Salish and Kootenai Tribes v. United States, U.S. Court of Claims Docket 50233, paragraph 10, decision Jan. 22, 1971.

21. See for example "(Schedule.) Inherited Indian Lands. (Advertised May 7, 1910. Bids opened July 7, 1910.)," DM, May 14, 1910, p. 7, col. 1–2.

22. Voggesser, *Irrigation, Timber*, 1–56.

23. Bellew to CIA, Mar. 30, 1905, 25,034/1905 NA CIA LR.

24. Voggesser, *Irrigation, Timber*, 89–114.

25. U.S. Statutes at Large, vol. 34, pt. 1 (1905–7), 355.

26. "Reservation Hot Springs," *Kalispell Bee*, Nov. 17, 1905, p. 1, col. 4–5.

Appendix A

1. Bigart, *Life and Death at St. Mary's Mission*, 238–40; *Challenge to Survive: Unit IV*, 64–69.

2. "Historical," WM, Feb. 3, 1882, p. 3, col. 4; "When the Indians Owned the Land," AS, Mar. 25, 1906, p. 13, col. 3–4; Bigart, *Life and Death at St. Mary's Mission*, 322–23.

3. Thomas W. Harris Diaries, SC 231, MHS Archives, Helena, folders 2 and 3.

4. Duncan McDonald to L. V. McWhorter, May 30, 1930, Lucullus Virgil McWhorter Manuscripts, Archives and Special Collections, Holland Library, Washington State University, Pullman, file 184.

5. "Historical," WM, Feb. 3, 1882, p. 3, col. 4; O'Connor, "The Flathead Indians," 104; Ronan, *Girl from the Gulches*, 182; "Missoula Mentionings," *Butte Semi-Weekly Miner*, Jan. 15, 1887, p. 1, col. 8.

6. Garfield, "Conference of Hon. James A. Garfield," 171–74; J. U. Sanders, "*When Garfield Visited Montana*," AS, May 24, 1908, part 2, p. 7, col. 1–4.

7. Peter Whaley to CIA, Sept. 12, 1874, ARCIA (1874), 263; Daniel Shanahan to CIA, Dec. 12, 1873, CIA LR NA 234, reel 496, fr. 153.

8. Chas. S. Medary to CIA, Sept. 13, 1875, ARCIA (1875), 306.

9. Bigart, "The Travails of Flathead Indian," 27–41.

10. Rappagliosi, *Letters from the Rocky Mountain*, 55–58.

11. S. S. Benedict to Secretary of Interior, July 10, 1883, NAmf M1070, 3093/1883.

12. Vest and Maginnis, "Report of the Subcommittee," xiv; Ronan letters, vol. 1: 232–34.

13. Arlee Antwine Skulep Squalshey to Supretenant of indian Afares, Feb. 17, 1887, 5,858/1887, NA CIA LR.

14. "Indians in State Celebrate Yule Fifty-First Time," DM, Dec. 23, 1937, p. 1, col. 5; p. 6, col. 3.

15. Bigart, *A Pretty Village*, 76–82, 148–53.

16. WM, Jan. 27, 1882, p. 3, col. 2.

17. White, "Garfield!: An Incident," 10–11.

18. Ronan, *Girl from the Gulches*, 155.

19. U.S. President, "Message," 1883, 8–18.

20. Ronan letters, vol. 1: 198–99; E. D. Bannister to SecInt, Oct. 20, 1888, NAmf M1070, 5,261/1888.

21. "The Kuntza-Marengo Murder Trial," NNW, Jan. 12, 1883, p. 3, col. 4.

22. "His Mystery," WM, Mar. 27, 1885, p. 1, col. 5–7; Rylett, *Surveying the Canadian*, 235.

23. C. H. Howard to SecInt, Dec. 4, 1883, NAmf M1070, 5,061/1883, pp. 27–29.

24. Ronan letters, vol. 1: 238–42.

25. Ronan, *Girl from the Gulches*, 205–7; Ronan letters, vol. 1: 343–46.

26. "Reduction of Indian Reservations," 71.

27. Ronan letters, vol. 1: 381–83.

28. Ronan letters, vol. 1: 50–58.

29. Ronan letters, vol. 1: 316–21.

30. Ronan letters, vol. 1: 322–26.

31. "Arlee Objects," WM, Jan. 9, 1889, p. 3, col. 3; "Frightful Atrocities," WM, May 1, 1889, p. 3, col. 3.

32. Ronan letters, vol. 2: 34–35, 45–48; "A Red Desperado," *Helena Independent*, May 14, 1889, p. 1, col. 7.

33. "To the Happy Hunting Grounds," *Helena Journal*, Aug. 13, 1889, p. 1, col. 5; "Death of an Indian Brave," *Butte Semi-Weekly Miner*, Aug. 21, 1889, p. 3, col. 2; Ronan, *Girl from the Gulches*, 212; Missoula Publishing Company, *Flathead Facts*, 15; Post, "Sweet Revenge," 15–16.

34. Ronan letters, vol. 1: 15–19.

35. See Ronan letters, vol. 1: 135–37.

36. Palladino, *Indian and White*, 85–86.

37. Will Sutherlin, "West Side of the Bitter Root—Sweat House Farmers," *Rocky Mountain Husbandman* (Diamond City, Mont.), Aug. 16, 1877, p. 2, col. 2–3.

38. Ronan letters, vol. 1: 243–54.

39. Ronan letters, vol. 1: 170–72.

40. Ronan letters, vol. 2: 126–27, 176–277, 198–200.

41. Ronan letters, vol. 2: 288.

42. Ronan letters, vol. 2: 342–43.

43. Menager, "Reminiscences of a Missionary Sister," 59–61.

44. Bigart, *Life and Death at St. Mary's Mission*, 252–54; Bigart, *Getting Good Crops*; *Challenge to Survive: Unit IV*, 12–15, 61–64, 82–86; Rappagliosi, *Letters from the Rocky Mountain*, 108–9.

45. "Kootenai Chiefs Memorial," 11–12; Chas. Hutchins to Montana Superintendent of Indian Affairs, June 30, 1865, ARCIA (1865), 246; Turney-High, *Ethnography of the Kutenai*, 134–39; Malouf and White, "Kutenai Calendar Records," 34–39.

46. Ronan letters, vol. 1: 42–45; Ronan, *Girl from the Gulches*, 182–83.

47. O'Connor, "The Flathead Indians," 104.

48. Chas. Hutchins to Montana Superintendent of Indian Affairs, June 30, 1865, ARCIA (1865), 246; Augustus Chapman to CIA, Apr. 20,1866, CIA LR NA 234, reel 488, fr. 178.

49. Ronan letters, vol. 1: 20–24.

50. Ronan letters, vol. 1: 111–14.

51. Ronan letters, vol. 1: 316–21.

52. Ronan letters, vol. 1: 360–64.

53. U.S. President, "Message," 1883, 11.

54. Ronan letters, vol. 1: 219–22, 391–93.

55. Ronan letters, vol. 2: 4–7.

56. Ronan letters, vol. 2: 32–33.

57. Ronan letters, vol. 2, pp. 42–45; E. D. Bannister to SecInt, Oct. 20, 1888, NAmf M1070, 5261/1888, p. 6.

58. "The Red Man's Story," *Helena Journal* (daily), Oct. 25, 1889, p. 5, col. 1–2; Ronan letters, vol. 2: 148–57.

59. Ronan letters, vol. 2: 75–83, 111–12, 142–45.

60. Ronan letters, vol. 2: 142–45, 157–60, 170–72; and newspaper reports in the footnotes to these letters.

61. Bigart, *Zealous in All Virtues*, 54.

62. "Four of a Kind," *Missoula Weekly Gazette*, Nov. 12, 1890, p. 3, col. 1–3.

63. Ronan letters, vol. 2: 186–88, 253–54.

64. Ronan letters, vol. 2: 219–22.

65. Ronan letters, vol. 2: 225–28, 262–63.

66. Ronan letters, vol. 2: 330–33.

67. Ronan letters, vol. 2: 312–16, 330–33.

68. Joseph Carter to CIA, Feb. 6, 1894, 6,591/1894, NA CIA LR; CIA to Carter, Feb. 21, 1894, land, letter book 274, pp. 394–96, NA CIA LS.

69. "Very Near a Good Indian," *Kalispell Graphic*, Mar. 13, 1895, p. 3, col. 1.

70. "All Same M'Kinley," AS, Aug. 24, 1898, p. 10, col. 2.

71. Augustine Dimier to Rev. Father Provincial, Apr. 1901, Bigart and Woodcock, "St. Ignatius Mission, Montana," 275–76.

72. "Noted Chief Dead," *Kalispell Bee*, July 27, 1900, p. 1, col. 5.

73. Ewers, *Gustavus Sohon's Portraits*, 50–52.

74. Teit, "The Salishan Tribes," 377.

75. Clark, *Indian Sign Language*, 301; Frank H. Woody, "Historical Sketch of Missoula County," WM, July 19, 1876, p. 2, col. 3–7 and p. 3, col. 1–4; Stone, *Following Old Trails*, 134.

76. Bigart, *A Pretty Village*, 78; Duncan McDonald, "More About Indian 'Medicine,'" NNW, Feb. 21, 1879, p. 3, col. 3.

77. "Accident," *Pioneer* (Missoula, Mont.), May 4, 1872, p. 3, col. 1.

78. Daniel Shanahan to CIA, Jan. 21, 1874, CIA LR NA 234, reel 500, fr. 262.

79. T. J. Demers to Martin Maginnis, May 2, 1874, Martin Maginnis Papers, MC 50, MHS Archives, Helena, box 1, folder 22.

80. Peter Whaley to CIA, Aug. 14, 1874, CIA LR NA 234, reel 500, fr. 1124; President to SecInt, Nov. 18, 1874, CIA LR NA 234, reel 500, fr. 190.

81. Peter Whaley to CIA, Sept. 12, 1874, ARCIA (1874), pp. 262–63.

82. Attorney General to SecInt, Jan. 8, 1876 [1877], CIA LR NA 234, reel 508, fr. 382; Chas. S. Medary to CIA, Sept. 13, 1875, ARCIA (1875), 304; Chas. S. Medary to CIA, Sept. 1, 1876, ARCIA (1876), 493.

83. Ronan letters, vol. 1: 15–19; Ronan, *Girl from the Gulches*, 158–59.

84. Ronan letters, vol. 1: 20–24.

85. Ronan letters, vol. 1: 50–58.

86. Ronan letters, vol. 1: 69–74; "Indian Matters," *Helena Independent*, July 21, 1878, p. 3, col. 3.

87. Ronan, *Girl from the Gulches*, 184–86; "Wayside Notes," *Helena Independent*, Nov. 22, 1878, p. 3, col. 3.

88. Ronan letters, vol. 1: 198–99; WM, June 30, 1882, p. 3, col. 3.

89. U.S. President, "Message," 1883, 11–19.

90. Vest and Maginnis, "Report of the Subcommittee," xxv-xxvii.

91. "Reduction of Indian Reservations," 58–60, 69–72.

92. Ronan letters, vol. 1: 316–26, 401–8.

93. Ronan letters, vol. 2: 58–60, 68–74.

94. "Cleverly Caught," *Missoula Gazette Daily*, Aug. 5, 1890, p. 1, col. 3–4; "One of Them Caught," *Missoula Gazette Daily*, Aug. 7, 1890, p. 1, col. 5; Bigart, *Zealous in All Virtues*, 54.

95. "Old Cheif [sic] Michel," DM, May 14, 1897, p. 1, col. 3; "Chief Michael Dead," AS, May 14, 1897, p. 10, col. 2.

Appendix B

1. Ewing to Van Gorp, about Apr. 19, 1875, BCIM Papers.

2. *Dictionary of American Biography*, vol. 12: 490–91; McMullin and Walker, *Biographical Directory*, 170–72, 199–201; Smith, *Samuel Medary*.

3. Ancestry.com.

4. Heitman, *Historical Register*, vol. 1: 704; Smith, *Samuel Medary*, 70, 142, 144.

5. NNW, July 9, 1875, p. 3, col. 4; WM, Sept. 1, 1975, p. 3, col. 4.

6. Medary to "My dear General," July 1875, BCIM Papers.

7. Medary to CIA, Aug. 16, 1875, CIA LR NA 234, r. 502, fr. 641; Potts to CIA, Oct. 12, 1875, CIA LR NA 234, r. 502, fr. 755; NNW, Aug. 20, 1875, p. 2, col. 1; "A Powerless Agent," WM, Aug. 25, 1875, p. 2, col. 3–4.

8. WM, Aug. 18, 1875, p. 3, col. 3.

9. Medary to CIA, Dec. 8, 1876, CIA LR NA 234, r. 505, fr. 698.

10. Medary to "My Dear General," Feb. 27, 1877, BCIM Papers; Medary to CIA, Feb. 28, 1877, CIA LR NA 234, r. 508, fr. 261; Medary to "My Dear General," Mar. 2, 1877, BCIM Papers; Medary to CIA, Mar. 2, 1877, CIA LR NA 234, r. 508, fr. 253.

11. Ewing to Medary, Mar. 28, 1877, BCIM Papers; Medary to Ewing, Apr. 15, 1877, BCIM Papers.

12. "Headquarters for Pure Austrian," 3; "German Carp Pond," 6; "At Democratic Headquarters," *New-York Times*, Aug. 16, 1892, p. 8, col. 2; "Deaths Reported April 25," *New York Times*, Apr. 26, 1901, p. 7, col. 7.

13. S. S. Benedict to SecInt, July 10, 1883, NAmf M1070, 3093/1883.

14. *Northwest Illustrated Monthly Magazine*, 46, col. 3.

15. P. McCormick to SecInt, Feb. 17, 1895, NAmf M1070, 1628/1895.

16. Ronan to CIA, Aug. 14, 1890, Ronan letters, vol. 2: 148–57.

17. Bigart, *Zealous in All Virtues*, 77; "Items from St. Ignatius," *Missoula Gazette* (daily), Jan. 9, 1891, p. 5, col. 2; Ronan to CIA, Jan. 2, 1891, Ronan letters, vol. 2: 183–85; Ronan to CIA, Jan. 31, 1891, Ronan letters, vol. 2: 186–88.

18. "Flathead Fears," *Helena Journal* (daily), Apr. 27, 1889, p. 1, col. 8.

19. Ronan to CIA, Aug. 1, 1890, Ronan letters, vol. 2: 142–45; Ronan to CIA, Nov. 1, 1890, Ronan letters, vol. 2: 170–72.

20. Ronan to CIA, Dec. 4, 1885, Ronan letters, vol. 1: 342–43.

21. Ronan to CIA, June 3, 1887, Ronan letters, vol. 1: 391–93.

22. Ronan to CIA, Nov. 16, 1892, Ronan letters, vol. 2: 337–38.

23. There is some disagreement in the sources about the exact year of Ronan's birth. This biographical sketch was compiled from: Ronan, "Discovery of Alder Gulch," 143–52; "Biographical," *Missoula County Times* (Missoula, Mont.), Aug. 31, 1887, p. 3, col. 3; "A Montana Pioneer," *Spokane Review*, Nov. 7, 1891, p. 3, col. 1–2; "Passed Peacefully Away," *Evening Missoulian*, Aug. 21, 1893, p. 1, col. 5–6.

24. *Northwest Illustrated Monthly Magazine*, p. 46, col. 3.

25. Estate of Peter Ronan, Probate file 339 (1893), Clerk of District Court, Missoula County Courthouse, Missoula, Mont.

26. Jackson, "The Irish Fox," 28–42; "Henry Bratnober," 579; "A Bear Story," *New-York Times*, July 21, 1890, p. 4, col. 7.

27. *Dictionary of American Biography*, vol. 4 (1930), 144–46; Mangam, *The Clarks*, 32–33; Patterson, *Montana Memories*, 22.

28. AncestryLibrary.com, 1880 United States Federal Census, Cicero, Cook County, Illinois.

29. WM, Sept. 4, 1885, p. 3, col. 4; WM, Jan. 15, 1886, p. 3, col. 3–4.

30. WM, Jan. 22, 1886, p. 3, col. 5.

31. *Missoula Gazette*, Oct. 27, 1890, p. 1, col. 4.

32. *Western Democrat* (weekly) (Missoula, Mont.), Aug. 27, 1893, p. 4, col. 2; "At the Flathead Agency," AS, Oct. 13, 1893, p. 1, col. 4.

33. Joseph T. Carter, Flathead Agency, 1893, appointment papers, RG 48, Office of the Secretary of the Interior, National Archives, Washington, D.C.

34. "At the Flathead Agency," AS, Oct. 13, 1893, p. 1, col. 4.

35. P. McCormick to SecInt, Feb. 17, 1895, NAmf M1070, 1628/1895.

36. Henry Matt, "How Former Agents Looked."

37. Joseph T. Carter, "Montana Marriages, 1889–1947," index, Familysearch.org.

38. Hon. T. H. Carter, U.S. Senate, to CIA, Mar. 9, 1896, 9,381/1896, NA CIA LR; Ronan letters, vol. 2: 399–401.

39. Carter to CIA, Mar. 4, 1895, NA CIA LR 10,563/1895.

40. Hon. T. H. Carter, U.S. Senate, to CIA, Mar. 9, 1896, 9.381/1896, NA CIA LR; "A Flathead Fracas," *Daily Democrat* (Missoula, Mont.), Mar. 5, 1895, p. 1, col. 8; "Went on the Warpath," AS, Mar. 6, 1895, p. 6, col. 3.

41. "Those Three Bad Indians," AS, Mar. 23, 1895, p. 6, col. 3–4; "The Indians Held," AS, Mar. 26, 1895, p. 6, col. 2; Carter to CIA, May 7, 1895, 20,518/1895, NA CIA LR.

42. Carter, Helena, Mont., to CIA, telegram, May 2, 1895, 19,118/1895, NA CIA LR; Carter to CIA, May 7, 1895, 20,518/1895, NA CIA LR.

43. "Will Walk Back," *Kalispell Graphic*, May 15, 1895, p. 2, col. 3.

44. Joseph T. Carter, Flathead Agency, 1897, appointment papers, RG 48, Office of the Secretary of the Interior, National Archive, Washington, D.C.; Schoenberg, *Paths to the Northwest*, 270; Ronan to CIA, May 5, 1884, Ronan letters, vol. 1: 263; Ronan to CIA, Oct. 22, 1889, Ronan letters, vol. 2: 96–98.

45. "New Church at Billings," *Butte Inter Mountain*, June 24, 1902, evening, p. 4, col. 5; "Will Start Work Soon," *Butte Inter Mountain*, July 3, 1902, evening, p. 9, col. 2; "Pride of Deer Lodge Is This New Kohrs Memorial Library," *Butte Inter Mountain*, Feb. 26, 1903, p. 1, col. 4–6; "Watching the Cash Lest It Be Wasted," *Butte Inter Mountain*, July 10, 1903, p. 1, col. 4–5, and p. 2, col. 4–5.

46. "Former Flathead Indian Agent Dies," DM, May 13, 1931, p. 3, col. 3.

47. AncestryLibrary.com, California Death Index, 1940–97.

48. Sanders, *A History of Montana*, vol. 2: 1284–85.

49. State Lumber Company, Montana Secretary of State, Business Entity Records, inactive, file D1535, MHS Archives, Helena; "New Incorporations," *Helena Independent*, Sept. 27, 1891, p. 5, col. 3.

50. "All After the Offices," AS, Sept. 6, 1894, p. 6, col. 1; "Picking Up the Pieces," AS, Nov. 11, 1894, p. 6, col. 1.

51. "The Flathead Reservation," DM, Jan. 29, 1895, p. 2, col. 1.

52. "Encouraging Progress," DM, Feb. 6, 1895, p. 2, col. 1; "Compliments for Bandmann," DM, Feb. 6, 1895, p. 1, col. 4.

53. "Is It a Scheme?" *Western Democrat* (daily) (Missoula, Mont.), Feb. 6, 1895, p. 1, col. 4.

54. "The Flathead Reservation," DM, Feb. 3, 1895, p. 2, col. 1.

55. "Passed the House," DM, Feb. 15, 1895, p. 1, col. 2; "Senate Joint Memorial No. 2," Montana Legislature, *Laws, Resolutions*, 65–66.

56. "All Home from Helena," AS, Mar. 13, 1895, p. 6, col. 1.

57. "Lots of Candidates," AS, Feb. 24, 1896, p. 10, col. 1; "Booms and Boomers," AS, Mar. 3, 1896, p. 10, col. 1; "It's Not Their Plan," AS, Mar. 17, 1896, p. 10, col. 1.

58. "Money for Pelts," AS, Mar. 21, 1896, p. 1, col. 5; "Money for the State," NNW, Apr. 3, 1896, p. 1, col. 5.

59. "Reading the Bills," AS, Jan. 8, 1897, p. 1, col. 2–3, p. 6, col. 2.

60. "Dead in the Senate," AS, Feb. 18, 1897, p. 5, col. 3.

61. "On the List," AS, June 4, 1897, p. 4, col. 4; "One Hundred and Fifty-Eight," AS, June 4, 1897, p. 4, col. 1.

62. Stout, *Montana*, vol. 2: 570; "Three Men for One Job," AS, Sept. 27, 1897, p. 10, col. 2.

63. "A Rattling of Bones," AS, Dec. 20, 1897, p. 10, col. 2.

64. *Daily Democrat-Messenger* (Missoula, Mont.), Jan. 11, 1898, p. 2, col. 1; St. Ignatius Mission House Diary, Jan. 24, 1898, PNTMC, reel 3, fr. 148.

65. *Plainsman*, Apr. 27, 1900, p. 4, col. 5.

66. "St. Ignatius Business Change," *Daily Democrat-Messenger* (Missoula, Mont.), Feb. 20, 1901, p. 1, col. 6.

67. W. McMillan, S.J., to Wm. H. Ketcham, Sept. 9, 1901, BCIM Papers; D'Aste to Smead, Sept. 11, 1901, FH Agency Papers LR.

68. "Disposes of Business," *Missoulian* (daily), Mar. 28, 1902, p. 1, col. 3.

69. "Indians Still Kicking," *Daily Democrat-Messenger* (Missoula, Mont.), Apr. 22, 1901, p. 1, col. 4; "Reservation Quarantine," *Missoulian* (daily), May 7, 1901, p. 3, col. 5; "Claim to Have a Grievance," *Missoulian* (daily), May 17, 1901, p. 1, col. 5, p. 4, col. 5.

70. "Remembered the Major," *Missoulian* (daily), July 3, 1902, p. 8, col. 2.

71. T. H. Carter to Joseph Dixon, Mar. 5, 1904, Joseph Dixon Papers, Toole Archives, Mansfield Library, Missoula, [filed under Mar. 26, 1904, letter from Dixon to Carter].

72. "Grave Charges Against Major Smead," AS, Apr. 28, 1904, p. 12, col. 1–3; "Serious Charges Made Against Smead," *Missoulian* (daily), Apr. 28, 1904, p. 1, col. 5–6, p. 8, col. 2.

73. Sanders, *A History of Montana*, vol. 3: 1683–84.

74. C. F. Nesler and Chas. S. McNichols to SecInt, June 21, 1904, inspection report on Flathead Agency, 6655/1904, Interior Department Inspection Report File, RG 48, National Archives, Washington, D.C.

75. Ibid.

76. "Indian Agent Smead Succeeded by Bellew," AS, July 2, 1904, p. 1, col. 4–5, p. 14, col. 4.

77. "Flathead Story Is Aptly Told," DM, Apr. 30, 1905, p. 10, col. 3–4; Smead, *Land of the Flatheads*.

78. "Major Smead Tells of Flathead Reservation," AS, May 15, 1905, p. 10, col. 3; "Reserve Has 1,500 Acres and Is a Fertile Domain," DM, May 16, 1905, p. 6, col. 1–2.

79. "Homestead Agency Is Established," DM, July 9, 1905, p. 8, c.2; "Smead & Hershey," DM, July 9, 1905, p. 7; Sanders, *A History of Montana*, vol. 3: 1427–28.

80. "Missoula to Have New Magazine," DM, July 2, 1905, p. 9, col. 7; "Flathead Reservation Information Agency," DM, July 9, 1905, p. 11; "William Q. Ranft Dies Suddenly in New York," DM, Mar. 13, 1914, p. 10, col. 3.

81. "Ten Massive Volumes To Hold Statistics," AS, Dec. 18, 1905, p. 12, col. 2.

82. "Wants Attorneys Disbarred," DM, Oct. 11, 1906, p. 10, col. 5.

83. "Taking of Testimony in Disbarment Case," AS, Dec. 4, 1906, p. 12, col. 3–4.

84. "Dunn Gives Testimony in Disbarment Case," AS, Dec. 5, 1906, p. 13, col. 1–2.

85. "Lively Scrimmage on Cedar Street," DM, Feb. 7, 1907, p. 2, col. 1.

86. "Disbarment Action Is Dismissed," DM, June 5, 1907, p. 6, col. 4.

87. "Six Thousand Registrants Mark First Day and Night," DM, July 16, 1909, p. 1, col. 1–2, p. 5, col. 3–4; "Major Smead Addresses Notaries," DM, July 19, 1909, p. 1, col. 7, p. 4, col. 5.

88. *Daily Inter Lake* (Kalispell, Mont.), Apr. 30, 1910, p. 5, col. 3; "Holders of Numbers on Flathead," DM, May 7, 1910, p. 2, col. 1–2.

89. DM, Apr. 4, 1911, p. 2, col. 4; "Ronan," DM, May 2, 1911, p. 2, col. 3.

90. DM, Aug. 1, 1915, p. 2, col. 5.

91. "Smead-Simons Building Corporation," DM, Feb. 22, 1920, p. 3, col. 1–7.

92. "New Wilma Theater Dedicated at Splendid Evening Concert," DM, May 12, 1921, p. 1, col. 3–5.

93. "Smead-Simons Building Affairs Are Settled," DM, June 2, 1922, p. 2, col. 2; "Another Knot Tied in the Theater Tangle," DM, Oct. 13, 1923, p. 2, col. 1.

94. "William Smead, 86, Rexburg Citizen, Dies at Home," *Post-Register* (Idaho Falls, Idaho), June 14, 1948, p. 3, col. 3.

95. Based on Bellew's obituary, "Major Sam Bellew, Missoula Pioneer, Is Taken by Death," DM, Sept. 28, 1921, p. 1, col. 5, p. 3, col. 4; and other sources as noted; WM, Mar. 1, 1878, p. 3, col. 3.

96. *Missoula Gazette* (daily), May 2, 1891, p. 8, col. 2.

97. "A Sad Demise," *Western Democrat* (daily) (Missoula, Mont.), Jan 24, 1895, p. 1, col. 6; "Death of Mrs. Bellew," DM, Jan. 25, 1895, p. 4, col. 4; "Bellew—Ralls," *Daily Democrat-Messenger* (Missoula, Mont.), Sept. 19, 1899, p. 4, col. 1; "Bellew—Ralls," AS, Sept. 19, 1899, p. 16, col. 3.

98. "The Local Call," *Daily Democrat-Messenger* (Missoula, Mont.), Mar. 28, 1900, p. 4, col. 2.

99. "Major Bellew Will Begin His New Duties To-morrow," AS, July 31, 1904, p. 13, col. 1–3.

100. "The Winning Ticket," WM, Mar. 23, 1892, p. 4, col. 3; "Sam Bellew Chairman," *Missoulian* (daily), Oct. 3, 1902, p. 8, col. 2.

101. *Morning Missoulian*, Sept. 3, 1892, p. 5, col. 1; "School Election," DM, Apr. 5, 1897, p. 4, col. 4–5; DM, Jan. 3, 1899, p. 8, col. 1; *Edwards' Fruit Grower & Farmer* (Missoula, Mont.), Mar. 15, 1901, p. 5, col. 1; *Missoulian* (daily), Jan. 21, 1904, p. 3, col. 3; *Missoulian* (daily), July 14, 1904, p. 3, col. 6.

102. "Major Bellew Will Begin His New Duties To-morrow," AS, July 31, 1904, p. 13, col. 1–3.

103. St. Ignatius Mission House Diary, June 4, 1906, PNTMC, reel 3, fr. 273.

104. L. Taleman, St. Ignatius, to Bellew, May 13, 1907, FH Agency Papers LR.

105. L. Taelman, S.J., to Wm. H. Ketcham, Aug. 16, 1907, BCIM Papers.

106. J. Daste, St. Ignatius, to Bellew, Feb. 10, 1908, FH Agency Papers LR.

107. L. Taelman, S.J., St. Ignatius, to Bellew, Sept. 18, 1908, FH Agency Papers LR.

108. John K Rankin, Flathead Res., to CIA, Aug. 25, 1906, 75,408/1906, NA CIA LR.

109. Jerome D'Aste, S.J., diaries, June 5, 1907, PNTMC, reel 30, fr. 209.

110. Reuben Perry to CIA, June 10, 1907, 55,396/1907, NA CIA LR.

111. "Bellew Not To Be Reappointed," *Missoula Herald*, Nov. 17, 1908, p. 1, col. 5–6.

112. "Major Sam Bellew, Missoula Pioneer, Is Taken by Death," DM, Sept. 28, 1921, p. 1, col. 5; p. 3, col. 4.

113. DM, June 18, 1898, p. 8, col. 1; "Flathead Club's Reunion," *Missoulian* (daily), Aug. 31, 1902, p. 9. col. 1.

114. *Missoulian* (daily), Sept. 6, 1903, p. 10, col. 3; *Missoulian* (daily), Sept. 17, 1903, p. 3, col. 3–4; "'Kamp Kootenai' as Hosts," *Missoulian* (daily), Sept. 27, 1903, p. 9, col. 6, p. 10, col. 1.

115. *Missoulian* (daily), Jan. 6, 1904, p. 3, col. 2.

116. DM, May 27, 1905, p. 6, col. 5; DM, Apr. 10, 1906, p. 6, col. 4.

117. Reuben Perry to CIA, June 10, 1907, 55,396/1907, NA CIA LR.

118. Bellew to CIA, Nov. 10, 1908, file 43,722/1908 Flathead 154, NA CIA CCF.

119. "Charged With Obtaining Money on Bogus Checks," AS, July 15, 1909, p. 5, col. 5.

120. "George Bellew Drowned in Hot Springs at Lolo," AS, Nov. 4, 1909, p. 2, col. 6; "George Bellew Dies in Plunge," DM, Nov. 4, 1909, p. 10, col. 4.

121. U.S. Census Office, "13th Census, 1910," Population Schedules, Montana, Missoula County, ED 72, sheet 15A, family 149, line 19, NAmf T624, reel 834.

122. "Fred Morgan Named As Agent," DM, Nov. 21, 1908, p. 10, col. 4.

123. "Missoula Matters," AS, Feb. 20, 1894, p. 6, col. 2.

124. "Republicans Nominate," *Missoula Journal*, Sept. 15, 1906, p. 3, col. 2; Waldron, *Montana Politics*, 118.

125. "Butte's Soiled Linen Will Not Be Washed by the State Legislature," DM, Jan. 11, 1907, p. 1, col. 1–2.

126. "Joseph M. Dixon Elected Senator on First Ballot," DM, Jan. 16, 1907, p. 1, col. 1–2; p. 4, col. 5.

127. Montana Legislature, *House Journal*, LXVI, 32–33, 294–95, 377, 383, and 434.

128. "List of Mayors of Missoula, Montana," Wikipedia.org.

129. "Caught on the Run About Town," DM, Nov. 6, 1907, p. 8, col. 2–3; *Plainsman*, Jan. 16, 1908, p. 3, col. 2; DM, June 12, 1908, p. 2, col. 5; "Fred Morgan May Get Plum," *Sanders County Signal* (Plains, Mont.), Nov. 19, 1908, p. 1, col. 6.

130. "Caught on the Run About Town," DM, June 10, 1908, p. 8, col. 2.

131. "Fred Morgan Named As Agent," DM, Nov. 21, 1908, p. 10, col. 4.

132. M. K. Sniffen, Missoula, Mont., to Mr. Welsh, Sept. 4, 1909, Incoming Correspondence, *Indian Rights Association Papers, 1868–1968* (Glen Rock, N.J.: Microfilming Corporation of America, 1974), reel 21.

133. "Major Fred Morgan Assumes Office," DM, Dec. 2, 1908, p. 10, col. 4.

134. L. Taelman, S.J., St. Ignatius, to Morgan, Dec. 28, 1908, FH Agency Papers LR.

135. Thomas Downs, Special U.S. Indian Agent, to CIA, Jan. 30, 1909, file 9,444/1909, Flathead 150, NA CIA CCF.

136. "New Flathead Indian Agency Near Town of Dixon: Model of Efficiency—Bits of History and Lore," DM, Dec. 12, 1915, ed. section, p. 1, col. 1–7; p. 7, col. 1–7.

137. Bigart and McDonald, *Duncan McDonald*, 107–74.

138. U.S. Census Office, "13th Census, 1910," Population Schedules, Montana, Missoula County, ED 72, sheet 15A, family 149, line 19, NAmf T624, reel 834.

139. "Major Morgan Offered Colville Agency Job," DM, Mar. 30, 1917, p. 2, col. 2–3.

140. Ortiz, *Handbook of North American Indians*, vol. 10: 817.

141. "St. Ignatius," *Flathead Courier* (Polson, Mont.), Mar. 5, 1925, p. 2, col. 1.

142. Tiffany Link, Maine Historical Society, Portland, Maine, to Bigart, Feb. 15, 2018, copy in possession of author.

Bibliography

Manuscript Sources

Marquette University Archives, Milwaukee, Wis.
  Bureau of Catholic Indian Missions Papers, St. Ignatius Mission, Montana, File

Missoula County Courthouse, Missoula, Mont.
  Clerk of District Court Records

Montana Historical Society, Helena, Mont.
  Thomas W. Harris Diaries, SC 231
  F. Jay Haynes photographs
  Thomas C. Power Papers, MS 55
  Martin Maginnis Papers, MC 50
  Montana Secretary of State, Business Entity Records, inactive, file D1535

National Archives, Washington, D.C.
  RG 48, Records of the Office of the Secretary of the Interior
  RG 75, Records of the Commissioner of Indian Affairs
  RG 279, Records of the Indian Claims Commission

National Archives Microfilm Publications, National Archives, Washington, D.C.
  M234, U.S. Office of Indian Affairs, "Letters Received by the Office of Indian
    Affairs, 1824–1880"

M1011, U.S. Bureau of Indian Affairs, "Superintendents' Annual Narrative and Statistical Reports from Field Jurisdictions of the Bureau of Indian Affairs, 1907–1938," reel 42

M1070, U.S. Department of the Interior, "Reports of Inspection of Field Jurisdictions of the Office of Indian Affairs, reel 11, Flathead Agency"

T623, U.S. Bureau of the Census, 12th Census of Population, 1900, reel 913, Missoula County

T624, U.S. Bureau of the Census, 13th Census, 1910 [Population Schedules], Montana, reel 832 (Flathead County), reel 834 (Missoula County), and reel 835 (Sanders County)

National Archives, Rocky Mountain Region, Denver, Colo.
RG 75, Blackfeet Agency Papers
RG 75, Flathead Agency Papers, letters received, 8NS–075–96–323
RG 75, Flathead Agency Papers, letters sent, local copy books, 8NS–075–96–318

Oregon Province Archives, Gonzaga University, Spokane, Wash.
Bro. Cyprius-Celestin, F.I.C. (Celestin Tregret), "Seven Years Among the Western Indians," unpublished manuscript

University of Montana, Mansfield Library, Toole Archives, Missoula, Mont.
W. H. H. Dickinson Papers, LC 23
Joseph Dixon Papers, MS 55
Morton J. Elrod Papers, MS UM 4
Frenchtown Historical Society Collection, OH 47–9
Samuel E. Johns Papers, SC 165, microfilm
Charles H. McLeod Papers, MS 1
Missoula County Records, MS 310

Washington State University, Holland Library, Manuscripts, Archives, and Special Collections.
Lucullus Virgil McWhorter Papers

Yale University, Sterling Library, New Haven, Conn.
Henry B. Carrington, "The Exodus of the Flathead Indians," Carrington Family Papers

Newspapers

Anaconda (Mont.) Standard, 1893–1910
Atlanta Constitution (Atlanta, Ga.), 1895
Benton Record (Fort Benton, Mont.), 1877

Bozeman (Mont.) Avant Courier, 1879

Butte (Mont.) Inter Mountain, 1902–3

Butte (Mont.) Semi-Weekly Miner, 1886–89

Catholic Sentinel for the Northwest (Portland, Ore.), 1886

Daily Democrat (Missoula, Mont.), 1895

Daily Democrat-Messenger (Missoula, Mont.), 1899–1901

Daily Inter Lake (Kalispell, Mont.), 1910

Daily Missoulian (Missoula, Mont.), 1895–99, 1904–39, 1949

Edwards' Fruit Grower & Farmer (Missoula, Mont.), 1900–1901

Evening Missoulian (Missoula, Mont.), 1893–94

Evening Republican (Missoula, Mont.), 1895

Flathead Courier (Polson, Mont.), 1910, 1925

Flathead Herald-Journal (Kalispell, Mont.), 1893–1905

Fort Benton (Mont.) Record, 1876

Fruit Grower and Farmer (Missoula, Mont.), 1901

Great Falls (Mont.) Tribune, 1955

Helena (Mont.) Daily Herald, 1875–82

Helena (Mont.) Independent (daily), 1875–83, 1889, 1891

Helena (Mont.) Journal, 1889

Helena (Mont.) Weekly Herald, 1881

Helena (Mont.) Weekly Independent, 1879

Inter Lake (Demersville and Kalispell, Mont.), 1890–1907

Kalispell (Mont.) Bee, 1900–1902, 1905–10

Kalispell (Mont.) Graphic, 1892–95

Kalispell (Mont.) Journal, 1907–10

Lake Shore Sentinel (Polson, Mont.), 1910

Livingston (Mont.) Enterprise, 1884

Mineral Independent (Superior, Mont.), 1933

Missoula (Mont.) County Times, 1884–87

Missoula (Mont.) Democrat, 1902

Missoula (Mont.) Gazette (daily), 1890–92

Missoula (Mont.) Gazette (weekly), 1888–89

Missoula (Mont.) Herald, 1907–10

Missoula (Mont.) Journal, 1906

Missoula (Mont.) Weekly Gazette, 1890–91

Missoulian (Missoula, Mont.) (daily), 1901–4, 1967

Montana Populist (Missoula, Mont.), 1893

Morning Missoulian (Missoula, Mont.), 1892

New North-West (Deer Lodge, Mont.) 1875–86

New York Times, 1883, 1890, 1892, 1901–2

Pioneer (Missoula, Mont.), 1872

Plainsman (Plains, Mont.), 1895–1910

Post-Register (Idaho Falls, Idaho), 1948
Rocky Mountain Husbandman (Diamond City, Mont., and other locations), 1877–82, 1932
Sanders County Democrat (Plains, Mont.), 1910
Sanders County Ledger (Thompson Falls, Mont.), 1966
Sanders County Signal (Plains, Mont.), 1906–9
Silver Occident (Missoula, Mont.), 1896
Spokane (Wash.) Review, 1891
Spokesman-Review (Spokane, Wash.), 1958
Times (Chicago, Ill.), 1881
Washington Post, 1907
Weekly Missoulian (Missoula, Mont.), 1875–91, 1904, 1907
Weekly Plainsman (Plains, Mont.), 1896
Western Democrat (daily) (Missoula, Mont.), 1895
Western Democrat (weekly) (Missoula, Mont.), 1893

Books, Articles, and Other Sources

Armstrong, Frank C. "Condition of Reservation Indians." *House of Representatives Document*. No. 406, 57th Cong., 1st Ses., 1902, serial 4361.

Beck, David R. M. *The Struggle for Self-Determination: History of the Menominee Indians Since 1854*. Lincoln: University of Nebraska Press, 2005.

Berthrong, Donald J. *The Cheyenne and Arapaho Ordeal: Reservation and Agency Life in the Indian Territory, 1875–1907*. Norman: University of Oklahoma Press, 1976.

Bigart, Robert, ed. *Life and Death at St. Mary's Mission, Montana: Births, Marriages, Deaths, and Survival among the Bitterroot Salish Indians, 1866–1891*. Pablo, Mont.: Salish Kootenai College Press, 2005.

———. "The Travails of Flathead Indian Agent Charles S. Medary, 1875–1877." *Montana: The Magazine of Western History* 62, no. 3 (Autumn 2012): 27–41.

Bigart, Robert J. *Getting Good Crops: Economic and Diplomatic Survival Strategies of the Montana Bitterroot Salish Indians, 1870–1891*. Norman: University of Oklahoma Press, 2010.

———, ed. *A Pretty Village: Documents of Worship and Culture Change, St. Ignatius Mission, Montana, 1880–1889*. Pablo, Mont.: Salish Kootenai College Press, 2007.

———, ed. *Zealous in All Virtues: Documents of Worship and Culture Change, St. Ignatius Mission, Montana, 1890–1894*. Pablo, Mont.: Salish Kootenai College Press, 2007.

Bigart, Robert, and Clarence Woodcock, eds. "St. Ignatius Mission, Montana: Reports from Two Jesuit Missionaries, 1885 & 1900–1901" (Parts I & II). *Arizona and the West* 23, no. 2 (Summer 1981): 149–72; and 23, no. 3 (Autumn 1981): 267–78.

———. *In the Name of the Salish & Kootenai Nation: The 1855 Hell Gate Treaty and the Origin of the Flathead Indian Reservation*. Pablo, Mont.: Salish Kootenai College Press, 1996.

Bigart, Robert, and Joseph McDonald. *Duncan McDonald: Flathead Indian Reservation Leader and Cultural Broker, 1849–1937*. Pablo, Mont.: Salish Kootenai College Press, 2016.

Brownell, Joan Louise. "The Genesis of Wildlife Conservation in Montana." Master's thesis, Montana State University, Bozeman, 1987.

Carriker, Robert C., and Eleanor R. Carriker, eds. "The Pacific Northwest Tribes Missions Collection of the Oregon Province Archives of the Society of Jesus." Wilmington, Del.: Scholarly Resources, 1987.

Challenge to Survive: History of the Salish Tribes of the Flathead Indian Reservation: Unit IV: Charlo and Michel Period, 1870–1910. Pablo, Mont.: Salish Kootenai College Tribal History Project, 2011.

Clark, W. P. *The Indian Sign Language*. Philadelphia: L. R. Hamersly, 1885.

Confederated Salish and Kootenai Tribes v. United States. U.S. Court of Claims Docket 50233, paragraph 10, decision Jan. 22, 1971.

Dana, Paul. "Among the Kalispel." *The Northwest* (New York) 1, no. 10 (Oct. 1883): p. 2, col. 2–3.

[DeRouge, Etienne Xavier, S.J.]. "Mission of St. Ignatius." *Letters and Notices* (Roehampton, London, England) 16, no. 77 (July 1883): 206–12.

Dictionary of American Biography. Vol. 4, 1930.

Dictionary of American Biography. Vol. 12, 1933.

Dixon, Joseph. "Young Joe Dixon in the Flathead Country." Edited by Jules A. Karlin. *Montana: The Magazine of Western History* 17, no. 1 (Jan. 1967): 12–19.

DuBois, Coert. *Trail Blazers*. Stonington, Conn.: Stonington Publishing, 1957.

Dusenberry, J. Verne. "Samples of Pend d'Oreille Oral Literature and Salish Narratives." In *Lifeways of Intermontane and Plains Montana Indians*, edited by Leslie B. Davis, 109–20. Bozeman, Mont.: Museum of the Rockies, Montana State University, 1979.

Ewers, John C. *Gustavus Sohon's Portraits of Flathead and Pend d'Oreille Indians, 1854*. Smithsonian Miscellaneous Collections, vol. 110, no. 7, 1948.

Foster, Morris W. *Being Comanche: A Social History of an American Indian Community*. Tucson: University of Arizona Press, 1991.

Fowler, Loretta. *Arapahoe Politics, 1851–1978: Symbols in Crises of Authority*. Lincoln: University of Nebraska Press, 1982.

———. *Tribal Sovereignty and the Historical Imagination: Cheyenne-Arapaho Politics*. Lincoln: University of Nebraska Press, 2002.

Garcia, Andrew. *Tough Trip Through Paradise, 1878–1879*. Edited by Bennett H. Stein. Boston: Houghton Mifflin, 1967.

Garfield, James A. "Conference of Hon. James A. Garfield, Special Commissioner, with the Indians of the Bitter Root Valley, Montana." *Fourth Annual Report of the Board of Indian Commissioners* (1872): 171–74.

"German Carp Pond." *Southern Cultivator* 41, no. 6 (June 1883): 6.

Glover, Eli Sheldon. *The Diary of Eli Sheldon Glover*. Fairfield, Wash.: Ye Galleon Press, 1987.

Gordon, Greg. *When Money Grew on Trees: A. B. Hammond and the Age of the Timber Baron*. Norman: University of Oklahoma Press, 2014.

Harmon, Alexandra. *Indians in the Making: Ethnic Relations and Indian Identities around Puget Sound*. Berkeley: University of California Press, 1998.

"Headquarters for Pure Austrian or German Carp." *Maine Farmer* 51, no. 18 (Mar. 22, 1883): 3.

Heitman, Francis B. *Historical Register and Dictionary of the United States Army*. Washington, D.C.: U.S. Government Printing Office, 1903.

Henderson, Palmer. "The Flathead Indians: A Visit to their Agency and to the St. Ignatius Mission." *Northwest Illustrated Monthly Magazine* (St. Paul, Minn.) 8, no. 8 (Aug. 1890): 1–3.

"Henry Bratnober." *Engineering and Mining Journal* 98, no. 13 (Sept. 26, 1914): 579.

Hoxie, Frederick E. *Parading Through History: The Making of the Crow Nation in America, 1805–1935*. Cambridge, U.K.: Cambridge University Press, 1995.

Indian Rights Association Papers, 1868–1968. Glen Rock, N.J.: Microfilming Corporation of America, 1974.

"Indians Recalled." *Montana Live Stock Journal* (Helena, Mont.) 2, no. 7 (Nov. 1885): p. 5, col. 3.

Ingersoll, Ernest. "The Last Remnant of Frontier." *American Magazine* 6, no. 2 (June 1887): 131–44.

Jackson, W. Turrentine. "The Irish Fox and the British Lion." *Montana: The Magazine of Western History* 9, no. 2 (Apr. 1959): 28–42.

Kappler, Charles J., ed. *Indian Affairs: Laws and Treaties: Vol. II (Treaties)*. Washington, D.C.: U.S. Government Printing Office, 1904.

Karlin, Jules A. *Joseph M. Dixon of Montana: Part I: Senator and Bull Moose Manager, 1867–1917*. Missoula, Mont.: Publications in History, University of Montana, 1974.

Koch, Elers. "Big Game in Montana from Early Historical Records." *Journal of Wildlife Management* 5, no. 4 (Oct. 1941): 357–70.

"Kootenai Chiefs Memorial Draws Hundreds." *Char-Koosta* (Dixon, Mont.) 2, no. 14 (Nov. 15, 1972): 11–12.

Lippincott, Joseph Barlow. "Grandeur in an American Forest." *The Forester* 6, no. 2 (Feb. 1900): 24–28.

MacTavish, Newton. "The Last Great Round-Up." *Canadian Magazine* 33, no. 6 (Oct. 1909): 482–91; and 34, no. 1 (Nov. 1909): 25–35.

Malouf, Carling, and Thain White. "Kutenai Calendar Records." *Montana: Magazine of History* 3, no. 2 (Spring 1953): 34–39.

Mangam, William D. *The Clarks: An American Phenomenon*. New York: Silver Bow Press, 1941.

Manning, Gladys. "Traveling in Montana in the Early Eighties." In "Sagas of Our Pioneers," Flathead County Superintendent of Schools, Kalispell, Mont., 8–10. Mimeograph. 1956.

Matt, Don. "Mary Ann Topsseh Coombs." *Char-Koosta* (Dixon, Mont.) 5, no. 14 (Nov. 15, 1975): 8–9.

———. "Blind Mose Remembers." *Char-Koosta* (Dixon, Mont.) 6, no. 5 (July 1, 1976): 6–7.

Matt, Henry. "How Former Agents Looked After Their Indian Charges." Clipping from unidentified newspaper, dated Jan. 26, 1914, possibly *St. Ignatius Post*. Copy in Henry Matt probate file, number 325, Flathead Agency Records, U.S. Bureau of Indian Affairs, Pablo, Mont.

McDermott, Louisa. "Ethnology and Folklore, Selish Proper." Master's thesis, University of California, Berkeley, 1904.

McKeogh, T. C., S.J. "The New Scholasticate Amid the Rockies." *Woodstock Letters* 26, no. 1 (1897): 71–85.

McLeod, Malcolm. *A Cowboy's Life Is Very Dangerous Work: The Autobiography of a Flathead Reservation Indian Cowboy, 1870–1944*. Edited by Mary Adele Rogers and Robert Bigart. Pablo, Mont.: Salish Kootenai College Press, 2016.

McMullin, Thomas A., and David Walker. *Biographical Directory of American Territorial Governors*. Westport, Conn.: Meckler Publishing, 1984.

Menager, Gabriel M., S.J. "Reminiscences of a Missionary Sister." *Indian Sentinel* 22, no. 4 (Apr. 1942): 59–61.

Meyer, Melissa L. *The White Earth Tragedy: Ethnicity and Dispossession at a Minnesota Anishinaabe Reservation, 1889–1920*. Lincoln: University of Nebraska Press, 1994.

Missoula Publishing Company. *Flathead Facts: Descriptive of the Resources of Missoula County*. Missoula, Mont.: Missoula Publishing, 1890.

Montana Legislature. *Laws, Resolutions and Memorials of the State of Montana, Passed at the Fourth Regular Session of the Legislative Assembly*. Helena, Mont.: State Publishing, 1895.

———. *House Journal of the Tenth Session of the Legislative Assembly of the State of Montana*. Helena, Mont.: State Publishing, 1907.

Northwest Illustrated Monthly Magazine (St. Paul, Minn.) 8, no. 7 (July 1890): p. 46, col. 3.

O'Connor, Rev. James. "The Flathead Indians." *Records of the American Catholic Historical Society of Philadelphia* 3 (1888–91): 85–110.

Ollason, James. "Canoeing on the Flathead." *Outing* (Albany, N.Y.) 19, no. 2 (Nov. 1891): 161–63; and no. 3 (Dec. 1891): 187–88.

Ortiz, Alfonso, ed. *Handbook of North American Indians: Volume 10: Southwest*. Washington, D.C.: Smithsonian Institution, 1983.

Palladino, L. B., S.J. *Indian and White in the Northwest: A History of Catholicity in Montana, 1831 to 1891*. 2nd ed. Lancaster, Pa.: Wickersham Publishing, 1922.

Patterson, Ida Smith. *Montana Memories: The Life of Emma Magee in the Rocky Mountain West, 1866–1950*. 2nd ed. Pablo, Mont.: Salish Kootenai College Press, 2011.

Peltier, Jerome. *A Brief History of the Coeur d'Alene Indians, 1805–1909*. Fairfield, Wash.: Ye Galleon Press, 1981.

Post, Hubert A., S.J. "A Model Indian Mission: St. Ignatius' Mission, Flathead Reserve, Montana, 1854–1893." *Messenger of the Sacred Heart* 28, no. 9 (Sept. 1893): 712–25.

———. "Sweet Revenge." *Indian Sentinel* 2, no. 1 (Jan. 1920): 15–16.

Rappagliosi, Philip. *Letters from the Rocky Mountain Indian Missions*. Edited by Robert Bigart. Lincoln: University of Nebraska Press, 2003.

"Reduction of Indian Reservations." *House of Representatives Exec. Doc.* No. 63, 50th Cong., 1st Sess., 1888, serial 2557.

"Rocky Mountain Mission, St. Ignatius Mission, Montana." *Woodstock Letters* 23, no. 1 (1894): 192–95.

Ronan, Mary. *Girl from the Gulches: The Story of Mary Ronan as Told to Margaret Ronan*. Edited by Ellen Baumler. Helena: Montana Historical Society Press, 2003.

Ronan, Peter. "Discovery of Alder Gulch." *Contributions to the Historical Society of Montana* 3 (1900): 143–52.

———. *"A Great Many of Us Have Good Farms": Agent Peter Ronan Reports on the Flathead Indian Reservation, Montana, 1877–1887*. Edited by Robert J. Bigart. Pablo, Mont.: Salish Kootenai College Press, 2014.

———. *Justice to Be Accorded to the Indians: Agent Peter Ronan Reports on the Flathead Indian Reservation, Montana, 1888–1893*. Pablo, Mont.: Salish Kootenai College Press, 2014.

Rothermich, Capt. A. E., ed. "Early Days at Fort Missoula." In *Frontier Omnibus*, edited by John W. Hakola, 385–97. Missoula and Helena: Montana State University Press and Historical Society of Montana, 1962.

Ruger, Col. Thos. H. "Report of Col. Thos. H. Ruger" [Sept. 21, 1880]. U.S. Secretary of War, *Annual Report of the Secretary of War* (1880): 76–78.

Ruger, Col. Thomas H. "Report of Col. Thomas H. Ruger." U.S. Secretary of War, *Annual Report of the Secretary of War* (1883): 119–24.

Rylett, R. M. *Surveying the Canadian Pacific: Memoir of a Railroad Pioneer*. Salt Lake City: University of Utah Press, 1991.

Rzeczkowski, Frank. *Uniting the Tribes: The Rise and Fall of Pan-Indian Community on the Crow Reservation*. Lawrence: University Press of Kansas, 2012.

Salish–Pend d'Oreille Culture Committee. "The Swan Massacre: A Brief History." In *The Gathering Place: Swan Valley's Gordon Ranch*. Condon, Mont.: Upper Swan Valley Historical Society, 2017: 62–93.

Sanders, Helen Fitzgerald. *A History of Montana*. Chicago: Lewis Publishing, 1913.

Schoenberg, Wilfred P., S.J. *Paths to the Northwest: A Jesuit History of the Oregon Province*. Chicago: Loyola University Press, 1982.

Seltice, Joseph. *Saga of the Coeur d'Alene Indians: An Account of Chief Joseph Seltice*. Edited by Edward J. Kowrach and Thomas E. Connolly. Fairfield, Wash.: Ye Galleon Press, 1990.

Sheridan, Gen. P. H., and W. T. Sherman. *Reports of Inspection Made in the Summer of 1877 by Generals P. H. Sheridan and W. T. Sherman of Country North of the Union Pacific Railroad*. Washington, D.C.: U.S. Government Printing Office, 1878.

Sisters of Providence. "St. Ignatius Chronicle, 1864–1938." Typescript. Spokane, Wash.: Provincial Archives, St. Ignatius Province, Sisters of Providence, 1975.

Smalley, E. V. "Among the Flathead Indians." *Youth's Companion* (Boston) 58, no. 49 (Dec. 3, 1885): 515.

——. "The New North-West: Third Paper: From the Rockies to the Cascade Range." *Century Magazine* 24, no. 6 (Oct. 1882): 863–72.

——. "Recollections of the Northwest: Chapter VII." *Northwest Illustrated Monthly Magazine* (St. Paul, Minn.) 16, no. 12 (Dec. 1898): 16–17.

[Smalley, E. V.?] "The Fertile Flathead Country: A Trip Across the Flathead Indian Reservation and Up the Flathead Valley." *Northwest Illustrated Monthly Magazine* (St. Paul, Minn.) 9, no. 7 (July 1891): 46–48.

Smalley, Eugene V. "The Kalispel Country." *Century Magazine* 29, no. 3 (Jan. 1885): 447–55.

Smead, W. H. *Land of the Flatheads: A Sketch of the Flathead Reservation, Montana*. St. Paul, Minn.: Pioneer Press Mfg. Depts., 1905.

Smith, Reed W. *Samuel Medary & The Crisis: Testing the Limits of Press Freedom*. Columbus: Ohio State University Press, 1995.

Staveley Hill, Alex. *From Home to Home: Autumn Wanderings in the North-West, in the Years 1881, 1882, 1883, 1884*. New York: O. Judd, 1885.

Stern, Theodore. *The Klamath Tribe: A People and Their Reservation*. Seattle: University of Washington Press, 1965.

Stone, Arthur L. *Following Old Trails*. Missoula, Mont.: Morton John Elrod, 1913.

Stout, Tom. *Montana: Its Story and Biography*. Chicago: American Historical Society, 1921.

Teit, James A. "The Salishan Tribes of the Western Plateaus." In *Forty-Fifth Annual Report of the Bureau of American Ethnology* (1927–28), edited by Franz Boas, 23–396. Washington, D.C.: U.S. Government Printing Office, 1930.

Trosper, Ronald Lloyd. "The Economic Impact of the Allotment Policy on the Flathead Indian Reservation." PhD dissertation, Harvard University, Cambridge, Mass., 1974.

Turney-High, Harry Holbert. *The Flathead Indians of Montana*. Memoir of the American Anthropological Association, No. 48, 1937.

——. *Ethnography of the Kutenai*. Memoir of the American Anthropological Association, No. 56, 1941.

U.S. Attorney-General. *Annual Report of the Attorney-General of the United States* (1886). House Ex. Doc No. 8, 49th Cong, 2d Ses., 1886, serial 2477.

U.S. Census Office. *Report on Indians Taxed and Indians Not Taxed*. Washington, D.C.: U.S. Government Printing Office, 1894.

——. "Twelfth Census of the United States: Agriculture: Montana." *Census Bulletin*. Washington, D.C., no. 205, June 24, 1902.

——. *Agriculture: Parts I & II: Census Reports: Volumes V & VI: Twelfth Census of the United States, 1900*. Washington, D.C.: United States Census Office, 1902.

U.S. Commissioner of Indian Affairs. *Annual Report of the Commissioner of Indian Affairs*. Washington, D.C.: U.S. Government Printing Office, 1865, 1874–1909.

U.S. Interior Department. *Official Register of the United States . . .* Washington, D.C.: U.S. Government Printing Office, 1887.

U.S. President. "Message from the President of the United States Transmitting a Letter from the Secretary of the Interior Respecting the Ratification of an Agreement with the Confederated Tribes of Flathead, Kootenay, and Upper Pend d'Oreilles Indians, for the Sale of a Portion of Their Reservation in Montana Territory." *Senate Executive Document* No. 44, 47th Cong., 2d. Sess., 1883.

———. "Message from the President of the United States Transmitting a Report Relative to the Compensation of Henry B. Carrington, a Special Agent for the Sale of Certain Indian Lands." *Senate Executive Document* No. 70, serial 2686, 51st Congress, 1st Session, 1890.

U.S. Senate. "In the Senate of the United States." *Senate Report* No. 2707, 50th Congress, 2d Sess., 1889, serial 2623.

U.S. Statutes at Large. Vol. 33, 1903–5.

U.S. Statutes at Large. Vol. 34, pt. 1, 1905–7.

Vest, G. G., and Martin Maginnis. "Report of the Subcommittee of the Special Committee of the United States Senate, Appointed to Visit the Indian Tribes in Northern Montana." In *Senate Report* No. 283, 48th Congress, 1st Session (1884), serial 2174, xiii–xxxvii, 225–49.

Voggesser, Garrit. *Irrigation, Timber, and Hydropower: Negotiating Natural Resource Development on the Flathead Indian Reservation, 1904–1945.* Pablo, Mont.: Salish Kootenai College Press, 2017.

Walcheck, Ken. "Montana Wildlife 170 Years Ago as Lewis and Clark Saw It." *Montana Outdoors* 7, no. 4 (July/Aug. 1976): 15–30.

Waldron, Ellis L. *Montana Politics Since 1864: An Atlas of Elections.* Missoula, Mont.: Montana State University Press, 1958.

Whealdon, Bon I., et al. *"I Will Be Meat for My Salish": The Buffalo and the Montana Writers Project Interviews on the Flathead Indian Reservation.* Edited by Robert Bigart. Pablo and Helena, Mont.: Salish Kootenai College Press and Montana Historical Society Press, 2001.

Wheeler, Olin D. *Indianland and Wonderland.* St. Paul, Minn.: Northern Pacific Railroad, 1894. 22–28.

Wheeler, W. F. "A Journey to the West Side." *Montana Live Stock Journal* (Helena, Mont.) 2, no. 2 (June 1885): 4–5.

White, Lucy S. "Garfield!: An Incident." *Christian Union* (New York) 32, no. 21 (Nov. 19, 1885): 10–11.

Woodworth-Ney, Laura. *Mapping Identity: The Creation of the Coeur d'Alene Indian Reservation, 1805–1902.* Boulder, Colo.: University Press of Colorado, 2004.

Index

Page numbers in *italic type* indicate illustrations.

Adams, T. M., 125
agents, overview, 186–204. See also *names of specific agents*
agriculture. *See* farming; land
alcohol: agents on, 102, 131; Chief Arlee on, 66, 171; Chief Charlo on, 131, 175; Chief Eneas on, 130–31, 177; Chief Michelle on, 132; regulations on, 31–32; sales and incidents involving, 4, 66–67, 130–33, 158–59, 171, 177
Allard, Charles, Jr.: bank investments of, 157, 158; buffalo exhibits of, 89–90, 110; businesses of, 123, 124–26, 141, 142, 153; hunting by, 130; land agreements of, 146; in outing club, 201; wage work for, 152, 155
Allard, Charles, Sr., *119*; buffalo business of, 3, 51, 66, 88; buffalo exhibits and Wild West shows of, 89, 109, 110, 124, 125; businesses of, 123, 124; cattle business of, 23, 82, 83; horse businesses of, 29, 47, 65, 75, 82; stage line business of, 4, 124–25

Allard, Joseph, 94, 136, 152, 162, 163
Allard, Levi, 154
Allicott, 97, 141
allotment system. *See under* land
Ambrose (chief), 167
Anaconda Standard (publication), 77, 98, 127
Anderson, Reese, 48, 111
Andre (chief), 18, 35
Antiste, Thomas, 140
Antoine, Pascale, 133
Antony, Michael, 152
apple businesses, 30, 97, 99, 124, 148
Arapahos, 7
Arlee (chief), *116*, 167–73; cattle stock of, 22, 49; Christmas service by, 15; dispute resolutions by, 183; on gun and ammunition sales ban, 16–17; on horse theft, 47; request for support of buffalo hunt, 19, 25. *See also* Bitterroot Salish
Arlee, Antoine, 19, 32
Arlee, Joseph, 159

Armstrong, Frank C., 83, 97, 103
Ashley, Alex, 111
Ashley, Frank, 146
Ashley, Joseph, 101
Ashley, Julian, 159
Ashley, Louis, 133
Assiniboines, 18, 35
Augustine (chief), 97
Auld, Mose, 154

bank stockholders, 157–58
Bannister, E. D., 55
Bannock Indians, 17
baptisms, 15
barley, 24, 92. See also farming
Barnaby, Adolph, 108, 131, 133, 168
Barnaby, Felix, 131
Barnaby, Joseph, 110, 127, 136
Barnaby, Leo, 160
bartering, 4, 36–38, 135–36. See also
    economic activity
Battiste, 175
Battle of Little Big Horn, 15
bear hunting, 45, 130, 156
Beauchene, John, 155
Beckwith, George, 156
Beede, Cyrus, 77, 80
Bellew, George, 141, 200, 201–2
Bellew, Samuel, 139–42, 146–47, 158,
    198, 200–202
Bellew, Zoe, 200, 201
Belmont, Sam, 93
Bendois, 68
Benedict, S. S., 53, 57, 169, 188
Berray, L. Casper, 46
Big Canoe (chief), 14, 17, 18, 19, 35
Big Jim, 171
Big Knife (chief), 175–79
Bigknife, Alex, 72–73, 130
Big Mouth Charley, 139
Big Pete, 156, 159
Big Pierre, 193

Big Semo, 94
Bisson, Camille, 155
Bisson, C. E., 154
Bisson, Raphael, 22
Bitterroot Salish: alcohol incidents with,
    131; buffalo hunting of, 17, 19, 21,
    173; cattle industry of, 22; farming
    of, 92–93, 98, 174; government aid
    for, 2, 33–36, 55, 56, 181, 187; gun
    and ammunition restrictions for, 16;
    relocation of, 60, 103, 108, 184. See
    also Arlee (chief); Charlo (chief);
    Salish Indians
Blackfeet: buffalo economy of, 5, 13–14,
    15, 18; cattle herds of, 143; warfare of,
    18, 35
blackleg disease, 23
blacksmith services, 104
Bliss, A. M., 139
Blodgett, Ashbury, 106, 110
Blodgett, Joe, Jr., 87, 156
Bobier, John, 33, 38
Boer War, 3, 78, 80
Bonaparte, Isaac, 87
Bonners Ferry Kootenai. See Kootenai
Booth, J. S., 70
Bratnober, Henry, 190
Breeden, George, 111
Brondel, John, 172
Buckman, James, 160
buffalo: exhibits of, 89–90, 110, 124, 125;
    herding businesses, 3, 51, 88, 144–45;
    hunting of, 2–3, 5, 12–21, 40, 173. See
    also cattle industry; grazing rights and
    taxes; hunting
Bureau of Indian Affairs, 163
Burland, Henry, 111, 155
Burns, James, 23
Bushman, John, 111
business exchanges: of 1875–1881,
    27–33; off-reservation, 128–34, 155–57;
    on-reservation, 134–37, 154–55. See

also economic activity; *names of specific businesses and industries*; wage work
Butte Butchering Company, 143

Cabell, Tony, 154
Calico, Peter, 110
Camas Prairie Kalispel Indians, 53, 103–4, 132, 147, 159
Camille, Louie, 133, 134
Campbell, A., 50
Campbell, George C., 50
Canada, 143–45
Canestrelli, Philip, 110
Carrier, Frank, 146
Carrington, Henry B., 92, 98, 105, 174
Carron, John, 109
Carron, Louis, 159
Carter, Joseph T., 191–94; on cattle industry, 76, 83; on farming, 93, 95; on hunting incident, 70–71; on reservation boundaries, 179; tribal opinion of, 188
Carter, Mary Ronan, 170, 192, 193, 194
casual labor. *See* wage work
Catholic Indian Missions, 186, 201. *See also* St. Ignatius Mission
cattle industry, 2; from 1875–1881, 22–23; from 1889–1904, 82–90; from 1905–1910, 140, 142–44; on Blackfeet Reservation, 5; cattlemen's association of, 87–88; of Comanche Indians, 7–8; of Crow Indians, 6; diseases of, 23, 144; grazing rights and taxes on, 78, 86, 104, 140; introduction of railroad and, 40–41, 44; wage work of, 108–9
Chapman, Augustus, 175
Charlo (chief), *115*, 173–75; on alcohol, 131, 175; cattle business of, 22; village farm by, 92–93, 94, 97. *See also* Bitterroot Salish
Charlo, Martin (chief), *122*
Charoline, Henry, 156

Cheyenne Indians, 6, 7
chiefs, overview, 167–85. See also *names of specific chiefs*
Chilten, Frank, 110
Chouteau, Mose, 81
Chowtay, Louie, 106
Christmas holiday, 15, 90, 169
Cisney, James H., 95
Clairmont, Alphonse, 99, 129, 156
Clairmont, Henry, 159
Clairmont, Louis, 159
Clairmont, Louis, Jr., 111
Clairmore, Eddie, 99, 105
Clark, William A., 190–91
Clark, Willie, 111
Clifford, Delima Demers, 177
Coeur d'Alene Indians, 7
Comanche Indians, 7–8
commercial exchanges. *See* business exchanges
Cone, Sam, 158
Conford, George, 37
Conrad, Charles, 90
Cook, Horatio, 76
Cooley, Sam, 137
Coombs, Mary Ann Topsseh, 108
Cory, F. M., 76–77
Coull-Coullee, Louis, 193
Courtois, William, 107
Courville, Alphonse, 128, 152
Courville, Louis, 109, 154, 155
Courville, Nazaire, 159
Courville, Oliver, 128, 147, 155
Courville, Zephyre, 111, 143, 153
Couture, Baptist, 154
Couture, David, 109
Couture, Emily Brown, 127
Couture, Jessie, 129
Couture, Louis, 64
Couture, Mack, 106
Couture, Maxime, 48–49, 52, 68, 127
Couture, Octave, 106, 129, 149, 151

Couture, Rose, 157
coyote hunting, 130, 156
Cramer, Ben, 82, 141
Cree Indians, 6, 112, 136
Crow Indians, 6, 68, 180
Cul-cow-wis-ka, Philip, 146
Cultis-toe, Louie, 26
Curran, Jack, 151–52
Cyr, Frank, 131
Cyril, Placid, 135

Daily, John R., 85, 142–43
Daily Missoulian (publication), 148, 154, 195
Daly, Marcus, 144, 191
Dana, Paul, 49–50
Dandy Jim, 29
D'Aste, Jerome: on farming conditions, 149; financial exchanges of, 66, 110, 135–36; last rites by, 172; on seasonal hunting, 46, 69; on theft, 136; on tribal disputes, 201; on wage work, 112–14
Dayton Mercantile Company, 158
Deaf Louis, 80, 136, 147
Decker, Frank, 25
deer hunting, 12, 20, 44, 72
Delaithe, Robert, 111
Delaware, Moses, 93–94
Delaware, Narcisse, 152
Demers, Alex L., 50, 55, 61, 64, 81, 133
Demers, Robert, 157
Demers, Telesphore Guillium "T. G.," 31, 64, 109, 128, 143, 153
Demers, Telesphore Jacques "T. J.," 23, 28, 37, 168, 181, 187
Denison, B. H., 112, 151
DeRouge, Etienne Xavier, 52
Deschamps, Ed, 94
Deschamps, Gaspard, 38, 85, 90
Deschamps, William, 159
Dewitt, William H., 193

Dexter, A., 152
Dimier, Augustine, 179
Dixon, Joseph M., 99, 123–24, 129, 138, 150, 162–63, 194
Dougan, Kennedy, 133
Dow, Alex, 77, 80, 110, 111
Dowd, David, 80
Dowd, William, 146, 152
Downs, Thomas, 203
drought, 29, 45, 55, 99, 149, 174. *See also* farming
Dubay, E., 155
DuBois, Coert, 110
Ducharme, Frank, 61, 127
Dugan, James, 22
Duncan, C. C., 95
Duncan, Tyson D., 65
Dunn, W. A., 199
Dupuis, James, 155
Dupuis, J. O., 158
Dupuis, J. S., 87
Dusold, Andrew, 14

Eaton, Charles, 155
Eaton, Howard, 90
economic activity, 2–4, 12, 65–68, 106–7, 128–37, 156–57. *See also* horse economy; sharing economy; theft economy; wage work
economic aid. *See* government aid
education. *See* schools
Eldred, Frank C., 80
elk hunting, 12, 20, 45, 72
Elrod, Morton J., 73
employment. *See* wage work
Eneas (chief), *117*, 175–79; on alcohol, 130–31, 177; arrest of, 185; government aid for, 34; on gun and ammunition sales ban, 16–17; on railroad right-of-way negotiations, 42–43; request for support of buffalo hunt, 19, 25; village farm by, 92, 98. *See also* Kootenai

Eneas, Baptiste: businesses of, 4, 30, 62; farm of, 24–25; land agreements of, 146

Enstata, August, 87

Evans, Richard, 32

Ewing, Charles, 186

farming, 120; from 1875–1881, 23–26; from 1882–1888, 51–55; from 1889–1904, 91–102; from 1905–1910, 145–50; drought, 29, 45, 55, 99, 149, 174; economic adaptations and, 3, 13; irrigation systems for, 5, 6, 98, 105, 145, 151; land agreements for, 25–26, 93–94; of Ojibwa Indians, 8; statistics on, 10–11. See also land; vegetable gardening

federal aid. See government aid

Federsohn, Peter, 85

Feidler, Victor, 111

Felix, Antoine, 135

Felsman, Henry, 148

Felsman, Herman, 61

ferry service businesses: of Antoine Revais, 62–63; of Baptiste Eneas, 4, 24, 30–31, 46; boat theft incident, 37; of Charles Allard, 153; of Tony Cabell, 154. See also business exchanges

financial assistance. See government aid

Finley, Abraham, 146

Finley, Alex, 133

Finley, Anthony, 160

Finley, Antoine, 75, 159

Finley, August, 32

Finley, Basham, 14

Finley, Basile, 52, 134, 155

Finley, Dave, 159

Finley, Espaniole, 26

Finley, Ignace, 135

Finley, Joe, 101

Finley, John Battiste, 61, 109

Finley, Koonsa, 66, 170–71, 183

Finley, Larra, 172

Finley, Modeste, 67

Finley, Moses, 32

Finley, Peter, 59, 130, 159–60

Finley, Phil, 154

First National Bank of Missoula, 88, 157, 158

Fisher, Conrad and Lena, 131

fishing, 8, 20, 45–46, 73–74, 139. See also hunting

Flathead, Sam, 67

Flathead Allotment Act (1904), 162–66

Flathead Indian Agency, 121

Flathead Irrigation Project, 145–46, 165

Flathead Reservation: Land of the Flatheads (Smead), 198

flour mill services, 104–5, 148, 150

food. See farming; fishing; gathering wild plants; hunting; vegetable gardening

Fordham, Ebb, 76

Forkner, Allen, 143

Gabe, Charley, 106

gambling, 75, 104, 131, 157, 168, 179, 188

Ganger, Joe, 143

Garcia, Andrew, 18, 27–28, 29

gardening, 2, 91–92, 97, 102, 147, 149–50, 161, 192. See also farming

Gardner, Robert S., 53, 95

Garfield, James, 33, 168, 170

Gates, C. F., 146

gathering wild plants: from 1889–1904, 73–74; from 1905–1910, 140; effects of government control on, 5; Hellgate Treaty provisions for, 17; as important subsistence activity, 2, 3, 8, 12, 20–21; white settlements and, 40

Gawith, Jesse, 125

Gebeau, Joe, 109

Gebeau, Oliver, 107, 111

Gibbon, John, 169

Gingras, John, 159–60

Gingras, Peter, 159
Glover, Eli, 24
Goodyer, William, 30
government aid, 2, 4; from 1875–1881, 33–36; from 1882–1888, 40, 55–58; from 1889–1904, 91, 102–7; from 1905–1910, 150–51. *See also* rations
Graham, S. W., 127
grain farming. *See* farming; *names of specific grains*
Grandjo, Aeneas, 159
Grandjo, Ignace, 151
Grass, Jim, 22
Gravelle, Francois "Savio" and Elizabeth, 126
Graw, Jean Jan (Gingras), 178
grazing rights and taxes, 78, 86, 104, 140–45, 165. *See also* buffalo herding business; cattle industry; land
Great Buffalo and Wild West Show, 89, 110. *See also* Wild West shows
Great Northern Railroad, 123, 124
Gregg, Omar G. V., 13
Grinder, Jim, 109
gristmill services, 24, 53, 56, 57, 58, 63, 104–5, 150
Griva, Edward, 154
Gros Ventres Indians, 14
Guidi, John B., 48
Guiznaiul, Paul, 136
gun and ammunition restrictions, 15–18, 29, 34

Hammer, Louie, 159
Hammond, A. B., 64, 88
Haney, Jon, 99
Harris, Thomas W., 167–68
Hauser, S. T., 191
hay farming, 21, 49, 51, 84, 96, 99–100, 148–49. *See also* farming
Haynes, F. Jay, 50, 60
Hee, Keat, 159

Helena Daily Herald (publication), 42, 43
Helena Independent (publication), 41–42, 172
Hellgate Treaty (1855): on government aid, 34, 35; on land allotment, 163; off-reservation provisions in, 13, 17, 45, 70, 140, 181, 196; on public road provisions, 41–42; on salaries of federal employees, 59; signing of, 1
Henderson, Palmer, 73
Hibler, G. F., 143
Higgins, Arthur, 72
Higgins, Christopher, 30
Higgins, Frank, 48
Hill, Alex Staveley, 46, 62, 63
Holland, A., 132
horse economy, 3, 21–22, 46–49, 74–82, 129, 140–42. *See also* economic activity
horse racing, 29, 65, 81–82, 130, 142
horse theft, 4, 14, 19, 36, 47, 67–68, 136, 137, 159–60. *See also* theft economy
Houle, Joe, 149
Houston, John, 132
Houston, William, 178, 185
Howard, C. H., 61, 63, 67, 171
Howe, C. W., 75
Howland, James, 155
Hubert Cattle Company, 143
Hull, D. D., 155
hunting, 20, 69–74, 98, 130, 139–40, 156. *See also under* buffalo; fishing
Hutchins, Charles, 175

Ignace, M., 101, 133
Ilimi, 97
Indian agents, 186–204
Ingersoll, Ernest, 49, 52, 62
Innias, Phil, 154
irrigation systems, 5, 6, 98, 105, 145, 151, 165. *See also* farming

Irvine, Peter, 29
Irvine, Robert H., 92, 107, 178
Irvine, William, 22, 86, 94, 127, 143, 144, 157
Isaac, Abraham, 130, 139

Jangraw, Joseph, 133
Jenkins, Jame E., 85
Jette, Baptiste, 101
Jette, Frank, 85
Jette, J. B., 143
Jim, Thomas Dandy, 109
Jones, Buffalo, 90
Jones, Joseph, 94
Jones, L. S., 134
Jones, Molly, 130
Joseph, Pierre, 75, 107
Junkin, William W., 131
justice system, tribal vs. U.S. government, 170–71, 183

Kakashe, Baptiste, 111, 136, 159, 185
Kaluia, Sophie, 135
Kennett, Percy, 48
Kickinghorse, Charlie, 132
King, John H., 125
King, Louis, 136
Kiupe, Isaac, 136
Klamath Indians, 8
Knowles, Frank, 146
Koch, Elers, 72
Konomakan, Gabriel, 108
Kootenai: chiefs of, 175–79; economic change and adaptations of, 2–4, 12; reservation boundaries and land allotments of, 176, 178–79; village garden of, 92. See also Eneas (chief)
Kooto, Joseph, 107
Ksanka Kootenai. See Kootenai

labor. See wage work
Laderoute, Isadore, 50

Lambert, H. A., 64
Lameroux, Ed, 128, 156
Lameroux, Mary, 147
Lamoose, Frank, 73
La Mousse, Joe, 135
land: allotment system, 100–101, 138–39, 147, 160–61, 162–66, 174–75, 189; economic implications of allotment system, 162–66; grazing rights and taxes on, 78, 86, 104, 140–45, 165; irrigation projects and, 5, 6, 98, 105, 145, 147–48, 165; poverty and, 4; proceeds from sales of, 127–28; tenure and farming agreements, 25–26, 93–94, 146–47. See also farming
LaRose, Anthony, 112–13
LaRose, Dan, 112–13
LaRose, David, 112–13
LaRose, Louis, 133
Larrivee, Arthur, 80, 87, 111, 124, 125, 141, 143, 152
Latattie, Joe, 146, 152
Laughlin, Denver, 37
Laughlin, James, 25–26
Lempro, John, 156
Leopold, Bernard, 131
Lewis, Jennie, 146
Lewis, Lee W., 143
Lewis & Clark Forest Reserve, 139
Link & Carter (firm), 194
Lippincott, Joseph Barlow, 72
liquor. See alcohol
Little-Claw-of-a-Grizzly-Bear. See Charlo (chief)
Little Plume (chief), 14, 36
Logan, Andrew, 61
logging. See timber industry
Lomprey, John, 134, 135
Lone Wolf v. United States, 162
Longpre, Dan, 73–74
Louison, 53, 107, 135, 151, 171, 192–93

Lower Kalispel Indians, 103–4
Lower Pend d'Oreille. See Michel (chief of Lower Pend d'Oreille); Pend d'Oreille
Loyola, Joseph, 29, 31
Lucier, Peter, 154
Lumpry, Dutch, 106
Lynch, Neptune, 37

Maginnis, Martin, 16, 183–84, 191
Magpie, Peter, 152
Maillett, George, 128
Marchant, Henry M., 102
Marengo, Baptiste, 154
Marengo, Frank, 66, 170
Marion, Joseph, 93, 111
Markle, Wilkes, 128
Mary, Sabine, 97
Matt, Alexander, 28–30, 59, 107, 122
Matt, Frank, 149
Matt, Gonsague, 59
Matt, Henry, 147, 156, 192
Matt, Joe, 149
Matt, Joel, 110
Matt, John, 107, 153–54, 156
Matt, Lomay, 158
Matt, Louis, 156
Matt, Maxime "Mike," 99, 129, 157
Matt, Peter, 29, 99
Matt, William, 151
Maxime, 37–38
McCammon, Joseph, 42–43, 52, 170
McCarthy, Eugene, 178
McClure, W. J., 106
McConnell, W. J., 81, 85, 101
McCormick, P., 83, 95, 102, 188, 191–92
McDermott, Louisa, 99, 127
McDonald, Angus P.: allotment policy and, 162; cattle business of, 82, 83, 86, 142, 143; on Chief Arlee, 168; death of, 124; farmland of, 101; horse racing

by, 130; horse theft of, 159; hunting by, 130; opposition to Smead's policies by, 80; wage work for, 111, 155
McDonald, Archie, 29, 136
McDonald, Duncan, 119, 167–68; 1882 purchases of, 65; allotment policy and, 162, 163; apple orchard of, 99, 124; as business chairman, 203; cattle business of, 22, 23, 124; on Chief Michelle, 180; on farm season, 55; horse theft of, 75; hotel of, 3–4, 123–24; as judge, 151; as railroad mediator, 41, 43, 58, 63; trading post of, 30, 57, 63–64; wage work of, 27, 109, 110
McDonald, John, 155
McDonald, Maggie, 66
McDonald, Thomas, 111, 171
McGowan, J. A., 71, 128, 132, 133
McKeever, James, 146
McKeogh, T. C., 73
McKinley, William, 193, 195
McLeod, Alex, 61, 153
McLeod, C. H., 88, 100, 126, 156, 157
McLeod, Dan, 106, 107, 156
McLeod, Hector, 154
McLeod, Malcolm, 49, 61, 89, 93, 109
McLeod, Richard, 154
McNichols, Charles S., 84, 85, 101, 104, 197
Medary, Charles S., 186–88; on cattle industry, 22; Chief Arlee and, 168, 172, 181; on farming, 24; on horse theft, 14, 37
Menominee Indians, 8
Merengo, Baptiste, 110
Michael, James, 134
Michand, Joe, 111
Michel (chief of Lower Pend d'Oreille), 132, 159
Michel (Kalispel man), 136–37
Michel, James, 107
Michel, Peter, 146

Michelle (chief of Upper Pend d'Oreilles), *116*, 179–85; on buffalo hunts, 18, 19, 25; farm of, 52, 55; on gun and ammunition sales ban, 16–17; on horse theft and sales, 38, 47; on Medary, 168; on railroad negotiations, 43
Miles, Frank R., 89, 166
military service, 3
Miller, George, 144
Miller, Jeremiah, 166
Missoula Mercantile Company, 29, 32, 88, 100, 126, 128, 156, 191, 195
Mitchell, Sam, 48
Moise, Antoine, 73
Montana & Columbian Buffalo and Indian Exhibit Company, 89
Montana Marble Works, 134
Montana Power Company, 166
Moran, Boston, 110
Morant, Joe, 131
Moremon, Charley, 105
Morgan, Eva E. Waterhouse Bean, 203–4
Morgan, Fred C., 139, 144, 149–51, 202–4
Morrigeau, Alexander, 28, 30, 47, 52, 129
Morrigeau, Eli, 94
Morrigeau, Joseph, 30, 86, 101, 128, 130, 147
Morris, M. C., 74–75
Moser, Gust, 195
Moss, Thomas, 94
Moss, William, 107
Murray, S. G., 199

native plants. *See* gathering wild plants
Neff, Milton, 111
Nenami, 157
Nenema, Antoine, 133
Nenema, Baptiste, 133, 159
Nenema, Benoit, 109, 132–33, 159
Nenema, Francois, 159

Nesbitt, Harry, 73
Nesler, C. F., 197
New North-West, 45
New York Times, 47, 137
Nez Perce: chiefs of, 167–73; gun and ammunition sales ban against, 15–16; horses of, 76–77; violence by, 17, 182
Nicolla, 193
Nile, Mary Finley, 110
Ninepipe, Antoine, 76, 134
Nine Pipes, 99, 106
NKuto, Michael, 136
Norman, Frank, 111
Northern Arapaho, 7
Northern Cheyenne, 6
Northern Pacific Railroad: boarding accommodations and, 124; construction and right-of-way negotiations of, 40–42, 183; labor workers of, 29, 30, 31, 58–59; liquor disputes and, 158; livestock deaths by, 44, 47, 50, 82, 129; tribal payments for, 65; water agreements of, 147
Northwest Illustrated Monthly Magazine, 124, 190
Northwest Indian Commission, 171–72

oats, 23, 24, 26, 92, 99. *See also* farming
O'Connor, James, 168
off-reservation business exchanges, 128–34, 155–57. *See also* business exchanges
Ojibwa, 8
open-grazing. *See* grazing rights and taxes

Pablo, Lorette, 32
Pablo, Michel: allotment policy and, 162; buffalo herd of, 3, 51, 88, 89, 90, 144–45; cattle business of, 22, 82, 83, 144; economic exchanges of, 29, 65; wage work of, 109
Packer/Parker, Alex, 132

Pain, E., 139
Pain, Joseph, 61, 78, 139
Palladino, Lawrence, 173
Parazo, Antoine, 93, 94, 134
Parsons, Harry H., 73, 133, 150, 197–98, 199
Parsons, W. B., 88, 150
Paul, Pierre, 156, 158
Paul, William, 159
Pearsons, George B., 55
Peh, Tsil, 137
Pend d'Oreille: chief of, 168, 179–85; fishing by, 20; horse sales by, 21; hunting parties of, 13–14, 18, 19, 139. See also Michel (chief of Lower Pend d'Oreille); Michelle (chief of Upper Pend d'Oreille)
penny capitalism. See economic activity
Perry, Reuben, 201, 202
Peter, John, 135
Peter, Michael, 130
Peyton, Charles B., 139–40
Piegan Blackfeet, 5, 14
Pierre, Cayuse, 174
Pierre, Joe, 106
Pierre, Louie, 136
Pierre, Sam, 129, 149
pig market, 77
Plainsman (publication), 78
Plant, Anthony, 29
Plant, Isaac, 156
Plant, Michael, 156, 159
plant food gathering. See gathering wild plants
Plouffe, Marcelene, 147
Plouffe, Mrs. Napoleon, 146
police forces, 59, 107, 168, 171
population statistics, 10
Post, Hubert A., 98, 105, 111
Post, John, 97
Potts, B. F., 187

poverty, 164, 174
Power, T. C., 52, 55, 56, 59–60, 64
Prescott, Clarence, 20, 28
Preuitt, W. G., 86–87
Prideaux, M. H., 133, 197
Proctor, Clarence, 178

Quinn, M. E., 159
Quinn, Michael, 132

railroad. See Great Northern Railroad; Northern Pacific Railroad
ranching. See under buffalo; cattle industry
Ranft, William Q., 156, 197, 198
Rankin, John, 201
Rappagliosi, Philip, 15, 168–69
rations, 5, 7, 57, 102, 108. See also government aid
Ravalli, Anthony, 180
Rawn, C. C., 21, 27
Raymond, Henry, 154
Raymond, James, 159
Redeker, Charles, 140
Red Thunder, 157
Resurrection, Sam, 152
Revais, Antoine, 22, 30–31, 62–63
Revais, Michel, 25, 59, 107, 174, 180
Rocky Mountain Husbandman (publication), 25
Ronan, Mary (wife of Peter), 37, 168, 172–73
Ronan, Mary E. (daughter of Peter). See Carter, Mary Ronan
Ronan, Peter, 118, 188–91; on alcohol and tobacco sales, 131; on buffalo hunting, 18; Chief Arlee and, 167, 169, 170–71, 172; Chief Charlo and, 173–74; Chief Eneas and, 175, 176, 178, 179; Chief Michelle and, 182; on farms, 54; on government assistance,

56; on gun and ammunition restrictions, 16, 34; on horse and cattle industry, 21, 22, 48, 84; railroad negotiations by, 41, 44; on seasonal hunting, 69–70; on tribal businesses, 64; on village garden, 92; wage work of, 59–60

Ronan, Vincent, 191

Roosevelt, Theodore, 162

Rothrock, F. M., 87

Roullier, Fred, 149

Rudolph, Herman, 140

Russo-Japanese War, 3

rye, 148. *See also* farming

Rzeczkowski, Frank, 6

Salish Indians: buffalo hunts of, 19; chiefs of, 167–75; economic adaptations of, 2–4; government aid for, 33–36; horse sales by, 21. *See also* Bitterroot Salish

Sapier, Gabe, 139

Sapierre, Anne, 75

Savage, H. N., 151

sawmill, 53, 56, 58, 104, *120*, 125–26, 150. *See also* timber industry

Saxa, Mary, 136

schools, 154, 155; Chief Charlo on, 131, 174–75; at Jocko, 99, 127; of St. Ignatius Mission, 48, 61, 181, 184, 188, 196

Scott, James, 132

Scullnah, Louis, 94

Scwi, Antoine, 139

Sears, J. R., 146

Sedman, Oscar, 126

See, Pa Las, 159

Seghers, Charles, 169

Selish Express Company, 64

Seward, Horatio L., 103

Shanahan, Daniel, 168, 181

sharing economy, 4, 36–38, 135–36. *See also* economic activity

Sheppard, Jack, 131

Sherman, Thomas, 193

Sherman, W. T., 16

shopping, 65–66, 128–29, 156–57. *See also* economic activity

Sieff, 74–75

Sine lo, Philip, 110

Sitting Bull, 182

sKaltemiger, Martin, 135

Sloan, Allen, 101, 129, 155, 162

Sloane, John, 148

Smalley, Eugene V.: on ferry business, 62; on Ronan as agent, 188; on shopping exchange, 65; on tribal subsistence, 46, 47, 49, 56; on wage work, 61

smallpox epidemic, 1, 78

Smead, William Henry, *118*, 194–99; agency appointment of, 193; on cattle industry, 85, 87–88, 140; denial of fishing permit by, 73; on employment preferences, 111; on government aid, 102–3; horse market and, 3, 75–81; on land disputes, 94; land transactions of, 128

Smead-Simons Building Corporation, 199

Smith, Thomas P., 191

Sniffen, M. K., 203

Southern Arapahos, 7

Southern Cheyenne, 7

Spokane Indians, 2

Spokane Table Supply Company, 158

Stair, Louie Tel Co, 159

Standing Bear, Joseph, 75

Stevens, Michael, 152

St. Ignatius Mission: Agent Smead and, 196; Chief Arlee and, 167, 168–69; Chief Michelle and, 179; schools of, 48, 61, 169, 181, 184, 188, 196;

St. Ignatius Mission (*continued*)
   wage work of, 60–61, 99, 151. *See also*
   schools
Still, Antoine, 107
Stillinger, C. A., 63, 124, 125
Stinger, Andrew, 82, 111, 129, 154
strawberries, 148
Stychen, Joseph, 87
suKoe, Michel, 136
Sullivan, Daniel, 22
Sullivan, Jerry, 142
Swasah, 193

Taelman, Louis, 149, 201
Taggart, S. L., 197
Tall Hat (chief), 36
T. C. Power & Co., 55
Teller, H. M., 44
Tellier, Isaac, 61
Terriault, Henry, 126
theft economy, 4, 36–38, 67–68, 136. *See
   also* economic activity; horse theft
Therriault, Fred, 155
Thomem, Victor, 110
timber industry, 6–7, 8, 88. *See also*
   sawmill
Tinker, Arthur M., 100, 164
tobacco, 29, 35, 47, 127
Todd, Albert, 110
Tomfohr, Caroline, 111
trade, 4, 36–38, 135–36, 157–60. *See also*
   economic activity
tribal *vs.* U.S. government justice system,
   170–71, 183
Trosper, Ronald, 164

Umatilla Reservation, 76, 77
Upper Pend d'Oreille. *See* Michelle
   (chief of Upper Pend d'Oreille); Pend
   d'Oreille
U.S. government *vs.* tribal justice system,
   170–71, 183

Vallee, Andrew, 154
Valley, Louis, 29
Vallie, John, 110, 154
Vandeburgh, Mary, 135
Vanderburg, Charlie, 110
Vanderburg, Jerome, 156
Vanderburg, Moses, 156
Vanderburg, Victor, 97, 130, 156
Van Gorp, Leopold, 55, 87
vegetable gardening, 2, 91–92, 97,
   102, 147, 149–50, 161, 192. *See also*
   farming
Vest, G. G., 43, 47, 50, 169, 183
Viloit, William, 132
Vose, Oliver, 123, 126

wage work, 27–33, 58–62, 107–14, 151–
   55. *See also* economic activity
Wallace, John T., 61
Walters, F. E., 80
Warrington, Colonel, 49, 169–70
water systems. *See* irrigation systems
Watson, Robert, 104
W. B. Russell Meat Company, 143
Weber, J. B., 71
Weed, Elbert D., 193
Weekly Missoulian (publication), 15, 27,
   31, 32, 62, 71, 133, 172
Wenger, John, 143
Westfield Importing Company, 81
Whaley, Peter, 13, 24, 181
wheat, 3, 6, 23–25, 51, 92, 97, 98, 148.
   See also farming
Wheeler, Olin D., 76
Wheeler, W. F., 50, 54
whiskey. *See* alcohol
White, W. W., 80
White Calf (chief), 14
White Earth Reservation, 8
W. H. Smead Company, 199
Wild West shows, 3, 89, 90, 109, 110,
   125, 126

Willis, C. C., 77–79
Willis, T. C., 125
Wilson, Charles, 158
Worden, Tyler, 128

Young, Charlie, 48

Zingele, William, 159

CPSIA information can be obtained
at www.ICGtesting.com
Printed in the USA
LVHW021958120922
728174LV00003B/261